PORNOGRAPHY
AND REPRESENTATION
IN GREECE AND ROME

PORNOGRAPHY AND REPRESENTATION IN GREECE AND ROME

Edited by Amy Richlin

New York   Oxford
OXFORD UNIVERSITY PRESS
1992

Oxford University Press

Oxford   New York   Toronto
Delhi   Bombay   Calcutta   Madras   Karachi
Petaling Jaya   Singapore   Hong Kong   Tokyo
Nairobi   Dar es Salaam   Cape Town
Melbourne   Auckland

and associated companies in
Berlin   Ibadan

Published by Oxford University Press, Inc.,
198 Madison Avenue, New York, New York 10016-4314

Oxford is a registered trademark of Oxford University Press

Library of Congress Cataloging-in-Publication Data
Pornography and representation in Greece and Rome /
edited by Amy Richlin.
p.   cm.
Includes bibliographical references and index.
ISBN 0-19-506722-3 (cloth). — ISBN 0-19-506723-1 (paper)
1. Pornography—Social aspects—Greece.   2. Pornography—Social aspects—Rome.
3. Feminist criticism—Greece.   4. Feminist criticism—Rome.
5. Erotic literature, Greek.   6. Erotic literature, Italian.
I. Richlin, Amy, 1951-.
HQ472.G8P67   1992
363.4'7'0945632—dc20-   90-43854

9 8 7 6 5 4 3 2

Printed in the United States of America
on acid-free paper

To the memory of Carolyn Hamm
To Barbara
To the memory of Saguiv Hadari
To my sisters, Nancy and Sarah
To the memory of Linda Jindra Zanmiller
For Deborah and Osias
For Annie and Eve
To Frances A. Joshel
To the memory of my sister, Joan Ellen Sorkin
To my sister, Susan Shapiro
To M, my brother
To Paul
To the memory of Kyle M. Phillips, Jr.

ACKNOWLEDGMENTS

The editor would like to thank the original *Pornography and Representation in Greece and Rome* collective—Madeleine Henry, Sandra Joshel, Molly Myerowitz, Terri Marsh, and Robert Sutton—for all their work and for many stimulating discussions; and all the contributors for their cooperation and joie de vivre. It was a great pleasure and excitement to read the drafts as they took shape, to talk over changes and ideas, and to see feminist theory applied to such a range of areas in Classics, often for the first time.

Thanks to the Berkshire Conference for hosting the first panel, on rape and Roman history; and to the Women's Classical Caucus of the American Philological Association for inviting the second one, on the pornographic in antiquity. One person must be thanked above all. To Marilyn Skinner I owe the idea of making this book, and in a way the book is a by-product of our ten years of epistolary debate, discussion, exegesis, and inspiration. Her example of commitment to excellence in both classical learning and feminist thought made this book thinkable, and I am deeply grateful.

Many thanks to Marleeta Wood of Lehigh University for her control of the project's communications, and to Ellen Bauer of the University of Southern California for coping with the bibliography.

To those friends, colleagues, and relatives who so generously gave of their time to help with the final editing, three cheers: Karen Banfield, Shelby Brown, Jane Cody, Carolyn Dewald, Alvin Lim, Martha Malamud, Samuel Richlin, Sylvia Richlin, Terry Seymour, W. Gregory Thalmann.

Special thanks to Peter Bingham, always good company.

Finally, I thank Rachel Toor, Herbert Addison, and the Oxford University Press for their enthusiastic support, which helped so much toward the timely completion of the book; and the National Endowment for the Humanities for some borrowed time.

CONTENTS

INTRODUCTION

This collection of essays is unusual in its content, its method, its authors, and the way it came together. It is one of very few large-scale applications of feminist theory to Greco-Roman antiquity; in fact, by starting from feminist theory we named and collocated a set of ancient phenomena that would otherwise not have received attention together. Many articles here are the first on their subject or of their kind, and the authors likewise include new and radical voices. What we have done constitutes part of an ongoing transformation of our field; it also serves to bring our material to a new audience. Yet as feminists we vary considerably in our approach, both in the kinds of theory we use and in the stands we take on the embattled issue of pornography. Finally, to an extent unusual in Classics, we wrote this book together; a collective made up of the six original panelists read all the papers, and rewriting took place in the context of group discussion and with much pooling of bibliography and ideas. Whatever effect we will have on our field, the experience has certainly transformed us as a group.

We share the following assumptions. (1) Our work fits into the discipline that is coming to be known as cultural studies. It is a methodological axiom of this volume that text and social context are interrelated, and we all consider issues of audience and conditions of production. (2) With this axiom firmly in place, the application of feminist or other modern theories to ancient material is not inherently problematical. Feminist theoretical models of the pornographic not only help us to understand what is going on in some ancient texts, images, and behaviors but also correspond with explicit Greek and Roman self-analyses. Furthermore, since some of the texts discussed here continue to enjoy canonical status, an adequate theoretical treatment of them must consider their content within a twentieth-century context as well. (3) Our use of the theory available to us has been wide-ranging, but most crucial here have been the issues raised by Susanne Kappeler's *The Pornography of Representation;* hence our title. As will be seen below, Kappeler draws a close connection between the power mechanism of pornography and the power mechanism of representation itself. Thus, the questions we raise and the materials we have chosen go beyond the purely sexual. (4) We seek a wider audience for the history of gender within Classics, and a wider audience outside of Classics for work on gender by classicists. Some of our material is known to most classicists but few nonclassicists, some to few people at all; we want to bring it to the attention of all those interested in the history of gender.

And so, since our audience is double, a double orientation seems in order.

Orientations: Classics for Feminists, Feminism for Classicists

Classics for Feminists

Classics is an area study and includes the work of linguists, literary critics, philosophers, historians, epigraphers, papyrologists, art historians, and archaeologists, among others. Its geographical and temporal boundaries take in the Mediterranean world between about 1500 B.C. and A.D. 500 but usually skirt the Near Eastern and North African cultures and embrace Greece and Rome. The discipline generally keeps its subfields separate and in addition has historically put a premium on positivist work: the recovery of facts, texts, and artifacts and their categorization and classification. But in this book we have overlapped boundaries and borrowed unifying approaches from anthropology, cultural history, and feminism, and our goal is the recovery of ideology.

The time line that follows this introduction will give you an idea of the range of periods covered. As it happens, we have clustered in some familiar investigative spaces: the fifth century B.C. in Athens, the late first century B.C. and early first century A.D. in Rome, and the "Second Sophistic," a pan-Mediterranean intellectual movement of the second century A.D. Though we have thereby covered basic and needful topics, still more remain: a consideration of the female gaze and the erotic in Sappho (seventh century B.C.) and Nossis (fourth century B.C.); further work on fifth-century tragedy and comedy; much in the Hellenistic period, from sculpture to the mimes of Herodas; the plays of New Comedy and the Roman stage; the histories of the first and second centuries A.D., with their love of *faits divers;* and much in late antiquity, from saints' lives to the *Secret History* of Procopius. We hope our work may spur further efforts in these and other areas.

Nonclassicists may not realize what is peculiar about our table of contents. First of all, it is unusual in the field for texts and works of art to be considered jointly, especially where the art is not overtly ideological. And it is unusual for the content of ancient art to be studied at all. Of what we show, Attic vase painting (Sutton, Shapiro) will be the most familiar, Roman wall painting (Myerowitz) less so; most of the mosaics presented by Brown are almost inaccessible to nonspecialists and are usually discussed as archaeological phenomena. The texts we present constitute a miscellany similarly incongruous to a classicist's eye: Greek tragedy and the Roman historian Livy are extremely well known—but then what are these archetypal Great Books doing *here?* Aristophanes is almost as well known but oddly enough has rarely been considered from a feminist standpoint. Ovid, on the other hand, is much more familiar as an erotic poet than as a misogynistic one; on this point, as on others, we differ in our final assessments (Myerowitz, Richlin). With the ancient novels discussed here by Elsom and Montague, we arrive at a body of ancient fiction almost unknown to nonclassicists yet highly pertinent to current debates on modern fiction, both highbrow and popular; it is also only beginning to be taken seriously on a large scale by classicists themselves. Finally, the materials dealt with by Henry and Parker—the anthologist Athenaeus and the fragments of the pornographers—have rarely, if ever, been considered as texts before; they are as little known within Classics as without. Terri Marsh's epilogue reflects our project as it brings *écriture féminine* to Classics; this kind of imaginative writing has been separate from the field.

The progress of feminism in Classics has been a slow one, and our collection must be seen in the context of previous work that itself is not widely known outside the field (for overviews, see Culham 1986, 1990; Fantham 1986; Skinner 1986, 1987a, 1987b). It first had to be suggested that ancient women were a legitimate subject for study; this began to happen in the 1960s, though acceptance of the idea is still far from widespread, and the study of women in antiquity has achieved only the status of a subfield (see Blok 1987), while work on male culture remains normative. There followed a period of rediscovery and of "images of women" criticism, which began later and has lasted longer than the similar stages experienced by the fields of English literature and European history. It is only since the mid-1980s that feminist theory has appeared in the writings of feminist classicists, as we struggle with the paradox of our occupation. For we work on cultures from which almost no women's voices survive, and so our relation to textual material is in some ways problematic (see the December 1990 issue of *Helios* [17.2] devoted to this question). Yet in the endeavor to write a history of gender, our examination of male-authored texts plays an important part, defining the cultural construction of the masculine as well as the feminine.

The writing of the history of sexuality in the cultures of Greece and Rome has developed both within and without the subfield of women in antiquity. It was long considered undignified for classicists to discuss sexuality at all, and several of the few studies before the 1970s were written in Latin. Space does not permit a full survey of what happened next, but groundbreaking works include Henderson's *The Maculate Muse* (1975), a study of obscene humor in Aristophanes, and Dover's *Greek Homosexuality* (1978), a comprehensive essay in cultural history that amassed evidence from both texts and images. These were followed by my *The Garden of Priapus* (1983), a feminist study of sexuality and aggression in Roman humor; and Keuls's *The Reign of the Phallus* (1985), a recovery of sexual realities in fifth-century B.C. Athens based on texts and images. Recently, David Halperin (*One Hundred Years of Homosexuality*, 1990), John J. Winkler (*The Constraints of Desire*, 1990), and, with them, Froma Zeitlin and others (Halperin, Winkler, and Zeitlin, *Before Sexuality*, 1990) have made use of French theory, both that of

Foucault and that of the structuralists Detienne and Vernant; as the title of their collection shows, they follow Foucault in positing a sexual experience in the cultures of Greece and Rome radically different from that of our own culture. Though the methodological assumptions of our collection are similar to theirs in an emphasis on cultural context, our political framework and goals differ from theirs, in some cases widely, and we focus on sameness rather than on difference.

As classicists, we bring to our subjects expertise in language and art; as feminist scholars, however, we have presented all texts in literal English translations and have tried to supply nonspecialist readers with enough background information to make each article intelligible. We hope classicists will understand that we want to bring our material to a new audience, readers who may not yet have heard of Athenaeus but who will be very interested in him once they make his acquaintance.

Feminism for Classicists

Classicists, in turn, may find themselves on unfamiliar ground with the inclusion of, for example, Greek tragedies and Roman gladiatorial games in a study of the pornographic, and indeed may not have much familiarity with scholarly discussions of the pornographic or know what *representation* is doing next to *pornography*. This connection has to be understood in light of fifteen years of debate among feminist theorists over the nature and effects of the pornographic.

Many people, if asked to define pornography, might respond that it has to do with obscene representations of sexuality, and might add that it is intended to titillate its audience. One influential feminist definition of pornography has focused more specifically on the way in which pornography tends to objectify women, sometimes literally and violently turning them into objects. And it is this way of framing the issue that has in turn enabled theorists to postulate analogies or identities between the pornographic and the process of representation itself. Thus, the concept of the pornographic has taken on great importance in the study of film, narrative, and representational art and in theories of fantasy, gender, humor, and violence. *Pornography,* then, as the term will be used in this book, refers to much more than the common meaning of the word and brings in a whole family of areas of scholarly inquiry.

Nonfeminists should also realize that there is great disagreement among feminists on the issue of pornography. The debate has generated deep divisions, a huge bibliography, and whole subfields of theory; like feminism itself, it spans the walls of the academy (see Gubar and Hoff 1989).

Feminist definitions of pornography started with the contention that pornography enslaves real women and children in a nonregulated industry (Barry 1979). The earliest feminist critique of the pornographic broadened the popular definition of the pornographic to include what are primarily representations of violence rather than sexuality, noticing how often these involved eroticized attacks on women and reinforcement of patriarchal institutions. Theorists argued that pornography contributes to the incidence of sexual violence against women (Lederer 1980; Beneke 1982); a number of psychological studies were launched to test this idea (e.g., Linz, Donnerstein, and Penrod 1987; Malamuth and Billings 1984; Malamuth and Donnerstein 1984). It was more generally argued that pornography is degrading to women and a major contributor to women's oppression (Brownmiller 1982; Dworkin 1981; Griffin 1981). Politically, this theory informed efforts by feminists, sometimes in uncomfortable coalition with the religious or political right, to regulate pornography and pornography-related institutions (from sex shows to exploitative advertising; see FACT Book Committee 1986: 26–29 for a chronology). In 1984, a feminist antipornography ordinance was nearly adopted by the city of Minneapolis and then, nearly or briefly, elsewhere (reprinted in *Film Comment* 1984). The Minneapolis ordinance gives its own detailed definition of what constitutes pornography:

> (1) . . . the sexually explicit subordination of women, graphically depicted . . . that also includes one or more of the following:
> —women are presented dehumanized as sexual objects, things or commodities; or
> —women are presented as sexual objects who enjoy pain or humiliation; or
> —women are presented as sexual objects who experience sexual pleasure in being raped; or . . .
> —women are presented in scenarios of degradation, injury, abasement, torture, shown as filthy or inferior, bleeding, bruised, or hurt in a context that makes these conditions sexual.
> (2) The use of men, children, or transsexuals in the place of women is pornography . . .

These political and theoretical positions are associated with what is known as radical feminism.

The antipornography movement produced a backlash within feminism, as feminists rallied in defense of pornography. Two anthologies countered the antipornography position (Snitow, Stansell, and Thompson 1983; Vance 1984). One line of argument was a classic liberal statement of the priority of the rights of individuals, and the pro-pornography political movement is indeed associated with the branch of the women's movement known as liberal feminism. For example, the Feminist Anti-Censorship Taskforce (FACT) fought against the Minneapolis ordinance in its various incarnations. Another and less conventional element of the pro-pornography position came from lesbian sadomasochists. It was cogently argued that feminists should not be in the business of legislating other people's sexuality (Rubin 1984), and especially that whereas sadomasochism is as legitimate a form of sexuality as any other, a fortiori so are representations of it. Women professed their enjoyment of sadomasochism, or sadomasochistic fantasy (FACT Book Committee 1986; Russ 1985). This movement produced a critique of the antipornography movement as the political program of "cultural feminism" (Echols 1983). Echols and others pointed out that those who argue against pornography by positing an ideally good, feminine sexuality as totally nonviolent replicate the kinds of generalizations about female nature that typify misogynist, "essentialist" theorists from Aristotle to Freud (see Thurston 1987; Atwood 1985). Feminist film critics attacked antipornography documentaries and reassessed violent films (Barrowclough 1982; Pally 1984, 1985; Stern 1982; Willis 1982; *Film Comment* 1984 gives a cross-section of opinions).

For classicists, the liberal position opens the possibility of theorizing some difficult elements in Greek and Roman societies. It allows for nonjudgmental appreciation of the value of sexual practices to the participants; it differentiates strongly between the literal and the figurative meanings of text, image, act, or play (a differentiation that is largely disallowed by a radical analysis). Moreover, the liberal position is eager for historical exempla, on which it often depends to substantiate arguments against repression of given behaviors. Thus, the debates between liberals and radicals provide classicists with new questions to ask and new goals and frameworks for asking. But these debates also give us a responsibility to a new audience unfamiliar with Greek and Roman cultures. We need to explicate Greek and Roman institutions like slavery, torture, prostitution, and gladiatorial combat, as well as ranges of sexual behaviors and norms.

One of the main centers of debate, as noted above, has come to be the theory of representation, especially within the discipline of film criticism. Feminist scholars in film studies defined the process of looking ("the gaze") as gendered, as in the claim "The gaze is male," and developed this model into a critique of the way sexual identities shape men and women ("gender construction") (e.g., Mulvey 1975; E. Kaplan 1983; de Lauretis 1984; compare esp. Carter 1978, Clover 1987, Gubar 1987). Many begin from John Berger's axiom that "men look at women. Women watch themselves being looked at" (1972). The pornographic here becomes a model for all representation. For those who study art and texts, issues of gender, audience, and cultural use thus become questions that must be dealt with, and self-consciously.

As E. Ann Kaplan put it (1983: 317), "to simply celebrate what gives us pleasure seems . . . both problematic and too easy." That is, radicals may be throwing the baby out with the bathwater, but liberals need to look more closely at the whole tub. The liberal permission to take the practices of others on their own terms allows neither for the elusive nature of those terms nor for the problematic nature of the taking (see Clifford and Marcus 1986). I have found the work of theorists of fantasy especially useful for defining the pornographic; depending on Lacanian psychoanalysis, they analyze *how* pleasure is given by fantasy (e.g., Benjamin 1983; Silverman 1984; Fletcher 1986; C. Kaplan 1986; Theweleit 1987). Such studies have contributed a consciousness of the oscillation of the subject—that is, the possibility that a reader could plug into a fantasy in a variety of ways and places, taking on both dominant and subordinate roles. Like the liberal feminist analysis above, this one also sometimes argues that the explicit content of fantasy is not its meaning (Russ 1985). This kind of theory allows a much more sophisticated analysis of the experience of consumer and artist alike.

Thus, these theories have been widely used to understand the experiences of the female reader in mass genres directed to women, which, oddly enough, often feature violence against women. In such areas of popular culture as the Harlequin romance, the Gothic, and the soap opera, the romantic overlaps with the pornographic. Early studies began from the observation that consumers of this material were largely women and that they consumed texts in great quantity, and hypothesized that they found the texts sexually stimulating and that the texts were meant to be so. The popularity of physical and mental abuse directed at the female heroine provoked debate over whether women's fantasies were inherently masochistic (Snitow 1983; Modleski 1982; C. Kaplan 1986); some actually carried out surveys of readers (Radway 1984), leading one critic to posit a paradigm shift in progress toward greater representation of female sexual autonomy (Thurston 1987). This body of approaches has been applied here to several ancient romances and suggests a strong new line of inquiry for work on the ancient novel. Unfortunately, the original readers of *Clitophon and Leucippe* are not available to be surveyed; both Elsom and Montague begin in this volume to raise questions about the novels and their audiences.

The most radical critique of the production of texts considers the intersection of class and gender (Berger 1972; Carter 1978; Soble 1986) and tends toward a literal iconoclasm. Most extreme is Susanne Kappeler, who speculates in her book *The Pornography of Representation* (1986): "Art will have to go." Her analysis of the politics of representation formed the starting point of most of the essays in this collection; she argues that the process of representation is like the process of pornography in that both involve a relatively powerful viewer and a relatively powerless viewed, and that images and texts are crystallizations of this power relationship and are further used to mark, enforce, reproduce, translate, and trade in power. (Like radical feminist analyses, this one is suspicious of differentiation between literal and figurative meanings.) We have all, in various ways and with various results, tested Kappeler's hypothesis for our Greek and Roman texts and contexts. At the least, theories like hers suggest that the social implications of texts and art can and should be considered. This, in turn, raises what is for some a dismaying threat to canons, and it problematizes the term *Classics* itself. One premise of our method is that we are reading and looking at *cultural artifacts of some cultures,* rather than at *The Classics.*

But even a conservative classicist will recognize Kappeler's argument about art and society as a Platonic one (see Sutton herein). We are back at the question of the place of art in a just state—a timely one, at the time of writing, as the U.S. Congress squares off against the National Endowment for the Arts over the funding of "obscene" art.

To recap: the feminist debate on pornography clearly applies to much more in antiquity than explicitly sexual art and literature; hence our inclusion of genres not usually considered pornographic, such as tragedy, and of performance and representation that is violent and not explicitly sexual. "Major" works rub shoulders with "minor" ones here because, in terms of this debate, they have important things in common.

As feminists, we have brought to classical topics our familiarity with theory, but we have tried to explain all terms and supply readers with enough background information to make each article intelligible. We hope feminists will understand that we want to bring feminist theory to a new audience, readers who may not yet have heard of Susanne Kappeler but who will be very interested in her once they make her acquaintance.

There is one special and important reason why we need to carry out these studies. Attention to the history of sexuality has flourished outside Classics, with the result that the best-known works on ancient sexuality have been written by nonclassicists, most notably Michel Foucault (but see above). One trend seems to be to seek salvation for humankind in a past golden age, much as the Greeks and Romans themselves did, or as Europeans did and anthropologists do in claiming nobility for cultures distant from their own. In vogue are arguments that the Greeks had no concept of sexuality per se (and therefore differ from us) or that homosexuality is a post-nineteenth-century concept (and therefore the Greeks and Romans had no homophobia) or that the Marquis de Sade's brand of sexuality is essentially modern (and therefore pleasure in cruelty does not predate him). The Greeks and Romans certainly had their differences from us and from each other, but not so much so that modern paradigms are inapplicable, and this collection should correct some current ideas about ancient societies (where, obviously, sexual norms also varied from class to class and region to region). Likewise, we can demonstrate that "modern" sexuality is not, pace Foucault and others, always significantly different in kind from ancient (see, e.g., Hoff 1989). Within this volume there is ample material to show that sexuality and pornography existed as concepts in Greek and Roman cultures (see Richlin 1983: 1–31), that the sexual was often consciously conflated with the violent by members of those cultures, and that the Greek and Roman hierarchical division of sexual ranks into penetrators and penetrated, noticed by Foucault, produced qualitatively different experiences for upper and lower ranks.

Specifics

As noted above, our assessments of the validity of Kappeler's hypothesis vary. I would draw the reader's attention to four positions in particular. Parker shows how ancient sex manuals and their attributions fit with the Hellenistic idea of taxonomic ordering, of control by listing; contrast Myerowitz, who defends the humanity of images. Joshel rejects the collapse of pornography with representation, sensing political oversimplification in a conflation of gender with other markers; Henry, on the other hand, uses Kappeler to provide models not only for ancient objectifications of women but also for modern accounts of ancient sexuality.

Of the observed phenomena that recur from study to study here, most striking are (1) inequity between partners; (2) objectification of women, with some emphasis on (a) nudity and (b) representation as food; (3) problematizing of the position of the female spectator. Several studies encountered and analyzed ancient uses of the term *pornographos*.

Inequity between Partners

Many contributors instance inequity as an essential framework of ancient gender relations. Sutton shows it on Greek vases, both pornographic (female prostitute services male customer) and romantic (society persuades, the bride is persuaded). Shapiro demonstrates equalities between male and male in courtship scenes that are lacking between male and female, as they are lacking, too, in rare scenes of homosexual rape that act out Eros's nature. Henry shows how Athenaeus's symposium constructs difference between male and female: men have communal consumption (of the female) and moderation; women have neither.

Moving from the specific to the abstract, Parker (following Myerowitz 1985) points to woman as *materia* of Ovid's *ars,* as for Aristotle the prime task was the subjection of matter (female) to spirit (male); Parker grounds his analysis in the Greco-Roman sexual dichotomy between passive (penetrated, symbolically female) and active (penetrator, male). On the same grounds, I argue that *pati* ("to be penetrated") and *vis* ("rape") are gendered in Ovid's poetry as female and male, despite any temporary cross-sex identification of the subjective with the female. The noninterchangeability of these sexual positions is stressed by Joshel, who presents Roman ideological recommendations for the male to rule his own body so he can rule others, while the female's only "choice" is to die; Elsom shows that woman in the Greek romance has the single "choice" of being a willing or an unwilling object; Henry shows prostitutes who "choose" always to act for men. Joshel's suggestion about class and power imbalance ties in with my analysis of pleasure and violence within hierarchy, and with Brown's reading of gladiatorial mosaics as symbols of power and ownership within the house. Marsh, on the other hand, claims that her cast of characters represents not genders but relative positions and holds out for fluidity of power.

Objectification of Women

I would direct the reader's attention most strongly to the examples of objectification of the female, shared by almost all our sources. To readers of Eva Keuls's *Reign of the Phallus,* such objectification will not come as a surprise, but I hope it will jolt those who may think of antiquity as a time somehow superior to others.

The most striking examples of objectification are those that present a naked woman to an audience, as in Aristophanes, discussed by Zweig; these women are both nude and mute, or, at most, make animal sounds (compare Joshel, Richlin). Sutton discusses naked women on Greek vases, while both he and Shapiro discuss "pinups." Those treated by Shapiro, however, are male, the boys beloved by older males; and Shapiro discusses how they are idealized and how they become signs: of a *kalos* inscription on a vase showing male rape, he remarks, "one can't help thinking this is a pointed message to the recipient." Shapiro goes on to compare and contrast the elements shared by this objectification of the male with objectification of the female. Female characters are presented nude to the reader or viewer, or spied on, in Ovid's poetry (Richlin) and in Greek romance (Montague); Ovid's poetry also mutilates and disfigures them. Parker connects ancient gastrologies with ancient sex manuals; Henry shows how Athenaeus commodifies women as food. Roman history prefers to present women's bodies as dead (Joshel), while sex manuals dismember women (Parker). On the symbolic level, this is the establishment of gender through the exposure of women to a public gaze (Elsom), the identification of the female with Iphigenia (Marsh): the text of gender demands the sacrifice. Many narratives take pleasure in terror, often stating women's fear to be beautiful (Joshel, Richlin, Elsom, Montague). Those who find some male identification with this female position agree that such identification basically confirms male normativity (Joshel, Richlin, Elsom). I suggest that the woman-objectifying content of these texts is essential to them and typical not only of their society but of all narratives produced within hierarchy.

The Woman Spectator

Many contributors deal with the problem of the woman spectator—both ancient and modern—confronting such narratives. In the ancient context, Rabinowitz and Zweig deal with the fact that we cannot even be sure women (which women?) could attend the Athenian theater; that if they were there, they saw plays in which the female was both everywhere and nowhere, in which female desire led to death and male suffering (Rabinowitz); plays which were produced by, for, and with men (Zweig). Likewise, in Roman ideology of the early empire, Joshel argues, uncontrolled female sexuality is said to lead to a "flood," an overwhelming of (male) structures. Several chapters touch on the cooption of the female voice: e.g. the male-identified character Lysistrata, who parcels out the mute nude Reconciliation (Zweig); the female pseudonyms attached to ancient sex manuals (Parker). Myerowitz, on the other hand, argues that married women as well as men saw Roman *tabellae* and that both were affected in equivalent ways. We also ask, how can women *now* read a canon that includes such texts? Montague suggests that her texts force us to become resisting readers, valuing the female characters and seeking the "muted text" within.

Pornographos

An argument from etymology has been a favorite of current theorists on pornography; we present analyses of the term as first used. Rabinowitz uses the parts of the word to correspond with (a) a Platonic focus on content (*pornê*) and (b) an Aristotelian focus on process (*graphê*). Zweig provides basic social background on prostitution, drawing a distinction between *pornê* and *hetaira*. Parker uses the (rare) ancient term *pornographos* to represent what he calls "whore-writing," the inscription of women as whores, and traces the outlines of the more common ancient term *anaischuntographos,* to represent what he calls "shame-writing," the rejection of behaviors as bad. Myerowitz discusses the term *pornographos* as it was used to mean "painter of whores"—that is, an easel artist who used prostitutes for models. Henry analyzes the first use of the term in Greek, in its second-century A.D. context. This multiplicity of approaches should counter any tendency to say "The Greeks had a word for it" and go from there. What Greeks? And what did it *mean* to them? Not what it means to us; but what it meant to them connects with things related to what it means to us.

Now What?

Kappeler's model, along with the material suggested above, leaves us wondering whether any form of representation *could* be all right. Livy's narrative of the Sabine women elides their experience of rape—that's no good. Ovid enjoys telling us about it—also no good. Talthybius's exposure of Polyxena's body is no good, but so is Hecuba's empathy, which leads to her replication of the strategies of the Greek army. Must we choose between these alternatives?

If our own enterprise in this volume has any credibility, there must be another way, a female gaze. Though it has historically been mythologized as destructive—the gaze of Medusa—maybe that is not the only possible method of representing it, as Hélène Cixous (re)wrote. Several contributors find a positive to accentuate. Myerowitz maintains that the sex scenes on Roman wall paintings are not hierarchically constructed but egalitarian; they objectify both men and women, and such objectification is an inevitable and necessary part of human socialization. Interestingly, both Elsom and Montague, in analyzing romance novels, are optimistic about the place of the female reader. And Marsh asserts the possibility of bootstrapping, instancing the book you now hold in your hands.

Meanwhile, have we recovered anything of real women in antiquity? For some would claim that feminists in Classics should concentrate on women's realities, not on more male ideology (Culham 1990). Parker, though noting that we are not allowed to know how real his female authors were, discusses the fragments of the purported female pornographers for nonclassicists for the first time. Myerowitz, though noting that we have little but ideology to testify to Roman women's experience, reconstructs a room in the domestic world some women inhabited. Henry recommends Athenaeus as a source for women's history; his huge collection of anecdotes about Greek prostitutes could tell us much about the conditions of their lives, if mediated by male imaginations. I would emphasize that the ideological systems that inform our materials are themselves important elements in women's history. But it is true that, as Joshel says, we are mostly looking at the male imagination and the process by which real women are elided. Where are the women of this history? The fact that Marsh so eloquently imagines them testifies sadly to our lack of them. And this lack is something big for us to know.

History and Change

One of our most important preoccupations turns out to be with our responsibility to history, with the (im)possibility of change. On the one hand, our research suggests that the *longue durée* of history for women stretches from antiquity to now; we can demonstrate pretty clearly that our material was pornographic within its society in the same way that current material is pornographic within ours. Nothing has changed. On another hand, our research suggests that what changes or differences did occur in antiquity, whether within a culture or from one culture to another, made very little difference in the bottom line for women—literally *plus ça change*. . . . Yet, on a third hand, it is clear that the specific shape of the phenomena we analyze is related to the particular construction of Greek and Roman societies as slave states. Where slaves are more or less naked, and free(born) or citizen women are heavily clothed, guarded, and/or sequestered, the available and the unavailable set each other off as objects of desire (see Lerner 1986: 123–40, on the ancient Near East). Several contributors (Sutton, Zweig, Joshel, Richlin, Henry) deal with the presence of slaves and/or prostitutes in the audience of our narratives, and with its meaning for them, for other women, and for the audience as a whole.

We do chart some changes in the history of sexuality in antiquity. Sutton outlines a tie-in between political changes in Athens and types of representation; both he and Shapiro trace changes in the popularity of different topics on vases, such as the fad for mythic rape scenes from 500 to 450 B.C. (Shapiro). Shapiro also sketches differences between Athenian and modern definitions of male homosexuality and the effect these have on what is represented. Parker's sex manuals appear, like Sutton's vases, at the time of the shift from an aristocratic and homosexual model to a bourgeois and heterosexual one. Myerowitz's egalitarian Roman erotic paintings, as she notes, are viewed in a domestic context rather than in a symposiac one as in Greece; these paintings contrast strongly with the Greek vases but also with Joshel's contemporary texts (so antierotic!) and with mine (so nonegalitarian!). Joshel suggests both how the changes Livy lived through—the civil war, the Augustan reforms—produced his text and how his stories mark changes in the Roman past. As for the larger context, if we did not believe change to be possible in history, we would be wasting our time in writing this book.

Yet our research produces some daunting evidence for lack of change, both in text and in context. Elsom and Montague both find that ancient romances share much with modern ones; Montague debunks the common claim that the romance novel began in the eighteenth century. Henry points to the long history of the pornographic, not only in Western civilization but within antiquity; her source, Athenaeus, recounts stories that were seven hundred years old when he quoted them, as if they were perfectly fresh and relevant. And I suggest that Sade need not be credited with inventing something new.

Furthermore, our analysis and methodology have ancient precursors. Rabinowitz cites Aristotle's view that tragedy renders the painful pleasurable. Joshel notes that in reading history through our present, we are only doing as Livy did. While indebted to Foucault, we here refute some of his claims about periodization in sexual history (Parker) and point out his replication of the structures he studies (Henry). As Joshel notes, it has been our business to explain, where images recur, what structures and practices reproduce them, what are their functions and effects.

Overall, we bear witness to a system that has reproduced itself in various cultures over a span of two thousand years, and our work shows clearly what the difference is between nonsubstantive and substantive change. But we all desire and by this writing work for substantive change. It is my hope that by exposing the workings of the pornographic, throughout history, we may contribute to its transformation.

We have also tried to make a serious contribution both to knowledge about antiquity and to the debate about pornography and representation. So we have chosen for the cover of this book an object discussed by Molly Myerowitz in her exploration of art and the erotic in Ovid's Rome: a bronze mirror cover from the first century A.D. Mirrors in ancient iconography were associated with the female; on this cover we see two lovers in bed and behind them on a wall a picture of two lovers in bed; a representation of the interrelation between art and life, a picture of it covers our book as once it covered a mirror that a Roman woman looked into and saw a face that we can only imagine.

NOTE

Many thanks to Diana Robin for critical reading and to Marilyn Skinner for close reading beyond the call of duty.

Time Line of Events, Sources, and Persons Discussed

GREECE

Mycenean culture—actual time of Troy.

Homeric poems sung about Troy.

GREEK DARK AGE

ARCHAIC PERIOD

Hesiod (didactic poet).

600

Hetairai and customers on red-figured vases.

CLASSICAL PERIOD

The Sophists flourish as teachers of rhetoric in Athens and elsewhere.

Aspasia, courtesan.

OLD COMEDY IN ATHENS

Aristophanes, comic playwright (c. 450–c. 385 B.C.) (*Wasps, Birds, Knights, Peace, Frogs, Acharnians, Lysistrata, Clouds, Congresswomen, Thesmophoriazousai*).

Euripides, tragic playwright (435–406 B.C.) (*Bacchae, Hekabe* [Hecuba], *Trojan Women, Hippolytus, Medea, Alcestis, Iphigenia in Tauris, Iphigenia at Aulis*).

Aeschylus, tragic playwright (525/4–456 B.C.) (*Oresteia* trilogy: *Agamemnon, Libation Bearers, Eumenides*).

Sophocles, tragic playwright (c. 496–406 B.C.) (*Oedipus Rex, Antigone, Women of Trachis*).

PELOPONNESIAN WAR (431–404) Thucydides, Athenian historian (c. 460–c. 400 B.C.), Pericles, Athenian leader (c. 495–429 B.C.). Xanthippe and Socrates.

ROME

LATE BRONZE AGE (1580–1120)

Aeneas leaves Troy to found Rome.

Rhea Silvia gives birth to Romulus and Remus.

753
Mythic date of the founding of Rome by Romulus and Remus—rape of the Sabines.

509
Mythic date of the start of the Roman republic; Lucretia's rape and death.

REPUBLIC

449
Mythic date of the killing of Verginia and overthrow of the *decemviri*.

GREECE

MIDDLE COMEDY

Parrhasius, painter (Ephesus).

Xenophon, student of Socrates (c. 430–c. 354 B.C.).

Philaenis, Athenian writer.

Plato, student of Socrates, philosopher (c. 429–347 B.C.).

Aristotle, student of Plato, philosopher (384–322 B.C.).

Salpe, (?) pornographer.

Botrys of Sicily.

HELLENISTIC PERIOD

(4th cent. B.C.) Pausias of Sicyon, painter.

Erinna, poet.

NEW COMEDY

Menander, playwright of New Comedy (342/1–291/0 B.C.).

Nikophanes of Sikyon, painter, pupil of Pausias.

Herodas, writer of mimes at Alexandria (3rd cent. B.C.).

Aristeides of Thebes, painter.

Theophrastus, student of Aristotle (*Characters*) (372/369–288/285 B.C.).

Apelles, painter

Nossis, poet (c. 290 B.C.).

ALEXANDRIA FLOURISHES AS CENTER FOR LITERATURE AND SCHOLARSHIP

400

300

ROME

REPUBLIC

GLADIATORIAL GAMES BEGIN TO BE POPULAR

GREECE

Paxamos, (?) pornographer.

Pamphile, writer-philosopher, of Epidauros.

Elephantis or Elephantine, pornographer.

200 100 44 31 AUGUSTUS 0 14 TIBERIUS 37 GAIUS 41 CLAUDIUS 54 NERO 68 69 VESPASIAN 79 TITUS 81 DOMITIAN 96 NERVA 98

Cicero, orator and philosopher (106–43 B.C.).

Murder of Julius Caesar.

Battle of Actium; Octavian (Augustus) becomes first Roman emperor.

JULIO-CLAUDIAN EMPERORS

FLAVIAN EMPERORS

ANTONINE EMPERORS

Sejanus, courtier (d. A.D. 31).
Valerius Maximus, anecdote collector.

Martial, epigrammatist, (c. 40–c. 104).

Elder Pliny (A.D. 23/4–79), natural historian.

Petronius, satirist.

79 POMPEII BURIED

Younger Pliny, letter writer and civil servant (61/62– before 114)

CIVIL WARS

Livy, historian (64 B.C.– A.D. 12).

Lucan, epic poet (A.D. 39–65).

Statius, epic and lyric poet (c. 45–96).

Augustan poets:
Virgil (70–19 B.C.).
Horace (65–8 B.C.).
Propertius (c. 50 B.C.–c. A.D. 2).
Tibullus (48–19 B.C.).
Ovid (43 B.C.–A.D. 17) (Ars Amatoria, Fasti, Amores, Heroides, Tristia, Ex Ponto, Metamorphoses).
Sulpicia, poet.

Elder Seneca, rhetorician (c. 55 B.C.–c. A.D. 40).

Younger Seneca, courtier–philosopher–dramatist (4 B.C.–A.D. 65).

Quintilian, rhetorician (c. 40– c. 100).

Calpurnius Flaccus, rhetorician (2nd cent.).

PANTOMIME POPULAR AS A THEATRICAL FORM

GLADIATORIAL GAMES CONTINUE POPULAR

*Year of 4 emperors: Otho, Vitellius, Galba, Vespasian.

LATE REPUBLIC   PRINCIPATE

ROME

GREECE

Longus, novelist (*Daphnis and Chloe*).

Lucian, satirist, of Samosata in Asia Minor (c. 120–180).

Achilles Tatius, novelist (*Leucippe and Clitophon*).

Chariton, novelist (*Chaireas and Callirhoe*).

Plutarch, of Boeotia, historian, essayist (c. 46–after 120).

SECOND SOPHISTIC

Epictetus, philosopher (c. 55–c. 135).

Dio Cassius, historian. Athenaeus, compiler-philosopher.

Hesychius's lexicon (5th cent.).

Suda compiled (10th cent.).

Macrobius, literary critic (5th cent.).
St. Augustine, theologian (354–430).

---

100 TRAJAN 117 HADRIAN 138 ANTONINUS PIUS 161 MARCUS AURELIUS 180 Apuleius of Madaura in N. Africa, rhetorician, priest of Isis, novelist (born c. 123). 200 218 HELIOGABALUS

SECOND SOPHISTIC

(?) *Priapea* collected.

Suetonius, historian (c. 69–c. 140).

Tacitus, historian (c. 55–after 115).

Juvenal, satirist (c. 50–c. 117).

Aulus Gellius, anthologist-philosopher (c. 123–c. 165).

Clement of Alexandria, Christian apologist (c. 150–sometime between 211–216).

GLADIATORIAL MOSAICS (through 4th cent.): (North Africa, Gaul, Germany, Italy)

GLADIATORIAL GAMES CONTINUE POPULAR . . . 5th cent.

ROME

PORNOGRAPHY AND REPRESENTATION
IN GREECE AND ROME

1

Pornography and Persuasion on Attic Pottery

Robert F. Sutton, Jr.

In *Antigone,* Sophocles lists various techniques by which the human race prevails, including "the emotions that sustain the city" (*astynomous orgas,* 355). This phrase transcends our notions of "civic spirit" or patriotism to cover the full range of cultural values on which classical Athenian society was based, including those related to sexuality and gender. Social patterns were both manifested and maintained by several means, including myth, ritual, and language (Versnell 1987: 78), as fused, for example, in Attic drama and the visual arts, particularly the paintings on Athenian vases. Vase painting was a popular medium that as the Democracy arose and flowered provided the Athenian people with a set of changing self-images with which they could define themselves as individuals and in respect to one another. While other scholars have recently explored a variety of themes through which this was accomplished (*La cité des images;* Hollein 1988), this chapter considers how attitudes on sex and gender were expressed and transmitted to various elements of Athenian society by comparing the explicit representation of sexuality on Athenian vases with representations of weddings and other scenes where sexuality is expressed in polite terms. In contrast to the analysis of Eva Keuls (1985; reviewed in Shapiro 1986), who recently surveyed much of the same evidence, the emphasis here is on vase painting as a medium of social communication.

In examining such products of popular culture, it is best to have evidence both of the work of art in question, whether text, object, or performance, and of audience attitudes and reactions. The model I adopt here is that used most notably in recent studies of the romance novel, especially Thurston (1987), who discusses the feedback response between consumer and producer. Unfortunately, in analyzing Greek vase paintings we have only the product to look at. My suggestion is that the change in content of these paintings reflects a change in their target audience; that, along with what we know about the oppressive nature of marriage at Athens at the end of the fifth century B.C. (e.g., from Xenophon's *Oikonomikos*), we must also consider the trend toward romance in popular art. Over the course of two centuries, vase paintings moved from a strictly male-oriented, egocentric eroticism to one that was emotionally based, aimed in good part at a feminine audience that had previously been neglected. Whether this represents an advance or a sidestep remains to be seen. The replacement of pornographic themes by romantic ones links this study to current feminist discussions of the romantic in terms of the pornographic (e.g., Snitow 1983). Meanwhile, before these ideas can be explored in detail, it may be useful to consider the nature of vase painting as an artistic medium and some difficulties encountered in interpreting its sexual imagery.

The vases under discussion were made in Athens and the surrounding region of Attica (whence the term *Attic*) during the sixth, fifth, and fourth centuries B.C.,[1] the Archaic and Classical periods. We shall generally avoid evidence from other times or places because each age and every Greek state had its own institutions, which were sometimes radically different from those of Classical Athens. By the middle of the sixth century, Attic potters achieved a virtual monopoly in the export of fine pottery painted with scenes drawn from both myth and daily life (Cook 1960; Boardman 1974, 1975, 1989; Scheibler 1983; Bron and Lissarague 1989). More than thirty thousand painted Attic vases survive from the seventh through the fourth centuries, apparently only a small proportion of the original production (Webster 1972: 3–4). This quantity indicates that we are considering a popular art that is comparable in relative scale to contemporary mass-market media. Around 530 B.C., the painters reversed the older black-figure technique (as seen below in Figure 1.1) to create the more expressive red-figure technique (below, Figures 1.2–1.12), and the two techniques coexisted until about the time of the Persian invasion in 480. The vases were decorated by several hundred painters, largely anonymous personalities whose individual styles can be recognized through the life's work of Sir John Beazley (Kurtz 1985; Boardman 1974, 1975, 1989).[2] These painters were drawn from a range of Athenian society including middle-class citizens, resident aliens, slaves, and even a few women (Scheibler 1983: 107–33; Kehrberg 1982; Beazley 1989). Almost all vases can be dated confidently on the basis of style to a twenty-five-year span, and most even more closely (see cautionary remarks in Robertson 1976; the revised chronology of Francis and Vickers 1983 is not persuasive).

To reconstruct the audience of the vase paintings, we must rely heavily on the evidence of the vases themselves and their archaeological context, for we cannot observe them actually in use or interview their users, and they are barely mentioned in surviving written sources (Scheibler 1983; Bron and Lissarague 1989). We must rely on inference and a statistical form of proof that makes our reconstruction necessarily hypothetical: we propose an ideal norm that reflects the apparent perception by the painters en masse of their intended market rather than the actual market itself as measured by objective means. The hazards of such an approach are obvious (see Thurston 1987: 4–7), and must be kept in mind.

Greek vases were designed for actual use, like china, although in Attica much red-figure and black-figure was reserved for ritual and special use (Scheibler 1983: 137–44). From its shape one can deduce the general use each vase was intended to serve, whether as drinking cup, water jar, or perfume bottle (see Moore and Philippides 1986). A demonstrated connection between vase shape and subject (Webster 1972) suggests that the painters had a clear notion of an audience and context in which various scenes were to be seen, regardless of what may actually have been done with the particular vases that survive, though that, too, is useful for our purpose. We know the city or region in which many were found and can trace general patterns of trade that can help identify pieces designed specially for domestic use or export (Webster 1972; Boardman 1979; Scheibler 1983: 136–86). Most well-preserved vases have been found in or near graves; some were intended specifically for the tomb, while others show wear and repairs indicating prior use. Sanctuaries yield many fragments of vases that were dedicated to the gods or used in mortal feasting. Domestic, commercial, and civic sites yield enough sherds, battered as they are, to suggest that painted pottery was also in everyday use. But there is virtually no detailed information on how vases were marketed at any level. While it is said that in Athens respectable women did not venture from the seclusion of their homes to shop, the evidence is scanty at best, delivered by males, and skewed to the ideal of a leisure class; it should not be used to suggest that women played only a minor role in selecting vases for their own use, whether individual women actually left their houses on occasion, dealt with itinerant vendors, or acted through second parties from their own households.

To understand the effect of sexual scenes in vase painting on ancient viewers, we must also understand Athenian sexual mores. Reflecting the articulation of ancient Athenian society, sexual norms varied according to one's social status as free or slave, citizen or foreigner, male or female, rich or poor, and young or old (Henderson 1988 and Pomeroy 1988 with earlier references; Foucault 1985; Halperin 1986, 1989; Blok and Mason 1987). Chastity was required of female but not male citizens, marriage was by arrangement, the seduction of respectable women was regarded as a greater threat to society than rape, prostitution was legal, homosexuality was relatively acceptable, and aspects of sex formed an important part of religious belief and cult. As a potential source of shame, sex was approached with discretion by the well-bred, although their boundaries were not the same as ours, and there were certain occasions (often ritual) when sexual matters were publicly displayed and discussed, such as in Old Comedy. To clarify this practice, we can follow Henderson (1975: 2) in distinguishing between obscenity and pornography (see Dworkin 1981: 1, 199–202), terms often used interchangeably. *Obscenity* signifies the mention or representation of sexual and other taboo matters (e.g., those concerned with bodily elimination) for nonsexual purposes, including good luck, apotropaic magic, and religion, and to insult, amuse, or enrage (Henderson 1975; Johns 1982: 38–96). In contrast, *pornography* is material designed to cause sexual arousal and pleasure (see Roth 1982: 1). The former is essentially extroverted and social, the latter introverted and personal, tied as it is to the individual psychology of the user. These are not strictly separate categories but two different aspects that must be considered in evaluating sexually explicit material from classical antiquity.

The current debate on pornography has focused on the social impact of sexual and other representations (including ethnic stereotypes, violence, and children's advertising), particularly their relation to socially undesirable action and attitudes (e.g., *Film Comment* 1984; Rubin 1984; Eysenck 1982: 305–12). A dominant school of thought argues that the representation of undesirable acts and attitudes is harmful since it actualizes them, thereby providing an external model that serves as a stimulus for imitation (see studies listed in Byrne and Kelley 1984: 6). Using the Greek term for "persuasion," we shall call this the *Peitho* model, since the representation can be said to persuade the viewer to imitation. Many psychologists believe that this model is valid for our own society (Donnerstein 1984; Zillman and Bryant 1984; but see Brannigan and Goldenberg 1987), and ancient Athenians believed it was operative in theirs (Aristophanes *Frogs* 1009–1097; Plato *Republic* 401). In opposition to the Peitho model, an opposing *cathartic* model has also been proposed, one whose name betrays its Aristotelian inspiration (*Poetics* 6.1449b). According to this model (whatever Aristotle may have meant by *katharsis*), images of undesirable acts can be a positive force by releasing dangerous passions that cannot be and are not actually realized. Though the validity of this model in our society is debated (Roth 1982: 18), it seems to operate in modern Japan, which has a very low incidence of rape despite prevalence of rape, bondage, and violence in its pornography and romantic fiction (Abramson and Hayashi 1984; Thurston 1987: 219 n. 2). Abramson and Hayashi connect this effect strongly to Japanese reliance on shame rather than guilt as a means of controlling antisocial impulses, factors that may make it applicable as well to classical Greece.

The Peitho model has been the basis of most contemporary feminist (and other) opposition to pornography. Some feminist critics target scenes that link sex and violence, others reject all heterosexual depiction because of the objectification implicit in the process, while yet others extend this objection to include all forms of representation on the grounds that it denies the existence of a female subject (Dworkin 1981; Kappeler 1986). The Peitho effect is, of course, not always thought to be negative, even when applied to sexual imaging. While most work on pornography assumes a male gaze, or the cultivation of a female market that reflects and advocates the values of patriarchy (Kaplan 1983), Thurston's (1987) study of modern mass-market romance novels suggests that this is not always the case. Using reader surveys and other information provided by authors, publishers, and readers, she shows that the rise of a new class of erotic romances aimed at a female audience reflects a new feminine outlook occasioned by the modern women's movement. The creators of these new romances are involved in a feedback loop with their mass audience: not only have producers solicited the reaction of their audience and responded to it by reshaping their narratives, but readers report that these novels have helped them reorient themselves and make major life decisions that fly in the face of traditional feminine roles and values.

Such discussion of representation is crucial to the ancient social historian, for most of our evidence is representational (Cantarella 1987: 5–6); the few hard data that survive are very hard indeed and rarely can be interpreted on their own. These modern studies help us recognize that the representations surviving from the ancient world are valuable not simply as passive, albeit biased, reflections of ancient life that can help us reconstruct it; in addition, they actively molded popular opinion and mediated between individual psychology and collective group identity. The following discussion will show how the popular, mass-produced genre (daily life) scenes on Athenian pottery of the sixth and fifth centuries B.C. helped the people (*dêmos*) of Athens acquire the sense of corporate identity that made possible the radical democracy of the fifth century. Whatever we living twenty-five centuries later may find deficient in this ideology with respect to the position it accorded (for example) women and slaves, the package formed a coherent whole that worked fairly well in its own day, was widely accepted throughout its own society (whatever the personal cost, to our eyes), and supported the discussion of far more liberal notions whose fruition has occurred only in our own day. This chapter does not seek to condemn or to glorify this ancient ideology but rather to identify one of the social mechanisms through which it gained popular acceptance even from those who would seem to have had little to gain from their adherence—Athenian women.

Copulation

We begin with the scenes that are most obviously pornographic, those showing sexual congress in explicit terms. Though earlier avoided by scholars or published with censored illustration, since the 1920s this material has been collected in a number of specialized picture books and is now one of the most completely illustrated and conveniently studied categories of the genre scenes on Greek vases (Brandt 1925–28; Vorberg 1932; Marcadé 1962; Grant 1975; Boardman and LaRocca 1975; Johns 1982; Keuls 1985). Otto Brendel's groundbreaking interpretative article of 1970 remains basic, despite correction of details occasioned by recent more specialized study. One should not from this abundance of illustration misrepresent the vase painters' lack of inhibition in portraying sexual themes, for only about one hundred fifty vases show figures actually engaged in copulation, a scant proportion of the thirty to forty thousand vases that survive. We only mention in passing the far more numerous (two thousand or more) scenes of male drinking parties in which there is often a strong sexual element even when graphic illustration of copulatory acts is avoided. Vase painters distinguish two distinct types of such parties: the more sedate *symposia* ("banquets") and the wilder *kômoi* ("revels"), the former characterized by horizontal arrangements of reclining figures set indoors, the latter by more varied compositions of more or less vertical ones set both in and out of doors. These relatively restrained scenes are often clearly pornographic in intent and show in more presentable form the same values expressed in the few really explicit examples. The sexually explicit representations are chronologically restricted almost exclusively to the years 575–450. There is a significant drop after about 480, very few after 450, and only one from the fourth century. Even if these subjects moved to other artistic media like (lost) painted panels and mirrors (Brendel 1970: 30), their eclipse on Attic vases is as significant a sign of changing taste as the later elimination of obscenity from Attic comedy.

Heterosexual

Explicit heterosexual intercourse is usually found on cups and other shapes used for the consumption of wine. Vases of the same types often appear in these scenes to define the setting as either komos or symposium, neither of which was attended by women with a reputation to uphold. The scenes would have provided models for imitation to elicit behavior appropriate to the occasion from both the men and their female companions in the sex industry. This argument is somewhat undercut by the observation that the overwhelming majority of these vases have actually been found in parts of central Italy inhabited by the Etruscans, the non-Greek neighbors of the Romans. As will be seen, Attic potters first introduce explicit sexual subjects on a special class of vases that seem from their geographical distribution to have been produced largely for export to the west; though painters quickly move the theme onto more generalized production, most still finds its way to Etruscan lands. While one is tantalized by this prospect of specialized Athenian production of pornography for the Etruscan market, we know virtually nothing of the way Attic vases were actually marketed for export, and there may be a variety of factors at work, including a marked Etruscan fondness for cups, or possible demand for commodities carried in certain types of vessels. The precise meaning of this remarkable distribution must therefore be set aside for exploration elsewhere, as must the interesting problem of how the scenes were interpreted by the Etruscans, whose imperfectly known culture was different from the Athenian in several respects, including the treatment of women (Bonfante 1981; Warren 1973a and b). Athenian painters, we assume, were reproducing their own cultural experience in these scenes; if so, the effect would likewise have been greatest on their fellow Athenians, to whom all details would have been familiar. Certainly Athenians and other Greeks did not eschew such scenes; they do occur in Greek lands, in unspectacular quantities but with consistency, throughout the period of their manufacture. Examples have even been found on the Athenian Acropolis; that they were dedications or used in religious feasts receives support from fragments of two votive plaques depicting explicit sexual subjects, one from the Acropolis, the other of unknown provenance (Greifenhagen 1976; Boardman 1975: fig. 18).

A probable explanation for the popularity of these scenes during the Archaic period and decline in the Classical period is that their representation of individualistic self-gratification, often shown in almost countercultural terms, runs contrary to the trends of vase imagery under the fifth century Democracy, which comes to stress a channeling of emotion into socially beneficial avenues. In most of the sexual scenes, one notices a strong connection between the drinking of wine and sexual activity; whether their original impulse is to be sought in the cult of Dionysos or not (pro, Brendel 1970: 15–18; con, Carpenter 1986: 86–90), they emphasize a release from social restraint that is similar to what is later associated with the god, as seen in Euripides' *Bacchae* and the unrestrained language of Old Comedy. These scenes seem to portray male emotional self-expression (*orgê*) of various forms; sex is not associated here primarily with affection and sensual pleasure, but more often with hostility and even anger. While in the earliest scenes the sexes appear on more or less equal footing, perhaps reflecting the release provided by Dionysiac worship, there soon emerges a pattern of male dominance and female submission that is appropriate to the social situation of ancient prostitution. The choice of sexual acts and the manner of their depiction emphasize male orgasmic gratification. Female pleasure and even comfort are often disregarded, and while women are several times shown performing fellatio (without pleasure), there is no explicit portrayal of cunnilingus (see Keuls 1985: fig. 131). While female pleasure is occasionally portrayed by the Archaic artist and then consistently developed in the Classical period, it serves only as an aspect or stimulus of male pleasure and is not treated as a theme of interest for its own sake.

Both hetero- and homosexual congress are introduced on Attic pottery in the second quarter of the sixth century on a large group of vases known as the Tyrrhenian amphorae, whose name derives from their discovery almost exclusively in Etruria (=Tyrrhenia) and the west.[3] On at least eleven of these vessels (*ABV*: 102.95–102; *Paralipomena* 41; Keuls 1985: figs. 135–36; Dover 1978: B51, B53; Boardman and LaRocca 1975: 76–78), sexual intercourse is included in komoi that descend from groups of padded dancers that appear on several Greek wares during the early years of the sixth century, and especially on Corinthian vases (Seeberg 1971; Boardman and LaRocca 1975: 76). These dancers, wearing costumes padded to emphasize the buttocks and belly, perform an unseemly drunken dance in which they often bend to extend and slap their prominent buttocks, occasionally display grotesque genitals (Seeberg 1971: 38–40, 73–74), and even defecate and conduct sexual intercourse in public (Stibbe 1972: no. 64). The general character of these activities in respect to Greek notions of propriety is illustrated by Herodotus's tale (6.126–130) of the noble Corinthian Hippokleides whose drunken dance at a public banquet cost him the hand of Agariste, daughter of Cleisthenes, the dignified tyrant of Sicyon. What seems to have particularly irked Cleisthenes was Hippokleides' finale, in which he inverted himself on a table, thereby exposing his genitals to public view (a natural consequence of Greek dress that Herodotus did not need to spell out to his audience), and waved his legs in the air. This notorious event is roughly contemporary with the vases under discussion, and Hippokleides' proverbial response to losing his bride, which might be rendered as "Hippokleides couldn't care less!" admirably sums up the irreverent, unconventional tone of the Tyrrhenian Group's revels.

Elements of "Hippokleidian" dance long continue in subsequent depictions of heterosexual copulation on Attic vases. As on a black-figure cup painted around 540 by the painter Beazley named Elbows Out (Figure 1.1), sex usually is shown in a group setting, often with the figures arrayed like chorus lines. The preference for standing positions, with an emphasis on the buttocks, which are often prominently extended, and for approaches from the rear betray their origin in the dance. A humorous, outrageous, and almost slapstick tone that emphasizes the kinetic over the sensual and the obviously formal, almost abstract manner of composition serve to remove many of these scenes from the realm of actual experience. Many might be regarded as a sign for social catharsis rather than a persuasive model to emulate. In some, the mood of good-humored obscene merriment seems almost a social leveler that places all actors, nude and devoid of all social trappings outside those of the moment, on an equal footing and eliminates any sense of power except to grant or deny a frantic or pathetic suitor's request.

A gradual transformation occurs, however, whereby the female partner becomes increasingly objectified into a piece of sexual furniture, and the male actor becomes the subject of the scene. This process is effected in part by recourse to compositions

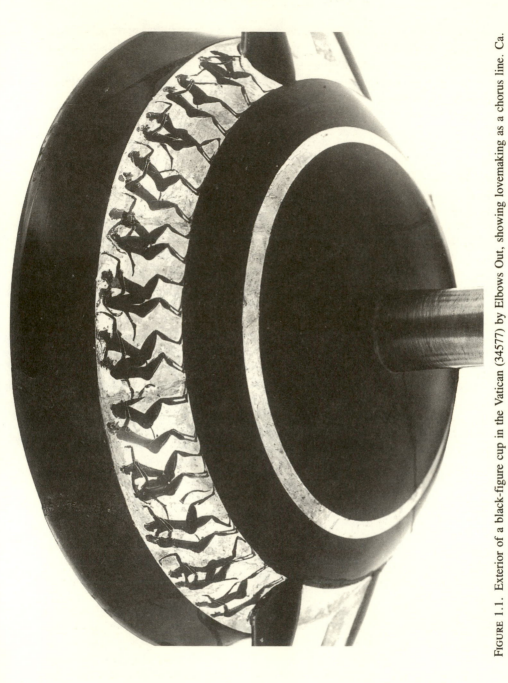

FIGURE 1.1. Exterior of a black-figure cup in the Vatican (34577) by Elbows Out, showing lovemaking as a chorus line. Ca. 540 B.C. (ABV, 250.23). Courtesy of the Vatican Museum.

featuring single couples framed by adjuncts (e.g., Marcadé 1962: 146–47) and compact, horizontal compositions in which male superiority in stance becomes visually translated into dominance.

In red-figure (Sutton 1981: 72–144), this domination is partially offset by compositional and thematic diversity coupled with growing social and psychological realism. We get our first isolated couples on the interior of red-figure cups, which become intimate representations that Brendel (1970) felt were the first to be truly pornographic in tone. There are a few tender scenes in which the female is treated as an active partner (Keuls 1985: fig. 173; *ARV²* 1208.41). The emotional engagement found here and elsewhere is achieved by the use of positions in which the lovers make eye contact (Marks 1978), a device that is characteristic of the Classical style in scenes that have nothing to do with sex.

Yet red-figure painters preferred to show rear-entry positions in which there is an emotional distance between lovers; very rarely does the woman look back to meet the eye of her lover in these scenes, though this device is exploited for its emotional effect in Hellenistic and later art (Keuls 1985: figs. 156–60, 162; see Brendel 1970: figs. 27–29). Although many who discuss these paintings assume that they portray anal rather than vaginal intercourse (Keuls 1985: 176–79; Dover 1978: 100), there is little to justify such a conclusion, for the small scale of the pictures vitiates discussion based on the position and angle of penetration (Marks 1978; Sutton 1981: 82–87). The issue of anal penetration was of insufficient interest to vase painters and their patrons to require the creation of unequivocal anal representations in the manner of modern pornography, for the appeal of these scenes is not so specialized in terms of sexual preference. Certainly the rear-entry stance allows the painter to show women being used impersonally, as mere sexual tools whose response and emotional reaction is of no concern to their male lovers. For example, in a cup by Douris in Boston (Figure 1.2), the impersonal rear-entry position without eye contact is enhanced by a stiff awkwardness in the figures that shows their lack of accord; that this is not simply a result of clumsy drawing is clear from the rare bit of dialogue that the painter has added: the man says *heche hêsychos* ("Keep still" or "Be quiet"), a peremptory command that captures well the master's voice.

Scenes in the old komos tradition show a variety of treatment, some merrily celebrating a zany Hippokleidian outlook (Sutton 1981: 106–7; *ARV²* 113.7, 132). Yet the tone changes, as seen especially on a number of well-published vases, moving from mere indifference to active hostility, and the abuse and degradation of prostitutes becomes the dominant theme (listed in Boardman 1976). These date from the years around 510 to 470 B.C., the period of the early Democracy and the Persian Wars, and find a parallel in a scene of brawling drunks found on a contemporary cup (Leningrad 651, *ARV²* 325.77). All express hostility, perhaps exacerbated by tensions in Athenian society during this turbulent time of class struggle and foreign threat, best characterized by the figure of the politician Themistocles. The most extreme example is a cup by the Pedieus Painter (*ARV²* 86α; Keuls 1985: fig. 166; Marcadé 1962: 138f.; *CVA* [France 28] III I b pl. 68–69), which Brendel (1970: 27, fig. 17) saw as social protest but which was surely intended to achieve a brutal humor. The women there are beaten with slippers as they serve male gratification fore and aft; they are shown as middle-aged and fat, in striking contrast to the idealizing conventions of vase painting, and the unusual creases shown around their

FIGURE 1.2. Interior of a red-figure cup in Boston (1970.233) by Douris, showing sexual intercourse between a man and woman; inscription running down from the man's mouth: "Keep still" or "Be quiet." Ca. 475 B.C. (*ARV²*, 444.241). Gift of Landon T. Clay. Courtesy of Museum of Fine Arts, Boston.

mouths express the disfiguration caused by performing fellatio. The power expressed here is not just male over female but also young over old, free over slave, and employer over employee. It stands as a clear statement of social dominance, and submission without protest. A cup in Florence by the Brygos Painter (Figure 1.3) belongs in this tradition but sounds a different note. There a man standing on the right edge of the scene with a lamp shouts in protest across the room beyond the couple beside him to a second man who threatens a flabby woman; this second man holds up what seems to be a wooden flute to strike her in order to force her to perform fellatio, as she pleads with him. This might be seen as a dispute between the two men over the possession of the woman rather than her treatment, but one would expect the men to be more closely engaged. Here alone, in the person of the man with the lamp, do we find the representation of a negative reaction. From modern psychological studies, one might suggest that this detail may have dissuaded ancient viewers from emulating the abusive activity depicted (Zillman and Bryant 1984).

Homosexual

The male homosexual analogues of these scenes are strikingly different, a graphic

FIGURE 1.3. Exterior of a red-figure cup in Florence (3921) by the Brygos Painter, showing orgiastic sex. Ca. 490 B.C. (ARV², 372.31). Courtesy of Soprintendenza Archeologica della Toscana, Gabinetto Fotografico.

illustration of the practice's relatively high status. Abuse between males in a sexual setting occurs very rarely (e.g., *ABV* 102.100; Koch-Harnack 1983: fig. 108). Most of the vases portray homosexuality as pederasty, a relationship between a boy or young adolescent who is the passive partner and an older male, either a beardless youth or an adult, who takes the aggressive role (see Shapiro, Chapter 3 herein). On vases, pederasty is treated with great sympathy in scenes that are radically different both in type and tone from the heterosexual scenes. Pederastic intercourse usually takes place not in the komos or symposium but in a new type of group scene called courting (Figure 1.4; compare Figures 3.1, 3.2). This new type emerges in the mid-sixth century B.C. and lasts for about a century, though most are Archaic (Beazley 1947; Dover 1978; Shapiro 1981b; Koch-Harnack 1983; Sutton 1985; Keuls 1985: 274–99). Men and older boys are shown as suitors who try to win the sexual favors of their young partners, making full use of gifts and other tactics. While there is a variety of responses, in a quarter to a third of these scenes the payoff is shown, invariably taking the form of standing "intercrural" intercourse in which the partners face each other, embracing, as the older partner thrusts his penis between the thighs of the younger (Figure 3.1; Keuls 1985: figs. 249–50). Penetration by anal intercourse or fellatio is scrupulously avoided, as is mutual masturbation, though the suitor may fondle his partner's genitals in foreplay. The tone is never impersonal or hostile, and affection is frequent. In contrast to the heterosexual scenes, one is struck by the idealized romantic tone found here.

Courting

Pederastic courting is popular in the second half of the sixth century but comes to be supplanted in the early fifth by its more common heterosexual analogue (Sutton 1981: 276–447; Keuls 1985: 187–273; Meyer 1988). These scenes, which clearly derive from their pederastic prototypes, are most popular in the years 480 to 450; they survive well into the second half of the fifth century and die out before its end. Both types of courting occur on a range of vase shapes and show a wide geographical distribution, a sign of their diverse appeal. The theme appears on cups and other symposium ware, but its common occurrence on small oil containers for scented oil and pyxides (boxes for toiletries, etc.), some of the former even inscribed *pros-agoreuô* ("I greet [you]"; *ARV²* 103–4) as the vase itself speaks to the viewer, indicates that many of the vessels were themselves designed as love gifts whose decoration was intended to enhance their persuasive power (Knigge 1964).

Despite their similarities, pederastic and heterosexual courting, with few exceptions, are treated separately. The suitors in a scene pursue either boys or girls, rarely both. This division only partially reflects the spatial distribution of the sexes in the city: boys in palaestrae and gymnasia, women and girls in private houses and brothels, with few places to encounter both together except fountain houses and public festivals. It more importantly suggests that the two forms of sexuality were conceived of as separate entities, each with its own clientele served by separate representations; similarly, heterosexual and homosexual intercourse are rarely pictured together (compare the situation today; see Shapiro, Chapter 3). Occasionally, as in later literature, the two worlds are contrasted on the same vessel, like a cup of the late sixth century in Berlin signed by a painter Peithinos (Figure 3.2; *ARV²*

115.2; Dover 1978: R196; Keuls 1985: figs. 37, 196–97)—a name, or perhaps a pseudonym (note Beazley's difficulties, *ARV²* 115), that bespeaks the artist's interest in persuasion. On the two sides of the exterior, heterosexual and pederastic Peitho are compared (the former surprisingly more demure, as many have remarked), while on the interior, Peleus's wrestling match with his divine bride Thetis is a heroic version of the same theme. The cup's total message is something like "Woo girls with sweetness, and boys more directly, but force may be needed to subdue an unwilling noble bride and sire a son like Achilles" (see Sourvinou-Inwood 1987; Shapiro, Chapter 3).

An even more important scene for illustrating the painter's personal involvement in the world he portrayed occurs on a contemporary psykter (wine cooler) in the Getty Museum by the painter Smikros that shows the vase painter Euphronios chucking the chin of Leagros in the company of other named pairs in the palaestra or gymnasium, including several youths who appear in a variety of other scenes (Melas, Ambrosios, Antias) and one (Euthydikos) who was later wealthy enough to dedicate a *korê* (statue of a girl) on the Acropolis (Figure 1.4; Frel 1983: 147–51). Euphronios, the mentor of Smikros, was the foremost vase painter of the day; Leagros, an aristocrat who was later elected general, has long been known as the youth whose beauty is most often praised in the *kalos* inscriptions common on Attic vases,[4] including eleven by Euphronios (*ARV²* 1591–94). This scene by a close associate of Euphronios seems, then, to reflect the artist's feelings, whether it accurately portrays reality or is simply a wishful or humorous fantasy. Members of the Pioneer Group of vase painters, to which Smikros and Euphronios belonged, are unusually fond of portraying each other and friends in a variety of gentlemanly leisure-time activities; Euphronios also shows Smikros at a symposium, and Smikros even portrays himself with the flute girl Helike at another symposium on one of his signed vases. That Leagros's family was resident in the township Kerameis (Davies 1971), which took its name from the potters' quarter, helps explain his popularity with vase painters and makes it likely that he was well known to Euphronios and even passed time at his shop in the manner of Socrates a century later. While Frel properly expresses reservations that a mere vase painter could have been romantically involved with a leading aristocratic youth, Scheibler (1983: 120–33) assembles evidence to suggest that the gulf between a successful artist-potter like Euphronios and a Leagros may not have been insurmountable in the social climate of the years that gave birth to the Democracy. For our purposes, in fact, it matters little whether the scene is historically accurate, for it and the others confirm the painters' interest in the courting and other activities of the city's leading circles: they interpose themselves in the same situations, becoming both represented and represented, creating and participating in the social feelings that made their city work.

While Euphronios and his companions on the Getty psykter rely entirely on nonmaterial means of persuasion, gifts are a prominent feature of courting scenes, and both species of courting show economic man writ large on both sides of the equation. This is probably not because the ancient Athenians were especially venal and prone to see money as an aphrodisiac (though one notes the theme of bribery running through contemporary literature and history), but because vase painters could illustrate the power of material goods much more clearly than intangible

FIGURE 1.4. Red-figure psykter (cooler) in Malibu (82.AE.53) by Smikros, showing the vase painter Euphronios embracing the fair Leagros, among other courting pairs. Ca. 510 B.C. Courtesy of the J. Paul Getty Museum, Malibu, California.

forces like social status, family connection, political favor, and natural charm. In both life and representations, there is an implicit inequality between the partners, and the exercise of power to persuade, as opposed to compel, is the major theme of these scenes, as it is in many modern romances (Thurston 1987). This is especially true of the heterosexual courting scenes where, in contrast to the homosexual type, intercourse is never represented. The emphasis is strictly on persuasion per se and on a woman's freedom to accept, reject, and even select a partner, for women and girls, unlike courted boys, sometimes take the initiative (Figure 1.5B). This last motif could appeal to viewers of both sexes who might appreciate the freedom to choose as well as the pleasure of being sought out.

The two sexes are also differentiated by the gifts they are offered. Boys receive hares, cocks, dogs, and other items connected to aggressive masculine pastimes appropriate to freemen and aristocrats: hunting, cockfighting, and active sport (Koch-Harnack 1983). Females, on the other hand, are offered flowers, fruit, wreaths, birds (but neither cocks nor hares), games, jewelry, and toiletries—items

FIGURE 1.5. Red-figure skyphos in Leningrad (4224) by the Penthesilea Painter, contrasting styles of courting. Ca. 460 B.C. (*ARV²*, 889.166). Courtesy of the Hermitage Museum, Leningrad.
Side A: Man offers woman a coin drawn from his purse.

FIGURE 1.5. *Side B:* Woman holds out a flower as she offers youth a lekythos (oil jar).

that characterize the feminine ideal as tender, sweet-smelling, sensuous, and child-like (Sutton 1981: 276–447). Members of both sexes, however, are offered purses, as in Figure 1.5A, where the coin is displayed as well, and uncooked meats, a nonmonetary form of payment; the purse is the most common gift for women, and for boys it is not rare (Sutton 1981: 290–304; Koch-Harnack 1983: 129–72; Keuls 1985: 260–66; Meyer 1988). There is little to suggest that the boys are not freeborn and even noble Athenian youths, aside from these purses, which are freely mixed with more noble offerings in the same settings, making it difficult or impossible to distinguish professionals from amateurs in the field of love. This is odd, for, at least in the fourth century B.C., a male citizen could be disenfranchised for prostituting himself to other men, and the very speech that reveals this law (Aischines 1.19-32 [*Against Timarchos*]; Dover 1978: 13–109) makes clear the difficulties of disproving such a charge and the dangers inherent in acquiring such a reputation. While it is possible that the risk was not as great in the era of these vases, we must remember that the paintings, themselves often evidently intended as gifts, are no more than hopeful expressions of what might be, shown largely from the suitor's point of view

(Shapiro, Chapter 3); some were presumably more acceptable to their intended recipients than others.

In contrast, most of the women, particularly those who are shown courted publicly in groups, probably were to be thought of as prostitutes and not as respectable citizen women. (Vase painters unfortunately use dress to mark status only imprecisely, evidently reflecting the situation in real life, to judge from the cranky complaints of a conservative writer known as the Old Oligarch that it was impossible to distinguish among free, slave, or citizen on the streets of Athens [ps.-Xen. *Constitution of Athens* 1.10–12].) In Athenian society, marriage was normally arranged and respectable women secluded; an unmarried woman who yielded to seduction could be sold into slavery, a husband was legally required to divorce not only a wife who had been willingly seduced but also one who had been raped against her will, and a male adulterer caught in the act could be killed by the offended husband (Pomeroy 1975: 86–87). Direct amorous approach to a respectable woman (other than one's wife) would therefore have been highly illicit and is clearly not shown in most of these scenes. The appeal of such forbidden fruit to certain individuals is noted in the fourth-century speech *Against Neaira,* which alleges that she could charge more as a prostitute once she claimed to be married (Ps.-Demosthenes, 59.41), a predilection apparently commemorated in a much-debated scene by the Pan Painter that has been convincingly explained as the attempted seduction of a married woman (*ARV*², 557.123; Crome 1966; Keuls 1985: 258–59). She, seated and properly veiled as she spins, is offered a purse by a youth; a snoopy maid turns around to watch, emphasizing the exceptional nature of the interaction (note her complacent counterpart in Figure 1.6, discussed below). This anomalous vase by an artist with a recognized taste for bawdy humor simply points out how conventional the interaction is in the majority of courting scenes.

The painters illustrate comparative approach and response by both male and female, including female initiation, competition by suitors for lovers, haggling over price, outright rejection, and probably even an attempt to seduce a respectable woman, as we have seen. A skyphos in Leningrad by the Penthesilea Painter (Figure 1.5A–B, above) compares a bearded man wooing a woman with a coin to a youth detained by a woman who offers him a flower and a lekythos (oil jar) presumably containing scent: the mature must pay, while the young get by on looks alone. The painter's interest here in showing a variety of action and response is typical, and the heterosexual theme is treated with far more complexity than one finds in the pederastic sphere, where initiative is pretty much a one-way street and response fairly formalized. What is interesting here is that both the freeborn youth and the female prostitute must be wooed and persuaded, both within and by means of the vase; this attitude toward prostitutes is familiar from later epigram and comedy, where prostitutes are often depicted as hard to get and lovers as importunate. We are a long way in iconography from the pleading woman of Figure 1.3; yet prose sources (see *Against Neaira* for some grim vignettes) suggest the reality had not changed much. The choice of what to depict has shifted; the mood is different.

Our word *courting* is more often employed in the context of intended marriage rather than the engagement of a prostitute or lover; by the early Classical period, the romantic courting theme is indeed adapted to the context of marriage, as sentimental gifts are exchanged by husband and wife. This surprising portrayal of married life in terms of iconography developed for pederasty and prostitution is consistent with the general transformation of the visual imagery of marriage during the fifth century traced below; such evidence is a welcome correction to those who use the one-sided testimony of works like Lysias's *On the Murder of Eratosthenes* to argue that in ancient Athens love and marriage were regarded as worlds apart. The transition is made absolutely certain by the combination of form and imagery in an unattributed alabastron (woman's oil jar) in Paris dated about 470–460 (Figure 1.6; Reilly 1989: 425, plate 80a). There, as a small girl looks on holding up a vessel of the same type, a youth identified by inscription as the fair Timodemos offers a head covering to a woman who sits holding a wreath, perhaps a nuptial wreath she has plaited either for herself or for him. Though she is identified in the inscription as the fair bride (*hê nymphê kalê,* in a unique transformation of the *kalos* formula), her name is not included, presumably reflecting the social convention whereby respectable women were left nameless in public (Schaps 1977). The depiction of the vase shape as an offering in the scene indicates that the persuasive power of the vase in the courting tradition was now extended to marriage, which, as we shall see, comes to be regularly portrayed in romantic terms at just this time.

FIGURE 1.6. Scene on a red-figure alabastron in Paris (Cabinet des Médailles, 508), showing courting adapted to marriage. Timodemos holds out a fringed scarf to his wife as a girl stands by with an alabastron; the two principals are identified in *kalos* inscriptions. Ca. 465 B.C. (*ARV²,* 1610). Drawing from Fröhner 1872, pl. 40.2.

Nudes

Via the evolution of courting scenes we have passed from the vase painters' "hardcore" treatment of sexual relations in explicit terms to scenes, though fundamentally pornographic in both intent and content, in which sex takes a back seat to social gamesmanship and sentiment. Before turning to marriage and other romantic scenes evidently aimed at a feminine audience, one should mention another soft-core pornographic subject: the many nudes, both male and female, on Attic vases. Male nudity was a common convention in Greek art which attracts little attention except when first encountered, whereas female nudes are rare in Archaic and Classical Greek art except in the private medium of vase painting (see now Bonfante 1989).

Pervasive male nudity is one of the more peculiar conventions of Greek art, one that is not easily explained (Bonfante 1989: 543–58; Ridgway 1977: 53–54). The naked men, youths, and boys that are ubiquitous in genre and mythological settings probably do represent an artistic convention as much as actual practice (*contra* Boardman 1985: 238–39), for the well-bred were evidently expected to keep themselves modestly covered in most social situations, as indicated by the tale of Hippokleides and the introduction to Plato's *Charmides* (see also Hollein 1988). This idealized nakedness is closely connected to the Greek custom of exercising in the nude, which they themselves recognized as peculiar (Herodotus 1.10). Though this idealized nudity in exercise and art may not have been motivated primarily by pornographic purposes, its pornographic effect cannot be dismissed, given the high visibility of pederasty and homosexuality in ancient Greek culture (Arieti 1975). Nude athletes and other figures could stand as both role model and a source of sexual pleasure not only for different members of society but even for the same individual. The Getty psykter (Figure 1.4) and the *kalos* inscriptions on vases indicate that vase painters were as susceptible as their (male) customers to the sexual charms of the many nude athletes, bathers, and workers they represented in a variety of settings.

Female nudity (Bonfante 1989: 558–62), in contrast, did not develop as an artistic convention until the transition from Classical to Hellenistic style during the second half of the fourth century, when Praxiteles created a nude cult statue of the goddess Aphrodite that established a canon for the female body (Richter 1970: 200–201). According to tradition (Pliny *Natural History* 36.20–21), this statue was one of two offered to the city of Kos, whose citizens preferred the other one that was modestly clothed, and so the nude passed on to nearby Knidos; there, set up in a circular temple (whose foundations were uncovered in the late 1960s by a colorful American archaeologist appropriately named Iris Love) where it could be seen and studied from all angles, it became one of the classical world's most renowned sights and spawned a number of poems (*Anth. Plan.* 4.159–70) and tales that highlight its pornographic effect on the ancient viewer. A famous anecdote, which goes back at least to the first century B.C. when it was apparently recorded by the Stoic philosopher Posidonius (Harmon 1925: 262n.), is noted briefly by several authors (Valerius Maximus 8.11.4; Pliny *HN* 7.127; Lucian *Eikones* 4; Tzetzes *Chil.* 8.375) and recounted with considerable embellishment in the anonymous fourth-century A.D. *Amores* (15–16) preserved among the works of Lucian. There it takes the form of an etiological tale told by a female temple attendant to explain a small dark blemish visible on one leg of the white marble statue. A youth had become so obsessed by the masterpiece that he surreptitiously had himself locked in the temple overnight and achieved intercourse with the statue, evidently in the intercrural mode (see Figure 3.1), leaving behind as evidence the discoloration on one of its thighs. Though this ribald "just so story" is much later than our vases, like the related tale of Pygmalion as told by Ovid (*Met.* 10.243–97) it illustrates the recognized hazards of combining the related powers of art and Aphrodite (see Henry, Chapter 12 on a similar tale from Samos).

Praxiteles' Knidian Aphrodite was shown as a bather, and it is in the same guise that we encounter, long before the development of the artistic convention, the first sizable group of female nudes in Western art: the bathing women on Attic vases (Sutton 1981: 46–48; Ginouvès 1962: 112–17, 163–78, 220–23; lists in Webster 1972, chap. 17, class N). It is easier to posit a pornographic intent for these bathers than for the male nudes; yet they evolve during the fifth century from soft-core images aimed at a primarily male audience to more generalized expressions of feminine sensuality that become appropriate for bridal themes and wedding gifts. They first appear in quantity on the interior of red-figure cups of the late sixth and early fifth centuries (Figure 1.7). These intimate scenes of single naked bathers, often shown with a small portable wash basin, are recognizable as a sort of peephole

FIGURE 1.7. Interior of a red-figure cup in Indianapolis (47.37) by the Chaire Painter, showing a woman bathing. Ca. 510 B.C. (*ARV²*, 144.5). Courtesy of the Indianapolis Museum of Art.

pornography aimed at an audience of males and disreputable females by their regular appearance in wine cups, the occasional inclusion of an *olisbos* (dildo) (see Keuls 1985: figs. 73, 80), and even a floating set of disembodied male genitals that appear in one scene in Berlin (Brandt 1926: II, p. 28; ARV^2, 1593.39). The figure would be revealed as the drinker drank.

The second quarter of the fifth century witnesses a shift in both the content and the audience of these feminine bathers. The subject moves from the interior of cups and onto larger vessels including kraters, hydriai (water jars), and, most significantly, alabastra and pyxides used by women. These vessels accommodate compositions with several figures, and the basin changes from the small portable one to a large permanent basin on a stand (Figure 1.8): the occasion becomes social, and

FIGURE 1.8. Red-figure stamnos in Boston (95.21) by a member of the Group of Polygnotos, showing women bathing at a wash basin. Ca. 440 B.C. (ARV^2, 1052.19). Catharine Page Perkins Fund. Courtesy of the Museum of Fine Arts, Boston.

the locale apparently shifts from the private chamber to the public bath. The switch from cups to hydriai and toilet shapes suggests that many of these vessels may have been designed for use in the baths and private bathing they portray; even the kraters may have doubled as wash basins (Ginouvès 1962: 55–57). Though some bathhouses seem to have had a reputation not very different from that of a modern massage parlor (Ehrenberg 1951: 180, citing Aristophanes *Knights* 1401 and *Frogs* 1279f.), and a pornographic purpose may still continue strong, it is clear that some of these later scenes were intended to be seen by a respectable feminine audience.

Certainly it cannot be maintained that all these naked women must be regarded as hetairai simply because of their nudity (contra Williams 1983: 99; Bonfante 1989: 559), for by around 430–420 a naked bride is shown bathing on an unattributed pyxis in New York (Figure 1.9) in a scene that shows the progressive preparations of a bride for her wedding, an occasion clearly indicated by the women tying fillets around a nuptial loutrophoros, a ritual shape discussed below (also Zevi 1937: 355–58, fig. 6; Bothmer 1961: no. 243, plates 91–92; Reilly 1989: 419, 421–22, plate 78b). The sensuous, erotic associations of the naked female image have not been abandoned, for Eros, the personification of love in the sense of sexual desire (Hermary et al. 1986), appears twice as a helper, and at the end he sits in the lap of a woman most plausibly identified as Aphrodite delivering final words of marital advice to the veiled bride. Female sensuality has been domesticated and brought in as a kind of Peitho to persuade the Athenian bride, and possibly her groom as well, of her proper sexuality.

Weddings

The romantic transformations of courting and bathing scenes described above are not isolated phenomena but are repeated also in Athenian nuptial imagery during the Classical period. The family (*oikos*) was the basic social unit of the Classical city-state (*polis*). The Athenians, like those in other Greek states, were jealous of their rights, and as the privileges of Athenian citizenship increased, became increasingly protective of membership in the citizen body. Although in Archaic Athens marriage between Athenian men and non-Athenian women was recognized by the *polis* and produced some of the city's leading politicians, after Pericles' citizenship law of 451/0 B.C., only marriage to an Athenian woman could produce legitimate children with full citizen rights (Patterson 1981; Pomeroy 1988). This new recognition of the importance of marriage to an Athenian bride seems to be reflected in the changing iconography of marriage during the fifth century. The naked bride on the pyxis in New York (Figure 1.9) is part of a general tendency to tame Eros and bring him into the service of the *oikos* and thereby of the Athenian state. In the new wedding scenes that appear in the second half of the fifth century, sexuality is shown in a polite but unmistakable manner as the bond that ties together the basic unit of the *polis*. Male sexual dominance and female submission, presented in a benign fashion attractive to male and female alike, serve as an emblem of the respective roles in society of the two sexes and provide a proper model for emulation, rather like the 1960s film comedies starring Doris Day and Rock Hudson.

FIGURE 1.9. Scene on a red-figure pyxis in New York (1972.118.148), showing the progress of a bride's preparations for the wedding: she bathes, dresses, and receives final advice from Aphrodite with the help of Eros. Ca. 425 B.C. Bequest of Walter C. Baker, 1972. Courtesy of the Metropolitan Museum of Art, New York.

Unlike other genre subjects, which show considerable variety in form and outlook, wedding scenes are strikingly uniform in composition and tone, reflecting the formal and public role of these vases in Athenian wedding ceremonies (Sutton 1981: 145–275; 1989). Gods and other elements of the mythical world are freely included in scenes that are only rarely (usually through inscription) connected to any particular mythical personality; while the two extremes of the mythical and contemporary worlds can be identified, most representations lie in an undifferentiated middle ground. This deliberate blurring of the boundaries between myth and genre makes elements of both felt simultaneously, presumably to enhance the actual weddings at which the painted scenes were viewed.

Archaic weddings are remarkably conservative. The black-figure technique is regularly retained well into the fifth century to depict a formal vehicular procession often attended by divinities (list in Webster 1972: 105 n. 1). The couple almost always rides in a chariot, an unrealistic heroic transformation of the rustic cart that was actually used (Krauskopf 1977; see Keuls 1985: fig. 92; Bothmer 1985: 182–84). The bride usually pulls the mantle from her head to reveal her face in an impersonal and formal expression of the sexual side of marriage, but there is no hint of physical or emotional contact between the couple riding rigidly side by side. These processions regularly occur on hydriai and amphorae (jugs) found throughout the Mediterranean (Webster 1972: 105).

A wave of innovation occurs at the outset of the Classical period (ca. 480) with the simultaneous adoption of the red-figure technique and of a new compositional type, the pedestrian procession, which may have seemed more democratic and certainly allowed a greater expressive range (Sutton 1981: 177–96). This new type is found most frequently on the loutrophoros, a ritual water jar represented in Figure 1.9; it is an impractical elongated version of both amphora and hydria that was used in Athens to carry the bridal bath from a special spring, and examples were often dedicated to the nymph of that spring (*nymphê* means both "bride" and "nymph").[5] Most of the red-figure weddings on all shapes were found in Attica and Greece; if they were indeed used at Athenian weddings, their romantic scenes could have worked to alleviate the anxiety that was surely felt by Athenian grooms and especially brides facing arranged marriage. In these scenes, male sexual possession and leadership are expressed by the groom's grasp of the bride's wrist or hand as he leads her into the house or bedroom; as he does so, he almost invariably turns back toward her to express his interest. She may meet his glance or look down as she acquiesces. A bridesmaid (*nympheutria*) usually sends her off by adjusting her veil. The groom is usually beardless and the bride mature, both sexually desirable. One of the finest of these scenes is on a loutrophoros in Toronto by Polygnotos (*ARV*[2], 1031.51; Lacey 1968: fig. 24; Boardman 1989: fig. 134), who politely emphasizes the sexual bond of marriage through the prominence of the bride's belt that the groom will shortly loosen, the rare inclusion of the traditional fruit she will eat in the bedchamber, and finally the glance in which the couple's eyes meet.

Our Figure 1.10 shows the type in its most developed form: the simple language of touch and glance was evidently not sufficient, and in the 430s (on current information) painters introduce the figure of Eros to make explicit what had previously been shown by more subtle means. Although in earlier genre scenes Eros had been associated with pederasty and prostitution, shortly after about 450 he

FIGURE 1.10. Scene on a red-figure loutrophoros in Boston (03.802), showing the procession to the nuptial bed. Ca. 425 B.C. (Drawing in Beazley Archive, Oxford). Courtesy of the Museum of Fine Arts, Boston, and the Beazley Archive, Oxford.

invades the domestic sphere of respectable women and then moves into the wedding itself (see below; Hermary et al. 1986: 902–17, 933–36, pls. 643–46; Shapiro, Chapter 3). The Eros of classical wedding scenes is associated especially with the bride, and to some painters he even seems to be a force she emanates rather than a simple attendant. This Eros operates in both an active and passive sense, expressing both the emotion felt by the bride and the feeling she engenders in the groom. One of the best expressions of this new nuptial imagery occurs on the illustrated loutrophoros (Figure 1.10; Sutton 1989; Keuls 1985: fig. 102). Here a usual wedding procession is embellished by two Erotes conventionally adorning the bride with wreath and necklace; a third Eros bounding down from the nuptial bed through the half-open door of the bridal chamber is a striking vision of love in marriage that astounds a bystander. The Classical Athenian bride, seeing herself surrounded by Erotes in such scenes, was perhaps inspired by this refined erotic vision with a passion to accept her sexual and social role in society.

Domestic Scenes of Women

The revaluation of respectable feminine sexuality described above is also seen in the ordinary portrayal of women on vases during the fifth century (Zevi 1937; Götte 1957; see now Reilly 1989). These scenes appear primarily on vessels that were intended for feminine domestic use, especially on toilet vessels and hydriai (whose nuptial use has been mentioned), but relatively rarely on cups and symposium ware (Webster 1972: 226). This evidence suggests that during the course of the fifth century, vase painters discovered and cultivated a feminine market. The find spots of these pieces are largely in Attica and Greece (Webster 1972: 227), indicating production for a largely Greek and Athenian audience. Comparisons between these scenes and modern romances are especially appropriate, for both represent reciprocal awareness and creation of a distinctly feminine sensibility. A reliable idea of an ancient Greek woman's outlook survives in the work of the Archaic poet Sappho, an almost isolated feminine voice speaking from antiquity (Hallett 1979; Stigers 1981; Winkler 1981; Snyder 1989: 1–37). Characteristic of her poetry is a delicate yet intense romantic sensibility focused on clothing, flowers, birds, Aphrodite, and feminine companionship, which finds close reflection in the vase paintings showing feminine life. Admittedly the aristocratic world of Sappho's Lesbos is different in many ways from democratic Athens, but we know that her work was popular there; Sappho is identified by name on four vases (Sutton 1981: 50 n. 165) and is therefore the most popular poet on vases save perhaps Anacreon; thus, her work was known even to vase painters and available to them as a source.

Over the course of a century, as is well documented by Erika Götte's dissertation (1957), Attic vase painters transform the unambitious scenes of women's domestic life that first appear regularly at the end of the sixth century into the sensuous, idyllic masterpieces of the Meidian style that were produced during the Peloponnesian War (for illustration, Haugsted 1977; Williams 1983; Bérard 1989; Keuls 1985; Reilly 1989). The feminine subject matter seems first to have been inspired by its suitability for small perfume jars and colored the content of the scenes, for women are shown at home occupied primarily with self-adornment and at leisure. A late example (ca. 430–420) in Chapel Hill (Shapiro 1981a: no. 50), remarkable only for the number of figures included, accurately conveys the scope and tenor of these scenes. This feminine world is inhabited by graceful creatures occupied almost exclusively with mirrors, hair bands, cosmetic chests, perfume, and sometimes games or pets; they cultivate beauty and charm in a sociable world of reassuring domesticity. Wool baskets and occasionally spinning and weaving are the only reference to labor, and one searches hard for reminders of unglamorous jobs—like cooking, cleaning, fetching water, or gardening—that were best left to slaves. That children (usually shown as infants) are rare is a sure sign that these vases celebrate feminine grace rather than any attribute considered useful in Athens. While these pleasant fantasies are interesting expressions of a prevailing feminine ideal appropriate for cosmetic containers, the theme achieves a higher level of expression and becomes a major artistic force in the service of two personal rites of passage: funerals and weddings.

As a mortuary subject (Götte 1957: 16–32), the theme of women at home acquires a noble monumentality on vessels designed especially for the tomb, in particular white lekythoi. These beautiful scenes are important here only for their expression of a restrained inner emotion, a feeling carried over as the subject of women passes into nuptial use (Götte 1957: 33–71). The subject becomes the adornment of the bride (see Figure 1.9; Reilly 1989), which is commonly portrayed

FIGURE 1.11. Scene on a red-figure lebes gamikos in New York (07.286.35) by the Washing Painter, showing a bride playing the harp amid companions as Eros appears. Ca. 425 B.C. (ARV², 1126.1). Rogers Fund, 1907. Courtesy of the Metropolitan Museum of Art, New York.

on hydriai and lebetes gamikoi (nuptial basins; Moore and Philippides 1986: 27–29), vessels associated with the bridal bath. The seated bride is brought various toiletries and clothing accessories by female companions (Keuls 1985: figs. 101, 104). The first step in elaboration during the second quarter of the fifth century is the inclusion of a winged female who flies in with items identical to those brought by the normal, wingless women (Götte 1957: 38–41). She could be Iris or Nike (Victory), both divine messengers, or perhaps some other figure more specifically nuptial. After mid-century, emphasis moves from the act of adornment itself to representation of the bride's emotional state, which is expressed through the introduction of another winged figure, Eros (Hermary et al. 1986: 906–7, 935–36), and a new interest in music and the Muses. These new themes, love and music, are united on a lebes gamikos in New York by the Washing Painter, dating from about 425 B.C. (Figure 1.11; Boardman 1989: fig. 207); here the seated bride playing the harp in the midst of her friends recalls the nuptial songs of Sappho. Eros suggests the romantic theme of the music, while the lush, clinging, transparent drapery creates an atmosphere of sensuous femininity.

This is the look of the extravagant Meidian style, characterized by rich drapery, mannered poses, and a romantic tone, which dominates the last quarter of the fifth century and represents the fullest development of the feminine theme in vase painting. Eros himself is displaced, or rather eclipsed, by his mother, Aphrodite, who sets the tone for all. The walls of the house dissolve to reveal an idyllic landscape where women sit in the open air with domestic adjuncts surrounded by birds, gilt-winged Erotes, sensuous lovers, benevolent feminine personifications (including Peitho), and Olympian divinities of both sexes (Götte 1957: 60–71; Burn 1987). A mostly nude long-haired Adonis lounges in the lap of Aphrodite, languidly allowing a lyre to slip from his limp left hand (Burn 1987: M1, pls. 22–25; Boardman 1989: fig. 285); a more vigorous but equally pretty Phaon serenades Demonassa in a gilded bower as Aphrodite flies overhead in a chariot drawn by Erotes, a Sapphic theme (Burn 1987: M2, pls. 27–29; Arias 1961: pls. 216–17; Boardman 1989: fig. 286). Though the origin of these compositions lies in the realm of genre representation, the subjects are now primarily those of myth and allegory.

On the painter's name piece in London (Figure 1.12; Burn 1987: plates 1–9; Boardman 1989: fig. 287), the abduction of the Leucippidae ("daughters of Leucippus") by Castor and Pollux is comparable in form and spirit to Fred Astaire and Ginger Rogers dancing to "Night and Day," with its similarly well-disposed flow of graceful drapery and mannered charm. The scene is set in a precinct of Aphrodite where the two girls have been gathering flowers in a rocky landscape; an archaic image of the goddess is set above in the center, while Aphrodite herself lounges against the altar to receive a flower from Chryseis ("Goldie"). Castor and Pollux, two handsome Spartan youths dressed in flowing robes of faintly Eastern look (Miller 1989: 327–29), have arrived in chariots and snatch up the girls as Zeus, the boys' father, looks on from the lower left. Agaue and Peitho flee off to the wings, demurely pulling their cloaks in theatrical alarm. Lucilla Burn (1987: 17) notes the way the traditional violence of the subject is replaced by romantic fiction: "[T]he Meidias Painter replaces the desolate Leukippos with Zeus, complacent father of the assailants, and Aphrodite, patroness of amorous intrigue. . . . [T]he Leukippidai

FIGURE 1.12. Detail of red-figure hydria in London (E 224) by the Meidias Painter, showing the rape of the Leucippidae by Castor and Pollux. Ca. 420 B.C. (*ARV²*, 1313.5). Courtesy of the Trustees of the British Museum, London.

themselves are rather calm and make no real effort to escape, their primary effort being to look pretty and pluck at their drapery with becoming elegance. This is no longer a rape, but a romantic elopement." The painter's novel reinterpretation of the old Greek theme of marriage as rape (Sourvinou-Inwood 1973, 1978, 1987) merely follows to its conclusion the romantic idealization we have seen in the genre wedding scenes. The trauma of a woman's compulsory removal to a new home through arranged marriage is artistically transformed into an agreeable abduction by handsome young heroes set in an idyllic fairyland. The Meidian style has been taken as a form of escapism from the horrors of the Peloponnesian War (Pollitt 1972: 123–25), similar in spirit to the romantic films of the Depression era, and as a romantic reaction to a general existential malaise of urban society, comparable to Tennyson's poetry (Burn 1987: 94–96). Acknowledgment of the scenes' feminine audience and Sapphic connections suggests a more immediate and specific inspiration: the concerns and aspirations of Athenian and other Greek women. These vase paintings, directed, like today's popular romances and romantic films, at a mass feminine audience (compare the sympathetic send-up in Woody Allen's *Purple Rose of Cairo*), may also have been a means by which ancient women were able to grapple with and transcend the cares of their existence.

An interest in romance is likewise reflected in the later fifth century's fondness for vase paintings showing the abduction of Helen by the Trojan prince Paris, the adulterous cause of the Trojan War (Ghali-Kahil 1955: 53–70). This theme is treated romantically and becomes so assimilated with the scenes of ordinary women that it is sometimes difficult to tell them apart. Both celebrate the goddess of love as an irresistible force whose destructive side is ignored in art or sublimated to the concerns of society at large. An acorn lekythos in a private collection in Switzerland by the Painter of the Frankfort Acorn (*ARV*², 1317.3; Delivorrias 1984: no. 1192, plate 120), dating to about 420–410 B.C., is a good example of the fusion of these two traditions to create a positive image of domestic love. Before an open door, a fleshy and beardless young man bends down behind a woman seated in a chair to embrace her as she turns back toward him in equal response; the two are swept away by the mutual passion aroused by the tiny female figure who flies over them in a miniature chariot drawn by two Erotes, and who Beazley suggests is the personification of Peitho.[6] Two female figures standing on either side are probably (as Beazley also suggests) Aphrodite and Hera, the two goddesses of marriage, for the great scholar is surely right to recognize the couple as bride and groom (yet note the skepticism of Delivorrias 1984 and Burn 1987: 81[F3]). Their model is Paris and Helen, but they seem to be characters of genre, not myth. This seductive image shows an idealized bride and groom swept away, yielding to the persuasion of divine lust, not to betray house and home, thereby bringing about the ultimate civic cataclysm that Troy represented to the Greeks, but rather to perform their expected role in society as husband and wife.

Conclusion

Such scenes in a popular medium like vase painting help one understand how Athenians, including prosperous and empowered male citizens as well as women and other disenfranchised members of society living in conditions that seem extremely restrictive to contemporary eyes, might have generated in themselves the allegiance to the values of their culture that allowed them to carry out the various roles society had decreed for them. In the Archaic period, we find in the sexual scenes on cups and other symposium ware an emphasis on male self-expression, frequently in defiance of social norms, that encouraged aggressive individualism. These scenes provided both images to emulate and social catharsis for their male viewers and creators, though we might suggest that it was not just these representations but the actual beating of prostitutes that provided catharsis through the displacement of aggression from fellow citizens to a socially acceptable outlet. (This is, we note, a one-sided catharsis.) Such scenes provided their servile female viewers with an image that reaffirmed their helpless standing; those presenting the positive results of demonstrative affection and compliance would encourage such behavior in response to male advances. Courting scenes idealized male pederastic sexual bonding at a time when that aristocratic ideal seems to have been especially important politically (Shapiro 1981b). Both types of scene express a relation between sex and power in rather blunt terms, and the evolution of new social structures attendant on the evolution of the radical Democracy, combined with other reasons, ensured that both types lost their appeal by the mid-fifth century. Antisocial individual self-expression was no longer popular on vases, probably reflecting both a need for a more refined public self-image for the Athenian *dêmos* and changing markets for painted pottery—or a tendency to reserve it for special occasions, as plain black-glaze wares became more elegant and suitable for daily use.

The radical Democracy of the fifth century was not opposed to love and other emotions unless they were directed at inappropriate objects that distracted individuals from benefiting the larger social group of the *polis*. It is Thucydides' Pericles, after all, that most outstanding proponent of democratic ideals, who asks the Athenians to direct their lust, that most personal of emotions, toward their city and become its lovers (*erastai*, 2.43). This rhetoric is reflected in the prominence given to Eros in contemporary vases. As the earlier erotic themes wane, the feminine atmosphere of women bathing and simply being women at home emerges as an erotic theme in heterosexual courting scenes. At the same time, women's life is idealized first on vases designed for female use and later for the display of feminine virtue at weddings and funerals. The celebration of women's beauty on cosmetic vessels contributed to the revaluation of female sexuality we have seen in Classical scenes of bathers, primpers, and weddings. In the second half of the fifth century, female eroticism not only becomes respectable but is portrayed as a means of personal happiness and social stability on vessels intended largely for feminine eyes. While wedding scenes always present highly idealized images, it is the increasing exploration of the specifically sexual elements that characterizes the Classical period. Such idealization served to provide positive role models with which the young bride could identify as she was led off to a strange house by a virtually unknown man, and the increasingly erotic tone that is found suggests that, like a reader of today's mass-market romances, the citizen woman of ancient Athens had high hopes of affection and sexual fulfillment. And perhaps males viewing the erotic visions on wedding and other feminine vessels would be encouraged to direct their erotic energies more exclusively to engendering future citizens.

Such artistic fictions contrast strongly with what is presented in Lysias's *On the Murder of Eratosthenes* (esp. 6–14), in which it is claimed that husband and wife saw little of each other, or Xenophon's *Oikonomikos,* a Socratic dialogue that includes the following famous interchange (12–13; Loeb trans.):

> "Is there anyone to whom you commit more affairs of importance than you commit to your wife?"
> "There is not."
> "Is there anyone with whom you talk less?"
> "There are few or none, I confess."
> "And you married her when she was a mere child and had seen and heard almost nothing?"
> "Certainly."

But while these literary representations may reflect actual experiences more faithfully than our vase paintings, they too are fictionalized interpretations reflecting ideology, and their intended audience is male. The paintings are important in suggesting how such a Xenophontic child bride, armed with only observation and the testimony of immediate family and friends, might have viewed the same situation in a way that she could accept and even embrace.

The evolution of erotic imagery on Attic pottery from Hippokleidian dance to romantic love in marriage during a century and a half of Athenian history marks a significant change in ideology. Like modern mass-market literature, these mass-market images must have both reflected and shaped the continually evolving self-images of the inhabitants of the Athenian *polis*. These changes in vase painting reflect both general changes in social ideology and persistent attitudes of particular segments of society that emerge and vanish as painters developed and abandoned (or lost) specialized markets for their products. Yet such changes do not necessarily reflect improvements in the circumstances of women's lives. Thurston's study of the modern romance is remarkable for its inclusion of readers' responses. What we lack, and mourn the loss of, are Athenian women's voices to speak for themselves.

NOTES

It is a pleasure to acknowledge the following help in preparing this chapter. Research and writing were supported by a grant from the American Council of Learned Societies and a leave from Loyola University of Chicago, with several small grants from the same university. Earlier versions were criticized by Amy Richlin, H. Alan Shapiro, and Keith DeVries. Keith DeVries generously sent me an unpublished manuscript with a catalogue of vases portraying ancient Athenian homosexuality. For the opportunity to consult photographs, I am grateful to Donna Kurtz of the Beazley Archive in Oxford and to Dietrich von Bothmer of the Metropolitan Museum of Art in New York. Additional assistance was provided by David M. Halperin, Kathleen G. Klein, and Stan W. Denski.

1. Hereafter, all dates are B.C. unless specified otherwise.

2. All vases attributed to painters by Beazley are identified by reference to his lists in *Attic Black-figure Vase-painters* (*ABV*) and the second edition of *Attic Red-figure Vase-painters* (*ARV²*); these provide full identification with citations of illustrations. I generally make no reference to the addenda of each volume, *Paralipomena*, or *Beazley Addenda²*, which should all be checked.

3. Carpenter's (1983) attempt to lower the Group's date is not compelling. See Moore 1985, which makes clear stylistic links to Sophilos, who was active around 580–70. In a subsequent article, Carpenter (1984) suggests that the Group may not have worked in Athens itself, though he still places its activity in Attica; technical studies might resolve such questions.

4. These are a kind of graffiti (in the nontechnical sense) which take the form *X kalos* ("X is handsome") and often have no obvious connection to the scene in which they appear. Those on vases presumably represent a small fraction of what was once written on perishable media. See Dover 1978: 111–24; Robinson and Fluck 1937; Shapiro 1987. Note the special examples in Figure 1.6, which *are* relevant to the representation.

5. Moore and Philippides 1986: 18–20. For preliminary reports on the shrine of Nymphe, see Wycherley 1978: 197–200; Travlos 1971: 361–63; *ARV²*, viii, 1747–48; pub-

lication of the myriad loutrophoros fragments found there may render details of my discussion of wedding scenes obsolete, though probably not the general picture.

6. Delivorrias 1984 suggests that this figure is Aphrodite herself, but also accepts Beazley's suggestion that Aphrodite is one of the flanking figures, which would seem to mean that Aphrodite appears twice.

2

Tragedy and the Politics of Containment

Nancy Sorkin Rabinowitz

If I tell my friends and colleagues that I am writing on pornography in Greek tragedy, the response is often "What pornography?" or "Where is it?" Obviously, by contemporary standards, there is none. But while it would be a mistake to conflate the theater of Dionysus and the 42nd Street movie houses, the *agora* and the bathhouses of New York City, the continuity between the two periods nonetheless bears analysis—there is a clear connection between the ideology and beliefs about sexuality then and now (Sedgwick 1985; duBois 1988). And part of this continuity derives from the status of the tragic myths and the status of tragedy itself. For tragedy is one of the founding texts of Western humanism, and simultaneously the place par excellence where the masculine has been read as universal.

We do well to remind ourselves that tragedy was a popular art form, more like film or TV in its accessibility, and that it developed at a particular time, in a particular place: fifth-century Athens after the Persian Wars. Let us also remember that although issues of gender are central themes, the genre was predominantly male—male actors, male poets, and possibly an all-male audience. Middle- and upper-class women lived a sequestered existence. As Pericles' famous statement puts it: "Your greatest glory is not to be inferior to what god has made you, and the greatest glory of a woman is to be least talked about by men, whether they are praising you or criticizing you" (2.45.2). In short, the transcendent "human" heroes of tragedy are gendered male and must be understood in that way. Such an emphasis on masculinity may underplay signs of female agency and may consequently reinscribe tragedy's elimination of the female subject. But to focus instead on gaps, contradictions, and female resistance (de Lauretis 1984: 29) is overly optimistic. For these plays did serve as an apparatus to construct gender, in Teresa de Lauretis's sense of a "technology of gender," in their own day. In fact, in most of the extant texts, female strength is associated with what we might call a male anxiety to control it; on the whole, these dramas achieve closure by foreclosing feminine resistance where it has erupted (Zeitlin 1985a: 81). Moreover, the scholarly tradition and universalizing performances have served to reinforce that gender hierarchy in succeeding centuries.

Feminist theorizing about pornography can help us to analyze tragedy's formation of sex difference and sex inequality. The etymology of the word *pornography*—from *pornê* and *graphê*, depiction of whores—suggests that we should consider it in terms of both content and form. If we focus on the *pornê* component, we find ourselves emphasizing what pornography is *about*. In the current feminist debate, there seem to be two contenders in this division: sex and violence. Theorists like Andrea Dworkin and Catharine MacKinnon emphasize the coincidence, not the divergence, of these two. MacKinnon holds that the subordination of women through the representation of violence *is* sex for men (1989; 1987: 86–87, 160 61, 172–73). Dworkin takes seriously the sexuality implicit in the etymology and consequently sees a continuity between past and present: "Contemporary pornography strictly and literally conforms to the word's root meaning: the graphic depiction of vile whores, or, in our language, sluts, cows (as in: sexual cattle, sexual chattel), cunts. The word has not changed its meaning and the genre is not misnamed" (1981: 200). The antipornography movement has taken the position that real women are being hurt in the production and reception of current pornographic representations; their argument focuses on the "object" imitated and on the specific ways in which women are objectified in the process. For my purposes, it will be helpful to combine this sense of object with a more literary one, using the terminology of Aristotle's *Poetics*. In this context, the plot of a play—what happens—constitutes the object, for it is in the plot that tragedy imitates an action (and that is what tragedy is, according to Aristotle).

Another branch of the discourse focuses on the *graphê*, drawing attention to pornography's status as representation: pornography resides not in the real world but in texts (or pictures). Susanne Kappeler argues that "pornography, like much other public imaging, is constructed for male viewing." It creates the male as subject and the female as object or victim (1986: 32, 51–53). This form of generalization risks obscuring important distinctions between "hard-core" pornography depicting violence against women, in which real women are used in the making of the "art," and other forms of representation under patriarchal conditions of production. But it performs an important task precisely in connecting pornography to those other forms of representation, most particularly film, and in connecting theory about pornography to semiotic/psychoanalytic work on film, which questions the way in which the spectator is engendered by the experience of watching (de Lauretis 1984; E. Kaplan 1983).[1]

But there is yet a third approach which would emphasize the Aristotelian final cause: effect. Traditionally, pornography has been said to arouse the (male) viewer sexually; more recently, radical feminists have argued that pornography leads to violence against women. Does pornography stimulate men to enact in the real world what they have seen in pictures? Or does it release those emotions harmlessly and effect a catharsis of them? That is, what is the relationship between representation and some referential reality? MacKinnon calls the catharsis or fantasy thesis a fantasy itself (1987: 190), and Dworkin similarly refuses to separate the representational from the material, rather seeing each as serving the other: "Woman as whore exists within the objective and real system of male sexual domination. The pornography itself is objective and real and central to the male sexual system" (1981: 200).

In one way or another, each aspect of this terrain—object, manner, and effect—is hotly contested, particularly regarding what one should do about pornography. Clearly, politics and aesthetics are related in this discourse, as they were in antiquity where art was held accountable to the social good and was meant to teach (as articulated, for example, by Aristotle and Aristophanes in *Frogs*). The pornography of our day is not separate from all other representational practices and technologies but is, as I hope to show, part of a spectrum of such practices. Advertising, film, and pornography share a structure of representation that can be argued to appear even in tragedy, which depicts neither nudity nor explicit sexuality, and where most violent action takes place offstage. As contemporary feminist theory points up, under male dominance and the hegemony of heterosexuality for women, there is currently ambiguity about and difficulty in distinguishing rape from intercourse (MacKinnon 1983b; 1987: 87–91). Similarly, under male dominance and the hegemony of heterosexuality for women, there is ambiguity about and difficulty in distinguishing representation of women from pornography. While we need to retain the distinctions, we need also to see the commonality. Behind MacKinnon's view of pornography per se stands a feminist theoretical position (1983a: 249), that the epistemological aspect of male power is the power to make its point of view seem like the truth (on tragedy and epistemology, see Zeitlin 1985a). Pornography and tragedy are two of the places where that epistemology is converted into ontology for women, where that knowing turns into being, where women are deprived of subjectivity.

We tend to overlook the more brutal aspects of tragedy, in part because we read the plays rather than seeing them, and because of a tradition that emphasizes the control exercised by the form, for example, in reporting rather than staging scenes of violence. Aristotle, however, gets to the heart of the matter when he asserts that tragedy takes the painful and renders it pleasurable: "Though the objects themselves may be painful to see, we delight to view the most realistic representations of them in art, the forms for example of the lowest animals and of dead bodies" (*Poetics* III.4, 1448b, trans. McKeon). Aristotle believes that the enacted imitation is effective because it teaches the audience and because humans instinctively like to learn. However, let us not assume the humanness of the experience but rather put together violence and gender in the tragic genre. Let us ask what tragedy teaches the audience about women's sexuality, whom it empowers, and to whom it is pleasurable. It is my hypothesis that the ideal spectator identifies as if "it" were male, regardless of whether there were women in the actual audience. Moreover, what happens to the spectator is also what happens to the "speculator," for watching is central to theory (the Greek word *theôrein* means "to be a spectator"), and as Mary Ann Doane has said, "ways of looking are inevitably linked to ways of speculating, of theorizing . . . and, ultimately, to ways of representing oneself" (Doane 1987: 37). In this pornographic structure of male subjectivity, what are the possibilities open to a female spectator?

Since each play is different, and since generalization has a flattening effect, we would be mistaken to seek every element presented in the same way in every play. But using the terms of the debate as I have outlined it, we do see certain recurring features that cohere into a pattern. In tragedy as in pornography, women are either desiring predators or passive victims (on these two models, see Kappeler 1986: 51, 90). Terri Marsh (in the Epilogue of this volume) turns her attention to the figure of the sacrificial maiden, while I will turn mine to those characters seen as having desire and acting on it. Their desire is represented as destructive of others and themselves; having disturbed the sexual hierarchy, they die like women—offstage, within their chambers (Loraux 1987: 20–21). The structure of the plays generally works to contain that destructive passion or will, so that in the end the audience is put into a subject relationship with the masculine protagonist (seen as a victim of women) (see Shaw 1975; Foley 1982). As I look at these plays, I will be taking women's sexuality as the object imitated and considering first how women's sexuality is constructed. Second, I ask whether the structure of representation and rhetoric creates a subject status for men, and object status for women. Finally, I will focus on the effect of the plays, inquiring whether they reproduce the pattern of domination in the audience—is there a space for a female spectator?

Sophocles' *Antigone* (442 B.C.E.) may serve as something of a paradigm for the ancient struggle between the sexes, in which hierarchy is sexualized and the subordinate position is marked as female. After a fatal battle between Oedipus's sons, Polyneices and Eteocles, Kreon has forbidden the burial of Polyneices, the aggressor. Antigone disobeys him and is sentenced to be buried alive in a cave. There she hangs herself, and her betrothed, Haemon, joins her in death by stabbing himself before the prophet Teiresias can persuade Kreon to have them released. After hearing the news, Eurydice (Haemon's mother and Kreon's wife) goes quietly to her own death. Even the virginal heroine is constituted as sexual; then she and the feminized male are exposed to view, so that the male spectator may learn a lesson. As he learns this lesson, he is taking artistic satisfaction in the spectacle, and in this way he consolidates his sense of self and morality from a pornographic experience.

While from Antigone's point of view the issue is one of contending laws—she believes that she enacted the gods' wish by burying her brother, even though she broke Kreon's law forbidding that burial—Kreon sees no such possibility of disagreement (639–80). He reduces her to her reproductive capacities and nullifies her subjectivity by asserting that there are other "furrows for his [Haemon's] plough" (569; see duBois 1988 on this metaphor). Kreon is an archetype of the phallocratic leader. From his point of view, the ruler is male, and the male is ruler. He is defensive about his rule and his masculinity: "I am no man and she the man instead if she can have this conquest without pain"; "No woman rules me while I live" (485, 525). He is anxious that his son honor and obey him (639–44) and calls him womanish or slave to a woman when he is "disloyal" (740, 746, 756). Kreon adheres to a division of responsibilities by age and sex; this hierarchy denies any other role to Antigone than that of mate, while she aspires to a spiritual and devotional role. Kreon sexualizes politics and eroticizes power: brutality is a civic act designed to firm up his rule, but also explicitly sexual since he means to teach Antigone to be a woman (577–81).

Not only does he sexualize his opponent, but the male tyrant emerges as a maker of language and, I would argue, pornography (he writes the script within the play). A central choral ode (332–83) significantly links Kreon's position to the human subject position in the world. The song begins with the free productivity of earth, but universal man (*ho anthrôpos*) enters to control both earth and sea; the implicit masculinity becomes explicit when man (*anêr*) begins hunting and taking the products of each realm. This male subject then teaches himself the arts of language, city building, and law giving. Such symbolic, coded activities define the human, which through the language is exclusively male. The transformation of nature into culture is central and brought about by Man. In this song, the Chorus celebrates male subjectivity but with ominous misgivings. The colossus who strides across the earth is terrible and strange (*deinos*), and if he is not careful, having founded cities, he may end up without one, as the stranger (*unheimlich,* according to Heidegger [1959: 150–51]). Kreon treats women and his son as Man treats the products of earth and sea—he hunts them and traps them—and in so doing he creates disorder rather than order. His language and law ought to constitute civilization but instead confuse the properly separated realms by treating the live woman as if she were dead, putting her beneath the earth (1068ff.).

At the same time that the text reveals Kreon's error, it gives support to his worldview. First, the play, no less than Kreon, sexualizes Antigone by referring to her as the Bride of Hades (1205). This is no mere conflation of themes, nor does it simply suggest Greek initiation rituals (which would be invoked at marriage and funeral) and a change in status. Rather, it serves to give a strongly erotic character to this heroine, whose salient feature is nonetheless her virginity (Michelini 1987: 76–77). Her strength in action is set against her vulnerability to re-action; she is open to capture. She remains feminine, even though she challenges the masculine, and femininity is vulnerability (Loraux 1987: 65). Because she has been effaced, the messenger speech gives only two small details about Antigone, both of them sexualizing: she hangs herself by the neck, in her veil linen; Haemon's blood is on her white skin.[2] The veil evokes the virgin about to be married, the blood the blood of defloration. In this way, desires that are ambitious are made to seem erotic from the male point of view, and the issue in the end is between father and son (on erotic and ambitious fantasies, see Miller 1981: 40–41).

Second, although Kreon has made a resounding error, for which he will pay dearly, it is nonetheless possible to read this play with sympathy for him, as is clear from Heidegger's concern for the stranger.[3] The structure of the play leaves him standing, the center of our attention, as a result of which there have been long debates about whose tragedy this is, particularly from those who are in search of *the* tragic hero of any given play.[4] He does not pay for his sadism with the loss of our attention. Antigone, however, slowly fades out. Her subjectivity stands out most sharply in the middle of the play when she has committed her act of defiance and defends it to Kreon and the Chorus. From this high point, alluded to by Haemon when he says that she deserves golden honor for her glorious deeds (695, 699), she enters into eclipse. She veers from her original stance, regretting that she is prevented from marrying (916–20) and pointing out that she would not have done what she did under any other circumstances; thus, burial is not an absolute duty but a relative one (904–15). Critics have even gone so far as to eliminate these troubling lines, so little do they seem to fit in with her character (Jebb 1971, ad loc. and 258–63), but they serve as a reminder, if we need one, that Sophocles does not write with a feminist agenda. Indeed, Antigone is gradually displaced as the tragic center; in the end the focus is on Kreon and his tragic experience.

Kreon is the masculine principle writ large, with all of its rigidity and emphasis on unity. He asserts control, condemns his son as a woman, and sexualizes the woman who opposes him. Although he fails and must acknowledge that he too is part of a script, one written for him by the gods, the play subtly supports his position. The structure of representation uses Antigone to make a lesson for men about their relationship to the divine; character/author and audience are put into relation through the objectified woman. In the end, we focus on the male protagonist in his suffering and his life as the stranger, as predicted by the ode, instead of the suffering of those controlled by him in his effort to establish his rule.

Antigone strives to act in conscience; in this she is unique among the active women I will consider. But surprisingly, the play has much in common with others centering in more typical ways on female desire and the more typically sexual figures, such as Clytemnestra, Deianeira, Phaedra, and Medea. Each is a mature woman, a wife and mother, and each is represented as the subject of desire, a desire that has excessive qualities and causes male suffering before leading to the death or suffering of the woman in question.[5] As Loraux (1981b, 1987) and Zeitlin (1985a, 1985b) have pointed out, male suffering is often then coded as female, but far from accepting this as necessary, natural, or freeing for the man, I see it as a sign of male dominance. Throughout these plays, gender boundaries seem to shift, not because the genre takes pleasure in undecidability but rather to restore the hierarchy by destroying the mother. When a woman becomes a subject, all hell breaks loose. As Teresa de Lauretis puts it, "The woman cannot transform the codes, she can only transgress them, make trouble, provoke, pervert, turn the representation into a trap" (1984: 35). In fact, I would challenge the illusion of feminine subjectivity and ask that we remain alert to the sex of the actor, and to the desire of the author/myth put into play in the fabrication of these "women."

One can hardly discuss sexual desire in antiquity without mentioning Clytemnestra—treated by all the tragedians but at greatest length by Aeschylus in the *Oresteia*. This trilogy (458 B.C.E.) tells the story of the house of Atreus beginning with the return of Agamemnon from Troy and his murder by Clytemnestra, followed by Electra and Orestes' matricide at the behest of Apollo, and culminating in the exoneration of Orestes at a trial in Athens, over which Athena presides.

As in *Antigone,* so here the gender hierarchy is at risk (N. Rabinowitz 1976; Zeitlin 1978). Clytemnestra has been ruling in Agamemnon's absence, and the Chorus of the city's elders mistrusts that power in a woman; there is a clear conflict between the queen and these old men. The Watchman she has herself employed speaks of her authority and her "man-counseling heart" (*androboulon kear,* 10–11), raising a fundamental question about whether a woman can and should rule, or whether this woman is not masculine by virtue of ruling. Clytemnestra is represented as straddling the positions of Kreon and Antigone—she shares Kreon's desire for rule, his arrogance, and pornographic tendencies, but the structure renders her a victim like Antigone, one who is, moreover, sexualized in order to be killed. While Kreon is punished, he is still a man acting like a man; the woman acting like a man seems twisted, and her perversity appears to justify her death.

In *Antigone,* the human (which initially seems to include woman) is the strangest thing, taming the earth and the sea; the *Oresteia* offers this formulation: "the earth and sea nurture strange echoes of fearful things, and send forth monsters" (*LB* 585–89), but male and female are explicitly distinguished. Man (*anêr*) has an "overdaring will" (*hupertolmon phronêma*), while woman is characterized by love that is no love (*aperôtos erôs*), which wins out over wedded union (594–601). In the subsequent lines, Clytemnestra is compared to the Lemnian women, who killed all their husbands. That is the risk that such a woman poses. Patriarchy must bring her under control.

Throughout antiquity Clytemnestra was characterized by infidelity; the *Odyssey* contrasts her with Penelope, and Agamemnon's fate serves as a warning to Odysseus to be wary of women. The *Oresteia* displays and uses her sexual drive, making her explicitly lascivious in several ways. First, she is jealous of Cassandra and kills her as well as Agamemnon. Second, she has a lover of her own, Aegisthus. Third, she takes sexual pleasure in the murder: Agamemnon's blood makes her rejoice like a plant in the dew (1390–92), and Cassandra's death adds an extra "dainty" to the luxury of her bed (1446–47). If in the rhetoric of *Antigone* death is made marriage, in the rhetoric of Clytemnestra murder is made erotic.

The second play of the trilogy shows the successful vengeance of the children. What does it take for the son (and daughter) to plot the murder of their mother? Her loss of status as parent, which logically follows from her sexual activity. Orestes and Electra emphasize the concupiscence of this woman (a pattern in Sophocles and Euripides as well) and find that her motherhood was lacking in contrast to her passion; they believe that she sold them for Aegisthus. Since the two roles, lover and mother, cannot coexist, her original motive—vengeance for Iphigenia—is forgotten in her characterization as adulterous queen. Clytemnestra offers her breast, a metonym for the female body in roles of lover and mother (compare Polyxena's breast as object of desire in *Hekabe*), as evidence that she gave suck, but a long speech by Orestes' Nurse negates that claim. Consequently, the audience is prepared to support Orestes when he rejects her bid for pity and carries out his oath to Apollo and his father (896–908).

The *Odyssey* version of Agamemnon's homecoming included his death and Orestes' vengeance; Aeschylus's rhetoric goes beyond that point, taking female power and rendering it repellent. The maternal here comes into the orbit of the "abject" (Kristeva 1982), culturally marginal and requiring that the subject control it. Not only is she identified with monsters (Skylla and Medusa), but once dead she is reduced to a shadow, a specter, trying to arouse the Furies, goddesses of maternal revenge. These Erinyes, snaky females—phallic, mothers of no man, daughters of Night by herself—heighten the audience's sense of disgust at Clytemnestra. Vile liquids flow from their eyes, and the Pythia (a priestess of Apollo) enacts an appropriate reaction when she runs from them in horror (see now Carson 1990).

Aeschylus's description of the Furies is echoed in Kristeva's definition of the abject ("A wound with blood and pus, or the sickly acrid smell of sweat, of decay . . . refuse and corpses *show me* what I permanently thrust aside in order to live," 1982: 3); the hero defines the border and rejects identification with the mother. Similarly, the play wards off danger from the city, by making the female serve the male—as maiden, woman, and crone. First, Iphigenia was sacrificed by Agamemnon to satisfy the crowd and his own war lust. Second, Clytemnestra's sexuality and power, her connection to the earth and the forces of blood, lose force in comparison with language, oaths, and marriage (duBois 1988: 70–71, on reproductive power of Clytemnestra). The sexual Clytemnestra gives way to the asexual Athena in the progress of the trilogy; the mother gives way to the father. Finally, this warrior goddess cleans up the Erinyes. The Pythia, who opens the last play, is an old woman under the control of a young god, speaking his words; even so, the Erinyes come under the control of the figures of light and *only speak their words*. Masculinity triumphs first when Orestes acts on Apollo's orders, and later when Apollo steps in to assert full rights of parenthood for the father, leaving the mother no longer capable (as were Earth and Night) of reproducing by herself but reduced to the nurse for the seed supplied by the father. Orestes' rule and status as speaking subject are firmly established, and Apollo's voice rings out in contrast to the mutterings of the Furies.

The *Oresteia* inscribes the woman as *pornê,* focusing on her sexuality in such a way as to make it seem perverse. The action makes this sexualized woman suffer for her crime; the effect is to eliminate sympathy for her and to justify her murder out of fear of that perversion. The audience is not meant to identify with Clytemnestra or the repulsive Furies but with the masculine position of subjectivity. Clytemnestra's strength could be awe-inspiring—did she not defend her daughter and oppose the senseless killing at Troy?—but not in a culture where femininity is a force to be abjected and contained either in the house or under the city.

Antigone and Clytemnestra challenge the gender hierarchy and are murdered; their texts serve to strengthen male subjectivity. Another group of females are, like Clytemnestra, defined as sexual beings, but they put themselves to death. The suicides share a form of incarceration with Antigone and the Furies, for they typically exit quietly to take their lives within doors, in the bridal chamber. These deaths are pornographic to the extent that they are gratuitous, not required by the plot, or even the myth, and are used to constitute the internal and external male viewer as a subject. Because Clytemnestra is delineated as a sadist, arranging for her own sexual pleasure in the violent death of Cassandra, she pays with her life. But no one pays for the rhetorical gain of these gratuitous deaths. Take, for example, Eurydice and Jocasta, who go in similar ways. The death of Eurydice in *Antigone* results from the Messenger's speech; his callous "why should I make it soft for you?" (1194) and his crude inattention to her silence mark his cruelty. But, in addition, the play makes its own use of her wordless disappearance and her suicide to complete Kreon's suffering.

The death of Jocasta is more sexual, more like what we associate with pornography, since *Oedipus* continually mixes the erotic with the deathly, notably when she (like Antigone, Alcestis, Deianeira) addresses her marriage bed. Like her sister-in-law Eurydice, Jocasta goes silently off stage; we only find her again when the

Messenger's narration re-presents Oedipus violently opening the doors of her room. Oedipus's anger at Jocasta suggests that he thinks her responsible for what has happened; he intends to kill her even after all they have been through. His words reduce her to her body, and her body to the sexual (field of double sowing). The specularization of Jocasta is overt: like the victim in pornography, she is displayed to viewers. Through her suicide she becomes a silent body for their perusal; by the play's verbal depiction of her hanging while they look, she has become an object of their and our gaze. She is the object of violence when Oedipus forcibly enters her room, and then an object for his use when he takes her brooches—a feminine adornment, articles of dress that hold her robes together—and blinds himself with them. Does he not humiliate her by ripping them from her corpse?

The representation of Jocasta's violation is a form of pornography, and it contributes to the creation of masculine subjectivity. She herself is another example of the marginalized and abjected maternal figure: "Jocasta is *miasma* and *agos*—that goes without saying. But Oedipus alone is *pharmakos*. He knows and bounds the mythic universe constituted by the question of (sexual) difference and preoccupied with the separation of the two powers: reproduction/production, feminine/ masculine" (Kristeva 1982: 85–86). Oedipus is the subject created by the discourse, and, of course, attention has remained on him for centuries. In *Oedipus Tyrannus,* Oedipus merely lives on with the knowledge that he has gained with such difficulty, but in the tradition that we have inherited, he becomes a hero of a cult at Colonus and a culture hero standing for the human condition (even in some feminist criticism).

Female desire is essential to the plots of *The Women of Trachis* (421–416?) and *Hippolytos* (428). Each picks up on the monstrosity we can see in Clytemnestra, for instance, and reaffirms masculine subjectivity by controlling that monstrous desire. Deianeira in Sophocles' *Women of Trachis* is the daughter of Oeneus and the wife of Heracles. Heracles, having been given up for dead, has just come home with many prisoners, one of them the beautiful Iole for whom he waged an entire war. Deianeira fears to lose her husband if she has to share him with the young woman, and so she anoints a robe with a "love potion" she got from the centaur, Nessus. The robe kills Heracles, who curses her and commands his son Hyllos to marry his intended concubine Iole. Deianeira is explicitly the woman at the boundary, depicted as looking on from the sidelines as Heracles saved her from marriage to the river Achelôos and from attack by the Centaur. Heracles is the hero who goes out in quest.

Deianeira is a prototypical woman in an economy that exchanges women; she, with her potentially active sexuality, imports a danger to the house, and yet that sexual capacity is crucial for the production of heirs. When she waits, she is the perfect wife, but when she departs from that role, going out herself (albeit through intermediaries), she destroys. The text clearly defines the female as destructive, since Deianeira's attempt to protect her marriage (inadvertently) kills Heracles. The language suggests that her sexuality per se destroys, for the inner regions (*mukhois*) where the potion was kept away from the light can also stand for the recesses of the body (duBois 1982: 95–106; 1988: 155). She and her genitals become a mediator for Heracles' destruction (duBois 1988: 155); he is killed because he cannot avoid her kind gift, the caress of the robe she offers him.

The representation of female desire as poisonous coexists with the representation of Heracles' pain as feminine (Loraux 1981b).[6] To suffer is to suffer like a woman (his death pangs are like birth pangs), for to be weak is to be womanish (compare Kreon, and the piteousness of Agamemnon's murder by a woman in the *Oresteia*). This play of sexual opposites is continued by the manliness with which Deianeira kills herself: with the sword, not the noose (Loraux 1987). Then, too, Deianeira is replacing Heracles at the play's opening by being in charge in his absence, as is pointed up by the quarrel between the messengers about what they owe her in the way of information (405–7).

Part of the blurring of cultural boundaries may occur when Deianeira gazes on Iole (306–13), the object of Heracles' desire. Iole is a vulnerable, pathetic, and noble young woman; because she is so clearly an object (of the war and of the gaze), she represents one pole of female experience. Deianeira seems to represent another, that of the mature wife, regent in her husband's absence. The irony of the play lies in that, although Deianeira thinks that she is pitying an other whose fate is different from hers (312–13), they turn out to be the same. She is not above Iole but is rather about to be displaced by her, for she has lost her status as desired object. In her sympathetic identification with Iole, we can see a doubling—two stages of women's lives are represented simultaneously. Just as Deianeira was at one time the prize sought by Nessus and the river Achelôos and rescued by Heracles, passive in her horror of sexuality, she will be turned into an object once again, for the text reestablishes a hierarchy of gender.

The play accomplishes its restoration of the gender hierarchy by constructing Deianeira as a jealous subject, so that she is rendered destructive of others, consequently the object of her son's hatred, and finally self-destructive. Not only the plot but also the discourse objectifies Deianeira. In the representation of her, her borderline status is stressed and controlled by various male subjects. First, Hyllos focuses on her as a hateful object. He wishes he were not her son (734–37). In the course of his speech she is doubly removed; she is mentioned in a description of the sufferings of Heracles, through *his* hatred of her and his marriage bed (791–92). Hyllos believes that Deianeira deserves to be cursed since she has thrown off all law and has killed the best of men (809–12). Silent as Iole, she becomes the vessel receiving this torrent of abuse, with no personhood, merely agency in Heracles' death. When the Chorus asks why she creeps off, they use a word appropriate to nonhumans, infants, and animals (*apherpeis*, 813). Hyllos agrees with the implication, suggesting that she is unimportant with his "let her creep" and his continued attack.

Second, she is objectified through the narrative representation of her death. After Deianeira's exit, she is once again the object of discourse of others, since the Nurse shadows her (914), observes her, and recounts what she does in the privacy of her quarters. She is not supposed to be a witness, and thus is intruding on Deianeira's space.[7] The narrated scene itself focuses on Deianeira's nostalgia for the place of *erôs* and procreation, the wedding bed; it therefore heightens the link between sexuality and death.[8] The pornographic quality inheres in her objectification and victimization, and the fact that her sex kills her.

As the effect of pornographic representation is to solidify relationships between male subjects, so here the ending unites men and eliminates the female almost entirely as subject. The prolonged description of Heracles' death may have rendered suffering feminine (1075), but he conquers in his combat with death and emerges a victor, able to assert his will over his son. The conclusion to the play establishes a male dyad, replacing the mother-son pair that dominates the play's beginning. Father and son are brought together by the woman, whose function is to provide heirs; she cannot possess the phallus but is necessary to pass it from father to son (Rubin 1975). At the base of patriarchy is the murder of the mother (Irigaray 1981: 16), and Hyllos may be said to kill his mother, since his hateful speech is the immediate cause of her suicide; he moves from his mother to his father, just as the structure of the play moves from mother-son couple to father-son-woman triangle. The woman is split into mother/wife, and both are silent displays, the ground on which the male child can come of age; his incestuous desires are displaced onto this woman, who is marriageable. He replaces his father and becomes a man; but being a man entails living in his father's shadow and marrying the woman he now believes responsible for his mother's death (1233–34). Obedience is the father's law. It is striking that the Chorus of maidens is silent from the entry of Heracles; the focus is now on the father and son and their bond through the exchange of this new (yet old) woman. The circulation begins again.

Drama is in its linguistic roots a doing, and this play does something to women and gender. No matter how much she wanted to be virtuous, Deianeira was dangerous; she resisted the double standard according to which she should have accepted Iole under her blanket. She is replaced by a totally objectified younger woman: Iole never speaks but is looked at and described. In the new attention to men, the man in the audience forgets about Deianeira and what the male traffic in women does to her subjectivity; if there were a woman in the audience, what position of subjectivity would be possible for her? There are only speaking men represented. Thus are pornographic structures of representation, tragedy, and the traffic in women mutually reinforcing.

These issues are even more complex when we turn to Euripides, one who seems the most interested in emotion of the three tragedians and, perhaps for that reason, in women. In fact, his attitude to women has been debated since antiquity. We might even say that he was thought to be a pornographer, for he was attacked by the women in Aristophanes' *Thesmophoriazousai* for telling the sexual secrets of women, forgetting Penelope and making all women like Phaedra, while Aeschylus in *Frogs* accuses him of "making whores" (*epoioun pornas,* 1043). Is *pornopoeia* so different from pornography? Attacks on particular women in *Antigone* and *Women of Trachis* here become generalized; in *Hippolytos* and *Medea* women's sexual activity elicits misogyny from men.

As we saw above, Phaedra is one of the whores Euripides is accused of having portrayed, thereby giving women a bad name. Froma Zeitlin has suggested that the extant version is not the play in which he did so (Zeitlin 1981: 320n), that it is rather a palinode, taking back that earlier vilification. Nonetheless, Phaedra's desire is rendered whorish and despicable to herself and to the audience. Since I have worked out elsewhere the relationship between Phaedra's speech and sexuality (N. Rabinowitz 1987; 1989), I will only mention here that her speech and text threaten Hippolytos and Theseus, and her silence or displacement is required for their harmonious reunion at the play's end.

If we turn to the depiction of Phaedra and female sexuality, we see an interesting confluence: she is objectified at the same time that she is asserted as the subject of desire. Phaedra is first presented as an object for the Chorus's and the audience's desire to know. While she is still offstage, the Chorus and Nurse discuss her physical malady at length, because they are curious about her. Like Deianeira, Phaedra is safe while she is inside, closed up. But the women who speculate on her illness will not leave her be; they open her to our view. This intrusion is a foreshadowing of the force the Nurse will use to pry loose her secret, and thus a foreshadowing of disaster to come. For if this subjected woman should become a subject—speak and act—there is danger for the men gazing at her.

When she is brought onstage, she is still passive, dependent on the Nurse to perform simple actions for her. She then goes fully into a hysterical state, which is erotic in tone and content. Although she is very strongly inscribed as the object of view, the Nurse's uncomprehending interrogation reveals that she is also the subject of desire. Phaedra, ringed about with spectators horrified at her utterances, is like a woman out of nineteenth-century studies of hysteria, like a pornographic image of a woman thrashing about in the throes of hysteria. Madness can be exciting in a woman—look at the role of Cassandra in *Trojan Women*—when she is out of her mind with desire, because she is a victim to be pitied. At the same time, the hysteric may pose a threat, because she might act on her fantasies. But as Catherine Clément points out in *The Newly Born Woman* (Cixous and Clément 1986), it is not much of a threat, for the masculine order will soon close over her head. In the case of Phaedra we can see this: her Nurse finds her discourse alarming because inappropriate, and when she returns to "herself" she is ashamed. Representation of the hysteric so that the masculine audience can take pleasure and see her as acting for him effectively takes her desire away from her and is one mechanism of control. It is interesting in this connection that Euripides only gives Phaedra images for her desire that are imitations of Hippolytos's actions. Let us not forget who creates Phaedra and enacts her. In her hysteria, we have a man in woman's dress pretending to be a woman longing to be the man she loves, longing to be like him, longing to be active. Aphrodite tells us that Phaedra fell in love with Hippolytos while looking at him; that gaze is not hers by rights, and the text takes it away from her.

Hippolytos explicitly makes female desire destructive, through Phaedra's deceitful text. As a result, both sexual and linguistic subjectivity are denied to her. Phaedra at first attempts to exert her will in the negative, by *not* speaking, *not* eating, so that she can peacefully slip from existence. When the Nurse approaches Hippolytos and upsets that plan, she moves into action and attempts to write her own story. But having actively desired Hippolytos, she writes a story of rape; she oscillates between the two pornographic scenarios, that of predator or that of victim, the only ones available to her; the traffic in women leaves no other position, and she can only be victorious by representing herself as a victim of male sexual drives.

The texts I have examined link female erotic desire to female desire for vengeance, which results in the victimization and pornographic representation of the male hero. In these cases (Clytemnestra/Agamemnon, Deianeira/Heracles, Phaedra/Hippolytos), the woman is not only an object set forth for the audience's viewing but the internal cause of another violent event. Like Heracles, in becoming a passive victim, Hippolytos shares the experience of the female (Loraux 1981b).

Phaedra and Hippolytos exchange places, imitate each other (Zeitlin 1985b; Loraux 1981b), and share the role of object in the pornographic plot; she is victimized by Aphrodite and Euripides, he by Phaedra and Theseus as well. As a young man, he too is subjected to the authority of the adult but becomes womanish in the process.[9] I have argued elsewhere that Theseus's violence toward his son may echo homosexual initiation rituals; surely the bull and horses are phallic in their own right (N. Rabinowitz 1989). The graphic description imitates and stands in place of that very violence (1173–1254); it is protracted, in order to wring out the last drop of pity and fear (or is it pleasure?) from the audience.

Such a strategy has the effect of removing audience sympathy from the "woman" who is responsible, at the same time as it justifies male hatred of women and control over them. In a striking mirroring of Heracles' farewell to Hyllos, the play moves to a father-son pietà; the men come together at the expense of the mother. The victimized men (unlike the women) survive their suffering and come onstage; as a result, audience pleasure at closure comes from the male reunion and settling of affairs. Heracles' pain resolves into the scene with Hyllos, and Hyllos's marriage to Iole; Hippolytos's pain resolves into his embrace of his father and a marriage cult that his patron Artemis promises in his honor. If we turn our attention to the intended effect of the plays, we see that just as the woman is eliminated by the father-son dyad in the action, so woman is displaced from the audience by the structure of its experience. Hippolytos suffers and is praised so extensively that it is impossible for the audience to admire Phaedra. She has failed to uphold her own noble standards of action and lowers herself by seeking vengeance. Hippolytos's misogynistic attack in which he calls woman a counterfeit coin (617) seems corroborated by her deceit. Given that fall from grace and the graciousness of the father-son scene, identification would have to be with this male pair. Texts do their cultural work in large part by their manipulation of the audience's desires. *Hippolytos* then combines a representation of female desire as vindictive and destructive, with the control of that desire by displacing the female from subjectivity. Male horror at female sexual activity is thus alleviated by a pornographic strategy that solidifies male subjectivity and the bond between men, shoring up the patriarchal men's club.

It is time now to turn to one last representation of female desire, Euripides' *Medea* (431 B.C.E.). Medea is like the other figures grouped here, in that she is sexual and faces a young rival (compare Clytemnestra, Deianeira), and she too kills (compare Clytemnestra, Deianeira, and Phaedra). Unlike them, she does not pay with her life. She was renowned in Athens for enabling Aegeus to have children; she was also well known for her role in the story of Jason and the Argonauts. Euripides' play takes place after the heroic episodes (her taming of the fire-breathing bulls and taking of the Golden Fleece, her murder of her brother and Jason's uncle), when Jason is about to forsake her and their children and marry the ruler's daughter in Corinth. As soon as Aegeus arrives, promising her safe haven in Athens, Medea arranges for her children to carry a poisoned robe to the princess, killing her and her father. She then murders the children and escapes in the dragon-drawn chariot sent by Helios.

The femaleness of sexual desire and the sexual desire of women are accepted by this text, as by *Hippolytos*. First, Medea's passion for Jason is asserted as a cause of the action. The Nurse, who takes her mistress's part throughout, says, "In Colchis she acted out of a heart (*thumos*) burning with desire for Jason" (8). Jason goes farther: since Aphrodite alone was responsible for all that Medea did for him, he therefore owes her nothing (520–31). Although Medea is in many ways exceptional—she is the granddaughter of Helios and endowed with magical powers—she claims commonality with other women (214–66). Her passion applies to them: Medea's vindictiveness is a measure of her desire, and she generalizes, saying that "once she [a woman] is wronged in the matter of love, no other soul can hold so many thoughts of blood" (265–66, Rex Warner trans.). Jason says, "Women think only about their bed" (569–73). There is a reason for this feminine preoccupation, since women limited, as Medea says, to one man have all their happiness wrapped up in him, while men are free to choose other companions (244–46).

As in *Hippolytos* and *Antigone,* this asserted female sexuality "calls forth" misogyny. The stereotype of women's burning desire seems the perhaps illogical corollary of the exchange of women, which posits and creates an object status for women. Women are obsessed with the bed because it is the source and site of their position in the house. Without that position, what is Medea? Admittedly, since Medea is a foreigner and one who has literally sacrificed her family to her husband, she is not typical, but her action is merely an exaggeration of, not different in kind from, those required of other women. Jason distinguishes himself from Medea, as a rational being from a passionate one; he argues that his purpose in his new marriage is not the gratification of sexual desire but children (563–65, 593–97; compare 876–78, where Medea deceitfully agrees with him) whose noble position would support his children by Medea. He believes that he can reassure her, eliminate her sexual jealousy, but her passion for him has caused a political problem: where can she and her children go if she is no longer his wife (511–13)?

As the plot develops, certainly this sexual woman is made dangerous. Although her suffering is described when she is offstage, she is never passive but from the first inspires fear in the Chorus and Nurse, and specifically fear for her children. Acting on her erotic desire, she sacrifices her role as mother. Although she depicts herself as vulnerable (889–90, 927–28), she is not. Rather, the plot moves Medea from the position of Jason's projected victim to the position of victimizer in her own right; she is the strategist of a successful revenge. We might expect Medea to kill herself after destroying the children, since she is compared to Ino (1282–90), who does so, and since it is usually a woman who is hanging or whose corpse will be revealed when the man yells for the doors to be opened, as Jason does (Loraux 1987: 23). She hurts herself twice as much as Jason, and one can argue that killing one's children is the surest form of suicide (Glass 1988), but the text stresses her intention of harming Jason. Her power extends to prophecy: she is able to foretell Jason's death, while she will have a long life (if not a merry one) in Athens. Her fearsomeness is not played down but placed in high relief by the play's ending.

The rhetoric and structure combine to make the audience experience her vengeance as pornography, with her as the pornographer. Like Kreon, Medea has arranged for a death, has sent a new bride to Hades, but she far surpasses him. She is the dramaturge behind the messenger speech, which constitutes a pornographic moment, excessive in its reporting of sexualized violence. The gruesomeness of the murder emerges slowly, with trivial details that in their banality reveal the princess as cold and narcissistic. While the servants dandled the children and patted their hair, the new mistress was not kind to them, until she saw the dress. This impression of her is reinforced when she puts on crown and dress: she looks at herself in the mirror, admires her legs before she dies (in an agony like Heracles'), killing her father with his own kindness to her. She becomes the spectacle, object for Medea's delectation and our horror. She is just an ordinary, shallow character, not attractive, without any understanding of what she has done to Medea. The combination of ordinary, commonplace events (the play with the children and her coldness) with a grotesque death heightens the pornographic pleasure in pain. To the extent that the audience supported Medea (or Phaedra, or Deianeira), it must now recoil from her.

Not only does Medea plan the death reported in such lavish and graphic detail, but she is the audience of the narration. And she also, like Clytemnestra, gets a thrill from it: "You will please us twice as much if they died very wretchedly" (1134–35). The woman with sexual desire, who aspires to act in the world, is represented as a perverse sadist, one who will kill her children if she thinks it is necessary. Listening to the account of the princess's death does not lead to her suicide (as is the case for other wives like Eurydice, Jocasta, or Deianeira) but rather confirms Medea in her plan to kill the children before someone else does. We are spared a retelling of that scene (although we do hear the offstage sounds); their pain is displaced onto the very long and drawn-out description of the justified other deaths, working to free Medea and us from the realization of the meaning of her act to *them*.

Euripides' Medea not only kills her children, but she escapes: the final tableau discloses no male couple standing over a figurative or literal female body but rather a woman standing in the position usually left to some divinity at the end of Euripidean drama. Medea, then, has established a subjectivity for herself through her powerful acts. What is the effect on the audience of this structuring of the action? Like Phaedra, this Medea gives up any claim on our sympathy by the vengeance she exacts. Having become masculine, a killer of young, she is like the aggressive woman in contemporary pornography, standing over her puny consort and attacking him with words (if not with a whip). A male might well be terrified of this vision of female dominance and male submission, unless he could console himself with the fact that *his* woman is safe at home, under control. At least comedically, Euripides had a real effect in the world; in Aristophanes' *Thesmophoriazousai,* the women object to Euripides precisely because his plays lead to increased male vigilance.

This text is very self-conscious about the power of representation—in particular, the women of the Chorus recognize that they have a bad reputation because men have had the use of the lyre (190–203); things would be different, they sing, if the female point of view could be represented. I remain suspicious of the feminine position seemingly taken by the playwright, and of the feminism attributed by him to Medea. There is no woman's voice represented in this play, only consciousness of its lack. The Medea who plans the death of the girl and hears it with glee is created in turn by Euripides. Although Medea appears to be a subject in her own right, she is, of course, a subject of Euripides' discourse, and ultimately of the discourse of his culture.

Euripides' Medea, who escapes the fate of ordinary women through magic and her grandfather Helios, who incarnates a sadistic model of instrumental use of her children for her own selfish ends, clarifies the problems facing the feminist theorist of representation. Jason describes Medea as a monster, Skylla, and critics have noted the extent to which she takes on the attributes of masculine heroism in her action. She must either kill her children or be a laughingstock—there are no other choices available to her. The only victory is achieved by becoming masculine, and it is a self-punishing victory at that. Who gives her those choices? To the extent that we are in the same culture, what are our choices? To beat men at their own game, or to validate the feminine? The terms facing her and us seem to be binary oppositions—passive/active, female/male. Without another term, we are doomed to continue the annihilation of our progeny.

In tragedy after tragedy, we see the female defined as sexual, possessed of a desire that destroys. When women are active and assertive like Clytemnestra and Medea, that sexuality is masculine and makes its object in turn a feminized victim; they usurp the phallocratic subject's privilege of pornography. The women who adopt the values of the culture—Antigone, Deianeira, and Phaedra—yield their place to the dominance of men. The effect is to bolster up the masculine and to justify cultural control of female desire. If in current times pornography (along with film) is shaping male sexuality and its design for what is feminine, tragedy worked in an analogous way in antiquity. Does this mythology and body of material not work in the same way today?

There are two congruent triangles at play in antiquity (and, though in different form, today): one of exchange and one of representation. The triangle formed by men exchanging women in marriage uses women to form and solidify relationships between men; that triangle is often visible in the plots of these plays (Deianeira/Hyllos/Heracles; Phaedra/Hippolytos/Theseus; Clytemnestra/Orestes/Agamemnon-Apollo). In marriage and the representation of gender, women, despite their resistance, are subordinated to relations between men. It is not merely the use of women that is at stake but a construction of their sexuality—necessary for procreation—as dangerous. That sexuality is contained by male control of the circulation of women and at the same time by male control of the circulation of representation. This brings me to another triangle, that among author, text, and audience. Here, I would argue, the audience is made masculine, asked to identify with the male protagonist, and in this way is put in relation to the author and the text. Through this experience masculine subjectivity is established. Tragedy participates in a pornographic structure of representation, accomplishing the solidification of the male subject at the expense of and through the construction of the female as object.

NOTES

1. Laura Mulvey argued in an early piece that sadism demands a story, thereby likening all narrative to pornography; Teresa de Lauretis draws an analogy between that position and Lotman's paradigm in which woman is positioned as obstacle, boundary, and limit for a mobile hero (de Lauretis 1984: 118–19). Does Lotman's typology hold true for tragedy, or

only for myth and film? Desiring females in tragedy refuse to stand and wait; by insisting on moving, characters like Clytemnestra, Phaedra, and Medea, for example, disrupt the phallic order and pay for it.

2. Feminists analyzing advertising have noted the vulnerability represented by the neck and its prominence in contemporary media images of women; perhaps that is why women in tragedy "get it in the neck."

3. I have in mind, for instance, the position Hegel takes on the play in *Phenomenology* (1910: 484–92) and *Ästhetik* (1920: 215), as popularized and simplified by A. C. Bradley in his essay "Hegel's Theory of Tragedy" (1909). For a cogent disagreement with Hegel, see Brian Vickers's chapter on Sophocles in *Towards Greek Tragedy* (1973).

4. Most of these plays have long philological and literary, although not necessarily theoretical, discussions attached to them; I have by and large dispensed with references to those debates, seeking to ground this essay in another problematic.

5. It is possible that the problem is simply desire itself, but tragedy tends to generalize about desire in these plays where women are overcome by lust. Male heroes, to be sure, are involved in plots of sexual desire, but because of the double standard, their desire is not problematized. The loves of Heracles or Menelaus, for example, have enormous consequences, but they are not themselves killers as a result.

6. There is an interesting mixing of genders in the wool. Deianeira first suspects what will happen when some of the unguent drops on a bit of wool and destroys it. The wool is a sign of the feminine (both female genitals and women's work), but it also stands for Heracles, who suffers like the wool and whose decomposition is adumbrated by its decomposition.

7. Messenger speeches about men most frequently report what could be known: Heracles is in a public place. Oedipus is looking for Jocasta in the palace and is followed into her room. Phaedra, Medea, Alcestis: these women are watched by other women in their quarters, who then make that information public.

8. There is a similar scene in *Alcestis;* she is another virtuous woman who dies voluntarily, though not a suicide.

9. Hippolytos and Pentheus suffer as children at the hands of their parents, as do the children of Heracles and Medea; other children are murdered in *Hekabe* and *Trojan Women*. In fact, in tragedy, the sacrifice of children is almost as common as the sacrifice of women; it appears more horrible (more sadistic?) because the children are obviously unwilling. The children remain outside the plot; since they are not the enemy but a way of attacking that enemy, their deaths always seem excessive because gratuitous, serving another end. Children strikingly share the role of women as victims of contemporary pornography; interestingly enough, the antipornography movement has been successful only in attacking pornography that uses children. Perhaps this is because children are presumed never to have consented, to be incapable of consent, while women are always presumed to have consented to pose for the picture. In tragic women's deaths, consent is provided: the virgins (Iphigenia, Polyxena, and Macaria) are all made complicit in their deaths, while the wives and mothers tend to commit suicide. Euripides is more interested in women and presents more child victims than either of the other tragedians, suggesting that there is a connection in his dramaturgy.

3

Eros in Love: Pederasty and Pornography in Greece

H. A. Shapiro

✗ Pornography and Art, Ancient and Modern

Though the origin of our word *pornography* is Greek, its first coinage in English, in the middle of the nineteenth century, was in response to Roman erotic paintings, then lately discovered at Pompeii (Kendrick 1987: 11). But by 1850, pornographic scenes, in the most literal sense ("drawings of prostitutes"), on much earlier Athenian vases were also widely known in Europe. Erotic encounters of hetairai (high-class prostitutes) and their customers are most prevalent on red-figured drinking cups of the period ca. 520 to 470 B.C. (Brendel 1970), the same years in which the export of fine Athenian ceramics to the Etruscans was at its height. When, in the 1820s and '30s, the rich Etruscan tombs began to be unearthed, we may be certain that these erotic vases, which were eventually dispersed to museums and collections all over Europe, were among their contents.

We know too little about the organization of the Athenian pottery industry, or of the Athenian household, to answer many of the immediate questions posed by such vases. Who determined the subject matter: painter, potter, proprietor of the workshop, or customer? Who bought these vases, and who used them, on what occasions? What did the Etruscans, in whose tombs they ended up, think of them? The most reasonable scenario is that erotic vases were used at all-male symposia, or drinking parties, the Athenian version of a stag party. Some were made for immediate export to the Etruscans, who had a well-documented taste for erotica, while others may have reached Etruria by a secondhand market (Webster 1972: 291). The symposium setting accounts for the concentration of erotic subjects on drinking vessels. The only women present at such symposia were flute girls and other hetairai hired for the evening. Pictures of the symposium are not uncommon on kraters, the large bowls used to mix wine and water at such occasions (e.g., *Cité des Images:* figs. 19–20, 25, 174). The bedroom scenes depicted on drinking cups may thus have offered guests a preview of what they might expect at the end of the evening.

Erotic scenes on Greek vases, then, illustrate perfectly the literal, etymological meaning of pornography (*pornê* = "prostitute," a more pejorative term than *hetaira,* or "companion"). There is no reason to think that the women shown are ever "respectable" (i.e., married or the unmarried daughters of Athenian citizens). Hetairai in Athens were typically foreigners (i.e., non-Athenian, if not non-Greek) and hence already outside the close-knit social fabric of Athenian society.

At the same time, many of these scenes also anticipate in certain respects modern notions of pornography (e.g., Boardman and LaRocca 1975: 97–99), in which the status of the women involved as prostitutes or not is usually irrelevant.[1] They include elements of (male) fantasies and exaggerated details (not limited to the women; the man's erect penis is often improbably large); there is group sex, with imaginative combinations of positions; there are hints of mild sadomasochism (e.g., a sandal wielded by one participant, Boardman and LaRocca 1975: 91); and there is often explicit abuse and degradation of the women involved. Indeed, this last element may take precedence over eroticism, as when aging hetairai are cruelly caricatured as toothless and fat, with double chins and spare tires (e.g., Keuls 1985: fig. 148). Here an element of reality intrudes which would be scrupulously avoided in mainstream modern pornography.

A few such discrepancies aside, one is tempted, in looking at erotic Greek vases alongside contemporary heterosexual pornography, to conclude "plus ça change. . . ." In the homosexual sphere, in contrast, the differences are far more radical and may tell us much about differences between the role of male homosexuality in Athenian society and that in our own.

Homosexual Pornography

Male homosexual pornography is a thriving industry in America and Western Europe, running parallel to heterosexual. Dirty bookstores and the X-rated back rooms of video stores typically display hetero- and homosexual wares on adjacent shelves. Customers have little difficulty finding their way to the appropriate shelf, and the tensions between the heterosexual majority and the homosexual minority often manifest in everyday life seem to disappear in this environment. Neither side is put off by the other's presence, or the other's pornography.

Despite the prevalence of homosexual pornography and its relatively open display in public places, it has rarely entered into the dialogue concerning pornography as a social, legal, and political phenomenon (see Kappeler 1986: 18). Peckham (1969: 213) notes the "strikingly asymmetrical relationship" of hetero- to homosexual pornography, for example in that female homosexual activity not infrequently figures in heterosexual pornography (e.g., two lesbians, for the titillation of the male viewer), while male homosexual pornography is strictly male and depends on an identification of viewer and actor. Clearly, this presents a different set of social issues. The offensiveness of heterosexual pornography to society at large, and to religious conservatives in particular, arises from its being regarded as a grotesque perversion of an idealized image of sex, that between monogamous married couples, especially for the purpose of procreation. Since, however, in the "hierarchical valuation of sex" (see Rubin 1984: 278–87), even a stable, monogamous relationship of two adult men has a very low status, the distance between this and pornography is not very great. There isn't that far to sink.

Meanwhile, heterosexual pornography is offensive to at least one school of feminist thought because, in its demeaning treatment of women and overtones of sadism, it is believed to encourage violence against women, specifically rape (see Kappeler 1986: 36). Rape is indeed a crucial issue which, whether one accepts this argumentation or not, cannot be entirely divorced from that of pornography, as we shall also see in some Greek representations. But homosexual rape is not a significant feature of our society, outside of prison, so it is difficult to argue that homosexual pornography has any negative behavioral effect on its consumers. Indeed, in the context of the current AIDS epidemic, the consumption of male homosexual pornography in private has acquired a new respectability, as a "safe" alternative to backroom bars, bathhouses, and street cruising.

In short, homosexual pornography is an issue of relatively little interest to a predominantly heterosexual society that is much more concerned with regulating what homosexuals actually do, rather than what they read or watch. Only when it involves minors would homosexual pornography impinge on another issue of great concern to society: the sexual exploitation of children. Meanwhile, within the male homosexual community, pornography has aroused little opposition. At worst, it might be argued that pornography perpetuates the ageism and obsession with perfect bodies that are unfortunate features of the modern homosexual subculture.

Greek Homosexuality

In Archaic and Classical Athens, sexual relationships between adult men and adolescent boys were, as is well known, a common and generally approved phenomenon (Dover 1978). And the same painters who depicted hetairai and their customers did not shy away from showing sexual encounters of *erastês* (mature lover) and *erômenos* (beloved youth). Such images were first labeled by Beazley, with Victorian propriety, "courting scenes" (Beazley 1947; see Shapiro 1981b). And, indeed, the difference between these paintings and modern homosexual pornography is as great as that between a society in which a man is put in prison for having sex with a boy under eighteen (and, once there, is especially despised by his fellow prisoners) and one in which a man of prominent family, a leading statesman or general, is expected to have a boy lover.[2]

Male prostitution certainly existed in Athens, and it was considered a sufficiently serious problem that legislation attempted to control it and punish offenders (Keuls 1985: 287–99; see now Halperin 1990: 88–112). But we do not have a single

certain representation of a male prostitute in Athenian art.[3] The *erômenos* in homoerotic scenes on vases is neither a slave nor a prostitute but a freeborn youth who
accepted from his *erastês* gifts (usually animals) but not money. Thus, these paintings are not pornographic in the etymological sense, nor do they have any of the
features that link their heterosexual counterparts on vases to modern pornography.
They are, rather, the reverse of the heterosexual scenes; while the latter exaggerate
and indulge in wild fantasies, the homosexual are restrained and understated (Figures 3.1, 3.2; contrast Figures 1.1–1.3). More specifically, they do not as a rule

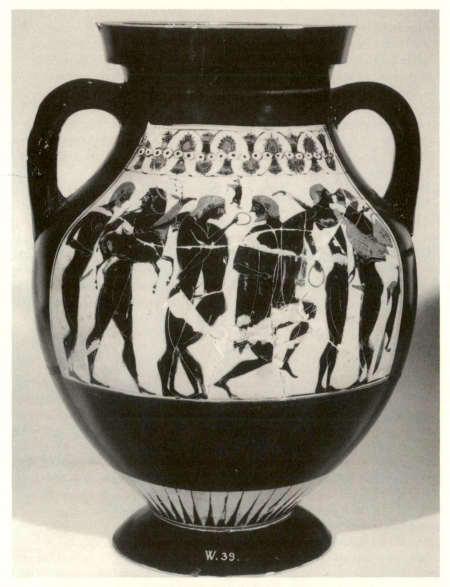

FIGURE 3.1 Men courting youths. Athenian black-figure amphora. Ca. 540 B.C. British
Museum W39. *ABV* 297, 16. Courtesy of the Trustees of the British Museum.

FIGURE 3.2 Youths courting boys. Athenian red-figure cup signed by Peithinos. Ca. 500 B.C. Berlin, Antikenmuseum 2279. *ARV*[2] 115, below, 2. Courtesy of Antikenmuseum, Berlin.

depict the one activity that written sources would lead us to expect: anal intercourse.[4] Instead, the *erastês* fondles his *erômenos*, offers him gifts, and, in the most explicit type of intercourse depicted ("intercrural"), rubs his penis between the boy's thighs. Oral sex, popular in depictions of hetairai, also is not shown.

I have argued in more detail elsewhere that the reason for the discrepancy lies not only in gender difference but in the difference in social status between the female prostitute (foreigner and/or slave) and the freeborn citizen *erômenos* (Shapiro 1981b: 136). Equality of social status of *erastês* and *erômenos* and respect for each other are the dominant motifs of the consciously idealized versions of the relationship presented on the vases. More than a century later, Plato would idealize the same relationship in his own way, often in language whose delicacy and refined innuendo reflect the restrained tone of the vases. In heterosexual scenes, the dominant motifs are power and abuse, and the hetaira is doubly subjugated, as a woman to a man and as an alien to a citizen.

If the intent of pornography is to arouse the viewer by portraying sexual activity in a heightened, exaggerated, and violent manner, then homosexual courtship scenes cannot be so designated. They show less than the reality, not more. But if the Greeks were so open about homosexuality, and so tolerant, then why not show, for example, an *erastês* penetrating his *erômenos*, as men are shown in both vaginal and anal intercourse with women? Presumably for the same reason that Plato, in his long discussions of *erastês* and *erômenos* in the *Phaedrus* and *Symposium*, uses "no explicit anatomical or physiological word" (Dover 1978: 44). Rather, he uses, for example, the verb *charizesthai* ("to grant a favor") of the *erômenos*, when he means "to allow himself to be penetrated." His interest is in the spiritual rather than the physical side of the love relationship, and his dialogues are a high literary form in which euphemism is appropriate. Obscenity and clinical descriptions of sex were reserved for medical writers or the comic stage. The vase painters are not, of course, philosophers, and theirs is not a particularly high art form. They would not hesitate to show an ardent lover with an erect penis or a man masturbating (Boardman and LaRocca 1975: 82). But there was still a boundary of decorum that was not to be crossed, and above all a clear distinction had to be made from heterosexual pornography, with its emphatic dominance of one partner over the other. Oral and anal sex, both viewed in antiquity as demeaning to the recipient (of either sex), are conspicuous in scenes with female prostitutes, thus are absent from homoerotic scenes. This distinction may not correspond fully with what happened in real life; it simply shows that art sometimes tells us more about how a society wishes to be seen than about reality.

Ganymede: Myth and Sexual Fantasy

When the Greeks wanted to express their deepest feelings, their fears and fantasies, they put them into myth. So, for example, satyrs, the mythological bestial followers of Dionysus thought to be in a permanent state of sexual arousal, are occasionally shown on vases performing sexual acrobatics (with each other or with maenads) far removed from the stylized poses and gestures of *erastês* and *erômenos* (Dover 1978: R1127).

Not surprisingly, several myths offer paradigms of the *erastês-erômenos* relationship (Sergent 1984). Indeed, in Classical Athens, where the homosexual ethos was so strong, there was even a tendency to homosexualize myths that did not in origin include an erotic element. Thus, from the time of Aeschylus (ca. 470 B.C.), the relationship of Achilles and Patroclus was assumed to be that of *erômenos* and *erastês* (or vice versa; Plato professes uncertainty), even though Homer, in the *Iliad*, never portrays the friendship in these terms (Keuls 1985: 287–89).

But the one myth that best embodies the fantasy of the perfect, beautiful *erômenos* is that of Zeus and Ganymede. Here, too, the myth evolved gradually toward a more explicitly erotic focus, then after the fifth century veered in the opposite direction (Mayo 1967: 2–5; Sichtermann n.d.: 13–14). For Homer, Ganymede is the most beautiful of mortals, and Zeus sweeps him up to Olympus to be his cupbearer (*Iliad* 22.230–35), but the logical implication of these two facts is never drawn. (This does not, of course, mean that the poet was unaware of it; see Sichtermann n.d.: 16). Only with the lyric poets of the sixth century are Zeus and Ganymede first treated as the ideal prototype of mortal homoerotic relationships (e.g., Theognis 1345–1350; see T. Lewis 1982–83: 165), and only in the early fifth century is the pair first rendered artistically, on Athenian red-figured vases (Figure 3.3). These at first overlap with the latest courtship scenes in red-figure, then for a brief time take the place of the latter, as the open celebration of the homosexual relationship among Athenians was discouraged for political reasons (Shapiro 1981b: 142). In the fourth century, when the motif of Zeus carrying off Ganymede in the guise of an eagle first appears, Ganymede himself gradually becomes a preadolescent boy (Mayo 1967: 13). Both iconographical traits clearly diminish the overt

FIGURE 3.3 Zeus pursuing Ganymede. Athenian red-figure kantharos. Ca. 490 B.C. Boston Museum of Fine Arts 95.36. Catharine Page Perkins Fund. Courtesy of the Museum of Fine Arts, Boston.

eroticism of the story in its High Classical form, and the end result is Rembrandt's Ganymede as a squawking, urinating three-year-old in the eagle's talons (Saslow 1986: 187 and fig. 5.9).

For our purposes, the depiction of Zeus and Ganymede on Athenian vases between ca. 490 and 450 B.C. is of greatest interest, since this is closest to the depiction of homosexual encounters of men and youths, yet at the same time shows other aspects possible (or permissible) only in myth. But Zeus and Ganymede cannot be considered in isolation from related heterosexual myths in vogue at this time. The first half of the fifth century B.C. witnessed an explosion of representations of myths that have been grouped under the heading "the loves of the gods" (Kaempf-Dimitriadou 1979). Some four hundred surviving vases were collected by Kaempf-Dimitriadou, all of them scenes whose iconography was a new creation after 500 B.C., not a revival, continuation, or alteration of subjects in the sixth-century repertoire. Each story combines a divine lover with a mortal love object, and several varieties of gender roles are equally popular. Gods fall in love with mortal women (Zeus and Aegina, Poseidon and Aithra or Amphitrite, Boreas and

Oreithyia), goddesses with mortal youths (principally Eos and Tithonos or Kephalos; Fig. 3.4), and gods with youths (chiefly Zeus and Ganymede). Several mortal men, such as Tityos and Ixion, try to violate a goddess. The only combination not seen is goddess and mortal woman, and this accords with the general lack of interest in lesbian love on the part of the Greek men who made art, wrote most of the literature (Sappho is the obvious exception), and ultimately determined which myths composed the canon. In addition, since mythological love affairs involving mortal women were important largely for the heroic children they produced (see Zeitlin

FIGURE 3.4 Eos pursuing Tithonos. Athenian red-figure pelike. Ca. 450 B.C. British Museum E381. Courtesy of the Trustees of the British Museum.

1986), a myth of lesbian love, even if it existed, would have lacked a crucial ingredient.

To these many vases we may add another large, contemporary group showing a hero, often Theseus, in amorous pursuit of a woman (Sourvinou-Inwood 1987). These scenes use many of the same conventions as the "loves of the gods." From the relatively large corpus of vase representations of both groups, some general observations may be made. Most of the encounters are conceived as pursuits, and there is no physical contact, or at most an outstretched hand on the shoulder of the fleeing victim. A minority of scenes shows a later moment, an abduction. This type occurs only with a male victim, Ganymede carried off by Zeus (e.g., Kaempf-Dimitriadou 1979: pl. 3, no. 39) or Tithonos by Eos (e.g., Kaempf-Dimitriadou 1979: pl. 10, nos. 193–94). The goddess of the dawn, Eos, has wings, and we assume that Zeus can fly without wings, so that in both instances we may imagine that the beautiful youth is being carried to a higher place (Mount Olympus) for the god's private enjoyment. The consummation is never shown—nor, for that matter, is a god or goddess ever shown having sexual intercourse anywhere in Greek art. Furthermore, the god in pursuit never has an erect phallus, so that the scene's eroticism is made even more abstract, less immediate than in generic *erastês-erômenos* scenes, let alone heterosexual orgies.[5]

Thus, the iconography of Zeus and Ganymede conforms in broad outline to a larger category of erotic pursuits, most of them heterosexual, while at the same time retaining a close association with a generic subject, *erastês* and *erômenos*. Within the conventions of Greek art of this period, difference in gender counts for more than difference in sexual orientation. For example, the female victims are always fully dressed, with at most their arms exposed. Even in full flight they manage to preserve their dignity, and such a detail as the garment slipping off the shoulder that might have offered some small titillation is studiously avoided. In this period, before the sensuous nude Aphrodites of the fourth century, female nudity was unacceptable for respectable women, and for this reason could be used to great effect for the rape of Kassandra (Figure 3.5) or the mortally wounded daughter of Niobe (part of a famous sculptural group of ca. 440 B.C. depicting the slaughter of the Niobids). The sadistic/pornographic connotation of the latter has recently been pointed out by Golden (1988: 12).

The males, by contrast, whether gods in pursuit or youthful victims, are often shown nude. This is entirely in keeping with the Greek artists' predilection for showing off the male body, whether as athlete, warrior, or lover. But the handling of nudity in pursuit scenes does occasionally suggest an even more deliberately erotic intent. The motif of the garment slipping off does, in fact, occur in Ganymede scenes (e.g., Kaempf-Dimitriadou 1979: pl. 2, no. 19). An instructive contrast is offered by the two sides of a famous kantharos (drinking vessel), pairing Zeus's pursuit of an unidentified woman with his pursuit of the young Ganymede (Kaempf-Dimitriadou 1979: pl. 1; Figure 3.3). The latter clings to the edge of his mantle as he runs, but almost his whole body is exposed. The woman lifts the hem of her chiton to facilitate her flight, revealing one leg and a bit of thigh but no more. Meanwhile, Zeus, in both scenes, wears his short mantle so as to expose most of his body, incidentally enabling the painter to add a detail of which he was especially fond, the

FIGURE 3.5 Rape of Kassandra. Athenian red-figure hydria. Ca. 490 B.C. Naples, Museo Nazionale 2422. *ARV*² 189, 74. Courtesy Deutsches Archäologisches Institut, Rome.

hairy chest of the mature bearded male. Here this has the effect of emphasizing the age difference between Zeus and Ganymede, on the one side, and, on the other, the contrast between the masculine, almost bestial pursuer and his delicate victim.

The contrast between Zeus—mature, hairy, and bearded—and Ganymede—smooth, boyish, and beardless—is, of course, a reflection of the rigid conventions of Greek pederastic relationships. Ironically, not only is the boy love so prized by the Greeks anathema to modern taste, but the mutual and reciprocal affection of two adult men now gaining some degree of acceptance was anathema to the Greeks. Once a boy's beard and body hair began to grow, he lost his appeal to an *erastês* (Richlin 1983: 34–38), and he was ready to seek an *erômenos* of his own (as well as the company of female prostitutes). Vase paintings show that the difference in age might be not more than a few years (see Figure 3.2), but sexual roles were nonetheless fixed, and any reversal would be strongly censured.

Ganymede may be fully dressed, fully nude, or almost any stage in between. In several striking instances, however, the painter has consciously turned him to expose his beautiful body in full frontal nudity that can only be meant to underline his erotic appeal. From the time of Homer, Ganymede was famous for being the most beautiful of mortals, and it was this that attracted Zeus to him. Clearly, the painters felt challenged to try to capture that beauty and let it work its magic on others.

Perhaps the best example of this motif is in the tondo of a cup that comes late in the series, ca. 460–450 B.C. (Kaempf-Dimitriadou 1979: pl. 3, no. 34). The well-muscled Zeus yanks Ganymede toward him as the youth tries to pull away, creating a powerfully centrifugal composition that threatens to burst the borders of the cup. Perhaps Zeus's unseen left hand is actually pulling off Ganymede's garment, or else it is about to slip off his left shoulder by itself. The youth's distraction is also evident in his having let go of the cock he was holding in his left hand (a love gift from Zeus; see Koch-Harnack 1983). He turns his head back, thus presenting a fully frontal torso, but his gaze avoids that of Zeus. Rather, he looks down, a sign of modesty typical of brides and other chaste girls and women. There is a striking similarity in the conventions of modesty expected of well-bred girls and of *erô-menoi*. If we apply E. Ann Kaplan's notion of the "gaze apparatus" (1983: 319) to the Greek situation, the demarcation of *erastês/erômenos* is more important than that of male/female. The boy was supposed never to be aroused at the sight of an older man.

Where scenes of Zeus and Ganymede come closest to those of mortal *erastês* and *erômenos* is in the motif of gift giving, in both cases the cock being the favorite gift. Where they diverge most sharply is in the element of force applied by Zeus, but never by an *erastês*. In addition to the sense of honor that required an *erastês* to win the favors of his beloved by force of his exemplary character and token gifts, the boy was protected from any physical violence by strict laws on *hybris* (Dover 1978: 34–39). But Zeus, of course, is different, not subject to the ethical and legal constraints of mortal men. As has often been observed, the Homeric gods are not only no better than mortals in their standard of moral conduct, but often notably worse. Certainly the gods are spectacularly lacking in sexual continence, as the huge body of vase paintings euphemistically labeled "the loves of the gods" makes very clear. In the *Iliad* (5.265), Zeus is said to have compensated Ganymede's father with a splendid set of horses for the loss of his son. This is the "justice of Zeus." The Athenian father also lost his son, in the sense that an *erastês* might well become more of a father figure (i.e., role model) to his *erômenos* than the boy's natural father was. His compensation could only be another father's son. But if Zeus, in his strong-arm tactics with Ganymede, does not live up to the moral standard of the ideal *erastês*, neither is he censured for it. Rather, he is envied, for his seizure of Ganymede represents an erotic fantasy the honorable Athenian might enjoy as he drained his wine.

If one goal of pornography is to enable the viewer to experience vicariously what he cannot act out in real life, then this may be as close as Greek art comes in the homosexual sphere. Yet *pornography* would surely be too strong a word for these rather stylized pictures. With his Homeric reputation as the most beautiful youth in the world, yet unattainable and fit only for a god, Ganymede corresponds rather to the sexy, unattainable "pinup" of mid-twentieth century America, the Betty Grables and Marilyn Monroes. And just as there was an air of coy playfulness, almost innocence, about the pinup girls (never fully nude), so Ganymede preserves the innocence of boyhood and the remoteness of myth. Greek myth, of course, has a female counterpart to Ganymede in Helen, the most beautiful woman in the world. She makes regular appearances in vase painting, in her first meeting with or abduction by Paris or, more often, recovered by an angry Menelaos at the end of the War. But her famous beauty is hard to discern (in scenes with Menelaos she is usually veiled and utterly submissive), and she is hardly a pinup.[6] Once again, we come closest to understanding the homosexual ethos of Classical Athens not by any analogy with modern male homosexuality but by substituting in our imaginations for the *erômenos* the stereotype of the (female) pretty, shy, sought-after "sweet young thing" (see Wender 1973).

Eros and Homosexual Rape

The scenes we have just considered are traditionally labeled "the rape of Ganymede," though they are far from the modern definition of rape (but closer to Latin *rapere,* "to seize or take"). The combination of eroticism and violence would indeed move them closer to the realm of pornography, though the conventions of Greek art prevent the pursuit from going beyond this preliminary stage.

In fact, only in a few exceptional instances does Greek vase painting offer us what we may recognize as a rape in the modern sense—forced sexual intercourse— with a most unexpected perpetrator. On the interior of an Athenian red-figure cup of ca. 480 B.C. now in Boston, unfortunately in a fragmentary state of preservation, is a unique depiction of homosexual rape (Figure 3.6). The god Eros, characterized as

FIGURE 3.6 Eros raping a boy. Athenian red-figure cup fragment. Ca. 480 B.C. Boston Museum of Fine Arts 13.94. *ARV*[2] 1570, 30. Gift of E. P. Warren. Courtesy of the Museum of Fine Arts, Boston.

a muscular nude youth with large, elaborate wings, has swept in from the left and, still hovering in midair, caught up in his arms a boy holding a large lyre. Of the victim only the legs and parts of a long, loosely fitting garment are preserved. His entire torso and head are lost, but we can be certain of his gender and can imagine what he must have looked like from other vases of the period. Not even pausing to undress his limp victim, Eros thrusts his erect penis between the boy's legs. Around the lyre are the remains of an inscription praising the beauty of an Athenian youth of the day ("Chairestratos is handsome"). While such inscriptions occur on hundreds of vases with nonerotic scenes, one cannot help thinking that here it may be a pointed message to the recipient of the vase.

This battered fragment may be the only representation in Greek art that combines the violence of rape with an explicit depiction of a sexual act. The much more popular subject of the rape of Kassandra by the Lesser Ajax, by comparison, depicts only violence and male domination. The hapless, nude, or seminude Kassandra clings to the statue of Athena (the Palladion), from which the Greek warrior wrests her away (Figure 3.5). There is no sex, though the frontal nudity of Kassandra, so rare in Archaic and Classical Greek art, was not only shocking but perhaps titillating to the male viewer. The scene often forms part of a larger, panoramic view of the sack of Troy by the Greek army, and Kassandra's rape becomes a kind of metaphor for the rape of her city.

The scene on the Boston cup thus falls outside the parameters of homoerotic subject matter on Greek vases that we have outlined above and goes beyond other mythological scenes, such as Zeus and Ganymede, in its unrestrained violence. This may account for a scholarly disagreement in identifying the figures at least since the time of Beazley, who called them Zephyros and Hyakinthos (1947: 31; repeated most recently by Schefold 1981: 325).[7] But the iconography of Zephyros, the West Wind, is familiar from other vases (clothed, with disheveled hair), and no erotic encounter of the god is attested in art. Certainly our figure does sweep down like the wind, and Greek poets recognized this trait in Eros as early as the sixth-century Ibycus of Rhegium, who likened his onslaught to that of Thracian Boreas, the North Wind (quoted by Athenaeus 13.601b). Sappho compares Eros to a storm (fr. 50), and her contemporary Alcaeus, in the late seventh century, even made Eros the son of Zephyros and Iris (fr. 8). That our rapist must be Eros was recognized by Vermeule (1969: 14–15), Greifenhagen (1957: 79–80), Sichtermann (1956: 121), and others.

Two contemporary cups, close in style to the one in Boston, show essentially the same scene with some slight variations: the victim is nude, Eros's penis is not visible as he presses the boy to himself, and, in one instance, the boy holds no lyre.[8] These three modest vases thus form a coherent group, but do they represent a bizarre aberration of a single mediocre artist, or can they be related to a broader iconography of Eros?

The figure of Eros as winged, youthful god, though strangely absent from Greek vase painting until the last years of the sixth century, is suddenly ubiquitous throughout the fifth. Yet in a narrow sense Eros has no mythology, in that there are no narrative tales in which he plays a significant role until the comparatively late story (more Roman than Greek) of Cupid and Psyche. Yet among the myriad representations of Eros in red-figure, we can piece together a sequence of several dozen where he pursues a boy with increasing aggressiveness, culminating in the three scenes of rape.

In the first of three phases, Eros approaches a boy from a discreet distance and offers him gifts (e.g., Greifenhagen 1957: 14, fig. 7)—sometimes the cock or hare familiar from courtship scenes of *erastês* and *erômenos,* sometimes a hoop (Ganymede's typical attribute, expressing his still puerile interest in toys). Sometimes the boy is not shown at all, but we can guess from Eros's attribute what his mission must be (Figure 3.7). In phase two, Eros swoops down and accosts the boy more directly, and usually he tries to flee (Figure 3.8). These resemble many of the "loves of the gods" scenes, both hetero- and homosexual, especially those with a winged lover like Eos, but with a few key differences. Most strikingly, Eros several times wields a whip, and on one vase two Erotes pursue the same boy from opposite directions, both armed with a whip (Greifenhagen 1957: 59, figs. 43–45). Finally, in phase three, Eros catches up the reluctant boy in his arms and forces him to submit to intercrural intercourse (Figure 3.6).

It is easy enough to string all these scenes together into a continuous story of erotic courtship, pursuit, and capture, more difficult to say what it all means. Who is the boy? No story of Eros's passion for a boy is recorded in any literary source. Is Eros even capable of falling in love (or lust), or is he, as most scholars maintain, simply the agent of his mother, Aphrodite, causing others (with his bow or otherwise) to fall in love but himself immune (Kaempf-Dimitriadou 1979: 6, 15)? What does the doubling or multiplication of Erotes mean? Interpreters of individual vases in this series have attempted to avoid treating Eros as a lover in his own right, first by denying that the rapist in phase three, and the pursuer on some vases of phase two, is Eros at all, then by arguing for a more metaphorical, less literal reading of all these vases. The epiphany of the love god to a boy represents the first awakening of passion in the adolescent. The whip symbolizes the driving force of the passion that love kindles.

There are certainly ample parallels in earlier poetry where the irresistible feeling of love within an individual (usually the poet himself) is personified as the onslaught of the god. Besides Ibycus's likening of Eros to Thracian Boreas, Anacreon uses a metaphor from the blacksmith's shop, saying that Eros hit him with a hammer and plunged him in a cold bath (fr. 45).

But Greek vase painters do not often trade in metaphor; they tend, rather, to be concrete and, through the use of attributes and other detail, to place their subjects in a specific setting and invite a specific reading. So, for example, in a typical example of Eros pursuing a boy (my phase two; Figures 3.8, 3.9), these are the determining elements: the boy's open cloak, the lyre he holds in his left hand (the object in his right hand is the *plêktron,* used in playing the lyre), the altar behind him, the whip carried by Eros, and the bearded man carrying a walking stick on the reverse of the vase.

Combining these elements, we obtain the following scenario. The boy is on his way to school when suddenly overtaken by Eros. The lyre may indicate that he is on his way to a music lesson, or, more generally, it is the attribute of the well-bred Greek youth. Tithonos, one of the objects of Eos's desire, regularly carries a lyre, as

FIGURE 3.7 Eros offering love gifts. Athenian red-figure neck-amphora. Ca. 470 B.C. British Museum E290. *ARV*² 653, below, 1. Courtesy of the Trustees of the British Museum.

does Paris, the handsome Trojan shepherd/prince visited by Hermes and the three goddesses. The altar implies an outdoor setting; many such simple shrines lined the roads of Attica. The bearded man is the boy's *paidagôgos*, a household slave whose job it was to accompany his charge safely to and from school. But he cannot protect him from the attentions of a god, and only gestures helplessly from a distance. The open cloak reveals what has caught Eros's eye, much as Ganymede's beauty and attractiveness to Zeus are often heightened by the modest yet revealing garment.

FIGURE 3.8 Eros pursuing a boy. Athenian red-figure neck-amphora. Ca. 470–460 B.C. Museo Nazionale di Villa Giulia 47214. *ARV*² 280, 13. Courtesy Deutsches Archäologisches Institut, Rome.

The whip is Eros's attribute, the symbol of his power, like Zeus's thunderbolt or Poseidon's trident—at least in the Early Classical period, before the bow and arrow became associated with him.[9]

Eros thus joins Zeus and other divinities as a pursuer of beautiful boys, but his passion is even more urgent, more irresistible and uncontrollable than theirs. The

FIGURE 3.9 Reverse of Figure 3.8: Paidagogos. Courtesy Deutsches Archäologisches Institut, Rome.

key to understanding this conceit lies in an observation made by Nikolaos Himmelmann-Wildschütz about the characterization of the gods in Classical Greek art. There is a paradox, as Himmelmann formulated it, that the gods fall victim to the same forces and emotions that they control in others: "This is the depiction of the divinity who displays his own powers, enjoys them himself, and falls victim to them. So, for example, Dionysos is seized by frenzied ecstasy, Apollo by the spirit of the oracle, Ares by dark lust for blood, Aphrodite by 'love that loosens the limbs' . . . the divinity is not only master of his own powers, but is himself possessed by them, is shown suffering from them" (Himmelmann 1959: 11). As examples, Himmelmann offers Dionysos, Apollo, Ares, and Aphrodite, but Eros perhaps illustrates the principle even better. For his passion is more sudden and, sometimes, more violent than that of any other god.

Admittedly, this explanation leaves a few unanswered questions. Could Eros be exclusively homosexual? Indeed he is not, for by the middle of the fifth century vases begin to show Eros pursuing a young woman (though he never catches or rapes her). The shift is symptomatic of a weakening of the homosexual ethos in Periclean Athens and a romanticizing of heterosexual love and marriage (Sutton 1981: 459–63). In Eros's cult as well, it is clear that throughout the Archaic period all the god's associations are with pederastic love (Furtwängler 1874: 19). Even if we accept that Eros falls victim to his own power, he looks like an unlikely *erastês,* this eternally boyish creature. But Plato's Diotima would later refer to Eros as an *erastês* (*Symposium* 203C 3–4), and in Platonic terms, Eros could *only* play the *erastês,* because only the *erastês* experiences *erôs* (the *erômenos* experiences *philia;* see Halperin 1986: 66). Seltman's idea of Eros as the personification of the *erômenos* (1923–25: 90) is thus untenable at every level. The vase painters themselves must have been aware of the seeming paradox, for at least some of them adjusted their image of Eros accordingly. The first few depictions of Eros in red-figure, in the last years of the sixth century, show him as a small, flitting *daimôn* or dolphin rider (Greifenhagen 1957: 33, fig. 26, 71), and this type recurs throughout the fifth century. But only in the years 480 to 450 do we encounter Eros as a full-grown, muscular adolescent. He is still beardless, to be sure, but then so are the *erastai* in many red-figure courtship scenes of the early fifth century (see Figure 3.2). Perhaps the beefiest Erotes in Greek art are on a well-known stamnos (storage jar for wine) in London.[10] Three winged Erotes fly over the sea, each bringing a traditional love gift for an *erômenos:* hare, sprig, and fillet. One is inscribed Himeros ("desire"), and we may assume that the other two are Pothos ("longing") and Eros. That they should hunt for boys in a pack is not so different from the earlier black-figure revelries with three or more pairs of *erastês* and *erômenos* (Figure 3.1).

The most exquisite scene of Eros in love decorates an object as enigmatic as it is beautiful (Figure 3.10). It is an unusual ceramic object composed of two disks joined by a small crosspiece (Greifenhagen 1957: 66, fig. 50; Schefold 1981: 327, figs. 478–79). The function is unclear. It has been called a bobbin or a yo-yo (Wehgartner 1983: 154–55), and I have argued elsewhere that it is meant to imitate a device used in love magic called an *iynx* (Shapiro 1985). Certainly the votive character (rather than functional) is clear in this instance, since there are two suspension holes, and the white-ground technique with which it is decorated was generally employed on vases not meant for use in everyday life.

The fair youth turns back and grasps the edge of his cloak, much like a Ganymede by the same artist, revealing himself to the viewer (cf. Harrison 1979). But the pursuer is not Zeus, but Eros. His large wings (now mostly lost), streaming hair, and the fillet fluttering from his arm indicate that he has just landed—a kind of divine epiphany—and caught his victim by surprise. There is less physical violence than in the struggle of Zeus and Ganymede by this painter (Kaempf-Dimitriadou 1979: pl. 3, no. 34), and, even more important, the gazes of lover and beloved now

FIGURE 3.10 Eros catching a youth. Athenian white-ground "bobbin." Ca. 460 B.C. Metropolitan Museum of Art 28.167. Fletcher Fund, 1928. Courtesy of the Metropolitan Museum of Art, New York.

meet. It is Eros's means of infusing himself (i.e., desire) into the love object, of transmitting desire like a contagious disease (see Halperin 1986: 63). That the boy responds to the gaze, instead of looking away, seems to suggest the kind of erotic reciprocity later defined by Plato (Halperin 1986).

Other details link this scene with those of my phase two: the lyre in the youth's hand and the altar, a small trace of which is preserved at the left. Simon has given the lyre a more specific interpretation, as marking the youth as the victor in a musical competition (the same youth is crowned by Nike on the other side of the object). Thus, it is his musical skill, as much as his beautiful body, that has aroused Eros's desire (Simon 1985: 70). In fact, Eros himself often carries a lyre (Greifenhagen 1957: 16–19), and the close association of eroticism and music did not escape Plato (*Republic* 3.403C).

At the time this object was made, about 450 B.C., no scene of mortal *erastês* and *erômenos* had been painted for a full generation, and the whole institution of pederasty, if not actually censured, was coming to be seen as old-fashioned, with elitist associations that were inimical to the Athenian democracy. Greifenhagen has rightly called this scene the last great artistic expression of Archaic male *erôs*. Ironically, from an art-historical point of view, it represents a new level of technical refinement, when, for the first time, an artist could transcend the limitations of conventional vase painting (through the use of shading and other techniques developed in wall painting) to create the most sensuous "pinup boys" ever seen in this medium—just when the demand for such images was on the wane. By the time Plato came to celebrate the beautiful youth, these pictures were heirlooms of a bygone age.

NOTES

I am grateful to Amy Richlin, not only for the invitation to contribute to this volume, but for much encouragement and many good suggestions along the way. Thanks also to Robert Sutton for his careful reading of an earlier draft and many helpful comments, and to Lucilla Burn and Dietrich von Bothmer for help in obtaining photographs.

1. See, however, Kappeler 1986: 152. Kappeler points out that the etymological derivation of *pornography* from "prostitute" is still accurately reflected in the power relationship of male and female.

2. In the remainder of this chapter, discussion of homosexual pornography or erotica is limited to that between males. There are, in my opinion, no depictions of explicit lesbian activity in Greek art, and attempts to recognize it (e.g., Keuls 1985: 87, fig. 81; Dover 1978: R207) do not convince. At most a scene like R207 might be intended for titillation of male viewers, as in the use of lesbianism in modern heterosexual pornography for men.

3. Keuls 1985: 297, fig. 166, reproduces a scene on the interior of a red-figured cup which she describes as "Man negotiating the price of sex with a boy." I doubt, however, that the money purse in the man's hand implies that the boy is a prostitute. Mature men often carry such a purse as an attribute (like the walking stick). It characterizes their status in society and signifies *ability* to purchase anything from sex to vegetables, but not necessarily *intent*.

4. A small number of black-figure vases show anal intercourse between men (e.g., Koch-Harnack 1983: fig. 108). All these vases belong to the so-called Tyrrhenian Group, made for the Etruscan market. The iconography of these vases is often eccentric, and they cannot be used in a discussion of Athenian tastes and expectations.

5. An exception would be the ithyphallic Pan pursuing a goatherd (Beazley 1963: 550, 1). But Pan falls more in the category of the bestial satyrs than of the Olympian gods.

6. The story that Helen distracted Menelaos from his wrath by baring her breast is depicted on a single remarkable vase of ca. 430. Beazley 1963: 1173 (Vatican).

7. Beazley was himself uncertain about the identification ("according to conjecture"), but it was taken up and repeated by others with more certainty; also in Dover 1978: 98, cf. 93. The suggestion had first been made by Friedrich Hauser in 1893 (references in Greifenhagen 1957: 79).

8. The vases are (1) a second cup in Boston, inv. no. 95.31; Beazley 1963: 443, 25; and (2) cup, Berlin (West) inv. 2305; Beazley 1963: 450, 31.

9. A unique, recently published red-figured vase of about 490 (Hermary 1986) is by far the earliest depiction of Eros as archer. The motif does not become popular until much later.

10. British Museum E440; Beazley 1963: 289, 1; Greifenhagen 1957: 32, fig. 25.

4

The Mute Nude Female Characters in Aristophanes' Plays

Bella Zweig

Considering the issue of the mute, nude female characters that have cameo appearances in many of Aristophanes' plays from the perspective of pornographic representation entails many problems, both of ancient scholarly criticism and of modern interpretation. Historically, the short, nonspeaking role assigned to these characters has resulted in comparably short scholarly attention to their dramatic and cultural significance. Classical scholarship has focused, in the words of Cedric Whitman (1964: 112), on "a minor, but enthusiastic, philological controversy," namely, were these characters portrayed by male actors in padded costume or by real, nude hetairai?[1] However enthusiastic the debate, and regardless of which position they espouse, critics curiously continue to discuss the thematic or dramatic significance of these scenes without regard to whether they were played by padded actors or real live women.

The situation is hardly better in the area of modern interpretations of pornography, where the scholarly literature is divided on both its definition and significance. How, or whether, one can distinguish between erotica and pornography continues in debate. Feminist, sociological, and psychoanalytical interpretations drastically oppose each other and are as often divided intra- as well as interdiscipline. Finally, once a coherent approach is proposed, whether it could validly be applied to the ancient material remains a serious question.

Undaunted by these multiple complexes of scholarly problems, I attempt in this chapter to accomplish several things. I first examine the role of the mute, nude female characters in Aristophanes' plays in their appropriate dramatic, religious, and societal contexts. I then briefly review some salient points in the modern debate on pornography. Since Old Comedy, as theater, is meant to be seen, I shall draw primarily upon feminist film analysis to formulate a critical approach by which to examine these nude female characters.[2] Finally, I assess whether we may judge these figures in Aristophanes' plays by the criteria of modern pornography.

The Mute Female Character in Aristophanes

Imagine these scenes:

1. A nude woman, gazed at by an assembly of clothed men, represents the abstraction Reconciliation. Her nude body functions as a map, as another female character, clothed, displays different parts of her body while calling them by sexually suggestive geographical names.

2. An adolescent female dancer is instructed by one older man—call him "the con"—to dance with her skirts held high to expose her genitals (a fifth-century can-can?), in order to entice another older man, who plays the dupe. The dupe eagerly paws the girl's breasts and genitals while the con negotiates her price.

3. Two young girls, nude and wearing piglet masks, are brought onto the stage in a wheelbarrow by their father, who designates them as "little piggies" he's bringing to market to sell. The buyer fingers "the goods" as he and the father negotiate their cost and exchange food jokes containing vivid, sexual double entendres.[3]

If these were contemporary scenes, there would be little doubt that they were culled from pornographic movies. For the central features of these scenes unmistakably characterize modern pornography: a nude or partially dressed female is exposed to the gaze, commentary, and sexual manipulation of others, especially men who are all dressed; sexual and/or obscene jokes are made of her body which serves frequently as a metaphor for animals, food, geography, or abstractions; the female object of this visual, verbal, and physical activity mutely and passively endures whatever use is made of her; at best she is allowed inarticulate animal sounds; and increasingly younger girls, and boys, are exploited by adults for sexually explicit scenes.[4]

But the scenes described above are not derived from modern pornography; instead, they are taken directly from the Old Comedy plays of Aristophanes. Out of context, these scenes lend themselves to the stark visual description presented here. Whether this description holds as accurate within the ancient context must now be determined.

Conditions of Dramatic Production

In the latter half of the fifth century, comedies were performed during the day at one of two festivals: the Athenians-only Lenaia, which produced only comedies, or the City Dionysia, which staged tragedies, satyr plays, and comedies and to which foreigners were also invited (Pickard-Cambridge 1962, 1968). The City Dionysia added comic plays to its program in 486, and a festival of comedies was officially established at the Lenaia about 440. Both festivals honored the god Dionysos; the

Frogs attests that Dionysos is here being venerated as vegetative god of the vine, ecstatic god of wine, sexual god of male fertility, transcendent god of mysteries, inspirational god of the dithyramb, and transformative god of the theater.[5] For Old Comedy, the overt sexual and fertility aspects are primary: the City Dionysia opens with a procession of phallos veneration, a rite characteristic of village *kômoi* (rural fertility bashes celebrating Dionysos as god of wine, male sexuality, and fertility); the Lenaia, as a festival of comedy, may have developed directly from such a village *kômos* as Athens grew to incorporate rural areas within its expanding city limits (Pickard-Cambridge 1962: 144–46).

Being part of an Athenian public and therefore male-oriented sphere, Attic Old Comedy presents a male-focused panorama: the plays were written by male playwrights, performed by male actors—including the roles of female characters—before a largely male audience, and judged by male officials. The actors wore padded, burlesque costumes, the male characters outfitted with large phalloi which provide comic props in many scenes (Pickard-Cambridge 1962: 169 ff.; Stone 1981). Mnesilochos's attempt to hide his phallos at *Thesm.* 643–48 surely provided opportunity for much comic play, and the Athenian Magistrate's reference to the Spartan Herald's huge erection as a spear hidden beneath his cloak (*Lys.* 985) could easily have inspired Mae West's comparable "Is that a gun in your pocket or are you glad to see me?"

Female characters are likewise depicted in padded costumes, with breasts and perhaps larger buttocks appended. As we will see, these costumes, too, inspired stage business, but of a special kind. For example, in the opening scenes of *Lysistrata,* the heroine first fondles the Spartan woman Lampito; then they, together with another Athenian female character Kalonike, fondle the Boiotian and Korinthian women (*Lys.* 83–92). What is unusual in this scene among extant plays of Aristophanes is that Lampito is the only speaking character with a major role to be manipulated this way on the stage. Indeed, she responds to Lysistrata's manipulations by rhetorically likening herself to a sacrificial calf (see Golden 1988: 11 n. 40), a remark that passes without further response. The Boiotian and Korinthian delegates remain mute; the dehumanizing nature of such scenes will be further considered below.

The typical humor of Old Comedy is lampoon and satire, whose subjects include issues of war and peace (*Acharnians, Knights, Peace, Lysistrata*); Athenian litigiousness and social institutions (*Wasps, Birds, Ekklesiazousai*); Sokrates and sophistry (*Clouds*); contemporary drama, the tragedian Euripides, and even the god of the theater, Dionysos (*Thesmophoriazousai, Frogs*). The figures satirized may be both type characters (such as the dithyrambic poet and sycophant at the end of *Birds;* old men in *Wasps, Clouds, Lysistrata;* and old women, *Ekklesiazousai*) or well-known figures, most notably the demagogue Kleon. Attacks on mothers-in-law and the political satires of Bob Hope or Mark Russell carry on this vein of satiric humor little changed from that of Aristophanes' day.

While much of the satiric content of Old Comedy may be seen to derive from the earlier tradition of iambic poetry, the obscenities and sexual play of the comedies are also publicly and ritually sanctioned expressions, integral to fertility festivals for both female and male deities (Henderson 1975: 13 ff.; Reckford 1987: 457 ff.). This aspect, so radically different from anything obtaining today, deserves strong emphasis and will be treated more fully below.

On the issue of women's presence in the audience, the ancient evidence admits no certainty. Many of the forty or more priestesses of city cults enjoyed front-row seating at dramatic festivals (Henderson 1987b: 114–15). Some passages in Plato state that women did attend (*Gorgias* 502d; *Laws* 658d and 817c, although the last citation, "educated women," may refer to educated foreign women or hetairai).[6] Similarly, the Chorus's exhortation (*Lys.* 1049–50) that "every man and woman (or wife) attend," suggests women's presence (Levy 1976: 104; *contra* Henderson 1987a: *ad loc*). In contrast, passages in other plays suggest their absence. At *Peace* 50–53, the Servant addresses the audience, as consisting of males only of all ages. This in itself does not necessarily rule out women's presence. As part of a male-oriented event, comedy regularly regards its audience as all-male, as the third-century plays of Menander still testify (see *Dys.* 967 and *Sam.* 733–34). In addition, true to Athenian custom, Old Comedy also avoids public naming of "respectable" women (Schaps 1977; Sommerstein 1980).

If women were present, one might expect the female characters in *Lysistrata, Thesmophoriazousai,* and *Ekklesiazousai* to throw asides to their female counterparts in the audience, comparable to those by male characters; but arguing from such silence is always fraught with danger.[7] More suggestive are two other passages. At *Thesm.* 395–97, Woman A, after summarizing the abuse Euripides heaps upon women on the stage, notes that the men come home from the theater in foul and suspicious moods, implying that they return home by themselves, not with their wives. Similarly, the joke at *Birds* 793 ff. assumes that wives are at home during dramatic performances. The ambivalent nature of the evidence makes Henderson's suggestion (personal communication) compelling, that rather than being legally debarred, the respectable wives of Athenian citizens chose not to attend.

But even if the men's wives absented themselves, hetairai may well have attended the plays. They were by definition outside the bounds of male-imposed *sôphrosynê,* "prudence"; the presence of hetairai may have been *de rigueur* at such men's gatherings as symposia or comedies, where respectable wives would incur shame by their appearance (Sutton 1981: 32). However small or great the extent of women's presence, it seems not to have altered the predominant male focus of the comedies intended for a male audience in a male-privileged realm of activity (Keuls 1985: 332; Zeitlin 1985a: 65).

Female Characters in the Plays

Female characters appear in various roles in the plays. They are featured as protagonists in only three extant plays: *Lysistrata, Thesmophoriazousai,* and *Ekklesiazousai.*[8] But though they may furnish the main characters, women are only incidentally the subjects of these plays, which deal rather with war and peace, Euripidean drama, and Athenian democratic institutions, respectively. The leading female characters exhibit the same qualities of resourcefulness, guile, and cleverness that characterize their male heroic counterparts (Whitman 1964; Rosellini 1979; Henderson 1987a; Reckford 1987) but are distinguished from comic male heroes by drawing inspiration for their schemes from the female sphere, by not engaging in generational strife with younger women, and by working in solidarity with other women for the good of the community (Foley 1982; Henderson 1987b). Female characters also appear as stock characters with minor speaking parts: the Baking Girl, *Wasps* 1388; the Maid, Innkeeper, and her female partner, *Frogs* 503–78; and Iris as messenger of the gods, *Birds* 1200 ff.

By far the most common type of female character appearing in the plays is mute. She may be cast as an abstraction: Treaties, *Knights* 1389; Peace, Showtime (Sommerstein 1985—Gk. *Theôria*), and Abundance, *Peace* 551, 849, 974; Reconciliation, *Lys.* 1114; as a hetaira (*Ach.* 1198), flute girl (*Wasps* 1341 and perhaps *Frogs*), or dancing girl (*Thesm.* 1172); or as a specific character: Procne, wife of Hoopoe, king of the birds (*Birds* 674), and the Boiotian and Korinthian women (*Lys.* 87–92). Except for the abstraction Peace (*Peace* 551, 974) and the mute Queen of Heaven (*Birds* 1720), these figures are all subject to exposure, actual or attempted molestation, and verbal objectification. The idealizations of Peace and the Queen of Heaven, whose marriage to Peisthetairos at the end of the *Birds* ushers in the utopian era, are expressions of purity rare in Old Comedy, and not even fully sustained in the case of Peace (see below). It is this group of mute characters that forms the subject of the following discussion.

Fragments from other Old Comedy attest to the appearance of hetairai as characters in some plays (M. Henry 1985: 13–31; Kculs 1985: 191). While several Old Comedies have a hetaira's name as a title, there is no concrete evidence they had speaking roles. Madeleine Henry (1985: 30) believes they were primarily an important part of the *opsis,* the visual presentation, of the comedy.[9] For Aristophanes' plays, Henry notes the ambivalence of references to hetairai. On the one hand, they are delightful and desirable, like the joys of peace; thus, Trygaios's request to Peace to reveal herself "fully and generously to us thy lovers" (*Peace* 987–89, trans. Sommerstein 1985). More frequently they are symbols of depravity, portrayed as vicious, greedy, drunken, and debased, associated with filth and corruption.

This accusation of lust, drunkenness, and greed is not limited to hetairai but forms a major accusation against younger wives and old women (M. Henry 1985: 28; Henderson 1987b: 117–20).[10] The spillover in attitude from hetairai to wives is significant. The plays *Peace* and *Birds* ambiguously portray the mute, abstract characters both as hetairai, available objects for men's lust, and as brides, symbols of legitimate marriage (see M. Henry 1985: 21–23). This conflation in imagery and verbal abuse betrays a fundamental notion that women, despite social and legal distinctions between wives and hetairai, share a basic capacity *qua* women to be controlled, used sexually, and possibly abused by men at will.

In general, remarks about women in Aristophanes' plays focus on them as objects for men's lust. Peace is notably a time for men's unfettered enjoyment of women's sexuality: Dikaiopolis implies that rape is a joy of peacetime (*Ach.* 271–76); as ruler the Sausage-Seller can turn the city into a brothel (*Knights* 167); and peacetime allows dreams of hetairai just as Peace herself is likened to a hetaira (*Peace* 440, 987). From words to action: Demos wants to "solemnize" the Treaties by fucking them ("thrice shoving in the old pole," trans. Henderson 1975: 67, *Knights* 1389); the old man Philokleon attempts to force the flute girl either to stroke his phallos or more likely to perform fellatio on it (*Wasps* 1341); Showtime (*Peace* 871) and Reconciliation (*Lys.* 1114) are exposed, their bodies discussed and manipulated on stage; Dikaiopolis fondles the little "piggies" and later two hetairai (*Ach.* 765, 1199); Peisthetairos and Euelpides paw Procne (*Birds* 674); Peisthetairos threatens to rape Iris (*Birds* 1255); and the Archer molests the dancing girl (*Thesm.* 1172).

Throughout most of these scenes, Henderson (1975: 148) notes that "the female body . . . was much exposed, both physically and verbally. . . . These physical acts of inspection and palpitation are usually accompanied by obscene verbal commentaries that make use of highly colored terminology intended to spice the humor of *exposure and/or degradation*" (my italics). Vulgar rather than proper terms for female anatomy are favored, and tend to signify "male sexual pleasure, rather than, say, to express any kind of female biological function apart from sexuality" (Henderson 1975: 148; cf. 64–66 on *Peace*, festive heterosexuality, and the gang rape of Theoria).

Henderson (1975: 151) further notes that "the vulgar *vox propria* for sexual intercourse in comedy is *binein*, which seems to have had the same force and flexibility in Greek as *fuck* does in English. The connotation is always of violent and/or illicit intercourse." The active voice is used exclusively of the male, the passive of the female, and in the passive voice *binein* "always connotes force or violence" (152). If the overall intent of Old Comedy is openly to promote male fertility and sexuality, the process for achieving this goal seems to entail a debasing and violent portrayal of women's bodies and their roles in sexuality.

Assessment of the effect of these scenes is critically affected by the question of whether these mute, female characters were played by costumed male actors or by nude hetairai. As so often in classical scholarship, the fragmentary nature of the ancient evidence prevents definitive conclusions. Whitman (1964), Vaio (1973), Henderson (1975 and more briefly 1980), and Stone (1981) all include summaries of the debate. Stone (1981: 149) further notes that "in general, the older scholars tend to favor the use of *hetaerae*, while more modern critics either suggest that men were padded to look like women, or else that the evidence is insufficient for a firm conclusion." This changing tendency in interpretation may itself reflect changing sensibilities on the part of scholars (a subject meriting its own further investigation), which further complicates our ability to reach a firm conclusion.

The issue was engaged by the contention of Wilamowitz (1958: 186–87) that the abstract figure of *Diallagê*, Reconciliation (*Lys.* 1114 ff.), was enacted by a nude hetaira. This view finds its most recent proponents in McLeish (1980: 153) and Walton (1987: 194). Opposition to Wilamowitz's view began at once with Holzinger (1928: 37 ff.) who held that the cold weather and the exigencies of theatrical production, which requires that all spectators be able to see the events onstage, precluded these parts being played by live, nude women. To these objections, supported most recently by Reckford (1987), Vaio (1973: 379 n. 48) adds that "the tendency of Old Comedy [is] not to reflect reality but grotesquely to distort it"; Stone (1981: 150), who remains undecided on the issue, further remarks that costumed actors would not violate the male-only rule of the Athenian stage; and Henderson (1987a: 195–96), first raising doubts that slaves would have an official role at dramatic festivals, consequently notes that employment records of prostitutes never mention dramatic activity.

These objections to the use of real, nude hetairai for these roles are varyingly cogent. Most easily dismissed is that of cold weather. Given the ill treatment to which hetairai, free or slave, were subjected in ancient Greece, in which conditions of convenience did not otherwise restrict male abuse of women, and adding the characteristic Greek disregard for physical comfort (Keuls 1985: 168), it is hardly likely that considerations of climatic comfort would have occurred to the ancient Greek producer. Secondly, it is not obvious that all stage business must be clearly seen by back-row viewers. Are we to imagine a giant blob of excrement sliding down Dionysos's legs at *Frogs* 480 ff., so it might be seen from the farthest reaches of the audiences? Rather, theatrical convention relies on verbal description for actions not so easily visible.

Nor can we so precisely determine ancient comic or festival customs as to assert either that theatrical rules of male-only participation would categorically exclude the presence of nude hetairai (Stone) or that slaves would have no formal role at official functions (Henderson). Some sixth-century Korinthian vases depict nude women among padded male dancers (Pickard-Cambridge 1962: 170). As for the latter point, Henderson implicitly attributes slave status to all hetairai, which is not the case. Hetairai are likely to have participated in the village *kômoi*, the fertility celebrations for Dionysos from which Old Comedy may have developed (see above), and from at least the fourth century, hetairai are believed to have been the main participants in the midwinter fertility festival for Demeter at Eleusis, the Haloa, which was subsidized and catered at public expense (Deubner 1956: 62). Thus, hetairai may have officially participated in Old Comedy. As for Henderson's second objection, that there is no record of hetairai being hired for entertainment at dramatic festivals, this is an *argumentum ex silentio* that cannot stand on its own.

Vaio's contention, based on the nature of Old Comedy, is not so easily dismissed. If the purpose of Old Comedy is to hold up for ridicule the topics it treats, we might prefer to opt for the padded male actor. But surely every subject and character of Old Comedy is not presented as being equal in kind or degree, and the role of these mute female characters differs significantly from that of most other characters. The characters that represent desirable abstractions, such as Treaties, Peace, or Reconciliation, would hardly be subject to the ridicule that a costumed male actor would naturally evoke. A real hetaira, nude or suggestively dressed, and who already embodies male sexual fantasies, would more aptly dramatize the pleasurable attainability of the personified goal. Thus, at *Ach.* 1198, Dikaiopolis's entry with two hetairai is dramatically similar to the entry of the desired abstractions symbolizing the joys of peace in *Knights, Peace* and *Lysistrata*.

Those characters representing hetairai may perhaps have been open to ridicule, since they are often portrayed as corrupt. Aristophanes, however, uses the depravity of hetairai to ridicule someone else, not the hetaira herself (M. Henry 1985: 29). The dancing girls and flute girls in *Wasps* and *Thesmophoriazousai* unmistakably hold Philokleon and the Archer up for mockery. As Dover (1972: 28) notes, "it is open to question whether dressed-up men would have been regarded as funny enough *per se* to contribute more to the theatrical effect than real dancing girls."

Since hetairai were so easily available, the possibility remains that they were engaged for such roles, among which I would also include Procne (*Birds* 674).

Of a different quality are the scenes with the girls as piggies (*Ach.* 730) and the fondling of Lampito and the Boiotian and Korinthian delegates (*Lys.* 83–92). Each of these forms a more integral part of the play's action and might well be played to better theatrical effect if enacted by costumed male actors.[11] This is certainly the case with Lampito, who has a substantial speaking role and must be played by a male actor. Dramatic consistency might tend to suggest, though by no means require (*contra* Henderson 1987a: 195), that the other two female delegates also be enacted by costumed men. Since the scene depicts only men's views of women's sexual play among themselves, the humor might have been strengthened if it were dramatically clear that all these characters were men playing women.[12]

It is worth exploring whether the fact that Reconciliation (*Lys.* 1114) is being manipulated by a speaking female character significantly changes the tone of this scene or the enactment of this abstraction. Victorious female protagonists such as Lysistrata display characteristics and behavior typical of leading male characters (Whitman 1964: chap. VI; Rosellini 1979; Loraux 1981b). Foley (1982: 9) and Henderson (1987a: xxxvii ff. and 1987b) concentrate rather on those female-affirming and sisterly characteristics that distinguish her from her male counterparts. But although she relies on women's skills—weaving, household management—as models for her plan, she achieves her goals through male-associated actions, and by the end her character speaks essentially "like a man" (Rosellini 1979). In contrast, the other female characters in her play function more like those of *Thesmophoriazousai* and *Ekklesiazousai,* who enjoy Pyrrhic victories over the male characters, and who disappear about two-thirds of the way through plays that unmistakably affirm male superiority by the end. If Lysistrata does not disappear altogether like these other leading female characters (but see Henderson 1987a *ad* 1184–88), we might, nevertheless, claim that her "feminine" side does.

Lysistrata's character displays a dramatic change after her reentry at 1112. Up to this point, distinctively female skills and talents, expressed in the company of women, are the source for her actions, even when speaking to men. Now, as the only speaking female among male characters, she is differentiated from the respectable Athenian woman she has apparently represented (Rosellini 1979) and may reflect the more independent and powerful roles assumed by city priestesses, notably the priestess of Athena Polias ("of the city"), who might well speak publicly in the city's interest (Loraux 1981a; Foley 1982: 8; Henderson 1987a: xxxviii–ix).[13] However, Lysistrata does not speak in the capacity of a priestess. In contrast to her earlier, confident reliance upon women's sphere, at 1124 ff. she begs indulgence for her gender and cites her schooling by her father and old men as her credentials, giving her the right to speak and to be heard. Where before she had embodied the powerful possibilities of women's roles, she now speaks for male values.

It is during this final, more masculine phase that she brings in and handles Reconciliation, much as Trygaios brings in and his servant *man*-handles Showtime in *Peace* (877 ff.). This latter action, not so incidentally, further indicates that males of even the lowest class positions have the right on the comic stage to abuse and humiliate desirable women, an action that in real life, if committed against a citizen woman, would be a grave legal offense (note the similar role of the servants in *The Story of O,* Silverman 1984). Thus, the superficial female trappings of Lysistrata at the end of the play do not significantly alter the dramatic and thematic functions of this scene, in which she plays a male role in a male way.

To summarize, costumed male actors may best have played out the broad humor of such scenes as the molestation of the piggies (*Ach.* 730), or of the Boiotian and Korinthian delegates (*Lys.* 83–92); and they may also have enacted the mock-tantalizing gestures of hetaira, dancing girl, and flute girl characters. Yet nothing precluded real hetairai or flute girls from portraying themselves in these latter roles, and it is equally imaginable that real women could increase the comic possibilities of these scenes. Consider the crazy antics provoked by the appearance of a flauntingly sexy, curvaceous woman in many films and in joke routines. Similarly, the appearance of the mute and desired female personifications of the Treaties (*Knights* 1389), Abundance and Showtime (*Peace* 705, 842), and Reconciliation (*Lys.* 1114) provoke gross sexual responses from the male characters.

At the same time, these abstractions present a truly desirable quality. Again drawing on modern cinema, we may compare the presence in Marx Brothers films, perhaps the closest modern analogue to Aristophanic Old Comedy, of the attractive young bride who generally remains free of the comic mockery of the film and innocently embodies the wishful dreams of the comic characters. Only the Queen of Heaven (*Birds* 1720) and Peace (*Peace* 551, 974) embody fully, or almost so, this innocence and purity. In contrast with contemporary acceptable practices (see Sutton, Chapter 1), ancient Greek male thought typically concentrated its desires in hetairai (thus, Sommerstein 1985 *ad Peace* 849; note the now infamous remark, "We have hetairai for our pleasure, concubines to serve us, and wives to bear us legitimate children," Ps.–Demosthenes *Against Neaera* 122). For the ancient Greek, nude or scantily clad hetairai would be a logical choice to embody the range of desires implicit in these abstract nouns.

Scholars invariably interpret these nude female characters as embodiments of the sexual exuberance and celebration that are central features of Old Comedy and of festivals of fertility, and the scenes in which they appear as contributing in one way or another to this comedic abandonment to sexual play (e.g., Whitman 1964; Spatz 1978: 39; Stone 1981: 150; Reckford 1987; and see further below). But a valid interpretation of these characters and their roles must also address women's position within the culture, to which we now turn.

Cultural Background

In ancient Greek religion, rites for both female and male deities of fertility, notably those for Demeter and Dionysos, whether in a dramatic, mythic, or ritual context, include *aiskhrologia,* ritual mockery or hurling of obscenities and insults, and open sexual play, in both word and action (Deubner 1956; Parke 1977; Simon 1983; on the "obscenities," see Henderson 1975 and Sutton, Chapter 1 above). Myth has it that the revered, matronly Demeter was finally brought to laughter by the frankly sexual antics of the woman Baubo (N. Richardson 1974: 82), which may have been enacted during certain women-only rituals for Demeter, and the initiates into the

Mysteries had to endure the insults hurled along the route of the sacred procession to Eleusis (on women's festivals, see now Winkler 1990: 188–209). Abusive language provides psychological release from social tensions, and sexual language and play accentuate the positive and pleasurable aspects of sexuality for the life of the individual and the community; the ritual context both sanctions these behaviors and provides a safe, nonthreatening environment for their expression (Kraemer 1979; Zeitlin 1982).

Susan and Robert Sutton, in the course of anthropological fieldwork, witnessed a modern parallel in the village of Langadha on Amorgos (Cyclades), on Easter Sunday, 1975. The brief event they describe is rife with sexual and scatological joking, much like that of Aristophanic comedy.[14] The annual, informal custom at Eastertime, "to while away the time" between the afternoon church service and the evening's secular dancing and feasting at the main *plateia,* is for the young men to play physical games such as tag and human pyramids in the small *plateia* next to the church. Organizing a comic vegetable market, two older men then arrange these younger men in a circle sitting cross-legged, while they, in the center, pretend to be a grocer and his customer come to buy various foods, all suggesting double entendres. (The young son of one even pretends to be a dog, crawling around, barking, biting his master's leg.) When the "customer" asked for zucchini or cucumbers, the "grocer" would pretend to grab the genitals of one of the younger men, or he would pretend to take feces from an upturned bottom when asked for honey. Concluding about ten minutes of this banter among the men, the "customer" asks for lemons, at which point the "grocer" lunges among the young women who have been watching and who now flee among shrieks of laughter. Robert Sutton notes that even in the context of the funny, good-natured humor of the event, the women exhibited a proper "giddy nervousness that attested to their true sense of shame." While shame does not seem to accompany the sexual mockery in ancient fertility festivals, as we shall see, assumption of women's sense of shame about their sexuality does figure in the comedic portrayals.

The comic theater of fifth-century Athens is another forum for such a celebration of sexuality, fertility, and life, here in honor of Dionysos; hence the classical scholarly emphasis on the celebratory dimension of open portrayals of nudity, obscenity, and sexual play on the comic stage. (The ecstatic and drunken celebrations of Mardi Gras or New Year's Eve, which are sometimes proffered as similar in their function for release in modern society, are, in contrast to the ancient festivals, both starkly secular and relatively muted in their exultation in human sexuality, both female and male.) Against the backdrop of ancient ritual practice, comedy's open displays of sexuality and of sexual or obscene language clearly function as life-affirming expressions.

Socially, male domination in marriage, in family lineage, in the economy, in the laws, and in political life is extensively documented for ancient Athens (Pomeroy 1975; Schaps 1979; Foley 1981; Cantarella 1987; Keuls 1985; Patterson 1986). Whether free citizen women or enslaved prostitutes, women led lives for the most part determined and circumscribed by men. At the same time, Athenian women raised the children, managed their households, contributed to the economy, and held respected roles, important for themselves and the community, in religious rituals and in deme life (Henderson 1987b: 114–17). Scenes throughout *Lysistrata* illustrate this spectrum of women's importance to the community. Friedl (1962, 1967) observes a comparable tension in regions of modern Greece between women's severe constriction by men in some spheres and respected power and ability in others.

This gap in real women's lives between areas of power and realms of exclusion or oppression is mirrored by ambivalence in images of women; even the earliest Greek literature exhibits this strain. Homer's epics of the late eighth century and the archaic poets Sappho and Alkman illustrate respect for women's roles. But Homer's own view is ambivalent: he opposes Briseis and Andromache, Klytaimestra and Penelope, and the views he presents of Helen vary widely (Foley 1978; Austin 1975; Arthur 1981; Bergren 1983). Roughly contemporary with Homer, Hesiod bitterly expresses suspicion and censure of women in both the *Works and Days* and *The-ogony*, while apparently praising them in his *Catalogue of Women* (Arthur 1984, 1983; Loraux 1978). This double strain continues: hostile misogyny is echoed by the sixth-century poet Semonides, by characters in fifth-century drama, and most emphatically by the fourth-century philosopher Aristotle, who provided the "scientific" and "philosophic" bases for continued misogyny in the Western tradition (see Okin 1979). Yet many dramas and early philosophy unmistakably portray women's power and value to the community, as well as their objections to constrictions imposed upon their lives.[15] And the figure of Helen continues to illustrate this ambiguity: note Euripides' contrasting depictions of the character Helen in *Andromache, Helen,* and *Trojan Women,* and Gorgias's two-edged praise in his *Encomium to Helen,* where he likens her power to that of a drug.

Art furnishes a similar picture. During the same period that the graceful statues of Korai are dedicated on the Acropolis, battles with Amazons, one of three conventional battle scenes appearing in both monumental sculpture and vase paintings of the Archaic and Classical periods, visually demonstrate Greek male violent conquest of women (duBois 1982). The mid-sixth to early fifth centuries witness a minor explosion of sexually explicit Attic vase paintings (see Dover 1978; Keuls 1985), of which a significant number portray violence against women (McNally 1978; Sutton 1981; Keuls 1985; see further Chapters 1 and 3 above).[16] These yield in the fifth century to images of women at various domestic and ritual tasks, both clothed and nude, and illustrations of marriage.

Because the sexually explicit vase paintings provide the only other visual analogue to the scenes in Old Comedy, a brief survey of this material is needed. These scenes appear primarily on the cups and bowls intended for the men's symposia, drinking parties which hetairai, but not "respectable" women, attended (Sutton 1981: 75; Keuls 1985: 165). Keuls (1985: 176, 182), moreover, believes that sexual violence was an integral part of the symposium, which served in part to develop male supremacist behavior in young men.

Few of these scenes demonstrate mutual affection (Sutton 1981: 108; Keuls 1985: 188 ff.), and the majority seem concerned only with male pleasure, the woman appearing degraded or at best uncomfortable (Sutton 1981: 85–86; Keuls 1985: 174 ff.). The rear-entry position is preferred for coitus, emphasizing male sexual dominance in emotionally impersonal situations.

Most disturbing are the scenes of sexual violence, which are both of a mythological nature (satyrs and maenads) and "realistic," showing apparently real men and women. The narratives of the two types of violent scenes differ markedly. In the scenes of satyrs against maenads, either the women pointedly defend themselves, or their potential for self-defense hovers in those scenes where they are attacked while asleep (McNally 1978; Keuls 1985: 366–67). But no such potential inheres in the female figures in the second type of violent scene. This type depicts group sex in which men beat or threaten women, to force them to submit to degrading acts of simultaneous oral and anal penetration and to perform fellatio, in general considered more demeaning than coitus (Sutton 1981: 88–96; Keuls 1985: 174–86; *contra* Henderson 1975: 51–52). The overwhelming impression presented by this collection of vase paintings is of male objectification, degradation, and abuse of women through sexuality.

The mythological stories that emerge from both literature and art teem with hostility between men and women. Women responsible for manslaughter are punished: Klytaimestra, Medea, Deianeira, the Lemnian women. But men or gods who abuse or kill women are heroized: Zeus, Apollo, Theseus, Herakles, Orestes, Perseus (see Keuls 1985: 47–62). Keuls notes that one of the most characteristic features of the Attic mythology which emerges at the beginning of the fifth century is the act of rape: "In no other mythology of which I am aware does rape play a more prominent part. . . . One can only marvel at the candor with which Greek myth fashioned and depicted these tales dramatizing the power of the male over the female" (51). Remembering the comedic readiness to engage in rape, we may observe artistic, literary, dramatic, and mythological expressions spanning more than a century that reflect views intensely hostile to women.

The sexually explicit vase paintings fade out about the time that Old Comedy is being officially established at dramatic festivals. As Sutton notes in Chapter 1 above, the increase in suppression of women and of open expression of sexuality during the fifth century may account for the shift in sexually explicit scenes from the medium of privatized vase painting to the more public forum of comedy. Despite the physical and temporal differences in setting, both drama and vase paintings, intended primarily for men's viewing, convey to men the same image of women's bodies and their sexuality, and the same message of men's right to control women through their sexuality and by violence. Like all cultural conventions, they both reinforce and perpetuate societal notions of appropriate male and female sexual behavior.

Furthermore, the public exposure and manipulation of the personified abstractions, shown above to comprise qualities of both hetaira and legitimate bride, reveal the function of sexuality in these scenes. Whereas Greek male social custom would not perceive this behavior toward hetairai as shameful, any public exposure of "respectable" women, whether visual or verbal, leads to shame, *aidôs* (like Phaidra's in Euripides' *Hippolytos*), and would destroy her *sôphrosynê* ("prudence"), the ideal virtue promulgated for proper Athenian women (North 1966). Aeschylus, as a character in Aristophanes' *Frogs* (1050 ff.), says Euripides' dramatizations of women's shameful acts caused the suicides of real women (see Henderson 1975: 3 ff.). Thus, exposure deliberately plays on shameful undertones and serves as an instrument of male control of women through sexuality, a realm designated as women's greatest vulnerability, whether free citizen woman or enslaved prostitute.

Like misogynistic literature, or myths of a primordial, topsy-turvy matriarchy, these scenes of open humiliation of women reinforce the highly skewed sexual rules of patriarchal society. We might add that, according to most psychoanalytic interpreters, such scenes probably also mask a deeply rooted male fear of sexual inadequacy (Horney 1932; Slater 1968; Keuls 1985; Gubar 1987: 737).

Conclusion

The cultural context attests to a climate that allowed or promoted male sexual abuse of women. More particularly, men's ceremonial celebration of male fertility and sexuality in Old Comedy entails a simultaneous objectification of women through deliberate degradation of women's bodies and of female sexuality. This degradation differs in kind from the conventional business of comedy that objectifies, mocks, and degrades men's bodies and sexual activity as well. Male characters mocked onstage are not mute, their exposure enacted for the comic play. The male domination of every level of the production automatically circumscribes any female role, both objectifying it and subjecting it to this male control. Additionally, the occasion of production of these scenes in a male-focused event accentuates the distancing and objectification of the female characters, thus immediately putting their mute, exposed portrayal in a different light from the comic mockery of male figures.

Nor is the ideological function of these scenes altered if the roles were in fact taken by male actors dressed as women. In some scenes costumed male actors would have heightened the comic effect; in others, the dramatic effect, as well as the social and psychological impact, seems better served if nude hetairai played these roles. While some critics claim that all this was simply funny (e.g., Sutton 1981: 95), or the violence mild (Shapiro, Chapter 3 above), to women, whether present in the immediate audience or removed to the background of the cultural context, such enactments of public degradation would have vividly confirmed male assertions of social supremacy and control.

The significance of these scenes, therefore, extends far beyond their immediate dramatic function. By depicting men, regardless of class, as always in control and women, again regardless of class, as always vulnerable to molestation, these scenes graphically legitimate the social and political inequality of Athenian patriarchal society. The intensity of this public humiliation is well reflected by the remarks of Walton (1987: 194), who finds it so distasteful that, even in the context of the humiliation male figures endure in many plays (consider especially Dionysos and Xanthias in the *Frogs*), he cannot believe these roles could have been played by men.

Modern Interpretations of Pornography

While the debates about the meaning and functions of pornography continue to rage, I would like here to expand on one aspect of a feminist, sociological analysis:

the idea that pornography depicts the unequal power dynamics of the society through sexual representation, and that by visually representing violence against women, it in turn contributes to a climate in which acts of sexual hostility directed against women are not only tolerated but ideologically encouraged (Brownmiller 1980: 32–33).[17] Since these characters and scenes in Old Comedy were meant to be viewed, I will base my analysis on recent feminist film criticism. Combining the work of feminist Lacanian analysis and semiotic theory, this literature regards representation as a mediation embedded through its art form in the dominant ideology (E. Kaplan 1983: 310; Kappeler 1986). This perspective addresses the issue of *viewing:* object viewed/producer of scene/subject viewing.

In this analysis, the sexual scenes in pornography reflect the dynamics of the society at large by portraying an active subject, male, who acts upon an object, female (Beauvoir 1953). The subject, as active agent, creates the entire scene in which the object, having no voice, plays only her assigned role (Kappeler 1986: 50). Stressing the distinction between active subject and passive object are not only gender but clothing (the men usually dressed, the women nude) and verbalization (the men speak, the women are mute, frequently actively silenced by gags or penises).

Furthermore, the very acts of gazing and of speaking are solely in the power of the controlling males, be they the producers, actors, characters, or spectators (E. Kaplan 1983). Again reflecting unequal social dynamics, the gaze and speech of the subject carry authority, both the power of action and the right to possession (E. Kaplan 1983: 311). The subject enforces acts of nonlooking and nonspeaking upon the object, which then signify submission in the subject's view. Contrasting images that demonstrate the destructiveness of the female gaze, such as Medusa, substantiate the need to enforce the gaze as a primarily male preserve (L. Williams 1984: 88). In contrast, mutual gaze, such as between lovers or between mother and child, would signify interactive subjects expressing mutual affection (E. Kaplan 1983: 324; Kappeler 1986: 81).[18] Instead, the one-way gaze in the subject-object scenario refuses human status to the object, avoids exchange and communication, which are possible only as reciprocal actions between subjects, and expresses the selfishness of auto-gratification (Kappeler 1986: 49–62). Consider the differing social conditions that must exist among the Dineh (Navajo), where it is the elder women who have the authority to look directly at another person (Morez 1977: 127; and from personal communication from elder women).

Since, in our culture, he who looks maintains social and political domination by his very presumed authority to gaze as subject at another who is cast in the role of object, feminist film theorists regard the cinema, like ancient drama, as essentially a male discourse, since its agents of production and primary audience are men (E. Kaplan 1983: 312; Kappeler 1986: 57). This subject-object cathexis in visual representations reflects a dominating/forcibly submissive social dynamics visible throughout the society in sexual, racial, class, and age inequalities. Some narratives within the cinema may appear to reflect differing social dynamics, as in *Witness,* where Kelly McGillis, the "good woman," with her breasts bare, gazes at Harrison Ford boldly as an assertion of her independent status, as well as hinting at sexual invitation. He atypically averts his gaze as a sign of modesty and respect. Most narratives, however, reproduce the actively male-dominant attitudes and behavior of patriarchal society.

Along with other forms of violent representation, pornography aims primarily at enforcing male social dominance. The particular form by which pornography achieves this aim is the representation of unequal societal power dynamics through the narrative of sexual activity. "The female body *is* sexuality," as Doane says (1984: 68), and Kappeler (1986: 52) regards the position of woman as object of the gaze as a structural feature of pornographic representation. Objectification, humiliation, and abuse of women are the lessons of pornography, which ever tries to render women and the female as passive, mute, nude, obedient, and available for sex at the whim of the male. *Clarissa* as high art differs not at all in its intent from the frankly pornographic *Story of O*.

Old Comedy Pornography?

Considering the scenes described above in this light, we find that in each scene the women are deprived of their rights as human beings: deprived of the clothing essential to maintain woman's *sôphrosynê* and to prevent her shame, they are denied basic human dignity; deprived of speech, they are denied the distinctly human form of communication; and by being abstracted or animalized, they are denied any claim to human status and their objectification is complete.

We may now be in a better position to determine whether the Aristophanic scenes herein described featuring mute female characters may be considered pornographic. Rather than joyfully celebrating the sexuality that brings forth life, as the sexual play in women's fertility rituals seems to have done, and as the vase paintings of mutually enjoyable sex seem to do, in these scenes there is no mutuality, no interaction between two active agents, and there is not even sexuality. In each scene the female is an object gazed at, lusted after, and manipulated by a subject. She is significant not as woman (human), but as body (text, symbol, abstraction). She is totally dehumanized. She is further set apart by her full or partial nudity when others are masked and costumed, by her muteness while others speak of her, by her passivity while others feel her body. Typical of pornographic representation, she is a sign in the iconography of patriarchal power dynamics.

As in contemporary society, these unequal power dynamics in sexual representation reflect extreme male domination in ancient Athenian life. This type scene in Aristophanic comedy may differ from modern pornography in many of the conditions of its production: in generic type it might be closer to live striptease than to the anonymous, even more distancing conditions of cinematic pornography; it also overlaps with the sanctioned, open, and liberating expressions of sexuality in ancient culture not paralleled by modern customs.

On the other hand, these scenes featuring mute, nude female characters match the conditions of contemporary pornography in their reflection of unequal social dynamics, in their control by and for essentially male view only, in their portrayal of objectification, degradation, and violence against women. They further parallel modern pornography in their production in a social environment that condoned and encouraged hostile attitudes and violent actions against women. Finally, the portrayal of these mute, nude female characters in Aristophanes' plays appears to be more like pornographic representation than like the expression of jubilant sexuality that many of us would wish they more truly were.

NOTES

My highest appreciation first to Amy Richlin for inviting me to contribute to this volume and for her constant encouragement. I am also grateful to the following readers for their supportive criticism on earlier drafts of this paper: Laura Stone Barnard, Jeffrey Henderson, and Robert Sutton.

1. The word refers most commonly to the educated and cultured "companions," both slave and free foreigner, whose services include intellectual companionship, entertainment, and sex. For general summations, see Pomeroy 1976; Sutton 1981: 34–35; Cantarella 1987; Keuls 1985, chaps. 6 and 7. (A note on orthography: in keeping with contemporary practice, I prefer transliterating Greek spellings. However, when citing others, I maintain their Latinate spellings in the quotation, which occasionally leads to inconsistencies.)

2. Although live theater might at first seem a more appropriate parallel for ancient comedy, scholarly literature on representations in film has treated the subject of pornography in a way not yet begun for live theater. I also wonder if both the formal distancing and social popularity of modern film may not better represent some of the roles ancient comedy played in its own society.

3. These descriptions are adaptations of (1) *Lys.* 1114 ff., (2) *Thesm.* 1172 ff., and (3) *Ach.* 765 ff.

4. For general characteristics, see Lederer 1980; Kuhn 1985; Kappeler 1986. On child pornography, Rush 1980.

5. In the *Frogs,* the fertile reveling Dionysos is celebrated by the first chorus of frogs (209 ff.). Next he is invoked by a chorus of mystic initiates (324 ff.). Finally, with Dionysos as its principal character addressing the notion of drama, both tragedy and comedy, the play unambiguously presents Dionysos in his guise as god of theater. See Reckford 1987: 403 ff.

6. My gratitude to Jeffrey Henderson for pointing this out.

7. M. Henry's contention (1985: 13, 24) that Mnesilochos actually sees the hetaira Kyrene in the audience (*Thesm.* 97–98) is inconclusive on its own. Mnesilochos might just as easily be stressing and ridiculing Agathon's effeminacy by addressing the tragic poet by this well-known hetaira's name.

8. Recent woman-focused yet highly divergent analyses of these plays are found in Rosellini 1979; Saïd 1979; Zeitlin 1981; and Foley 1982.

9. Henderson (personal communication) finds it hard to imagine that none spoke. He points out further that one comic actor, Pherekrates, is said to have specialized in hetaira roles.

10. In the article here cited, Henderson notes the general respect accorded to older women protagonists in these three plays.

11. For a more sinister analysis of the identification of the young girls with pigs, see Golden 1988.

12. We know almost nothing about Greek women's mutual sexuality. Sappho's references suggest a tenderness (fr. 126), passion (fr. 47, 48), and mutuality (fr. 94) missing from these comedic scenes (see Dover 1978: 171–84). Women's fertility rituals may also have occasioned joyous sexual play among women, as the all-male sources suggest (see further below). For this scene, we can state with certainty only that it portrays men's perceptions of women's sexual interaction, based no doubt on what the men envisage themselves doing in comparable situations.

13. D. Lewis (1955: 1 ff.) first suggests that Lysistrata is modeled on the contemporary priestess of Athena Polias, Lysimache. The names are similar in sound and meaning, "releaser of battle/armies," and Lysimache may well have held the conciliatory attitudes expressed by the play's heroine (Henderson 1987a: xxxv).

14. I am grateful to Susan Buck Sutton for sharing copies of her field notes and to her husband, Robert F. Sutton, Jr., for bringing the incident to my attention and providing interpretive observations.

15. The ambiguity of women's roles in fifth-century Athenian drama is well reflected in these works: Pomeroy 1975; Shaw 1975; Gould 1980; Foley 1981; and see Chapter 2 above. On philosophy, see Okin 1979.

16. Sutton, in Chapter 1 above, notes that these scenes appear on about a hundred vases out of the thousands produced in this period.

17. Sutton, Chapter 1, distinguishes between the persuasive and cathartic functions of pornography, and interprets these scenes in antiquity as cathartic. This interpretation is debatable.

18. Thus, Sutton (1981: 86–87) interprets the lovemaking scenes on ancient vases in which the couple holds a mutual gaze.

5

Love's Body Anatomized: The Ancient Erotic Handbooks and the Rhetoric of Sexuality

Holt N. Parker

Illustrated Guide to Sexual Positions
—title in *Publishers Clearing House Catalogue*

"Lady Chatterley vs. Fanny Hill" (British; 1979) Sexploitation tale of two madams trying to win a wager.
—listing in *TV Guide*

One of the things that the study of sexuality in the art and literature of the ancient world can do is to force a reexamination of our own society's notions of sexuality, the categories that we accept as natural and given. Specifically for this collection, ancient ideas about sexual content in art and literature call into question our very notion of pornography.

Pornography, in the dominant ideology, is defined by content. Despite the work of much recent feminist criticism in pointing out the inadequacies of the prevailing definition, and instead focusing on the act of objectification itself, the theme of violence, and the power relations encoded in pornography, most current definitions of pornography rest on the notions of intent and content. As a recent instance, Soble (1986: 8–9) gives a working definition which he intends to reflect a representative view: "Pornography refers to any literature or film . . . that describes or depicts sexual organs, preludes to sexual activity, or sexual activity . . . in such a way as to produce sexual arousal in the user or the viewer; and . . . this effect in the viewer is either the effect intended by both producer and consumer or a very likely effect in the absence of direct intention."

Though this definition begs a number of important questions (notably what constitutes the "sexual"), it incorporates the two most commonly used criteria in determining pornography: the producer's intent to arouse (see Joyce 1946: vii–xii) and a specifically sexual content. Since intentionality is largely unknowable and unverifiable, any judgment of whether a particular work is pornographic tends to be based on whether it contains any member of a particular list of words, body parts, or physical acts, which varies from society to society.[1] Pornography so defined cuts across boundaries of media and genre to form a separate genre of its own. Paintings, sculptures, films, novels, poems, and songs all may be deemed pornographic by one segment of the community or another. A sexual content is held to be the defining characteristic of pornography. The essence of pornography thus is embodied in its objects.

This idea of pornography finds little correspondence with the way the ancient world conceptualized and subdivided its artistic universe. For both the Greeks and the Romans, genre is determined principally by form and only secondarily by content (Arist. *Poet.* 1447a13–47b29). In poetry, for example, genre is determined simply by the meter, and a certain content is appropriate to each meter (Hor. *Ars Poet.* 73–92). Homer's *Iliad* and Hesiod's didactic treatise on farming, the *Works and Days,* are both *epos,* epic poetry, by virtue of being written in hexameters. Content is secondary, appealed to when distinguishing subdivisions. So Aristotle laments the lack of a word to distinguish the (martial) epic of Homer from the (philosophical) epic of Empedocles (*Poet.* 1447b16–20; for types of drama, see 1448a16–18).

For the Greeks or the Romans, obscene content did not therefore in itself determine a specific genre. Explicit sexual matter and obscene language are permissible in a wide variety of genres: Old Comedy, satyr plays, mime, iambic verse, hendecasyllabic verse, satire (cf. Ovid *Trist.* 2.353 ff.; Quint. 10.1.9). Yet obscene language or sexual material is not a necessary or a defining characteristic of any of these genres. A hendecasyllabic may express wit, love, grief, complaint, anger, or sexual arousal (Pliny 4.14). Iambic covers a wide variety of topics, of which the sexual is only one of the possibilities. There is little in antiquity corresponding to the modern general idea of pornography, as shown by the very word itself, *pornographos,* which refers not to our general idea of pornography but to a specific subcategory of biography—tales of the lives of the courtesans—which may not contain any obscene material at all (Ath. 13.567b; but see Kappeler 1986: 155–58; Dworkin 1981: 199–202).

Yet there did arise one subspecies of literature for which the defining characteristic was uniquely its erotic content, thus more nearly approaching the common modern idea of pornography: works where the erotic content is both a necessary and a sufficient feature. These were the works not of *porno-graphoi,* "writers about prostitutes," but *an-aiskhunto-graphoi,* literally "writers of shameless things."[2] Note how the genre is defined by the content of the works. This class was itself curiously restricted in subject, being confined strictly to "sex manuals," handbooks whose primary stock in trade was a careful listing, enumerating, and limiting of the positions for heterosexual intercourse (still a flourishing type). There are a number of striking features about these works, which can give us a vivid insight into the way in which the Greek male culture of the late Classical and Hellenistic period and its continuation under Rome constructed its worldview and its corresponding "experience of sexuality," which Foucault (1985: 4) defines as "the correlation between fields of knowledge, types of normativity, and forms of subjectivity in a particular culture." I will here focus on this genre as a technology of social control.

Documents

Sexuality must not be thought of as a kind of natural given which power tries to hold in check, or as an obscure domain which knowledge tries gradually to uncover. It is the name that can be given to a historical construct.

—Foucault 1978a: 105

Space forbids a detailed discussion of all the sources that mention these handbooks; the relevant texts are listed in the appendix below and will be cited here by the letters *A* through *T*. *A,* a paradigmatic case, illustrating many of these features and running themes, is the creation of a founder for the genre: Astyanassa ("Ruler of the City"), who is not a traditional character of Greek mythology.[3] One of the concerns of Alexandrian and later Greek scholarship was to identify a *heuretês,* a discoverer or first exponent, for each genre. Indeed, the creation of Astyanassa as *heuretês* is itself an excellent demonstration that the sex manuals were thought to form a separate genre. The Byzantine encyclopedia, the *Suda* (compiled in the tenth century A.D.), identifies her as the inventor of the genre of sex manuals: "Astyanassa: the maid of Helen, the wife of Menelaus. She was the first to discover the ways of lying in bed (*katakliseis*) for intercourse, and wrote 'On the Postures (*skhêmatôn*) for Intercourse,' which Philaenis and Elephantine later imitated, who carried further similar licentious acts (*aselgêmata*)."

Although much here is typical of ancient biography (see Lefkowitz 1981b), already we can note several themes that will recur throughout the history of this genre. (1) The work is ascribed to a woman. These sex manuals were almost without exception circulated under the names of women. (2) The woman is a fiction, a male-created mask, which authorizes and privileges a male-created text. (3) The work is said to be the result of the (female) author's own personal experience in the erotic arts, and there is a corresponding conflation of the author with her book.[4] (4) The social status of the woman is frequently that of a slave or a prostitute, that is, of a class the audience would expect to have a wider sexual experience than citizen wives (Finley 1980: 94 ff.; Pomeroy 1975: 10, 26, 80–83, 192); or else, by having written on sex, she can be attacked as having acquired the necessary experience personally, and so further attacked as being a slave or a prostitute. Astyanassa is specifically a *therapaina,* a body servant, one who cares for (*therapeuô*) her mistress's personal appearance and health (see *F*). This brings up a further point. (5) There is a close connection between the sex manuals and other genres, principally medical writings,[5] and other encyclopedic, scientific, and culinary works. (6) The principal objection made by other authors to these handbooks is that they are licentious things (*aselgêmata*), that is, excessive, immoderate, self-indulgent. (7) The subject matter is restricted primarily to a tabulation of schemata for intercourse, though some of the works appear to have included sections on techniques of seduction and perhaps oral sex.[6] That is, of the wide possibilities for different modes of representation in pornographic writing, the Greeks recognized as a separate genre only the handbook format, and of the wide variety of possible subject matters, the genre chooses the narrowly heterosexual and phallocentric.

The case of Astyanassa also illustrates two further points about these hand-books. The first is the question of authorship. I have written that the work is *ascribed* to a woman. This is, of course, the case for the fictional Astyanassa, but did women write any of the other works bearing their names? Is there any chance of making visible a group of literate women, even if they were only the Dr. Ruths or Xaviera Hollanders of their age? We cannot know. We are not allowed to know. The fragmentary evidence is subject to the same double bind that has historically af-flicted women and their writing. The social constraints on women's voices, es-pecially on the expression of desire, are stringent. The double movement of social repression and heuristic uncertainty can be expressed in Joanna Russ's terms (1983: 20–24, 25–39): "She didn't write it" (denial of agency) and "She did, but she shouldn't have" (pollution of agency). No proper woman writes about sex; there-fore, the writing is not by a woman. And if she does write, she's not a proper woman. If there were any women in antiquity who wrote on sexual subjects, their identities have been taken away from them, their names made into pseudonyms, their gender made generic. A mask is the rule in pornography. Thus, the most famous author of these sex manuals is said to be a woman named Philaenis, but it is clear that her name is later used as a cover term for writers of sex manuals, for prostitutes, for whatever the user of her name considers to be sexually depraved (*A–N*). We cannot know if a real Philaenis wrote any of the works under her name or even if the citations refer to the same book. On the other hand ("She did, but she shouldn't have"), where works are attributed to women, we cannot be sure of the truth of the attribution, which may have been made as an attack, a distortion, or a misunderstanding.[7] On analysis we find a tendency to use this kind of attribution to attack learned or literary women in particular, or other persons by comparison to the author, or else to attack by attributing to the author or others the practices she supposedly recommended. Thus, the entry in the *Suda* for Pamphile of Epidauros, a remarkable woman scholar, philosopher, and historian of the age of Nero, lists among her works *On Sex* (*Peri Aphrodisiôn,* "On the Things of Aphrodite") and says, "Some ascribe all these to her father . . . but others ascribe them to her husband Sokratides." With her we see the double motion described by Russ, where-in her works are stripped from her and assigned to her father or husband, stemming from a general reluctance to credit women with intellectual abilities, and a sexual work is (possibly falsely) ascribed to her, again stemming from a general belief that even the best of women is sex-obsessed. Therefore, as with so many women authors of the past, we are kept from knowledge. We can have no certainty of whether she wrote such a work or of its nature. Is the title a misunderstanding of a work of some other type, perhaps ethnographic (parallel to her historical works), a species of *The Sexual Life of Savages,*[8] or biological, or dietetic (see below)? The title *Peri Aphro-disiôn* is, however, only used of sex manuals. Was it inserted into the list of her writings as a slanderous forgery,[9] or was it genuinely hers? If hers, what was its purpose, its methods and form?

Second, the case of Astyanassa illustrates the nature of evidence for this genre. We are speaking of a vanished literature, known only secondarily and from scraps. Yet if we wish to know anything about the lives of women or how the ancient cultures constructed their views of women, it is to such fragments that we must turn. For the sex manuals, besides the references in scattered authors, we have a passage from Ovid's *Art of Love,* which uses them as source material, and most remarkably a recently discovered papyrus fragment that gives us our first look directly at this genre and the works attributed to Philaenis.

The sources give us the names of nine writers of sex manuals, besides Astyanassa, the mythological founder of the genre. They are Philaenis (fl. ca. 370 B.C.), Botrys (ca. 340 B.C.?), Salpe (ca. 340 B.C.?), Elephantine (first century B.C.?), Paxamos (first century A.D.?), Pamphile (fl. ca. A.D. 65), Niko of Samos, Callistrate of Lesbos, Pythonicus of Athens. The last three are mere names (*G*).

The earliest attested and most famous is Philaenis. Hers is the most frequently cited name for an author of a sex manual, referred to in passing in thirteen texts for a variety of rhetorical purposes (*A–N*), including the passage from the *Suda* on Astyanassa quoted above. Until 1972, these few references, with no direct quotation, were all we had about Philaenis. Then Lobel (1972: 51–54) published fragments of a papyrus, dated to the early second century A.D., containing the beginning of a work ascribed to Philaenis. The text,[10] though damaged, can be translated as follows:

> Frg. 1 [col. i]: Philaenis of Samos, daughter of Okymenes, wrote these things for those who plan to lead their life with knowledge and not off-handedly . . . having worked at it myself . . . [col. ii] Concerning seductions: So then, the seducer must go unadorned and uncombed so that he does not [appear] to the woman to be on the job . . . Frg. 3: . . . with the thought . . . we . . . saying the [ ] woman is like a goddess . . . the ugly one is charming, the older one is like a young girl. Concerning kisses . . .

A word of warning: there is nothing to show that this text is directly related to any of the ones known to the various authors who mentioned Philaenis. A pseudonymous writing is by nature inauthentic, and the name Philaenis had proliferated and become simply the cover name for sex manuals.[11] There is therefore no easy identification of these scraps with any of the descriptions of works under the name Philaenis. The papyrus is, however, roughly contemporary with later texts that mention Philaenis (*I–N*). The papyrus is brief and tantalizing, not only because of its fragmentary nature but because it has the quality perhaps of a précis and so sounds like just the sort of *Philaenis's Notebook* that the critic in Pseudo-Lucian's *Erôtes* is accused of keeping handy (*M*).

However, in these few lines we can note a number of the running themes that have already been pointed out. The work is a full manual of sexual activity, not just a list of positions. It includes sections on seduction and kisses and is thus much closer to the full range of Ovid's *Ars Amatoria* than the testimonia might lead us to imagine (Cataudella 1974: 847–57). The connection to other genres is made explicit. It claims to be a didactic work, an objective and scientific guide "for those who plan to lead their life with knowledge and not off-handedly." It also claims to be the result of personal experience: "having worked at it myself."

Analysis

All knowledge which does not recognize, which does not take social oppression as its premise, denies it, and as a consequence objectively serves it. . . . Knowledge that would take as its point of departure the oppression of women would constitute an epistemological revolution.

—Delphy 1981: 73

Parody and Essence

I begin my analysis of this problematic genre with a text that stands in a problematic relation to it, Ovid's *Ars Amatoria,* since it is from Ovid's parodistic use of his sources that we can form our clearest picture of the form and content of the sex manuals. I cannot hope to provide an overall treatment of this polysemic work (for which see Myerowitz 1985), a summary of the major themes (Hollis 1973; 1977: xi–xix), or even a detailed treatment of what Ovid borrowed from his sources, including Philaenis (Cataudella 1973, 1974). Rather, I want to focus on the ambiguity of the relation itself.

The *Ars* is, among many other things, a brilliant and witty parody of the conventions of elegiac poetry, of didactic poetry, and of the sex manuals. Yet simply to call it a parody does not constitute an explication. The *Ars,* like other parodies, is subject to a peculiar and recursive relationship to the genre on which it depends for its existence: it is simultaneously a commentary on that genre, claiming to stand outside it and observe it, and an example of it (see Culler 1975: 152–153).

A parody is ambiguous; it may contain the message of its original while denying it. It does not demand seriousness; neither does it exclude it. In general, parody operates by creating a more literal reading of the original text which exposes the codes (linguistic, ideological, cultural) that underlie its exemplar, but at the same time it necessarily makes use of them. It thus undergoes the same paradox as the linguistic-philosophical distinction between mention and use. Any mention is a use. A parody is always an example of its genre.

Accordingly, we can divide our analysis of this passage of Ovid into the notions of Ovid with his predecessors and Ovid against his predecessors. At the end of Book 3, devoted to advice to women (added to his original two-volume work addressed exclusively to men), Ovid includes a section giving explicit advice to women on positions for intercourse (*Ars* 3.769–88):

> I am ashamed (*pudet*) to teach the rest, but kind Venus
>   says "What makes you ashamed (*pudet*) is my job especially." 770
> Let every woman know herself; take your standard method
>   based on your body: one position (*figura*) is not suitable to all women.
> The one who is remarkable for her face, let her lie on her back;
>   let them be viewed from behind, those whose backs are pleasing.
> Milanion used to carry Atalanta's legs on his shoulders: 775
>   if they are lovely, let them be seen in this way.

> Let the little one be carried on her horse; because she was so tall
>   the Theban bride [Andromache] never rode Hector like a horse.
> Let her press the covers with her knees and bend back her neck a little,
>   the woman who is worth looking at for her long flank.   780
> For the one whose thighs are youthful and whose breasts are flawless,
>   let the man stand and let her spread out crosswise on the bed.
> And don't think it sinful to let down your hair, like the Phylleian Mother
>   [the goddess Cybele],
>   with your locks spread out and your neck bent back.
> You also, whose belly Lucina [childbirth] has marked with wrinkles,   785
>   like the swift Parthian use horses turned backward [i.e., straddle the
>   man facing his feet; Parthian archers proverbially sat backward on their
>   horses to shoot while in retreat].
> Venus has a thousand joys; the easiest and the one of least effort
>   is when you lie down on your right side.

Ovid's text as a whole shares many features with the Philaenis fragment. Both are complete manuals of seduction, not just pillow books. There is the same didactic tone, the notion of imparting useful and scientific knowledge. There is the theme of *usus*, that the knowledge is not purely theoretical but practical, both in deriving from the author's own experience and in being applicable to the reader's own experience (*Ars* 1.25–30; Myerowitz 1985: 147–48). As for specifics of the positions, though we lack the portion of the Philaenis papyrus that dealt with the actual postures, the continuity between Aristophanes and Ovid, the two authors we possess who give details, is interesting for sharing certain specific types.[12] We may deduce that the writers of sex manuals, like other didactic authors, may have learned more from each other than from experience, and despite the claim of *usus*, may owe more to literature than to life.

Ovid mentions some eight positions, each geared to one particular physical type. It is this one-to-one correspondence between somatotype and sexual position that reveals an important feature of Ovid's humor and technique. Employing the process of literalization of trope central to parody, Ovid enjoys taking a literary convention and reducing it with relentless logic to its absurd conclusion, such as *Am.* 1.6.3–6 (the wasted lover is so thin, he can slip through a small crack in the door) or the exhaustive examination of *militia amoris* (love as soldiering) in 1.9 (see Lyne 1980: 243–52). So here Ovid takes the advice present in his sources on suiting different classifications of bodies to different classifications of sexual positions and makes manifest the underlying rhetorical notion of objectification of women's bodies, that a woman's body determines everything about her, that she is only her body. He then draws the logical conclusion: only one body, only one style of sex. The short woman will never do anything other than ride her lover, the postpartum woman never do anything but ride him backward. The joke is subtle, ironic, expressed with great sincerity, and is a perfect example of the way Ovid deconstructs the very constructions he writes.

Ovid is almost alone in classical literature for paying attention to the woman's pleasure during sex (*Ars* 2.679–84, 717–32; see *Am.* 1.10.35–36; also Ar. *Lys.*

163–66). Yet, despite the parodistic framework, his advice necessarily partakes of these same acts of objectification and dismemberment. He advises a woman to use each position not according to the degree of pleasure that each affords her but in order to keep a single physical feature in sight of the man, or else to hide a blemish from him. This objectification can be seen in the difference between the sexual advice given men which concludes *Ars* 2 (703–32) and that given women which concludes 3 (771–808). After all Ovid's advice on seduction, the man is explicitly said not to need advice on what to do with what he has caught; he will know by instinct. In this poem of *ars,* the Muse is to wait outside the door, and *natura* will take over. He is advised to control himself, to take his time and aim at a simultaneous orgasm, but he is given none of the detailed advice on mechanics that the woman needs. The man is still the master of the situation. The woman, on the other hand, is the *materia* of the *ars,* the raw natural substance on which art works (Myerowitz 1985). She is given instruction on how to look good, how to reduce her body to a single desirable part, how to objectify and anatomize herself. Soble's analysis of what he terms "the dismemberment syndrome," the reduction of women to an assemblage of parts, and its relation to the social construction of male sexuality "with the concepts of objectification, fixation (or partialism), manipulation (or conquest) and performance" (1986: 55–61; cf. N. Vickers 1982) reads like a commentary on the *Ars Amatoria.* This ana-tomy (cutting apart) of sexuality, then, is not an accidental by-product of subjecting sexuality to ana-lysis (taking apart). It is an essential feature of the ancient genre.

Shame-Writers: Ancient Attitudes

The sources, together with Ovid, provide a sketch, if not a portrait, of this important and fragmentary genre. In light of these texts, several statements by Foucault need to be modified (1985: 92–93, 114; cf. 38, 138):

> Putting it schematically, we could say that classical antiquity's moral reflection concerning the pleasures was not directed towards a codification of acts, nor towards a hermeneutics of the subject, but towards a stylization of attitudes, and an aesthetics of existence. . . . The textual record is clear in this regard: neither the doctors who made recommendations about the regimen one should follow, nor the moralists who demanded that husbands respect their wives, nor those who gave advice concerning the right conduct to manifest in the love of boys, ever say what ought or ought not to be done in the way of sexual acts or practices.

> The preoccupation with regimen was never focused on the *form* of the acts: nothing was said about the types of sexual relations, nothing about the "natural" position or about unseemly practices. . . . The *aphrodisia* were considered in the aggregate, as an activity whose significance was not determined by the various forms it could take.

These observations are certainly true as regards "moral reflection," but Foucault has been misled to some extent by the texts he chose to study: precisely the prescriptive works of doctors and the like (1985: 12). Prescriptive lists did exist, but in texts that stand opposed to the "dietetic" works that Foucault made his primary object of investigation.

These texts form a coherent genre, viewed by the ancients as unique, singled out for its content and its treatment in a way that resembles the current popular notion of pornography. But why did this genre of sex manuals draw so much more opprobrium than the genres of Old Comedy, iambic, satire, and so on, which appear to feature a more direct and explicit obscenity?[13] A simple answer would be that obscenity was "allowed" in these genres. This is true, but it merely restates the question. The answer can be seen in their rhetorical deployment, in the way these manuals were used by other writers. They are used primarily as a standard of excess, a measure against which individual behavior can be judged. Thus, the emphasis throughout is not so much on the specific sexual acts they recommend as on the genre itself as a symbol of immoderation and overindulgence in sexual pleasure. They are attacked not only by Christians (*J, K, N*) but by Greek philosophers of schools that preach moderation, for example the Peripatetic Clearchus (*E*) and the Stoic Chrysippus (*F*). The attack is based on two different grounds and finds expression in two different sets of words. The sex manuals are blamed as *anaiskhuntos,* "shameless" (*D, H, N*), that is, for their content. Rather than treating the pleasures of sex (*aphrodisia*) as an unspecified aggregate, as the dietetic texts do, the *aphrodisia* are broken down, listed, particularized, in explicit detail. The sex manuals are also blamed for *aselgeia* (*A, M*) or *akolasia* (*F*) "licentiousness," that is, for their treatment of the contents. The basic meanings of *aselgeia* and *akolasia* are a lack of self-control, excess and extravagance in physical pleasure or psychological passion, and they are both opposed to *sôphrosunê,* the virtue of moderation.[14] Foucault is right in that the moral concern with *aphrodisia* is not based on an act of listing which divides the licit from the illicit. The sex manuals are not blamed so much for being immoral—that is, offering forbidden pleasures—but for being fussy, self-indulgent, and overelaborate about those pleasures. Both classes of guides go beyond the simple life and the simple satisfaction of basic needs, whether for food or for sex.[15]

Thus, the constant coupling of these works with the cookbooks and gourmet guides of Archestratus of Gela, whom Athenaeus (6.310a) calls "the Hesiod or Theognis of gourmandizing," and others (*E, F, G, S*) is part of a general coupling of *aphrodisia* with the pleasures of food and drink. "This association between the ethics of sex and the ethics of food was a constant factor in ancient culture" (Foucault 1985: 50; see 50–57). It is precisely the fact that they do not counsel moderation in food and sex, as dietetic texts and good doctors do (Plato *Symp.* 187e), but simply list possibilities, that causes them to be seen not as handbooks to pleasure but as inducements to luxury.[16] The people who like Archestratus also like the sex guides: they overindulge in sex just as they overindulge in food, even to the extent of drinking unmixed wine, a wild and barbarian custom that can drive people mad (*E*).[17] The manuals are gourmet guides to sex (the subtitle to Comfort's 1986 book, *The Joy of Sex*).

The associations of this idea of luxury are also vital for understanding the position of the sex manuals. Sexuality in our society is constructed on the choice of object, heterosexual versus homosexual. Both Greek and Roman male sexuality was constructed on the division between active and passive.[18] The active one, the one who penetrated, who moved, who fucked, was "male," and was acting the role of a free man, whether he used as object a woman, a boy, or a man. The passive one, who was penetrated, who did not move, who was fucked, was "female," and servile, whether woman, boy, or man. The active role could also be shown not only in mastery over others but in self-mastery. Thus, paradoxically, the ability to withstand desire, to abstain from sexual pleasure, in classical society is conceived of as essentially masculine. The opposite is also true: the inability to withstand desire, indulgence in pleasure, is essentially feminine, and so equally women's sexuality is feared as unrestrained, uncontrolled, uncontrollable (see Arthur 1984). Thus, the whole genre, viewed as guides to luxury, is condemned as *mollis* (*Q*); that is, soft, weak, inherently "feminine" (see Richlin 1983: 39, and passim, esp. 258 n. 3). It is only suitable for men who act like women (*D, E, L*), for moral weaklings or impotent emperors (*D, L*). It is used by insatiable women (*F, I, R*). It is only "natural," therefore, that the inventor was a woman (*A*) and that the authorial voice throughout is feminine.

Whore-Writers: Modern Theories

The ancient sex manuals, therefore, by their explicit contents fit the prevalent notion of pornography. Whether we wish to label these ancient sex manuals as "pornography"—that is, whether they fall on a given side of a particular boundary line—is problematic at best and perhaps ultimately unhelpful. The inadequacy of such content-oriented definitions either to distinguish pornography from other representations (if they can be so distinguished) or to capture any essential facts about pornography has been pointed out frequently in recent criticism (e.g., Brown 1981: 6–7). Rather, what we can do to elucidate their nature and the structures of signification that inform them is to point out features that they share with pornography as described by modern feminist theories, that is, use our own sexual discourse to understand theirs. The two features I wish to examine are the fact of objectification and its connections with technologies of power.

One of the most striking features of the sex manuals is the objectification of women and the dismemberment of their bodies. MacKinnon (1983a: 541) speaks of objectification as "the primary process of subjection of women. It unites act with word, construction with expression, perception with enforcement, myth with reality." Pornography is singled out primarily because of the immediacy of the objectifications (Kappeler 1986: 49–62). So Brownmiller (1982: 32) writes of pornography as "a male invention, designed to dehumanize women, to reduce the female to an object of sexual access"; and the Dworkin-MacKinnon model amendment on pornography (Blakely 1985: 46) defines pornography in part as "the graphic sexually explicit subordination of women through pictures and/or words, that also includes one or more of the following: (i) women are presented dehumanized as sexual objects, things or commodities; . . . or (vi) women's body parts—including but not limited to vaginas, breasts, and buttocks—are exhibited, such that women are reduced to those parts; or (vii) women are presented as whores by nature."

Besides the act of objectification, feminist theories of pornography seek to deconstruct the power relationships that pornography encodes and which make the objectification possible. So Dworkin (1981: 24): "The major theme of pornography as a genre is male power, its magnitude, its use, its meaning." Thus, if we apply Steinem's definition of pornography (1980: 37)—"sex in which there is clear force," in which the audience "must identify with either conqueror or victim"—it is clear from the equation mentioned above of male-active-fucker-conqueror and female-passive-fucked-victim that the ideological formation of what was constituted as normal sexuality in Greek and Roman society was inherently pornographic (see Richlin 1983: 78–80).

Knowledge

Foucault's analysis of the rise of sexual discourse in the seventeenth and succeeding centuries provides a valuable framework for investigating the ancient sex manuals. For Foucault (1978a: 97), the essential question is: "In a specific type of discourse on sex, in a particular form of extortion of truth, appearing historically and in specific places . . . what were the most immediate, the most local power relations at work? How did they make possible these kinds of discourses, and conversely, how were these discourses used to support power relations?"

Sexual discourse is a particular class of speech, a specialized *langue,* that is a linguistic code.[19] It consists of a set of values which define ontological categories, corresponding to the semantic level, and a set of rules for employing those categories, that is a deontology, corresponding to syntax. These can be reformulated in Foucault's terms as knowledge and power: "It is in discourse that power and knowledge are joined together" (Foucault 1978a: 100), and sexual discourse in particular "appears as an especially dense transfer point for relations of power" (1978a: 103). The two are interdependent, but I wish to concentrate first on knowledge, the way in which the sex manuals establish women and women's sexuality as their domain, and then on power, the way in which the manuals form a medium for the social control of women. The two together constitute a rhetoric of sexuality.

"If sexuality was constituted as an area of investigation, this is only because relations of power had established it as a possible object; and conversely, if power was able to take it as a target, this was because techniques of knowledge and procedures of discourse were capable of investing it" (Foucault 1978a: 98). One of the reasons the sex manuals arise in the fourth and early third centuries B.C. is the deployment of techniques of knowledge that could create them. The most powerful of the techniques of knowledge was the rise of the detailed systems of taxonomy and classification of the natural world associated with Aristotelian philosophy. The sex manuals have their origins in several major tendencies of philosophy, literature, and society that characterize the period of the dissolution of the Classical Greek polis and the emergence of the Hellenistic era, and are themselves symptomatic of what we might call the Age of Aristotle.

Philosophically, the sex manuals show a continuance of the Aristotelian and Peripatetic tradition of analysis and classification, wherein the continua of the world are broken into discrete, nameable, and hence controllable quanta.[20] The Greeks had always had a liking for catalogues, for lists of gods, heroes, and heroines,[21] but it is in the philosophy of the time of Aristotle that the technique of categorization is fully deployed as a conscious tool of rigorous analysis. The phenomena of the natural world were analyzed and described as separate ontological entities. Hence the well-developed taxonomies according to genus and species of the biological works, in particular the *Historia Animalium*.[22]

This taxonomic principle was extended not only to the phenomena of nature (minerals, plants, animals) but also to the human and social sphere. So we hear of ethnographic works by Aristotle, such as the lost *Customs of the Barbarians* or the systematic collection of the constitutions of 158 Greek cities, of which only the *Athenian Constitution* survives (see *Pol.* 1279 a22 ff., 1290a1 ff.). More directly relevant are the studies that concern *ethos,* the attempt at a classification of human types and types of behavior, best known to us from Theophrastus's *Characters,* a series of sketches of thirty personalities each marked by a single "distinctive feature" (*kharaktêr*): the ironical, the flattering, the talkative, the tactless, and so on.

This classificatory and systematizing urge was also brought to bear on human speech, in the form of the science of rhetoric. So Kennedy writes (1963: 32): "The second sign of the birth of rhetoric was the new interest in dividing speeches into parts, each with a special function. This interest no doubt reflects the beginning of a fondness for definition and classification which became stronger among the Greeks." Indeed, rhetoric represents one of the earliest attempts at controlling a body of knowledge as a teachable system, that is, a *tekhnê* (Latin *ars*). The first uses of *tekhnê* in the sense of "an art or craft, i.e. a set of rules, system or method of making or doing" (*LSJ,* s.v. III) refer to rhetoric, that is, *the* art, so that *tekhnê* is employed simply as the title for numerous rhetorical handbooks, already a flourishing genre in the time of Plato (*Phaedrus* 245a, 271c; *Phaedo* 90b; Arist. *Rh.* 1354a11–12). Rhetoric was part of the Greek cultural universe from the time of Homer (*Il.* 9.443), but its systematic exposition begins first with the philosophical movement of the Sophists and especially Gorgias (Dodds 1959) and is continued by numerous authors, especially Isocrates and his school and Aristotle and the Peripatetics.[23] The scientific classification extended not only to the parts of a speech but also the figures of speech, the *skhêmata* (Latin *figurae*), a word ambiguous between the positioning of words in a sentence and the positioning of bodies in a bed.[24] The use of the same vocabulary points to the generic similarities between both types of handbooks. We may speak of a rhetoric of sexuality.[25]

Thus, the analysis and classification of human actions extended to sexuality itself. We hear of various analytical works from the Academy: Aristotle's own dialogue *Eroticus*[26] and various works by others entitled *On Love,*[27] as well as books called *Erôtikê Tekhnê (The Art of Love)*.[28] The same impulse that leads to the systematic taxonomies of the biological works creates a taxonomy of sex.

The genre associations of the sex handbooks are most revealing. Sexuality is simply one of the new areas into which the desire for encyclopedic learning that characterized the Sophists and later authors has extended: zoology, ethnology, rhetoric, and so on. The variety of works by Paxamos (*S*)—*Alphabetical Cookbook, Foods, Art of Dyeing, Georgics,* as well as the sexual manual *The Twelvefold Art*—is a case in point. Equally revealing are its associations with medical writings, which also take as their starting point the classification of natural phenomena—especially with medicine as part of a universal system of knowledge.[29] Indeed, like medical treatises and other encyclopedic writings, these sex manuals acquired illustrations precisely because they were part of the genre of handbooks on the natural world,[30] and it is perhaps through the medium of such illustrated texts that the genre of the sex books had its schematizing influence on Roman art.[31]

Thus, we are given love's body anatomized. Sexuality is on the same basis as animals, plants, and minerals, as an object of intellectual inquiry. The continua of sexual activities are broken down into separate actions, each given a name, a description, and so constituted as a separate ontological category. However, a necessary prerequisite of such classification is to establish sexuality as a natural phenomenon, while at the same time this treatment of sexuality as part of natural philosophy is part of the discourse that establishes a "sexual essentialism," defined by Rubin (1984: 275) as "the idea that sex is a natural force that exists prior to social life and shapes institutions. Sexual essentialism is embedded in the folk wisdoms of Western societies, which consider sex to be eternally unchanging, asocial, and ahistorical"—not only within folk wisdoms but within academic philosophy as well (see Padgug 1979: 5, Winkler 1990: 17).

Pornography represents an attempt to place human sexuality, viewed as a natural phenomenon, under intellectual control. To be precise, in the act of analyzing sexuality, pornography creates it. Pornography is part of the discourse that both posits and constructs the phenomenon of sexuality as mysterious, unfathomable, synthetic, indiscrete—that is, in its essence feminine—and desires to subject it to the mastery of the intellect, which it both posits and constructs as rational, comprehensible, analytic, discrete—that is, in its essence masculine. This is a recapitulation of the primary act of identification of the natural with the feminine and the masculine with the cultural (Ortner 1974, Mathieu 1973). Pornography is therefore not only culture's revenge on nature, the subtitle of Susan Griffin's *Pornography and Silence* (1981); it is also a literalization and realization of what is, according to Aristotle, the fundamental philosophical and ethical action: the subjection of matter (female) to spirit (male).[32]

The philosophical role of the sex manuals can be made clear from an economic exchange model of pornography (as used by Kappeler 1986: 5–10; J. M. Davies 1988: 136–38). Lévi-Strauss (1969: 65, 114–15, 481, 496) has identified the ways in which the exchange of women between men in patriarchal social groups establishes woman as sign. The producer of pornography, however, gives to the consumer not a real woman but a representation of one, a symbol of a woman. Most pornography insists that it is realistic; it claims to represent accurately an individual. Thus, the reader is given not just the picture of the Playmate of the Month but her name and a list of her "turn-ons and turn-offs." The objective scientific stance, however, can do something much more powerful. By claiming to describe not an individual but a class, the producer of what we might call "objective pornography" can give to the consumer not one woman but all women; can purport to delimit not what a woman is as an individual but what woman is as an essence. The consumer of pornography possesses one woman who is made to declare her desire. The consumer of the handbooks possesses all women, who are made to declare that they are desire. The producer of the handbook thus has a total control over determining and defining the meaning of the symbol of woman. That is, the handbooks offer an unrivaled power of objectification.[33]

Power

"Relations of power are not in a position of exteriority with respect to other types of relationships (economic processes, knowledge relationships, sexual relationships), but are immanent in the latter" (Foucault 1978a: 94). "Knowledge is power," said Francis Bacon more briefly. The power to name is the power to control. The act of Adam is not only over the natural world but over Eve as well. As the economic exchange model of pornography illustrates, the ability to define a symbol is also the ability to control its use.

Again, the genre associations of the handbooks are extremely revealing. They are part of the general type of didactic poetry and prose. The sexual manuals belong to the same genre as Aratus on astronomy and weather or Nicander on snakes and poisons (see Easterling and Knox 1985: 598–606), as well as the rhetorical and medical handbooks. As noted, the ancients made no distinction (except on the basis of medium) between didactic works and the natural philosophical works mentioned above: didactic poetry seeks to delight as well as instruct, and to instruct in that which delights (Lucr. 1.936–50; see Sen. *Ep.* 86.15).

However, didactic works also aim at the practical control (i.e., control over *praxis*) of the phenomena they describe. The reader is given knowledge about the nature of a given mass of material in order to acquire power over it. The act of classification of phenomena, even of the natural world, is preparatory to their control.[34] Likewise, the ethical works and political works, dealing with social constructs, are not merely descriptive but prescriptive. These works concern not only what people do but what they should do. Constitutions are collected and catalogued, as a necessary preliminary to judging which one is best (cf. Arist. *Pol.* 1288b10–89b26; *EN* 1181b6–9).

The relation between knowledge and power is most clear in the association between the sex manuals and the various medical and rhetorical works. Like the medical works, the manuals do not confine themselves to description. The medical handbooks cover treatment as well as diagnosis; they are descriptive in order to be prescriptive.[35] Likewise, rhetoric is not the abstract study of speech. Its purpose is to persuade, to gain control (Plato *Gorg.* 453a, 454e).

Thus, the sex manuals are guides to a *tekhnê,* a skill or teachable art (*ars*). Foucault draws a distinction between the "two great procedures for producing the truth of sex": the *ars erotica* and the *scientia sexualis*. In the *ars erotica*, "truth is drawn from pleasure itself, understood as a practice and accumulated as experience; pleasure is not considered in relation to an absolute law of the permitted and the forbidden, nor by reference to a criterion of utility, but first and foremost in relation to itself" (1978a: 57). The model of the *ars erotica* is that of initiation, master to pupil. The *scientia sexualis,* on the other hand, is geared to forms of knowledge-power and is unique to modern Western civilization. The model of the *scientia sexualis* is the confession (Foucault 1978a: 58). Foucault's distinction (essentially that between the Classical and the Christian world), however, is largely illusory. The claim to *usus*, personal experience, is a mark of the didactic genre as a whole, and the authors claim to pass on this knowledge as master to pupil.[36] On the other hand, the sex manuals as well as the other prescriptive works Foucault follows are intimately tied in with rituals of power and knowledge. While it is true that they do not divide sexual acts into the permitted and the forbidden (cf. Foucault 1986: 124), they operate with subtler forms of linking knowledge and power. One of the most effective forms of the technology of power resides in the very act of listing itself. As with any process that claims to be normative, especially canon formation, the basic move is exclusion. When the taxonomy claims to be objective and exhaustive, it can reduce the unlisted to the nonexistent. Rather than the "logic of censorship" (Foucault 1978a: 84) which takes the form of an act denying that the thing exists, the power of the list lies in silence, so that the possibility of anything outside the list does not even occur. What is unspoken becomes unspeakable; what is uncatalogued becomes impossible.

The intellectual control (description) and practical control (prescription) given by the manuals are both male- and female-directed, for they seek not only to describe a reality of sexual praxis but to construct and control it. As Kappeler says (1986: 2): "Sex or sexual practices do not just exist out there, waiting to be represented; rather, there is a dialectical relationship between representational practices which construct sexuality and the actual sexual practices, each informing the other." As the genre shows, there was a clear didactic and psychological function, present today in similar works. Pornography has been defended and disseminated as educational, while at the same time sex education has been condemned as pornographic. These pillow books, constructing sexuality from the male point of view and for the male consumer, serve to create a normative intercourse and to reassure the male initiate that he will meet with nothing unexpected. Manuals of sexual positions therefore make their appearance at the time of a fundamental shift in Greek society from a predominantly aristocratic and homoerotic code to a bourgeois and heteroerotic code, of which the domestic concerns of New Comedy are indicative.[37] The fear of sexual contact with the Other is removed, not only by advance familiarity with certain basic physiological facts but by the construction of a carefully delimited sexual cosmos. The reduction of the possibilities of human sexuality to heterosexual intercourse is an essential feature of the genre.

Besides a psychological, male-directed aspect, there is a social, female-directed aspect of practical control. This is pornography in the passive sense, writings about whores, writing about women as whores, purporting to tell them how to behave in bed, whose purpose is to convince the female nonresisting reader to become a whore, that is, a compliant sexual object, who will not do (or ask to have done) anything not on the menu. Ovid is overinsistent in stating that he is writing for the prostitute (*Ars* 1.31–34, 2.599–600, 3.57–58). In choosing positions, she is to consider not her pleasure but her appearance. This type of pornography represents a very evident attempt at the control of women's space, or rather women's bodies in space, a reduction of the female to a hole and four limbs that may be positioned around it in a limited number of permutations (see *M*). Thus, the ancient sexual manuals reveal in a very clear form what may be the defining characteristic of pornography: the reduction of its subject matter to object and matter.

Clearchus, Chrysippus, and Athenaeus associate the sex manuals with the gastronomic treatises of Archestratus as examples of didactic literature (*E, F, G*). The two species of handbooks are equally lists of the variety of sensual pleasures that exist as well as the manners in which they should be enjoyed. That is, as guides to bodily pleasures they also function to control the body. The gourmet handbooks tell not only what foodstuffs exist and where they are to be found (description, knowledge) but how they are to be cooked (prescription, power). The sex handbooks not only list what sexual positions exist (description, knowledge) but tell how to employ each one (prescription, power). Thus, the controlling metaphor of the genre is how the material, the natural, the feminine is to be transformed into the logical, the cultural, the masculine. The object of the gastronomical works is to transform the raw into the cooked. The object of pornography is to transform women into whores. Woman is a species of meat. Pornography is a species of cookbook.

The Female Authorial Voice

Most of the major themes of this analysis can be seen in one of the most striking features about these ancient sex handbooks: the consistent assumption of a female authorial voice (*A–R, T; C, H,* and perhaps *O* refer explicitly to men writing under women's names). The obvious question arising from a consideration of the testimonia is why so obviously a male-generated and phallocentric genre is so often fathered off on women. Here I am not denying the possibility that women might have produced pornography in antiquity even as they do now, but the evidence points to a literature that was as male-produced as it was male-consumed.

The use of a female authorial voice is a recurring feature of pornography. It appears at first to be a counterexample to the objectification of women. Women appear to be making themselves subjects and controlling their own sexuality. Carter draws attention to the paradoxical nature of this move (1978: 15–16): "Many pornographic novels are written in the first person as if by a woman, or use a woman as the focus of the narrative; but this device only reinforces the male orientation of the fiction. John Cleland's *Fanny Hill* and the anonymous[38] *The Story of O*, both classics of the genre, appear in this way to describe a woman's mind through the fiction of her sexuality." So, too, Kappeler (1986: 90): "The assumption of the female point of view and narrative voice—the assumption of linguistic and narrative female 'subjectivity'—in no way lessens the pornographic structure, the fundamental elision of the woman as subject. On the contrary, it goes one step further in the total objectification of woman. . . . The so-called female point of view is a male construction of the passive victim in his own scenario, the necessary counterpart to his active aggressor."

The use of a woman's voice is part of the deployment of knowledge and power. Donning this authorial mask is an act to authorize the knowledge. It is another form of Diderot's *Les bijoux indiscrets:* the male author forces the woman's body to speak the "truth." The producer of pornography usurps the act of writing the body.

The female authorial voice in the handbooks plays an important psychological role in the male construction of female sexuality. These works are presented as the writings of women, especially *hetairai* and maidservants (*therapainai*), professional sexual entertainers, who speak with the authority of vast experience.[39] This is pornography in the active sense, writings by whores. Freud's famous question "What does woman want?" is here answered with feminine authority. The answer, comforting the male reader, turns out unsurprisingly enough to be that women want exactly what men want them to want.

There is a further aspect to the assumption by pornography of the female authorial voice. The inscription of a woman's name provides a reinscription of the dominant culture's ideas about women's nature. They are proved out of their own mouths to be sex-obsessed. Their nature is only sexual. They are their bodies. They spend their whole lives doing nothing but talking about the things of Aphrodite and, if they are taught to write, writing about the things of Aphrodite. The sex manuals reinforce a conceit going back to Semonides (7.91; see Bergren 1983: 69–95; Arthur 1984). We have already seen how the genre from its associations with Archestratus and the food writers has been attacked as a guide to luxury and extravagance. The genre is condemned as excessive, weak, and thus essentially feminine. On the other hand, women can be shown to be luxurious, incapable of self-control, totally given over to passion and appetite by their association with the genre. Thus, the genre is used to belittle women; women are used to belittle the genre.

This leads to a final aspect of the social control of women. For the sex manuals act as a check specifically on the clever woman. The recurrent feature of their ascription to learned women in particular inscribes the notion that as women's nature is sexual, so are their attempts at learning. Their desire for knowledge is merely the knowledge of desire. This is especially clear in the cases of Salpe (*O*) and Elephantis (*A, K, P–R*). Each is the name of a famous midwife and writer on her craft, and each has a "doublet" who is a whore and a writer on her craft. The gynecological and obstetric works are confounded with the pornographic works to such an extent that it is impossible to separate out the realities of authorship.[40] So Pliny, in a remarkably revealing passage (*HN* 28.70) about the magic powers of menstrual blood, gives as his authorities "not only midwives but prostitutes themselves," equating the two as the only sources of knowledge about women's sexuality.[41] The sexual slander of the intellectual woman as a form of social control has not vanished, and it is a frequently attested move in antiquity (note the attacks on the poets Nossis and Erinna in Herodas *Mime* 6). The philosopher Nicarete of Megara was called a hetaira, as was Leontion, the pupil of Epicurus (Ath. 13.596e; Diog. Laert. 6.96–98; *contra* Cic. *Fat.* 5.581; see Pomeroy 1977: 58). Valerius Maximus's spleen against Gaia Afrania (8.3) comes to mind, as well as Sallust on Sempronia (*Cat.* 24–25; see Lefkowitz and Fant 1982: 205–6). The coercion of the intellectual woman by slander as sexually obsessed or deviate is paralleled by the case of Aphra Behn, whose outspoken poetry on love earned her similar accusations of unchastity. These women's excessive knowledge, particularly on matters of *erôs,* and their intrusions into masculine fields of expertise (medicine, poetry, literature) render them liable to social sanctions. In particular, their works are controlled because of the threat they pose to the canon, not just of authors but of knowledge, because of the threat that writing by women might offer other ways of knowing, other languages, other entities that differ from the received list. Rhetoric and gynecology can equally be forms of control and areas in which it is necessary to retain control.

Sade makes pornograms. The pornogram is not merely the written trace of an erotic practice, nor even the product of a cutting up of that practice, treated as a grammar of sites and operations; through a new chemistry of the text, it is the fusion (as under high pressure) of discourse and body ("You see me completely naked," Eugénie says to her professor: "dissertate on me as much as you want"), so that, that point having been reached, the writing will be what regulates the exchange of Logos and Eros, and that it will be possible to speak of the erotic as a grammarian and of language as a pornographer.

—Barthes 1976: 158–59

APPENDIX

Texts Relating to the Writers of Sexual Handbooks

Philaenis

A: Suda, s.v. Astyanassa (also mentions Elephantine).

B: P. Oxy. 2891 (Lobel 1972).

C: Aeschrion *A.P.* 7.345.

D: Timaeus of Tauromenium in Polybius 12.13.1 (also Botrys).

E: Clearchus of Soli in Athenaeus 10.457d–e.

F: Chrysippus in Athenaeus 8.335.

G: Antisthenes in Athenaeus 5.220 (also Niko of Samos, Callistrate of Lesbos, Pythonicus of Athens; these only mentioned here).

H: Dioscorides *A.P.* 7.450.

I: Priapea 63.15–18.

J: Justin Martyr 2.15.3.

K: Tatian, *Oratio ad Graecos* 34.3 (also Elephantine).

L: Lucian, *Pseudologista* 24.

M: Pseudo-Lucian, *Erotes* 28.

N: Clement of Alexandria, *Protreptikos* 53P; quoted by Myerowitz (Chapter 7 in this volume).

Others

O: Alcimus and Nymphodorus of Syracuse in Athenaeus 7.321f–322a (Botrys, see *D;* also Salpe).

P: Suetonius, *Tib.* 43 (Elephantis).

Q: Martial 12.43 (Elephantis).

R: Priapea 4 (Elephantis).

S: Suda, s.v. Paxamos.

T: Suda, s.v. Pamphile.

NOTES

I owe a considerable debt to Amy Richlin, Sandra Joshel, Molly Myerowitz, and the other contributors to this book, as well as to my friend and colleague Barbara Burrell. All translations are my own.

1. For Greek and Roman concepts of obscenity, see, respectively, Henderson (1975) and Richlin (1983).

2. Timaeus of Tauromenium (ca. 356–260) in Polyb. 12.13.1; already by the time of Timaeus, there was a recognized genre of sex manuals by *anaiskhuntographoi*.

3. First mentioned by Ptolemy Chennus, first–second century A.D. (Photius *Biblio.* 149a28), who may have created this figure of Helen's maid. See Cohn, in Pauly-Wissowa 1894: 23.2.1862 (77).

4. *C* (a mock epitaph which implies that Philaenis wrote sex manuals by pretending to deny the charge), *G, H, M* (a complete fusion of author and text: "Let all our women's quarters be a Philaenis").

5. Note that *kataklisis*, "posture," is a technical medical term for "position for resting in bed." See Hp. *Art.* 33; cf. *Prog.* 3, Gal. 16.578K: *to tês katakliseôs skhêma*.

6. Seduction: So *B* (quoted below); implied by *G* and Ovid's use of his sources in the *Ars Amatoria*. Oral sex is perhaps implied by *D* and *L*.

7. For the case of Sappho, see esp. Page 1955: 110–46; Lefkowitz 1981a: 59–68; Hallett 1979: 447–64.

8. See Ath. 13.601e, 609c; Hp. *Aera* 20–22. Part of the appeal of ethnographic works lies precisely in their sexual content. The pose of the detached scientific point of view and the fact that it is turned on the culturally Other authorizes discourse and representations otherwise forbidden. The success of Malinowski's title is a case in point.

9. For an example: Philostr. *V.S.* 1.22.524; cf. Suet. *Aug.* 51. For the *Phoenicica*, attributed to Lollianus, see Easterling and Knox 1985: 686.

10. For text, see Merkelbach (1972: 284); Tsantsanoglou (1973: 183–95); Cataudella (1973: 253–63); Luppe (1974: 281–82); Marcovich (1975: 123–24). My text differs slightly from Tsantsanoglou's, principally in retaining Merkelbach and Luppe's [νέ]αν (Parker 1989: 49–50).

11. *Pace* Tsantsanoglou (1973: 194). For a modern analogue, compare the "Emmanuelle" movies, all the more so since the novel *Emmanuelle* by "Emmanuelle Arsan" is pseudonymous, possibly written by a man. The name Emmanuelle does not indicate authorship but is simply a signal to the consumer of pornographic content.

12. See Henderson 1987a: 96, and 1975: 151–83, esp. 164–66 (no. 274–78), 173 (no. 317), 178–80 (no. 358–64). Artemidorus 1.79 also contains a similar list of sexual positions used for interpreting dreams of mother-son incest; see Winkler 1990: 42.

13. But see Arist. *Nic. Eth.* 1128a22–25 on Old Comedy. Roman sources in Richlin 1983: 1–31.

14. So *aselgeia:* Plato *Rep.* 424e, Polyb. 36.15.4; coupled with *hubris*, Dem. 21.1, etc. For *akolasia*, Thuc. 3.37.3; Aristotle *Eth. Nic.* 1118b–9a, 1150a–51a; *Eth. Eud.* 1230b, etc.; see North 1966: 202–3.

15. E.g., in food, Xen. *Mem.* 1.3.5, 2.1.33; Hp. *Aphorisms* 2.4, 17, 22 (but see 2.38); food and sex, Diog. Laert. 6.2.69; Plato *Rep.* 389e, 580e; Xen. *Symp.* 4.38. This is, of course, a vast topic in Greek philosophy (see North 1966 for a survey) and one that forms the staple diet of Roman philosophers and poets; see Henry, Chapter 12 in this volume.

16. On luxury, extravagance in sex joined with food and drink, see Xen. *Mem.* 2.1.30; Plato *Rep.* 573a–e; Aesch. 1.42, 1.75; Dem. 18.296, 19.229; Crates frg. 13–14; Hp. *Epid.* 3.10, 14. See Dover 1974: 178–80.

17. Hdt. 6.84. For women and wine in invective, see Herodas *Mime* 1; Juv. 6.319.

18. See principally Dover 1984: 143–57, esp. 148–49; Foucault 1985: 84–86. For Rome, see Richlin 1983, esp. 131–39 (see index s.v. "effeminacy," "'pathic' homosexual"); Wiseman 1985: 10–14.

19. See Saussure 1976: 13–15; Culler 1975: 6–11; Ray 1984: 110–13.

20. Thus, the *Categories, Top.* 101b–3b22, etc. So, too, Xenocrates, frg. 12 H; Hermodorus (in Simpl. *In phys.* 247.33–248.20 D).

21. E.g., the "Catalogue of Ships" and the *aristeia* of various heroes in the *Iliad*, the Hesiodic catalogues and genealogies in the *Works and Days* and *Theogony* as well as the *Catalogue of Women* (*Eoiae*). See Semonides 7 (the taxonomy of women, purporting to give their essential natures): Pomeroy 1975: 40–52; Lefkowitz and Fant 1982: 14–16; and Arthur 1984: 46–47.

22. E.g., *Hist. An.* 491a7; *Meteorologica* 4. For statements on method and classification, see *Part. An.* 644a16–23; *Hist. An.* 486a14–b22, 490b7 ff., 497b6–13. See Jaeger 1948: 19; Rose 1953: 112–17; Lloyd 1968: 68–102 (esp. 86–90), 173–75; Lloyd 1983: 7–57.

23. Besides Aristotle's *Rhetoric* and *Art of Poetry*, there was the *Sunagôgê Tekhnôn*, a collection and survey of previous writers, a preliminary research effort similar to the collection of constitutions (Cic. *Brutus* 45–51). For the *skhêmata*, see Longinus 18.1–29.2 (Russell and Winterbottom 1972: 480–89).

24. Rhetoric: first in Zoïlus (fourth century B.C.; *FGH* IIA.71; cf. Quint. 9.1.14); cf. Plato *Ion* 536c. Sexual *skhêmata*: *A, F, N, S; figurae: I, P, Q, R.* See note 5, above.

25. The idea that the *Ars Amatoria* is simply a direct parody of the rhetorical handbooks (no mention of the sexual handbooks) has been rightly questioned (Myerowitz 1985: 31, 195n 54). Rather, they resemble each other because they share the same taxonomic and analytic approach that is endemic to all the handbooks, natural historical, medical, or rhetorical.

26. Athen. 13.564b, 15.674b; Plut. *Erot.* 17; *de Erot.* 17, etc.

27. E.g., the *Erôtikos* and *Peri Erôtos* by Theophrastus (Diog. Laert. 5.43), Persaeus (Diog. Laert. 7.36) and Antisthenes (Diog. Laert. 6.16; *G*); *Erôtika* by Clearchus of Soli (Athen. 12.533e, 13.564b, 15.669f; *E*), by Ariston of Ceos (Athen. 13.564b, 15.674); *Erôtikoi Dialogoi* by Sphaerus (Diog. Laert. 7.178), etc. For a full list and testimonia, see V. Rose 1863: 105–7.

28. Zeno (Diog. Laert. 7.34; not at 7.4) and a similar work, the "Pastimes" (*Diatribai*); Cleanthes (Diog. Laert. 7.175): not manuals of sexual positions. Rather, they show the way in which love in all aspects has become a *tekhnê*.

29. See Hp. *Epid.* 1.23; *De Arte* 9–14; *Prognosis;* Celsus *prooem.* 52–54, 57. Compare the Roman inclusion of agriculture, rhetoric, and medicine in the encyclopedias of Cato, Varro, and Celsus.

30. Thus, the earliest extant illustrated papyrus (Louvre, *P. Letronne* 1) is of Eudoxus's astronomy. Cf. Pliny on illustrated herbals, *HN* 25.8. See Weitzmann 1977: 9; Lloyd 1983: 114 n. 4. Aristotle's *Historia Animalium* was illustrated with diagrams (510a29), as was *The Anatomy* by his father, a doctor (497a32). In gynecology the original text of Soranus was certainly illustrated; see Ilberg 1911: 16–21; Burguière et al. 1988: lii–liii.

31. See Ovid *Ars* 2.679–80; Prop. 2.6.27–32; Suet. *Tib.* 44 (cf. *P*), etc. See Brendel 1970: 62–63, and Myerowitz, Chapter 7 in this volume.

32. See *Pol.* 1254b2–16, 1277b27. For woman as the *materia* of the male, *Met.* 729a11, 726b30; *Gen. An.* 716a7, 732a5, 738b20, etc. For the proper subordination of matter, see *Met.* 988a5, 1024a35, 1070b17, 1071a3–25, etc. On Aristotle and women, see Clark 1975: 29, 44, 48, 106, 206–11; Horowitz 1976: 183–213; Morsink 1979: 83–112; Fortenbaugh 1977; Spelman 1977: 17–30; Saïd 1983: 93–123; Clark 1982: 177–91; Lloyd 1983: 94–106; Lange 1983: 1–15; Sissa 1983: 83–145, esp. 139–45; Manuli 1983: 162–70.

33. See Kuhn's observation that pornography "in constructing certain representations of women . . . codes woman in a general way as sign, as an object, that is of (implicitly male) looking" (1982: 114); and J. M. Davies's definition (1988: 137): "The name feminists give to this process of limiting what a person can be by predetermining how her or his behavior or appearance is to be interpreted is 'objectification.' "

34. Cf. Arist. *Met.* 1025b25. See Guthrie 1981: 337, 345–49, 356.

35. Note the very apposite remarks of E. Phillips (1973: 72; cf. 32), contrasting the Coan and Cnidian schools of medicine: "These clinical books [such as the *Epidemics*] bring the reader into direct contact with ancient patients, the more so because no theory is obtruded, nor any explanation explicitly offered. But other books, which are Cnidian in origin, laboriously describe, classify and attempt to explain the variety of diseases. They are harder to read and more technical; passing to them is like passing from Plato to Aristotle. . . . Unlike the *Epidemics,* which from time to time mention persons and places, their attitude to disease approaches the modern ontological theory in which diseases are treated as if they were entities in themselves. . . . These books are also therapeutic, unlike most of the *Epidemics* and *Prognostic,* so that the descriptions of diseases are supplemented with lists of suitable foods, drinks and treatments, along with herbal remedies." See Galen 5,760–61K; 15, 427–28K.

36. Ovid *Ars* 1.1–30; and *B.* Archestratus's own work stated that it was based on *historia* (research), gathered from the whole world (frg. 1 and 2 Brandt).

37. See Foucault's analysis (1986: 211–27) of Pseudo-Lucian's *Erôtes* (cf. *M*).

38. Rather, pseudonymous. The ascription of the book to "Pauline Réage" is an intimate part of the process.

39. For a modern analogue, *Penthouse* runs a sexual advice column by the Happy Hooker, rather than Masters and Johnson or even Dr. Ruth.

40. Brendel (1970: 66 n. 70) and Jones (1963: VIII.58) assume that there was only one Elephantis. The articles in Pauly-Wissowa distinguish them. Elephantis: Pliny *HN* 28.51, as a writer on abortifacients; Galen 12.416K, as a writer on cosmetics. Salpe: Pliny *HN* 28.38, 66, 82, 262; 32.135 (*obstetrix*), 140.

41. See Hp. *Carn.* 19 (8.610.3–10L).

6

The Body Female and the Body Politic: Livy's Lucretia and Verginia

Sandra R. Joshel

Brutus, while the others were absorbed in grief, drew out the knife from Lucretia's wound, and holding it up, dripping with gore, exclaimed, "By this blood most chaste until a prince wronged it, I swear, and I take you, gods, to witness, that I will pursue Lucius Tarquinius Superbus and his wicked wife and all his children, with sword, with fire, aye with whatsoever violence I may; and that I will suffer neither them nor any other to be king in Rome!"
—Livy 1.59.1, LCL[1]

Reality, robbed of its independent life, is shaped anew, kneaded into large, englobing blocks that will serve as the building material for a larger vista, a monumental world of the future. . . . Empires can be built only on, and out of, dead matter. Destroyed life provides the material for their building blocks.
—Klaus Theweleit, *Male Fantasies*

Pretext: The Conditions of a Reading

I read Livy's history of Rome's origins, its earliest struggles with neighboring states, and the political events that formed the state that conquered an empire. The historian writes within an immediate past he regards as decadent, a fall from the glorious society of ancestors who made empire possible; he stands at a point where his Rome is about to be reinvigorated by a new imperial order. Raped, dead, or disappeared women litter the pages. The priestess Rhea Silvia, raped by the god Mars, gives birth to Rome's founder, Romulus, and leaves the story. The women of the neighboring Sabines are seized as wives by Romulus's wifeless men. When the Sabine soldiers come to do battle with the Romans, the Roman girl Tarpeia betrays her own menfolk by admitting their foes into the citadel. She is slain by the enemy she helped. By contrast, the Sabine women place their bodies between their kin and their husbands, offering to take on the violence the men would do to each other.

112

Later, a young woman, named only as sister, is murdered by her brother Horatius because she mourns the fiancé he killed in single combat. "So perish every Roman woman who mourns a foe!" he declares, and their father agrees that she was justly slain. Lucretia, raped by the king's son, calls on her menfolk to avenge her and commits suicide. The men overthrow the monarchy. Verginia, threatened with rape by a tyrannical magistrate, is killed by her father to prevent her violation. The citizen body ousts the magistrate and his colleagues. In these stories of early Rome, the death and disappearance of women recur periodically; the rape of women becomes the history of the state.[2]

I read Klaus Theweleit's study of Freikorps narratives, written by "soldier males" who would become active Nazis. They write of World War I, of battling Reds, of living in a time they experience as chaotic and decadent in a Germany fallen from former greatness. Dead, disappeared, and silent women litter their texts. Sexually active working-class and communist women are slain brutally; chaste wives and sisters are made antiseptic, are killed tragically, or do not speak.

And I read Livy and Theweleit in the United States in the summer of 1987, at a time when the title of a recent Canadian film evokes what is often not explicit—*The Decline of the American Empire*. A time of concern about American power abroad and American life at home. The war against drugs and the battle against uncontrolled sex. Betsy North, Donna Rice, and Vanna White litter the TV screen, newspapers, and magazines. Betsy, silent and composed, sits behind her ramrod-straight husband, stiff and immaculate in his Marine uniform. Donna Rice appears in private, now public, photographs with Gary Hart; she has nothing to say. He gives up his candidacy for the presidency, guilty of extramarital sex. Vanna White turns letters on the popular game show "Wheel of Fortune." She does speak. "I enjoy getting dressed as a Barbie doll," she tells an interviewer. An image on our TV screens gotten up like a doll that simulates a nonexistent woman named Barbie, she is rematerialized by her dress in some sort of fetishistic process: "Speaking of *Vanna White*, a polyester magenta dress, one worn by the celebrated letter-turner, is on display at a Seattle espresso bar, where fans may touch it for 25 cents" (*Boston Globe*, June 9, 1987).

I look here at gender relations and images of women in Livy's history of early Rome, focusing on his tales of Lucretia and Verginia, but I do so within my own present. Freikorps narratives and the current mediascape are the "conditions of my narrative," to borrow a phrase from Christa Wolf. I am not equating Rome, Fascist Germany, and the United States of the 1980s; nor am I making the images of women in their histories and fictions exactly analogous. By juxtaposing images, I raise questions about the representations of gender within visions of building and collapsing empires. As Theweleit suggests of fascism, the Roman fiction should be understood and combated not "because it might 'return again,'" but primarily because, as a form of reality production that is constantly present and possible under determinate conditions, *it can, and does, become our production*" (1987: 221). Whether our own fictions include tales similar to Lucretia's and Verginia's with names changed or whether, as academics, we dissect Livy's tales, we retell the stories, bringing their gender images and relations into our present (cf. Theweleit 1987: 265–89, 359).

Livy and the Conditions of His Narrative

Livy (64 B.C.–A.D. 12) lived through the change from aristocratic Republic to Principate, a military dictatorship disguised in republican forms. For more than a century before Livy's birth, Rome's senatorial class had ruled an empire; by the time of his death, Rome, its political elite, and the empire were governed by one man. He grew up during the civil wars that marked the end of the Republic, and his adult years saw the last struggle of military dynasts, Octavian and Antony, and the reign of the first emperor, the victor in that struggle. Raised in a Padua known for its traditional morality, Livy was a provincial; he did not belong to the senatorial class and was uninvolved in politics, although he did have friendly relations with the imperial family (Ogilvie 1965: 1–5; Walsh 1961; Syme 1959; see J. Phillips 1982: 1028, for bibliography).

Livy wrote the early books of his history after Octavian's victory over Antony and during the years in which Octavian became Augustus *princeps*—in effect, emperor (J. Phillips 1982: 1029, for the debate on the precise date). Shortly afterward came Augustus's restoration of the state religion and his program of social and moral reform which included new laws on marriage and adultery aimed primarily at the upper classes. The adultery law made sexual relations between a married woman and a man other than her husband a criminal offense. Ineffective and unpopular, the law nonetheless indicates the regime's concern with regulating sexuality, especially female (see Dixon 1988: 71ff). The program was to return Rome to its ancestral traditions, renew its imperial greatness, and refound the state.

The state to be refounded was a Rome uncorrupted by wealth and luxury, greed and license, the supposed conditions of the late Republic. The stories in which Lucretia and Verginia figure record critical points in that state's formation, marking the origin of political and social forms which, along with the behavior of heroes, account for Rome's greatness and its rise to imperial power. The rape of Lucretia precipitates the fall of the monarchy and establishment of the Republic and the Roman version of liberty. The attempted rape of Verginia belongs to a struggle between privileged and unprivileged groups (patricians and plebeians) known as the Conflict of the Orders; the event resulted in the overthrow of the decemvirs, officials who had abused their original mission of codifying the law, and began a long process of reform that eventually changed the form of Roman political institutions.

To modern historians, Livy's stories of Lucretia and Verginia are myths or, at best, legends that include some memory of actual events. Current historical reconstructions of Rome in the late sixth and mid-fifth centuries B.C., the society in which Lucretia and Verginia are supposed to have lived, depend on archaeology, some early documents, antiquarian notices in later authors (Heurgon 1973; Gjerstad 1973; Bloch 1965; Raaflaub 1986 for historical methodology), and, as has recently been suggested, the "structural facts" obtained when Livy's accounts have been stripped of their "narrative superstructure" (Cornell 1986: 61–76, esp. 73; Raaflaub 1986: 49–50). This evidence usually leaves us without a narrative or the names of agents (see Raaflaub 1986: 13–16). But Livy invented neither the outline of events nor the characters in his stories. First written down in the third and second centuries B.C., the tales were perpetuated as part of a living historical tradition by Roman writers of the early first century B.C. who were the major sources for Livy's retelling (for Livy's use of his sources, see Ogilvie 1965; Walsh 1961; Luce 1977). The history of the roughly contemporary Dionysius of Halicarnassus allows us to see how Livy used the tradition.

This tradition "was neither an authenticated official record nor an objective critical reconstruction, but rather an ideological construct, designed to control, to justify, and to inspire" (Cornell 1986: 58). For historian and audience, the past provided the standards by which to judge the present: the deeds of great ancestors offered models for imitation and supported the claims of the ruling class to political privilege and power. Each historian infused his version of events with his own (and his class's) literary, moral, and political concerns. The past, Cornell notes, "was subject to a process of continuous transformation as each generation reconstructed the past in its own image" (1986: 58). For many modern historians, Livy's account of early Rome better reflects the late Republic than the late sixth and fifth centuries B.C. (Raaflaub 1986: 23).

Even if we view Livy's "description of the monarchy and early Republic as prose epics or historical novels" (Raaflaub 1986: 8), we should not ignore the power of his fictions of Lucretia and Verginia. For Livy, they were history, and, as history, they should inform a way of life in an imperial Rome ripe for refounding. In good Roman fashion, Livy views history as a repository of illustrative behaviors and their results: "What chiefly makes the study of history wholesome and profitable is this, that you behold the lessons of every kind of experience set forth on a conspicuous monument; from these you may choose for yourself and for your state what to imitate, from these mark for avoidance what is shameful in conception and shameful in the result" (*praef.* 10, LCL). Before he begins his historical narrative per se, Livy urges a particular kind of reading. His stories will proffer an array of subject positions, beliefs, and bodily practices. The reader should recognize and identify with them and should understand the consequences of assuming particular subject positions. Bodily practices fit into a vision of building and collapsing empire: some result in imperial power; others bring decadence and destruction. The reader should pay close attention to "what life and morals were like; through what men and by what policies, in peace and in war, empire was established and enlarged; then let him note how, with the gradual relaxation of discipline, morals first gave way, as it were, then sank lower and lower, and finally began the downward plunge which has brought us to the present time, when we can endure neither our vices nor their cure" (*praef.* 9, LCL).

Thus, the question for us is not whether victims, villains, and heroes are fictional, but the way Livy tells their story, offering up a blueprint for his imperial present.

Livy's Stories of Lucretia and Verginia: Rape, Death, and Roman History

Lucretia and the Fall of the Monarchy (1.57–60)

In 509 B.C., the king of Rome, Lucius Tarquinius Superbus, wages war on Ardea in the hope that the booty will lessen the people's resentment at the labor he has imposed on them. During the siege of the city, at a drinking party, the king's sons and their kinsman Collatinus argue over who has the best wife. On Collatinus's suggestion, they decide to settle the question by seeing what their wives are doing. They find the princes' wives enjoying themselves at a banquet with their friends; Collatinus's wife, Lucretia, surrounded by her maids, spins by lamplight in her front hall. Lucretia makes her husband the victor in the wife contest. One of the princes, Sextus Tarquinius, inflamed by Lucretia's beauty and her proven chastity, is seized by a desire to have her. A few days later, without Collatinus's knowledge, he returns to Collatia, where he is welcomed as a guest. That night when the household is asleep, he draws his sword and wakes the sleeping Lucretia. Neither his declarations of love nor his threats of murder nor his pleas move the chaste Lucretia. She submits only when he threatens to create an appearance of disgraceful behavior: he will kill her and a slave and leave the slave's naked body next to hers, so that it will look as if they had been slain in the act of adultery.[3] After the rape, she sends for her husband and her father, instructing them to come with a trusted friend (Collatinus brings Lucius Junius Brutus). To her husband's question "Is it well with you?" she answers, "What can be well with a woman who has lost her chastity? The mark of another man is in your bed. My body only is violated; my mind is guiltless; death will be my witness. Swear that the adulterer will be punished—he is Sextus Tarquinius." The men swear and try to console her, arguing that the mind sins, not the body. She responds, "You will determine what is due him. As for me, although I acquit myself of fault, I do not free myself from punishment. No unchaste woman will live with Lucretia as a precedent." Then she kills herself with a knife she had hidden beneath her robe. While her husband and father grieve, Brutus draws the weapon from Lucretia's body and swears on her blood to destroy the monarchy. Lucretia's body, taken into the public square of Collatia, stirs the populace; Brutus incites the men to take up arms and overthrow the king. Brutus marches to Rome, and in the Forum the story of Lucretia and Brutus's speech have the same effect. The king is exiled, the monarchy ended; the Republic begins with the election of two consuls, Brutus and Collatinus.

Verginia and the Fall of the Decemvirate (3.44–58)

In 450 B.C., the decemvirs have taken control of the state. They have displaced the consuls and the tribunes, protectors of the rights of plebeians. The chief decemvir, Appius Claudius, desires the beautiful young Verginia, daughter of the plebeian centurion Lucius Verginius. When Appius fails to seduce her with money or promises, he arranges to have Marcus Claudius, his *cliens* (a dependent tied to a more powerful man or an ex-master), claim Verginia as his (Marcus's) slave while her father is away at war (apparently the client will give the young woman to his patron Appius). Marcus grabs Verginia as she enters the Forum. When the cries of her nurse draw a crowd, Marcus hauls her before Appius's court. The decemvir postpones his decision until her father arrives but orders Verginia turned over to the man who claims her as his slave until the case can be tried. An impassioned speech by Verginia's fiancé Icilius incites the crowd; Appius rescinds his order. The next day, Verginius leads his daughter into the Forum, seeking support from the crowd.

Unmoved by appeals or weeping women, Appius adjudges Verginia a slave, but he grants Verginius's request for a moment to question his daughter's nurse in Verginia's presence. Verginius leads his daughter away. Grabbing a knife from a butcher's shop, he cries, "In the only way I can, my daughter, I claim your freedom," and kills her. Icilius and Publius Numitorius, Verginia's grandfather (?), show the lifeless body to the populace and stir them to action. Verginius escapes to the army, where his bloodstained clothes, the knife, and his speech move his fellow soldiers to revolt. The decemvirate is overthrown, and when the tribunate is restored, Verginia's father, fiancé, and grandfather (?) are elected to office.

Flood: Bodily Desire and Political Catastrophe

Livy's narrative of Rome's political transformation revolves around chaste, innocent women raped and killed for the sake of preserving the virtue of the body female and the body politic; Roman men stirred to action by men who take control; and lustful villains whose desires result in their own destruction. Although the basic elements of Rome's early legends were present in Livy's sources, he could have dispensed with the tales in abbreviated fashion or minimized the role of women in stories of political change. Instead, he carefully constructs tragedies, drawing on all the literary techniques and models so meticulously noted by scholars (Ogilvie 1965: 218–32, 476–88; J. Phillips 1982: 1036–37 for bibliography). Why *this* writing of Roman history in Livy's present?

Livy's view of the immediate past engages him in Rome's ancient history. He elaborates that history, because he finds pleasure in it and relief from recent civil war, social upheaval, and military disaster:

> To most readers the earliest origins and the period immediately succeeding them will give little pleasure, for they will be in haste to reach these modern times, in which the might of a people which has long been very powerful is working its own undoing. I myself, on the contrary, shall seek in this an additional reward for my toil, that I may avert my gaze from the troubles which our age has been witnessing for so many years, so long at least as I am absorbed in the recollection of the brave days of old. (*praef.* 5, LCL)

"The troubles" haunted male authors of the first century B.C.—Sallust, Cicero, Horace, and Livy himself. As in the imagination of Theweleit's Freikorps writers, political chaos and military failure are associated with immorality. Although this vision is familiar to modern historians of ancient Rome, the strikingly similar images of chaos and men's experience in Weimar Germany compel reconsideration of the Roman images. I attend here only to how two elements, marked in these tales of origin, both deaden and kill: male excess and female unchastity.

Ancient authors attributed the crises of the late Republic to political ambition and to male bodies out of control in the social world, guilty of, in Livy's words, *luxus, avaritia, libido, cupiditas, abundantes voluptates* (luxurious living, avarice, lust, immoderate desire, excessive pleasures). Uncontrolled bodies bring personal ruin and general disaster (*praef.* 11–12). For his contemporary Horace (*Odes* 3.6.19–20; cf. 1.2), disaster floods country and people. The body and its pleasures are present only as excess in this vision. The slightest infraction seems dangerous. A single vice can slip into another or into a host of moral flaws, as in Livy's description of Tarquinius Superbus and his son Sextus (Phillipides 1983: 114, 117). Any desire becomes avarice or lust and must be rooted out.

> The seeds of vicious avarice
>> must be rooted up, and our far too delicate
> characters must be moulded by
>> sterner training.
> —Horace, *Odes* 3.24.51–54 (trans. J. P. Clancy)

Men of the Freikorps feared a "Red" flood affecting the entire society, "piercing through the ancient dam of traditional state authority" (Theweleit 1987: 231; see 385 ff., esp. 392, for Freikorps images of chaos). It "brought all of the worse instincts to the surface, washing them up on the land" (Theweleit 1987: 231). Ultimately, comments Theweleit (231), this flood flows "from inside of those from whom the constraint of the old order has been removed." A man could feel "powerless" and "defenseless" before what flows—fearful yet fascinated. The flood solidifies in a morass; men can hardly extract themselves from a mire that softness produces within them (404, 388). Indulgence must be rooted out: "If you want to press on forward, you cannot allow this mire of failure of the will to form inside you. The most humane way is still to go for the beast's throat, to pull the thing out by its roots" (388). The "defense against suffocation in flabby self-indulgence and capriciousness" (389) lies in toughness and self-control: men should "stand fast . . . think of, and believe in, the nation" (405).

Livy focuses on what he imagines to be the ancient and necessary virtue of the soldier: *disciplina*. Roman tradition offered him tales of discipline instilled by floggings, sons executed by fathers to preserve *disciplina* for the state, and men hardened to fight both the enemy without and the weakness within themselves (see Valerius Maximus, 2.7.1–15, esp. 2.7.6, 2.7.9, 2.7.10). Neither exceptional bravery nor victory should be allowed to undermine *disciplina*. When Livy's Manlius Torquatus orders the execution of his own son because, although successful in battle, he had ignored a direct order that no one was to engage the enemy, he makes the execution and the sacrifice of his own feelings a model for future generations of Roman men:

> As you have held in reverence neither consular authority nor a father's dignity, and . . . have broken military discipline, whereby the Roman state has stood until this day unshaken, thus compelling me to forget either the Republic or myself, we will sooner endure the punishment of our wrong-doing than suffer the Republic to expiate our sins at a cost so heavy to herself; we will set a stern example, but a salutary one, for the young men of the future. For my own part, I am moved, not only by a man's instinctive love of his children, but by this instance you have given of your bravery. . . . But . . . the authority of the consuls must either be established by your death, or by your impunity be forever abrogated, and . . . I think you yourself, if you have a drop of my blood in you, would not refuse to raise up by

your punishment the military discipline which through your misdemeanour has slipped and fallen. (8.7.15–19, LCL)

Whatever his motives (8.7.4–8), the son had not simply disobeyed his commander and father; implicitly, he had failed to maintain the necessary self-control.

In Livy's view, control must be absolute. A slight crack in the edifice brings down the entire structure. *Disciplina* resulted in conquest; its gradual relaxation precipitated a slide, then collapse (*praef.* 9)—personal, social, political. A man, and Rome, would seem to have a choice between obdurate victor and pusillanimous loser, between fighter and pulp in the Freikorps vision (cf. Valerius Maximus, 2.7.9 and Theweleit 1987: 395).

The heroes of Livy's history, the men who act when women are made dead, are disciplined and unyielding. Noble Brutus chastised men for their tears and idle complaints (1.59.4) when they lamented Lucretia's death and their own miseries. He urged them as men and Romans to take up arms. Later, he would administer as consul and suffer as father the scourging and execution of his own sons as traitors. Founder of the Republic and the consulship, he is a model for future consuls and fathers, like Torquatus, whose defense of the state's tradition and existence will require dead sons and numbed affections. No *luxus* here or in the likes of Cocles, Scaevola, and Cincinnatus. These men are stern and self-controlled, bodies hardened to protect Rome and fight its wars. They must have been to have become the foremost people of the world (*praef.* 3)—the rulers of world empire. Like Virgil's Aeneas, Trojan ancestor of the Romans, conceived within a few years of Livy's heroes, they endure pain and adversity to create a Rome whose imperial power is portrayed as destiny (*Aeneid* 1.261–79): "so great was the effort to found the Roman race" (*Aeneid* 1.33). So disciplined, so self-controlled, so annealed, the body as a living, feeling, perceiving entity almost disappears.

Livy's instructions to imitate virtue and avoid vice invoke the *mos maiorum*— the way of the ancestors as a guide for the present. Bodily excess as manifested in the lust of Tarquin and Appius Claudius brings personal ruin and the collapse of their governments. Not incidentally, at the same time, Rome's wars with its neighbors are waged unsuccessfully. Tarquin desires Lucretia during the inactivity (*otium*) of a long siege which is blamed on the king's extravagance and his consequent need for booty. His avarice and his son's lust become "two sides of the same coin, a metaphor of the City's moral sickness," and explain Rome's military failure (Phillipides 1983: 114–15). For the sake of Rome's martial and moral health, father and son as desiring agents must go (Phillipides 1983: 114). The actions of disciplined men like Brutus result in personal success and Roman power. They set the example for Livy's present: the male body must be indifferent to material and sexual desire.

So Woman poses a particular problem.[4] The Roman discourse on chaos often joins loose women with male failure to control various appetites.[5] Uncontrolled female sexuality was associated with moral decay, and both were seen as the roots of social chaos, civil war, and military failure.

> Breeder of vices, our age has polluted
> first marriage vows and the children and the home;

> from this spring, a river of ruin
>   has flooded our country [*patria,* lit. "fatherland"] and our people.
>   —Horace, *Odes* 3.6.17–20 (trans. J. P. Clancy)

Livy's view of control makes it appropriate that his narrative tends toward a simple dichotomous vision of female sexuality: woman is or is not chaste.

This vision may account for the satisfaction Livy's tales find in the point of the knife. Where he omits words about forced penetration, he offers a precise image of the dagger piercing Lucretia's body and her death (1.58.11; cf. Verginia, 3.48.5). Perhaps that knife is aimed at "any unchaste woman," real or imagined, of Livy's age (cf. Freikorps worship of asexual "high-born" women and attack on sexual "low-born" women; Theweleit 1987: 79 ff., 315 ff., esp. 367). In Rome's imagined past, the knife constructs absolute control. It eradicates unchastity and kills any anomaly in female sexuality, such as the contradiction between Lucretia's violated body and her guiltless mind, or the blurring between the "good" and the "evil" woman (see Theweleit 1987: 183).

In Livy, the "good" woman's threatening element is her attractiveness. While Livy never explicitly questions the innocence and chaste spirit of Verginia or Lucretia, the beauty of each woman is marked and explains the rapists' actions. Lust seizes each man, as if desire originated outside him in beauty (1.57.10; 3.44.2). If, as the object of desire, a woman's beauty is the condition of male lust, then good as well as evil men are potentially affected. Her existence threatens men's *disciplina.* "The affective mode of self-defense in which [the annihilation of women] occurs seems to be made up of *fear* and *desire*" (Theweleit 1987: 183). Once Woman has played her role—to attract the villain whose actions set in motion other active males who construct the state, empire, and therefore history in the Roman sense—she must go.

As Theweleit suggests, what is at issue in this construction is male uncontrol. "What really started swimming were the men's boundaries—the boundaries of their perceptions, the boundaries of their bodies" (1987: 427). The dagger stems the flood, at least in the imagination. In effect, the aggression men visit on women is really aimed at their own bodies (note Theweleit 1987: 427, 154–55). Woman must die in order to deaden the male body. Aggression toward Woman and self produces *disciplina* (or is it the other way around?). The pathos of Livy's stories displaces the relief at the removal of the threatening element. "How tragic!" sigh author and reader, finding pleasure in the pain of noble loss. Ultimately, the pleasure of the narrative lies in killing what lives: women, the image of Woman as the object of desire, and male desire itself.

Discipline was necessary not only for the acquisition of empire but also for ruling it. The denial of the body to the self speaks the denial of social power to others; a Roman's rule of his own body provides an image of Roman domination and a model of sovereignty—of Roman over non-Roman, of upper class over lower, of master over slave, of man over woman, and of Princeps over everyone else (note Livy's use of a Greek metaphor likening a disordered body to the plebs' revolt against the *patres,* 2.32.9–12). In particular, the morality of control served Rome's new ruler. Augustus presented the required image of control and sacrifice

(*Res Gestae* 4–6, 34; Suetonius *Augustus* 31.5, 33.1, 44–45, 51–58, 64.2–3, 65.3, 72–73, 76–77; cf. 71); denial and the morality of control enabled his authority to be "implanted into subjects' bodies in the form of a lack in overflowing" (Theweleit 1987: 414). In the Princeps' new order, there were to be no more selfish desires like those which had precipitated civil war. Woman was to be returned to her proper place. Marriage was to be regulated by the state; women's sexuality was to form the images and establish the boundaries so necessary to secure Rome's domination of others and Augustus's structuring of power. Harnessed, chaste, and deadened, Woman became the matter of a new order designed to control men and the free movement of all bodies. "Women within the new state once again provide the building blocks for internal boundaries against life" (Theweleit 1987: 366).

Woman as Space: Not a Room of Her Own

Within imperial constructions and the political context of the late first century B.C., Livy's account of early Rome creates Woman and her chastity as space, making her a catalyst for male action. She embodies the space of the home, a boundary, and a buffer zone. She is also a blank space—a void, for Livy effectively eliminates her voice, facilitating the perpetuation of male stories about men.

As is well known, a woman's chastity is associated with the honor of her male kin (Dixon 1982; Ortner 1978). Lucretia's behavior makes her husband the victor (*victor maritus*) in a contest between men (1.57). The praise awarded her is for chastity, measured by conduct outside the bedroom. Lucretia, spinning and alone but for her maids, acts out the traditional virtues of the good wife; the princes' wives, banqueting with friends, presumably display Woman's traditional vice, drinking wine, an offense tantamount to adultery (A. Watson 1975: 36–38; MacCormack 1975: 170–74). Verginia's fiancé Icilius (3.45.6–11) equates an assault on female chastity with violence done to male bodies and accuses Appius Claudius of making the eradication of tribunes (whose bodies were sacrosanct) and the right of appeal, defenses of men's *libertas,* an opportunity for *regnum vestrae libidini* ("a tyranny of your lust").

The association of male honor and female chastity makes a different kind of sense when we observe the narrative role of other women in Livy's early books. Women function as obstacles or embody spaces, often between and separating men. The Sabines put their bodies between their battling fathers and new husbands, offering to take on the anger the men feel toward one another and the violence they would inflict (1.13.1–4). Tarpeia fails to use her body in this way. Bribed by the Sabine king when she fetches water outside the city wall, the girl admits Rome's enemies into the citadel (1.11.6–9). The women whose actions preserve the physical integrity of both husbands and fathers are treasured by both; the girl whose treachery leaves her male kin vulnerable is crushed by the very enemy she aided.

As Natalie Kampen has pointed out, Tarpeia crosses the boundary of the city and appropriate behavior; the Sabines make themselves a boundary between warring men and observe appropriate behavior (1986: 10). If the issue is the control of female sexuality, control means the deployment of the female body in relations between men. Proper deployment founds relations between men, making society possible in Lévi-Strauss's terms (1969; cf. Mitchell 1975: 370–76). Not surprisingly, friezes depicting these tales "appeared at the very heart of the nation in the Forum," thus violating a convention that made women "extremely rare in public state-funded Roman sculpture" (1, 3). Kampen dates the friezes to 14–12 B.C., arguing that these representations served Augustus's moral and social program (5 ff.). In effect, the friezes made visible the narrative role of women in Livy's story of origin: within an emergent imperial order, women are fixed within the frame as boundary and space.

The move from animate life to inanimate matter is repeated in etymology. In each case, the Romans used a story of Woman's body to explain the name of a fixture of Rome: from Tarpeia the name of a place, the Tarpeian rock associated with the punishment of traitors, and from the Sabines the names of political divisions of citizens (the *curiae*). Whether the story follows the naming or vice versa, women's bodies literally become building material—the stuff of physical and political topography. Women who are supposed to have lived are transformed into places and spaces.

The Sabines, *matronae* (respectable married women) who voluntarily take up proper control of their own bodies, are reflected in Lucretia, the noble wife who will herself act and speak the proper use of her body. Tarpeia, *virgo* (unmarried girl) in need of paternal control, finds her counterpart in Verginia, whose father administers the necessary disposal of his daughter's body. Livy's *matrona* and *virgo* become spaces within the husband's or father's home. Unlike Dionysius of Halicarnassus (4.66.1), Livy never moves Lucretia out of Collatinus's house. She appears fixed in every scene—spinning in her hall, sleeping and pinned to the bed by Tarquin, and sitting in her bedroom when her kin come to her after the rape. This fixity in space informs her identity in the narrative and constitutes the grounds for male praise (1.57.9). And Verginius (3.50.9) literally equates his daughter with a place within his home (*locum in domo sua*).

In both narratives, the space that is Woman is equated with a chastity that should render the space of the home or between men impenetrable. Thus, rape or attempted rape appears as the penetration of space. The chastity of both women is described as a state of obstinacy or immobility (1.58.3–4, 5; 3.44.4). However, alone or accompanied only by women, wife and daughter are vulnerable to non-kin males who can use force combined with the threat of shame or the power of the state in order to satisfy their lust. Lucretia is a *place* where Tarquin intends to stick his sword or his penis. She appears as an obstacle to his desire, impenetrable even at the threat of death. When she gives way at the threat of a shame worse than rape, Tarquin conquers (*vicisset, expugnato*) not a person but her chastity (*pudicitiam, decore*). The rape of a Lucretia fixed in and identified with Collatinus's home seems equivalent to a penetration of his private sphere, his territory.

Male heroes, not raped women, carry forward the main trajectory of Livy's work—the history of the Roman state (see de Lauretis 1984: 109–24 on Oedipal narratives). They lead citizen males to overthrow a tyrannical ruler, advancing from the sphere of the home to that of the state, from private vengeance to public action. The transition from domestic to political is represented in a shift in the scene of action from Collatia and the private space of Collatinus's home to Rome and the public space of the Forum. Brutus, not Lucretia (1.59.5; cf. Dionysius 4.66.1), effects the change of scene, just as he transposes her request for the punishment of the rapist to his own demand for the overthrow of the monarchy. His oath of vengeance begins with the determination to avenge Lucretia and finishes not with an oath to dethrone Tarquin's family but with the promise to end the institution of monarchy itself.

The connection between the rape of an individual woman and the overthrow of monarchy and decemvirate finds its model in the Greek stereotype of the tyrant whose part Tarquin and Appius Claudius play (Ogilvie 1965: 195–97, 218–19, 453, 477; Dunkle 1971: 16): they are violent and rape other men's women.[6] Livy's rewriting of the Greek paradigm, however, has a particularly Roman subtext: imperial conquest and its product, large-scale slavery. In both tales, men complain that they, Roman soldiers, are treated as Rome's enemies (1.59.4), the conquered (3.47.2, 3.57.3, 3.61.4), or slaves (1.57.2, 59.4, 59.9, 3.45.8). In effect, king and decemvir behave as if citizen males, like slaves, lacked physical integrity. Very importantly, the "slave" makes possible the victimization of both women. Lucretia gives in when Tarquin threatens to kill her in a simulation of adultery with a slave. Appius Claudius intends to rape Verginia by having her adjudicated a slave, thus legally vulnerable to a master's sexual use (cf. Dionysius 11.29–33, making clear the issue of the slave's lack of physical integrity). Tarquin, his father, and Appius Claudius are made to do to Lucretia, Verginia, and their male kin what Roman "soldier males" do to the conquered. Roman wives and children are assimilated to the conquered and slaves (3.57.4, 61.4), and the physical vulnerability of the latter is unquestioned. This was the empire that needed *disciplina*.

Verginia's story sets out a logic of bodies: between the rape of a woman and direct violence to the bodies of her male kin lies male action. "Vent your rage on our backs and necks: let chastity at least be safe," Icilius exclaims to Appius Claudius early in Livy's account (3.45.9). Verginia's betrothed offers to substitute male for female bodies. Appius's lust, inflicted on wives and children, should be channeled into violence, inflicted on husbands and fathers. The switch never occurs, because male action intervenes and removes the source of lust and violence. At the end, Icilius, Verginius, and Numitorius are alive, well, and sacrosanct tribunes; chastity is safe; Verginia is dead.

But Verginia's father makes clear that her rape poses a direct threat to the male body. After slaying her, he states that there is no longer a *locus* in his home for Appius's lust, and he now intends to defend his own body as he had defended his daughter's (3.50.9). The buffer between himself and Appius is gone.[7] Woman's chastity signifies her, and hence his, imperviousness to assault; her rape endangers his body. Thus, the raped woman becomes a *casus belli*, a catalyst for a male response which stems the threatened violence. Men halt the invasion before it gets to them.

Icilius's speech suggests the nature of the threat to the male body (see Douglas 1984: 133 ff. and Donaldson 1982: 23–25, on the fear of pollution). His words effect a displacement.[8] As "rage" (*saevire*) replaces rape, male necks and backs replace female genitals. Although rage and lust seem interchangeable, Icilius's proffered exchange excludes an assault on the body's most vulnerable place—its orifices (Douglas 1984: 121). The very substitution of necks and backs for orifices masks an apprehension about male vulnerability: invasion of woman as boundary threatens penetration of the male body (see Richlin 1983: 57–63, 98–99).

In Livy's accounts, men experience the offense of rape as tragedy. They grieve and are moved, but they do not directly suffer invasion; they remain intact. Moreover, they can feel like men, because they have taken out their own swords. In a most satisfying way, the invader loses ultimate control of the woman's body. While Appius Claudius and Tarquin wield their penises or try to, the father and, even better, the woman herself wield the knife.

Male action against the tyrant (it should be emphasized) begins not with rape but with the woman's death. Narratively, it appears as if Lucretia and Verginia must die in order for male action to begin and for the story to move on. Three logics seem to account for the slaying of the women and explain why the violence done to woman does not end with rape.

In the first place, a living Lucretia or Verginia would stand as evidence of disorder and chaos (see above on Horace *Odes* 3.6). Livy's Verginius and Icilius speak of the social disorder Appius Claudius's desire introduces for the men of their order and the destruction of the social ties between them. Verginius accuses Appius of instituting an order of nature—rushing into intercourse without distinction in the manner of animals (3.47.7). By killing his daughter, he halts the plunge into animality. Of course, animality and the disorder it signals mean that father and husband no longer control the bodies of "their" women. Appius robs Verginius of the ability to give his daughter in marriage to a man of his choosing (3.47.7). Icilius loses a bride *intacta,* and the bond between Icilius and Verginius would be flawed if Verginius offered him "damaged goods." Icilius asserts that *he* is going to marry Verginia, and *he* intends to have a chaste bride (3.45.6–11). He will not allow his bride to spend a single night outside her father's home (3.45.7).

Appius denies plebeian males membership in a patriarchal order. And where the decemvir offends an already existing patriarchal order, only the political change motivated by his assault on the chastity of a plebeian woman assures paternal power to the men of her social class. In versions of the story earlier than Livy's first-century sources, Verginia was a patrician. By changing her status, Livy's sources invested meanings from current political struggles into the fifth century Conflict of the Orders (Ogilvie 1965: 477). Yet the updated political story is essentially a story about patriarchy, for the political events turn on the control of a daughter's/bride's body.

Second, alive, the raped woman would constitute another sort of threat: once invaded, the buffer zone becomes harmful to what it/she once protected. If women are boundaries, rape, which assaults an orifice, a marginal area of the body, creates a special vulnerability for the "center," that is, men. The danger of a living Verginia is noted above. Her life is dearer than her father's own, but only if she is chaste and "free" (3.50.6), a body intact whose access lies in her father's control. A raped Lucretia, still alive, would display the violation of her husband's home. The mark of another man in Collatinus's bed apparently cannot be erased, at least not without his wife's death. Livy's Lucretia speaks as if she and the marked bed are one: although her mind is guiltless, her body is violated and soiled. Only death, self-inflicted, can display her innocence (1.58.7). Soiled, the body must go (see Douglas 1984: 113, 136, on inadvertent pollution and efforts made to align inward heart and public act).

For history to be a source of models for emulation (*praef.* 10), it must demonstrate an unequivocal pattern. The relation of a moral present to its imagined origins constructs chastity as an absolute quality (see Dixon 1982: 4). The pleas of Lucretia's husband and father that the mind, not the body, sins frame her suicide as a tragic martyrdom. Correcting them, Lucretia makes herself an *exemplum:* "no unchaste woman will live with Lucretia as a precedent" (1.58.10). On the surface, the pleas of father and husband imply that men do not require Lucretia's death: suicide appears as woman's choice. This construction of female choice and agency disguises the male necessity at work in Lucretia's eradication. Alive, even Lucretia would confront a patriarchal order with a model, an excuse, for the woman unchaste *by volition*. Lucretia's statement admits no distinction: her suicide leaves no anomaly for the patriarchal future.

Third, and perhaps most important for the narrative: dead, the female body has other purposes. Dead, the woman whose chastity had been assaulted assumes other values. Dead, her body can be deployed, and the sight of it enjoyed, by all men. Without the stabbing of Lucretia and Verginia, there is no bloodied knife, no blood to swear on, no corpse to display to the masses. Brutus, Icilius, and Numitorius use the dead female body to incite themselves and other men (1.59.3, 3.48.7). The woman's blood enlivens men's determination to overthrow the tyrant. Her raped or almost raped and stabbed body kindles thoughts of men's own sufferings and feeds mass male action (note Theweleit 1987: 34, 105–6); in an almost vampiric relation, the living are enlivened by the dead. He becomes free (i.e., comes alive) when she becomes an inert, unliving object.

Actually, Livy's narrative deadens both women before the knife ever pierces them (Theweleit 1987: 90 ff.). Lucretia is introduced as an object in a male contest, as Verginia is an object of contention, pulled this way and that by the men who would claim her body. In the rape scene, Lucretia is inert; appropriately, she sees death from the moment Tarquin enters her bedroom. The stories "record the living as that which is condemned to death" (Theweleit 1987: 217). Narratively, Lucretia and Verginia become ever more dead, as action moves progressively further from them: from the sight of their deaths to the bloodstained knife to the raped, almost raped dead body to the story of that body told to men not present at the murder. The farther removed from the body, the wider the audience, the more public the action, and ultimately the larger the arena of Roman conquest and rule. Male action secures the form of the Roman state and *libertas*. Most immediately, this results in "soldier males" winning wars that, until these episodes, were stalemated.

The tragic effects and pathos evoked by the woman's death veil the necessary central operation of the narrative: to create a purely public (and male) arena. Although presented as tragedies, Lucretia's suicide and Verginia's slaying remove the women from the scene, from between men. With the buffering space gone, there will now ensue a "real" struggle between men, a struggle that moves forward the central narrative, that of state and empire (on the primacy of public and male concerns, see 3.48.8–9 and Theweleit 1987: 88).

While consulship, tribunate, Senate, and assemblies mark the shape of the state whose development Livy traces, each rape, each body willing to bear the wounds men would inflict on each other, and each dead body sets in place a block of a patriarchal and imperial order. The rape of Rhea Silvia gives the Roman state its *pater* (no room here for a queen mother). The rape of the Sabine women makes possible patriarchy by supplying it with its one necessary component: the women who produce children. Lucretia and Verginia precipitate the overthrow of a tyrant and the confirmation, or indeed establishment, of patriarchy for patricians and then plebeians. Assured at home that their wives and children will not be treated as the conquered, these men can go forth, conquer an empire, and do to other men and women what they would not have done to their own wives and children.

It is in this context that we should see the silence in Livy's narrative, the silence of Lucretia and Verginia, and the dead matter these women become. Verginia never speaks or acts. Livy remarks on her obstinacy in the face of Appius's attempted seduction, although, in fact, he speaks not of her but of her *pudor* (3.44.4). When Appius's client grabs her, her fear silences her; her nurse, not Verginia, cries out for help. The girl is led here and there by kin or grabbed by Appius's client. There is no notice of tears, clinging, or interaction with her father, as in Dionysius's telling (11.31.3, 32.1, 35, 37.4–5). Even the women who surround her are moving by the *silence* of their tears (3.47.4). At the moment she would become a slave, Appius shouts, the crowd parts, the girl stands alone *praeda iniuriae* ("prey to sexual assault," 3.48.3). A moment of silence. Her father takes Verginia's life; he acts and speaks the meaning of her death. Nothing of or from Verginia. "From the start, indeed, she [a Freikorps bride] is no more than a fiction. She never appears in her own right; she is only spoken *about*" (Theweleit 1987: 32).

Throughout the events leading up to and including the rape, Livy's Lucretia is also silent. Although the rape scene is highly dramatic, Livy gives us only Tarquin's actions: he waits until the household is asleep, he draws his sword, he enters Lucretia's bedroom, he holds her down, he speaks, pleads, and threatens. Lucretia is mute. Like Verginia's, her terror eliminates speech, and her chastity makes her obdurate: she is a silent stone.

Silence is what Tarquin demands of her: "*Tace, Lucretia, Sex. Tarquinius sum*" ("Be quiet, Lucretia, I am Sextus Tarquinius"). His speech could not connect silence and erasure more directly. The command and direct address (*Tace, Lucretia*) imply "I give the orders," and since he orders Lucretia's silence, the command is almost tautological. Then he asserts his own name (*Sex. Tarquinius*) and existence (*sum*). The insistence on his own existence follows from his demand for her silence. Indicative, statement of fact, replaces imperative, command—here an order that she erase the fact of herself as a speaking subject; his name replaces hers. In effect, he says, "I am; you are not, although since I must order your silence, you are and I shall have to make you not be." Implicitly, his existence as a speaking (here, an ordering) subject with a name depends on her status as an object without speech (see

Kappeler 1986: 49). Like Brutus's later deployment of her body in the overthrow of the monarchy, Tarquin's words and act are vampiric: her silence (erasure), his existence.

Her silence constructs a pleasure of terror like that of the horror film, where the audience is held in expectation that what it fears will occur. Certainly, tension and terror cannot exist without Lucretia's silence, without her presence as an actionless body. The description of Tarquin's actions delays what every Roman would know to be the inevitable. Livy's account allows the reader to dwell on the details of power asserted—drawn sword, hand on breast, woman pinned to the bed, woman starting out of sleep to hear "*Tace, Lucretia, Sex. Tarquinius sum.*" The mute, immobile victim sets the escalating movement of violation in high relief. As in the cinema, the construction of powerlessness provides a perverse thrill.

What are the pleasures of this silence for male author and reader? Did Livy, "pen" in hand, identify with Tarquin and his drawn sword, experience the imagined exertion of force, and take pleasure in the prospect of *pen*etration with sword or penis (on pen and penis, see Gilbert and Gubar 1979: 3–16)? Is this the titillation found by the male reader? Or does Lucretia's silence also open a space for the flow of the reader's feelings, permitting his entry into the forbidden pleasure of the penetrated, imagined from the place of one required to be a penetrator (Silverman 1980, and Richlin in Chapter 8 of this volume)?

About the act of penetration itself, no words and a gap filled with the language of chastity conquered. Despite rules of taste or convention, such language erases the moment of Lucretia's violation and silences her experience as a subject of violation. Livy comments only, and only after her violation, that she was *maesta* ("mournful"). The place of Lucretia's pain is absent. Without words about her experience at that moment and without that moment, Lucretia is dead matter—not feeling, not thinking, not perceiving. Present is Lucretia's chastity, but not Lucretia. Livy or convention—it doesn't matter which—creates rape as a male event, and an imperial one. Rape consists of male action and female space, the exertion of force and chastity.

After, and only after, the rape, Lucretia speaks and acts as Verginia does not. Donaldson sees Lucretia's act as a sacrifice of self, contrasting it with Brutus's sacrifice of his feelings and his sons (1982: 12). Brutus achieves political liberty, Lucretia personal liberty (8). Higonnet focuses on Lucretia's speech as an explanatory text for suicide (1986: 69). She argues that Lucretia's use of language is "revolutionary" because she sets her own verbal constructs against those of Collatinus which make her a verbal boast and a sexual object (75). With Donaldson (1982: 103 ff.), she views the stress on Brutus's role as the "masculine domestication of an essentially revolutionary heroic instance of female suicide."

This assumes that we can return to some origin where women occupied some other role and misses the male production of origin. The sacrifices of Brutus and Lucretia are "radically different," but not for the reasons noted by Donaldson (12). Brutus's words and actions bring a political order in which men like himself can act; his sacrifice preserves that order. Lucretia's actions result in her own eradication. She is sacrificed so the men of her class may win their liberty—their ability to act. Her language kills no less than her actions: like the Sabines, she "asks for it." Together, words and actions set an example for the control of female sexual activity; in other words, she founds an order in which her female descendants can only enact their own destruction. As with Rhea Silvia, the Sabines, Tarpeia, Horatia, and Verginia, men's liberation and political advances require the sacrifice of Woman.

Moreover, both Lucretia's words and her act silence any difference that would disturb the structural boundaries of an ideal patriarchal order. I find it difficult to see Lucretia's speech (given her by the male historian, it should be emphasized) as revolutionary, when she is made to speak as well as act the absolute, objective quality of chastity and herself as a space invaded. Soiled is soiled: "No unchaste woman will live with Lucretia as a precedent." To see or hear anything else would make Lucretia anomalous—innocent yet penetrated—and alive. Patriarchy in Livy's good old days apparently cannot tolerate a subject whose speech would evoke the disorder of anomaly; it depends on woman's silence, or at most speech that enunciates the role men set out for her (note Theweleit 1987: 123; Gilbert and Gubar 1979: 14).

Theweleit's analysis of the "mode of production of [his] writers' language" is instructive. Freikorps authors employ the postures of description, narration, representation, and argument "only as empty shells" (1987: 215). Rather, their linguistic process is one of transmutation. The events depicted serve a preconceived idea which is not directly described. The "ideational representation" impresses itself on perceived reality and devours it (87). While every linguistic process "appropriates and transforms reality" (215), Freikorps authors deaden what they depict. Theirs is a "language of occupation: it acts imperialistically against any form of independently moving life" (215). The life that especially draws the onslaught is the "living movement of women" and the whole complex of feelings and experiences, sexual and emotional, associated with women.

The thrust of Livy's narrative kills, but with certain effects. Women are made dead, and men come alive. Women as a presence disappear from the narrative and leave the stage of history to men struggling with one another, winning wars, and building an empire which, of course, means making other women and men physically dead in conquest or socially dead in enslavement. Lucretia and Verginia endure and are removed from the scene by the activities of the conqueror—rape, death, enslavement. In effect, Livy builds Rome's origin and its history with what deadens in the imperial present.

Where it would seem that women in Livy are made dead with the result that the men who make empire come alive, this operation of the narrative veils the deadness of the men who build imperial society. *Disciplina* requires bodies insensible to desire. Brutus holds aloft the bloody knife drawn from Lucretia's body and swears the overthrow of tyranny. He evokes the more recent image of his descendant, beloved by Caesar and one of his assassins. Livy seems simply to have replaced one dead body with another; Lucretia's corpse hides another, not of the past but of Augustus's emerging imperial order—Gaius Julius Caesar, a man who controlled neither his ambition nor his bodily desires.

Epilogue: The News, History, and the Body of Woman

The story of Lucretia, Donaldson says, has disappeared from popular knowledge not on account of "moral disapproval, but neglect: the explanation lies in the modern decline in classical knowledge and classical education" (1982: 168). We are too distant from ancient Rome and the eighteenth century that found meaning in its virtues. Instead, "we celebrate the 'heroes' of the sports field and the world of entertainment more readily than the heroes of the battlefield and the deathbed; the word is drained of its moral sense."

I cannot share Donaldson's perception of distance and difference. The news, that raw material of political history, seems to belong to the "world of entertainment": fiction and fact meld, working on and with the same images. Through them echo the women and gender relations in Livy's stories of early Rome, his narrative of origins constructed in apprehension of decadence and decline. The Iran-Contra hearings slip into the air time of the soap opera. The cases of Bernhard Goetz and Baby M become news and made-for-TV movies. In the newspaper, extramarital sex costs a politician his chance at the presidency; in the cinema, it nearly costs a man his family and his life. In Rambo films and *Fatal Attraction,* "the world of entertainment" does offer us heroes of the battlefield and the deathbed (more precisely, death *and* bed). Daily, images of woman as space and void cross my TV screen. Often, the news seems written on the bodies of women; at least, she is there—a part of the landscape of what becomes history.

This is not a Roman landscape. The women belong to seemingly different narratives: hostages, not raped women, catalyzed action in Reagan's White House. Women are not slain in current political narratives, yet seemingly different stories proffer words flooded with "moral sense," implicitly urging correct bodily behavior, generally the practices of self-control—"just say no." These stories, too, require the bodies of women, made dead by their silence and their allocation to a holding place in stories of men. And when these women speak, they enunciate this place or their pleasure as inanimate matter, like a Barbie doll available for purchase.

The "decline in classical knowledge" has not spelled the disappearance of these features of Roman fictions, however unfamiliar the specific narratives. The deadening or silencing of Woman perpetuates the fictions and history of the bodies politic, female, and male. Since the eighteenth century, when some celebrated Lucretia's story, the commodity has taken the place of honor in systems of value as a bourgeois order replaced an aristocratic one, but the images of Woman have followed the displacement. "Her image sells his products" (Pfohl 1990: 223–24); it "sells" Livy's history, too.

NOTES

This essay has grown out of extended discussions with Amy Richlin, Avery Gordon, and Andrew Herman, and I have benefited from their insight, critical comments, and constructive suggestions. To each, a special thank you.

1. Translations from ancient sources are the author's own, unless indicated otherwise. LCL refers to the Loeb Classical Library.

2. Lavinia, daughter of King Latinus, married to Aeneas in order to cement an alliance between Latins and Trojans, disappears from the text (1.3.3), as do the politically and/or sexually active Tanaquil and Tullia (exiled 1.59.13). On this and related issues, see now Jed 1989 and Joplin 1990, which unfortunately appeared too late to be considered here.

3. By "submits" (or, later, "gives in"), I do not intend to imply consent on Lucretia's part (*contra* Donaldson 1982: 24 and Bryson 1986: 165–66). To speak of consent in conditions of force and violence is meaningless; in Lucretia's situation, it seems perverse. She can die or live through the rape only to defend her honor by suicide.

4. I distinguish an individual woman or women from Woman, "a fictional construct, a distillate from diverse but congruent discourses dominant in Western cultures" (de Lauretis 1984: 5).

5. Appetites include a decadent concern with food, table servants, and dining accoutrements. For discussion and sources on Roman luxury and decadence, see Earl 1961: 41ff; 1967: 17–20; and J. Griffin 1976. Uncontrolled sexuality and decadent eating fit Lévi-Strauss's observation of a "very profound analogy which people throughout the world seem to find between copulation and eating" (1966: 105). See Modleski's analysis of the "ambivalence towards femininity" played out in a woman's function "as both edible commodity and inedible pollutant" in Alfred Hitchcock's *Frenzy* (1988: 101–14).

6. It is well known that Livy drew on other paradigms and stereotypes, literary genres, and Hellenistic historical practices; however, for my purposes, tracing the elements from diverse sources is less important than how they work within Livy's historical discourse. As Phillipides (1983: 119 n. 20) points out, "the elements taken from a prior sign system acquire a different significance when transposed into the new sign system." Following Julia Kristeva, she notes that "this process of transformation involves the destruction of the old and the formation of a new signification."

7. Ironically, the removal of Woman in both stories returns Roman "soldier males" to the conditions of their mythical *patres* Romulus and Remus, two men without a woman, not even a mother, between them (1.6.4–7.3). Quite literally, the twins try to occupy the same space at the same time and do violence to each other. Like the Romans and the Sabines, they cannot coexist without the body of woman between them, without the space and place of "not us."

8. Tales of male bodies that suffer violence and penetration focus on those who occupy the place of the son *in potestate*—sons killed by stern fathers and young men raped (often unsuccessfully) by evil army officers and magistrates (Valerius Maximus 5.8.1–5, 6.1.5, 7, 9–12); see Richlin 1983: 220–26, esp. 225–26. In effect, Roman patriarchy associates all women with sons in paternal power. Apprehension about their vulnerability to aggressive non-kin males would seem to stem from the "rightful" power that fathers (and husbands) wielded over their bodies.

7

The Domestication of Desire: Ovid's *Parva Tabella* and the Theater of Love

Molly Myerowitz

Beauty is momentary in the mind—
The fitful tracing of a portal;
But in the flesh it is immortal.
    —Wallace Stevens, "Peter Quince at the Clavier"

During the summer of 1986, I traveled to Italy for a seminar at the American Academy in Rome on Roman art in its social context.[1] Putting objects together with words as complementary expressions of social reality was a new experience for a classicist who had hitherto confined her wondering to words alone. For years my imagination had been occupied by Ovid, the poet exiled in A.D. 8 by the emperor Augustus in the most notorious case of literary censorship from antiquity. Our seminar's sober vocabulary of "decorative programs" and "realia" often seemed very remote from the deceptively insouciant sparkle of Ovid's poetry.

One day, in an experience familiar to many visitors to Pompeii, our bedraggled group of unsuspecting pedants wilting under the summer heat was ushered into a small dark room off the kitchen of the House of the Vettii by a happily leering guard. When the flashlights clicked on to the display of explicit erotica painted on the walls, apathy was no longer a problem, although equanimity was (Figure 7.1). The House of the Vettii was not a *lupanar,* a brothel (literally, a wolf den), but a private villa, richly decorated with mythological wall paintings, owned by two wealthy men (Mau 1902: 321–22, 508); the purpose of their little room near the kitchen— whether cook's bedroom (Archer 1981: 63) or *camera d'amore* for the entertainment of guests (L. Richardson 1988: 325–26)—defies conclusive explanation. In our classes on Roman wall paintings, no one had ever touched on this particular scheme for the decorative program of a Roman villa.

A week later, in the tranquil retreat of the Academy library, I came across a passage in Ovid's *Tristia* 2, one of the poet's sad songs from exile to the emperor Augustus, which seemed to speak directly to the mystery of the little room off the

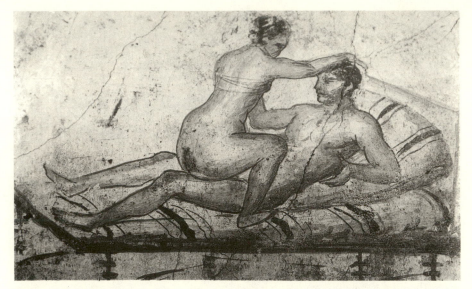

FIGURE 7.1 Erotic scene from a small room off the kitchen of the House of the Vettii, Pompeii VI.xv.1.x (Schefold 1957: 149). Grant 1975: 52 bottom; cf. second erotic scene from the House of the Vettii in Grant 1975: 52 top (=Marcadé 1965: 129). Photograph by Antonia Mulas.

kitchen in the House of the Vettii. Here Ovid argues for his condemned *Ars Amatoria,* the poem on the art of love which had enraged the emperor and helped to earn the poet banishment from Rome. Into a roll call of literary works on erotic themes of which none had been previously singled out for imperial disapproval (*Tr.* 2.361–470, 497–546), the poet inserts a brief passage on the visual arts (*Tr.* 2.521–28). In it Ovid claims that somewhere in the imperial residences (*in domibus vestris,* "in your houses") the august emperor himself housed a *parva tabella* ("small painted picture"), illustrating *concubitus varios Venerisque figuras* ("various sexual unions and positions"):

> In your homes bodies glimmer, it's known:
> artists have painted great men of old
>   and somewhere a small picture
>   portrays the diversity of sex,
>   the calculus of Venus.
> Telamonian Ajax sulks glowering ire
> barbarian Medea glares infanticide
>   and nearby a damp Venus
>   wrings her dripping hair dry
>   barely covered by the waters that bore her.

Did this passage mean that the paintings on the wall of the little room in the House of the Vettii were less of an anomaly in the upper-class houses of Augustan Rome than either the delighted guard or his discomfited charges had assumed? A glance at the critical apparatus and then at several other editions of the Ovidian text revealed yet another curiosity. The precise ownership of the houses with the *parva tabella* had been turned into a textual problem with the readings of *vestris* ("your")—found in the better manuscripts—and *nostris* ("our")—found in the inferior manuscripts—tossed back and forth by perplexed generations of editors starting with the turn of this century. They had been troubled by what seemed to them an undiplomatic *faux pas* on the part of the beleaguered poet. Could the exiled Ovid be seriously attempting to win reprieve by accusing Augustus of harboring "salacious" pictures in the imperial residence? Or, no better, could the poet in his defense (which includes a conventional declaration of the purity of his personal life) be claiming that such a collection is harbored in his own and his own friends' homes? But a choice between your place and ours could only be a decision on the lesser of two incriminating evils for Victorian editors, more certain than we are both about their own definition of "indecent" and of the applicability of this definition to Ovid's Rome.[2]

My sidetrack down the path of textual confusion wound full circle back to the pictures themselves. Ovid's contemporary witness to the presence of such pictures in upper-class Augustan homes was what counted; the dispute over the precise ownership of the *parva tabella* belonged in the history of scholarship as a footnote on the relation between mores and editing. But it seemed that whichever possessive pronoun Ovid really had written, the same questions raised by the pictures in the House of the Vettii remained. What was the place of erotic art in Augustan villas, and what were the attitudes of Roman men and women toward such representations? How frequently were such paintings found on the walls of rooms in which real men and women led their everyday lives? Were Roman definitions of pornography/obscenity/indecency as clear-cut or confused as our own? Can we recover the response that such pictures evoked in the *matronae,* the upper-class matrons, in whose villas these pictures appeared? And finally, as is always the case in engaged scholarship, a personal motive. I had left a loved one to study in Rome and keenly felt the erotic deprivation. Would looking at these ancient pictures provide a measure of consolation to the ragged imagination of a twentieth-century feminist? The search for answers led beyond the ancient sources to the ever-changing critique of the pornographic, including the provocative and creative contemporary discussions that today issue from feminist scholarship and polemic, both anti and pro.

My discussion then begins with the Roman erotic pictures themselves, familiar enough to the average classicist or connoisseur from lavishly illustrated volumes (Barré 1877; Marcadé 1965; Marini 1971; Grant 1975; Boardman and LaRocca 1975; Johns 1982); from the sites, primarily Pompeii; or, for those privileged few who have actually been admitted, from the once infamous *Gabinetto degli Oggetti Osceni* (Cabinet of Obscene Objects), now renamed, more circumspectly, the *Raccolta Pornografica* (Pornographic Collection), in the National Museum of Naples. The erotic paintings I discuss here are straightforward, almost reportorial scenes of anonymous and (almost invariably) heterosexual couples, found in brothels and "respectable" dwellings alike. Scholarly works tend to limit this category of picture to scenes of intercourse itself (often captioning them with the Greek *symplegmata,* "entwinings," or Latin *figurae veneris,* "configurations of sex"), but I shall broaden the group somewhat to include all representations depicting heterosexual pairs of anonymous mortals in various stages and styles of sexual expression where the focus, whether explicitly or by suggestion (Figure 7.2), is on sex and the various ways in which it can be accomplished. The challenges for the artist seem to be

FIGURE 7.2 Erotic scene with *cubicularius* in background from the House of L. Caecilius Iucundus. Pompeii V.i.26, Museum of Naples R.P. 110569. Marcadé 1965: 15. (Schefold 1957: 68; =Grant 1975: 156–57=Marini 1971: 95). Photograph by Antonia Mulas.

primarily what to do with all the arms and legs; the contrast between textures of cushions and bodies; the creation of moods of isolation, intimacy, domesticity, and desire.

Erotic scenes such as these represent a small fraction of the hundreds of wall paintings that have been recovered in more than two centuries of excavation primarily from Campania, the region around Naples, which was frozen in time under the great eruption of Mount Vesuvius on August 24, A.D. 79. Far fewer paintings in general, and proportionately fewer erotic scenes, survive from Rome. However, statistical proportions of extant works may be misleading; content may well have impeded the survival of erotic scenes at Rome. Certainly, even while allowing for their uneven quality, these pictures have been conspicuous by their absence from general works on Roman wall painting (e.g., Maiuri 1953; Picard 1968) and have been detached from the literary corpus of Latin love poetry to which they form a natural complement and analogue.

My purpose here is also to make a start at the latter by integrating these pictures into Ovid's *Ars Amatoria,* in such a way as might enable us to read both the pictures and the poetry within the social context of first-century Rome. I choose the *Ars Amatoria* not simply because of superficial resemblances between the poem and the art works (both deal with sex in an atmosphere of "refined sensuality," Marcadé 1965: 105–8), nor because Ovid himself called for the comparison, as we have seen. Among ancient erotic poems, the *Ars Amatoria* raises most directly and profoundly the business of culture's conceptualization and representation of sex— also the issue in reading these paintings as pornographic or erotic—even as the ultimate fate of the author and his poem (exile for the author, removal from public libraries for his poem) embodies social attitudes, both ancient and modern, toward certain ways of erotic representation. Within the frame of this discussion, I shall also raise the issue of the status of these pictures (and by implication the poetry they parallel) as "pornography" in light of contemporary feminist debate on the subject. It says a lot about the elusive and mercurial definition of pornography to recall that these graphic depictions of heterosexual intercourse, which were assumed to be unquestionably pornographic in the late eighteenth and nineteenth centuries— whose discovery, in fact, as Walter Kendrick argues, gave rise to modern definitions of pornography—seem relatively mild erotica, at the most "soft porn," to most contemporary eyes (Kendrick 1987: 1–32; cf. Johns 1982: 13–35; Grant 1975: 168–69).

Painted pictures of explicit sexual scenes are mentioned by, among others, the Augustan elegist Propertius, the Roman encyclopedist Pliny the Elder, the Roman biographer and scholar Suetonius, the Greek essayist and biographer Plutarch, the Greek author Athenaeus, and the *Priapea* (an anonymous collection of obscene poems in honor of the god Priapus), as well as by Ovid.[3] Although moderns may naturally take such paintings primarily to be a means of "sharpening desire,"[4] most ancient sources take erotic paintings to be didactic paradigms as well as aphrodisiacs, and Ovid himself may well have such pictures in mind when he alludes generally in his erotic poetry to sexual positions as *modi* or *figurae* (e.g., *Amores* 3.7.63–64, 3.14.24).

Positions are discussed in the two sections of Ovid's *Ars Amatoria* that offer explicit instruction on making love (see Parker, Chapter 5 above). But the first of these, a passage in Book 2 (*AA* 2.703–32) which tells the male lover what to do (touching, pacing) in order to bring the most pleasure to the woman and to himself, with a goal of simultaneous orgasm (*AA* 2.725–28), reserves mention of *figurae* (with specific reference to a *tabella*) only for a preliminary aside on the sexual prowess of older women (*AA* 2.679–80): "However you wish, they make love in a thousand positions [*figuras*]; no picture [*tabella*] has invented more ways [*modos*]." In other words, *figurae* seem to be "women's business." And, indeed, Ovid's most elaborate recitation of *figurae* is reserved for the close of Book 3 of the *Ars Amatoria* (771–88), a book addressed to women:

"Know thyself": your body should determine your positions [*modos*].
 no single pose [*figura*] suits [*decet*] all women.

A woman with a pretty face should lie on her back,
  women with nice backs should be seen [*spectentur*] from behind.
Milanion bore Atalanta's legs on his shoulders: 775
  good legs should be taken in this pose
A small woman should ride astride; Andromache
  was too tall ever to ride on Hector's horse.
Kneel on the covers, bend the neck back a bit:
  good for a long-waisted attractive woman.   780
If her thighs are youthful and her breasts perfect,
  have the man stand, let her sprawl aslant on the bed.
Don't be ashamed to undo your hair—like the Phylleian mother—
  bend back your neck, let your hair pour down.
You, too, if childbirth has marked your stomach,   785
  like the swift Parthian, take your horse turned around.
A thousand modes [*modi*] of lovemaking exist; simple and easiest:
  for the woman to lie half-reclined on her right side.⁵

In the *Ars Amatoria, figurae* are primarily a female concern because they offer women a means to manipulate their own bodies in order to make themselves attractive to men. As in all of Book 3, the female here is encouraged to look upon her body as *materia,* the raw material for the operation of art (Myerowitz 1985: 104–28). In this work—which is entirely concerned with "appearance" rather than "reality," objectivity rather than subjectivity—women are told to select sexual positions not with an eye to what *feels* best but to what *looks* best, as underlined by the programmatic word *spectentur* (774). The self-knowledge of the opening line (a sly echo of the Socratic dictum) is the woman's knowledge of her own body as an object for her art. The principle that informs her art is decorum (appropriateness): suit *figura* to *materia* (Myerowitz 1985: 129–49). The woman, of course, is told to arrange herself for a male spectator; that is, she is told to objectify her own body and see herself through masculine eyes. Men, in the *Ars,* are remarkably absent from decisions on the choice of *figurae;* women are taught to seize the initiative and use it to their advantage. Only in the *Remedia Amoris,* a kind of codicil to the *Ars Amatoria,* filled with good advice (to men) on how to disengage from an unhappy love affair, are men encouraged to take the lead (*Remedia Amoris* 407–8): "and make love in a position [*figura*] which you think is least helpful for sex and which least becomes [*decere*]." Here, the male's refusal to allow his partner to appear at her best despoils the female of her edge in the game of love. That women are assumed to be more concerned with how they appear than how they feel, and are better at this self-objectification than men are, is consistent with Ovid's view of women throughout the *Ars* as being better artists since they are able to work on their own bodies as *materia,* in addition to the *materia* of their men. (Book 3 spends more time teaching women to manipulate themselves than their male love objects.) That is to say that the price paid in subjectivity—which makes this passage sexist, even pornographic, by the criteria of much feminist criticism—would earn women, as a group, higher marks than their male counterparts from Ovid's *praeceptor,* who counsels self-objectification at every possible opportunity *and* to both sexes.
Ovid's enumeration of sexual *figurae* points to two branches of the tradition of

paintings of explicit sexual scenes: generic scenes of anonymous couples in sexual poses, and representations of famous mythological pairs (both hetero- and homosexual), which have literary precedents as early as Homer's depiction of Aphrodite and Ares caught in their bed of adultery by an irate Hephaestus (*Odyssey* 8.266–366). Although this latter type of explicit sexual representation was essentially satiric (Brendel 1970: 44 n. 47), it could be put to didactic use as well. No exemplars survive, but Ovid may be alluding to well-known paintings in his references to Milanion and Atalanta (above), Hector and Andromache (above; cf. *AA* 2.709–10; cf. Martial 11.104.14), and Briseis and Achilles (*AA* 2.711–14; cf. Martial 11.43.9)—as if they would be familiar to his cultivated audience of first-century Roman aristocrats. At the same time, they provide yet another opportunity for the humor of incongruity which pervades the *Ars* by setting gods and heroes in all-too-mortal situations (see Richlin 1983: 156–58). The Roman comic poet Plautus (*Menaechmi* 143–44) mentions a wall painting of the rape of Ganymede by Jupiter, and of Adonis by Venus; the playwright Terence refers to what sounds like a sexual representation of Jupiter impregnating Danaë (*Eunuchus* 583–85). And Suetonius refers to both types of picture in his famous passage (*Tiberius* 43–44) on the decorative scheme of the bedroom of the emperor Tiberius at his Capri retreat: the room held Parrhasius's probably obscene "Archigallus" (the title refers to the chief eunuch-priest of Cybele; Pliny *HN* 35.70, with Jex-Blake 1896 *ad loc.*); lascivious *tabellae* (apparently, generic pictures); and an expensive and famous erotic *tabella* by Parrhasius depicting Atalanta and Meleager in a very unheroic pose.[6]

Most of the written sources on these pictures date from the first century B.C. through the early second century A.D. However, the artistic tradition of erotic *tabellae* in which the Romans apparently found their inspiration is said to go back to early Hellenistic times (fourth century B.C.) and is associated specifically with the name of Parrhasius and, indirectly—perhaps misleadingly—with Pausias of Sicyon, an encaustic painter; Nicophanes of Sicyon, a pupil of Pausias; and Aristeides of Thebes, a contemporary of the famous Apelles.[7]

Parrhasius of Ephesus (fl. 420–390 B.C.) was highly praised for his draftsmanship (Pliny *HN* 35.65, 67–70; Quintilian *Institutio oratoria* 12.10.5; Xenophon *Memorabilia* 3.10; cf. Propertius 3.9.12) but criticized for his luxurious life and for arrogance supposedly unbecoming an artist (Pliny *HN* 35.71–72; Athenaeus *Deipnosophistae* 12.543c–f, 15.687b; Aelian *Variae historiae* 9.11; Rumpf 1951). He is the earliest easel painter known to have painted sexual pictures: "He also painted little pictures [*tabellis*] of sex [*libidines*], refreshing himself by this kind of wanton humor" (Pliny *HN* 35.72). In addition, he was associated with sexually explicit mythological burlesques, such as the infamous Meleager-Atalanta scene (Suetonius, *Tiberius* 44).

Athenaeus (for whom see Henry, Chapter 12 in this volume) groups Aristeides, Pausias, and Nicophanes together (*Deipnosophistae* 13.567b). He characterizes them as *pornographoi,* a word that ought to mean painters of *pornai,* whores. And indeed Pausias painted his mistress Glykera, possibly a hetaira by the sound of her name ("Sweetie"), although tradition has it that she was the inventor of flower wreaths (Pliny *HN* 35.125, cf. 21.4); Aristeides painted Leontion, pupil and friend of Epicurus and mistress of the philosopher's favorite pupil Metrodorus (Pliny *HN*

35.99; Athenaeus *Deipnosophistae* 13.588b). Was she a prostitute? Cicero calls her a *meretricula* ("little whore") while praising the style of her critique of Theophrastus (*Nat. D.* 1.93). The "pornographic" tradition persists at Rome with the story of the painter Arellius, who lived close to the time of Augustus and painted goddesses to resemble his (many) mistresses who were *scorta,* prostitutes (Pliny *HN* 35.119); Plutarch also reports (*Pompey* 2.4) that the courtesan Flora, former mistress of Pompey, was so beautiful that when Caecilius Metellus was decorating the temple of the Dioscuri with statues and paintings, he also set up a painted portrait of her.

This tradition of literal "pornography"—"whore depiction"—in painting thus parallels a tradition of stories about famous hetairai, popular in the Hellenistic age, such as Xenophon's account of a flirtatious encounter of Socrates with the hetaira Theodote (*Memorabilia* 3.11), the work of the grammarian Aristophanes of Byzantium on 135 Athenian hetairai (Athenaeus *Deipnosophistae* 13.567a; 583d, f), or the story of Epicurus's infatuation with the witty Leontion.[8] There is nothing particularly sexual about these literary and artistic works except for the fact that they are, as the name suggests, supposed to be representations of prostitutes, whose work is sex. (The issue of whether artists used these women as models because they were prostitutes, or whether these women were considered prostitutes because they posed as artist's models opens an interesting line of inquiry.) Whether Athenaeus's *pornographoi*—Aristeides, Nicophanes, and Pausias—ever painted *libidines,* like Parrhasius, must remain an unanswered question.

Scenes of sex are, of course, by no means inconspicuous in Greek sympotic pottery from the late archaic and early classical periods (530–470 B.C.). But when, after a hiatus of some seventy years, erotic representations come back into vogue, the pictures look different (see Sutton, Chapter 1 above). The Hellenistic representations of sex differ from the earlier traditions, as Brendel has pointed out (1970: 42–43), in their iconography: the couple is invariably heterosexual and presumed alone; much attention is paid to the bourgeois "comforts of life" (e.g., pillows, bedding, etc.). The erotic ambience is one of domesticity and middle-class romance, rather than the group orgy depicted on sympotic pottery, with its hetairai and aristocratic young men. The province of erotica shifts to other types of vases, gems, mirror covers, and easel pictures, abandoning the confines of ware destined for the all-male symposium. It is from this new Hellenistic context that Roman painters took the inspiration and designs for their erotic *tabellae.*

Visual evidence for erotic *tabellae* is, of course, most abundant from Pompeii, but there is no reason to assume Pompeii to have been an erotic *hapax legomenon.* As the historian Michael Grant remarks: "If we had even a fraction as many paintings, sculptures, and graffiti from other towns as have survived from Pompeii and Herculaneum, they would probably tell a not altogether different story" (Grant 1975: 69). Indeed, much finer versions of this type of picture (Figures 7.3, 7.4), wonderfully evocative of Augustan erotic poetry with its twilight haze of Greek and Roman (one rare signed exemplar bears the Greek name of Seleukos), come from the remains of the Villa della Farnesina in Rome. The paintings are housed in the Museo delle Terme—for years notoriously inaccessible to viewers—but are newly available in reproduction (Bragantini and de Vos 1982). The villa itself is thought to

FIGURE 7.3 Lovers in bed with attendant *cubicularii,* from a *pinax* with shutters on the left wall of *cubiculum* B of the Villa della Farnesina. Bragantini and de Vos 1982: 145, Tav. 40, Inv. 1128, Rome, Museo delle Terme. The same scene appears in a mosaic design, probably of later date, now in the Kunsthistorisches Museum of Vienna, illustrated in Curtius 1929: 101, pl. 69.

have been decorated after 20 B.C., when it served as residence for Julia, daughter of Augustus, and her second husband, Agrippa (Bragantini and de Vos 1982: 23). The wall paintings from the villa brilliantly limn erotic *Peitho* (Persuasion), directed at the woman and presumably necessary in the case of the dynastic marriage of the nineteen-year-old Julia to the middle-aged Agrippa (Suetonius *Augustus* 63). They differ from most of the Pompeian exemplars in the fineness of their execution far more than they do in their content, reflecting the sophisticated taste of the villa's owners (Maiuri 1953: 28–31) and bearing comparison only to the Pompeian paint-ing from the house of the rich banker and auctioneer L. Caecilius Iucundus (Figure 7.2).

Explicit erotic scenes are also conspicuous on Arretine pottery (Figure 7.5), mass-produced red ware from the town of Arezzo popular on the tables of the Augustan upper classes (Johns 1982: 124–25, figs. 101, 102, pl. 30; Boardman and LaRocca 1975: 164–67). The designs produced by the workshop of Marcus Peren-nius begin in about 30 B.C. to offer a variety of serial generic sexual scenes at a strikingly high level of artistic execution which in some ways recalls Athenian sympotic pottery and which has been thought to reflect the retrospective "classiciz-ing" spirit of the Augustan age, although the "stock sexual poses" appear to have drawn on the same Hellenistic sources as the *tabellae* and wall paintings (Brendel 1970: 57–60).

FIGURE 7.4 Woman embracing a man in bed with *cubicularius* visible, from *cubiculum* D of the Villa della Farnesina. Bragantini and de Vos 1982: 198, Tav. 86, Inv. 1188, Rome, Museo delle Terme.

FIGURE 7.5 Arretine bowl mold. 40–20 B.C. Berlin, Antikenmuseum. Boardman and LaRocca 1975: 166 bottom. Courtesy of Antikenmuseum, Berlin.

It is helpful in thinking about these representations to go beyond content to consider the questions of their location and intended audience. These pictures are not exclusively brothel decor, as has often been assumed (e.g., Brendel 1970: 61). Michael Grant notes that "many [erotic paintings] have been found not only in brothels but also in the bedrooms of private houses, as if they were private collections of erotic art" (Grant 1975: 154). Most of the pictures reproduced here were found in private houses, and I can detect little difference in content between exemplars from brothels and those from private dwellings that is not a function of the level of artistic execution, which in turn depends on the taste and wealth of the patrons. Brothel and mansion often seem to have drawn their designs from common patterns. Compare, for example, Figure 7.6 from the wall of a brothel in Pompeii and Figure 7.7 from the so-called House of the Centenary, a vast private dwelling extensively remodeled and inhabited by a rich magistrate during the last period of Pompeii (L. Richardson 1988: 126–27). Unfortunately, the provenance of many scenes of *figurae veneris* is unknown or unpublished; the paintings, removed hastily from the sites, are now identified only by a number in the *Raccolta Pornografica*. However, the (scanty) literary and archaeological evidence points to the *cubiculum*, usually a bedroom, as the favored locale for the paintings in villas, either as murals painted directly on the walls or as small portable painted pictures (*tabellae*).[9] Whether or not Roman couples actually shared a common bedroom, these pictures certainly belong not to a male sympotic provenance but rather to an integrated domestic world: the Roman *domus*.[10] Their audience included Roman married women, who, as both the first-century B.C. biographer Cornelius Nepos (*Praefatio* 6–7) and the Augustan architect Vitruvius (*De Architectura* 6.7.4–5) inform us, not

FIGURE 7.6 Erotic fresco from a brothel at Pompeii. Grant 1975: 33 top. Photograph by Antonia Mulas.

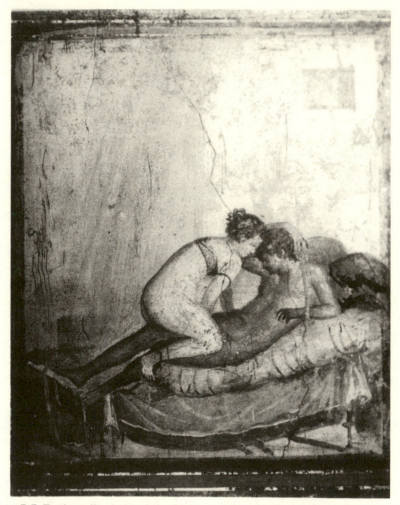

FIGURE 7.7 Erotic wall painting from the House of the Centenary. Pompeii IX.viii.3/6 (Schefold 1957: 280, room 43). Grant 1975: 36 (=Marcadé 1965: 79 = Johns 1982: pl. 2). The room also contains a second *figura veneris* (Marcadé 1965: 126) and a Hercules with amoretti (Marcadé 1965: 7). Photograph by Antonia Mulas.

only shared living quarters with men but participated with men in mixed social occasions. Furthermore, many of the stock scenes on these pictures, including those from *lupanaria*, turn up repeatedly on items intended for daily domestic use, objects that would be in everybody's hands (Brendel 1970: 47): pottery, gems, lamps, and, most noteworthy, mirrors, intended exclusively for feminine use (Johns 1982: 117). Compare, for example, the scenes in Figure 7.8 (a painting from a Pompeian brothel), 7.5 (an Arretine bowl mold) and 7.9 (a lamp from Herculaneum), which are very similar in design. Thus, the erotic scenes in the paintings on the walls of the Roman villa are but one expression of the extent to which desire had become feminized and domesticated in first-century Rome.

FIGURE 7.8 Erotic wall painting from a brothel at Pompeii. Marcadé 1965: 71. Courtesy Les Editions Nagel, Geneva.

Our curious passage from Ovid's *Tristia* 2 provides the most specific contemporary written witness for location and spectators. Whichever house Ovid specified— his own or the emperor's—the passage testifies to the presence of erotic *tabellae* in Augustan homes. Pictures such as these existed in upper-class Roman villas, but did the Romans view them in the same way as had nineteenth-century editors of Ovid? The *Tristia* passage suggests that such pictures were no more or less incriminating in the context of Augustan Rome than were the dice games, mime shows, and other less than exalted pursuits enjoyed by Augustus and his friends (Suetonius *Augustus* 70–71; Plutarch *Antonius* 33.3; *Moralia* 319f–320a); certainly no more or less "pornographic" than the *Ars Amatoria,* which in itself was not sufficient to earn Ovid immediate punishment when the poem first appeared. To charge a political opponent with harboring such pictures (or dicing or putting on mime shows) may have been as conventional a thrust as to parry with poetic disclaimers, such as Ovid's, that though his page may be lascivious, his personal life is pure.[11] Ovid in Tomis had learned the harsh realities of politics; he clearly wanted reprieve. His mention of the erotic pictures merely points to a gap between Augustan public ideology and personal practice (note the biographer Suetonius's portrait of the emperor as a homespun lecher)—a political chasm persisting through our own times. Ovid defends his *Ars* by comparing it to games where great men fritter away their time and money (*Tr.* 2.471–96); mimes where defenders of the family laugh at adultery (*Tr.* 2.497–516); and sexually explicit pictures that hang in the same house with the revered images of Roman ancestors and icons of world conquest—all trivial, but licit, for men wearied by the burdens of power. But what of women, unburdened by the cares of state? The *Ars* was not for married women (*Tr.* 2.237–

FIGURE 7.9 Erotic scene on a lamp of brown-painted terra cotta, dating from the first half of the first century A.D., found at Pompeii. Museum of Naples, R.P. 109412. Grant 1975: 107 top right (=Marini 1971: 19). Photograph by Antonia Mulas.

52), the poet counters, and besides no one pure of heart was ever corrupted by a book (*Tr.* 2.253–76). It almost works. However, unlike the *Ars,* which, it could be claimed, might not fall into the hands of *matronae,* explicit erotic art was part of the everyday experience of those same *matronae.*

This difference raises the interesting, if moot, question of the response of women to such pictures. Impassivity might be the ideologically proper Augustan reaction for *matronae,* as evidenced by the second-century historian Dio Cassius's anecdote about Livia, wife of Augustus. Once when some men were about to be put to death for having met her while they were naked, she saved their lives with the claim that "to chaste women such [naked] men are no whit different from statues" (Dio Cassius *Historiae Romanae* 58.2.4). Dio's anecdote enunciates an idealized Roman model for matronly behavior. Thus, Ovid defends himself in *Tristia* 2.309–

14 with the argument that "stern-browed matrons" often see naked women standing ready for every type of sex and Vestal Virgins see whores' bodies for sale (i.e., the conduct of matrons is expected to be on a par with that of Vestal Virgins), and yet their master goes unpunished (Ovid is here to his book as pimp is to whores). Proper women are expected to turn a blind eye, and certainly to distance themselves from possibly salacious vistas. Caveats such as these may attract even while they repel, and are often intended to do so (Richlin 1983: 11–13). As is the usual case in such issues, reality goes unrecorded. But it should be recalled that this same Livia is described as the ideologically proper "one-man woman" (the famous *unico gaudens mulier marito* of *Odes* 3.14.5) by her contemporary, the poet Horace, although in reality she had married Augustus while pregnant with a son, the future emperor Tiberius, from her first husband (Suetonius *Augustus* 62.2). It should also be noted that this same poem begins by calling the people to a public celebration of Augustus's return from his Spanish campaign in 24 B.C., but concludes with a summons to a private celebration featuring wine and Neaera of the lovely hair, dulcet voice, and unquestionably loose morals. Which half is fictive, which is real? Or are both parts of the poem as real as they are fictive, reflecting a real chasm between obverse mirror images of reality?[12]

It is probably no accident that our most explicit Augustan source on these paintings should be Ovid, himself exiled for a book that Augustus claimed was harmful to public sexual morality (*Tr.* 2.345–46; *Epistulae ex Ponto* 3.3.57–58), thus anticipating some modern definitions of pornography. Augustus had objected to the *Ars Amatoria* on social grounds, claiming that it undermined the institution of marriage—which at the time he was trying to promote by public policy.[13] It has even been suggested that Augustus's action against Ovid was inspired by Platonic views on the relation of artistic representation to education in the ideal society (Hammond 1958), a curiously modern-sounding precursor of the arguments for censorship of some antiporn activists who feel pornography writes the script for rape, although Augustus was worried about promiscuity in married women rather than in men (Horace *Odes* 3.6). However, even more curious is the coincidence between the nature of that banned book and these *tabellae*. For Ovid's *Ars Amatoria,* by virtue of the poet's transformation of the material of subjective love elegy into the didactic form, accomplished in words what these pictures do in images.

A generic scene which makes its way onto the back of a Roman mirror from Flavian times and is now in the Capitoline Museum in Rome (Figure 7.10) suggests a way of reading such pictures which most clearly integrates them into Ovid's own *Ars.* The design, which is a stereotypical scene of an aristocratic Roman couple (the woman is heavily jeweled and elaborately coiffed), clearly depicts among the conventional domestic appurtenances of the room (including a puppy and a mouse) a *tabella* of lovers hanging on the wall above the couple, themselves shown making love. This scene of a picture within a picture is notable for its absence from earlier but otherwise analogous Hellenistic scenes on mirror covers, such as a widely reproduced mid-fourth-century B.C. bronze mirror cover (Marcadé 1962: 130 = Boardman and LaRocca 1975: 134 = Johns 1982: 135, fig. 112), which has been linked to the "pornographers" Pausias and Parrhasius (Boardman and LaRocca 1975: 133–34). The picture within a picture is subsequently retained, I think signifi-

FIGURE 7.10 Scene of two lovers on a bed with domestic details including an erotic *tabella* on the wall above the lovers, from a bronze mirror cover from the first century A.D. Rome, Capitoline Museum. Johns 1982: pl. 35 (=Johns 1982: 116 = Boardman and LaRocca 1975: 162–63). Courtesy of the Capitoline Museum, Rome.

cantly, as illustrated by some later (second-to-third-century A.D.) fragments of pottery medallions from Roman Gaul, and is perhaps visible in some of the Pompeian pictures themselves.[14]

The Flavian representation answers one question and raises another, more important one. First, it demonstrates the conventionality of erotic *tabellae* as domestic decor in aristocratic Roman *cubicula*. Second, it raises the issue of the "mirror effect," the fact that Romans saw as appropriate decor for their walls scenes that imitate, qualify, and even magnify the real life activity of the self within the room; the *trompe l'oeil* effect, so prevalent in garden rooms, in which the bird on the wall parallels, mirrors, and qualifies the living bird in the garden while always keeping the viewer in the center (e.g., Maiuri 1953: 125, from a recently discovered house in Pompeii, II.vi.3). Do such scenes imply art imitating life or life imitating art, or perhaps purposely confound the lines between the poles of art and life? This is precisely the issue raised by Ovid's didactic poem on love. Such scenes must be the natural outgrowth of the Roman insistence on decorum taken in its widest sense, to mean that art must imitate or conform to nature, an ideal of harmony and sameness rather than dissonance and otherness, which E. H. Gombrich has described as the passage from making to matching (1969: 93–145). But from the "matching" comes a different kind of "making." Art of this type serves as a mirror, affecting the viewer's grasp of himself as the mirror affects the formation of the child's ego in what Lacan has called the mirror stage. The child once glimpsing himself in the mirror immediately responds with "a series of gestures in which he experiences in *play* [my emphasis] the relation between the movements assumed in the image and the reflected environment, and between this virtual complex and the reality it reduplicates—the child's own body, and the persons and things, around him" (Lacan 1977: 1). Even while prefiguring the possibility of alienation, the world is recreated on walls of rooms with the self at its center; and this artifact ultimately yields a highly contextualized, constructed, artificial, and theatrical reflection of the self.

This idea of decorum pervades Augustan aesthetics; it can be seen applied to poetry in Horace's *Ars Poetica,* to love in Ovid's *Ars Amatoria* (Myerowitz 1985: 129–49, on Horace and Ovid), and to architecture and painting by Vitruvius in his *De Architectura.* The concept not only implies the appropriateness of the parts to the whole but of the whole to the context, art to nature (Vitruvius 7.5.1–7). When applied to room decoration and paintings on the walls of rooms, decorum can be seen in the custom of decorating walks with landscapes, interiors with construction material (Vitruvius 5.1–2), wrestling and anointing rooms with portraits of athletes (Pliny *HN* 35.5), "garden rooms" with garden scenes, libraries with busts of philosophers (Pliny *HN* 35.9–11), the *atrium* with masks and busts of ancestors that anchor the persona of the inhabitant within the public traditions of his family (Polybius 6.53; Pliny *HN* 35.6–7), and perhaps even bedrooms with portraits of Epicurus (Pliny *HN* 35.5), when the bedroom is seen as a retreat from public activity and the place for Epicurean *ataraxia* (calm detachment). The true subject of all of these representations is the self in its various public and private roles, a self that art serves to contextualize and enlarge. When Pliny (*HN* 35.4) is disturbed by the substitution of heads on statues or the vagueness of outlines on portrait shields and the custom of buying portraits of total strangers in a time when "the display of material is preferred universally to self-recognition," it is because the idea of art as the representation of others unrelated to the self is not congenial to the Romans. Pliny (*HN* 35.22–23), for example, records the custom of triumphant generals exhibiting paintings of their own victories publicly from as early as the third century B.C. For the Romans, self-objectification seems to be a proper, even desirable role for art, perhaps because, in the Roman world, art still is genuinely powerful.

Representation does not simply reflect, enlarge, and/or contextualize the self, but art also still retains its primitive power, bordering on magic, to efface the self. This "flip side" of the power of art is seen in the report of the *damnatio memoriae* which took place after the death of the hated emperor Domitian in 96 A.D. All statues of the emperor were ordered effaced or destroyed as if to efface retroactively the persona of the detested ruler (Suetonius *Domitian* 23). According to Procopius (*Anecdota* 8.18–21), Domitian's dismembered body was pieced together by his wife Domitia to give the sculptor a model for a posthumous statue! In Heliodorus's *Aethiopica*, a 3rd-century A.D. Greek romance, a picture of a white woman on the wall of the bedroom is responsible for the conception of a white child by a black couple (*Aethiopica* 4.8). These stories, however fantastic, reveal much about the ancient notion of the relationship of the self to the representation of the self, life to art, subject to object. Art creates, kills, and can even resurrect the objectified self.

Thus far, scholarly speculation regarding the role of erotic pictures in ancient Rome has been limited to passing remarks on titillation or an aesthetic of pleasure; elements of both must indeed be present (Marcadé 1965: 105–8; Grant 1975: 154; Croisille 1982: 259; Klinger 1983: 58). Schefold's (1972: 65–66) attempt to give a religious interpretation to scenes such as those on the wall of the little room in the House of the Vettii—as popular expressions of attitudes toward love that are more seriously expressed in mythological scenes—fails to convince. Only Otto Brendel has offered a theoretical model that can be taken further to explain these pictures within their domestic context, although Brendel himself has not taken a domestic context into account. He suggests (1970: 62–69) a quasi-didactic function characteristic of serial iconographies (from which he proposes these representations to have been taken), in which pictures are meant to be seen as part of a series and serve as the visual analogues of an implied accompanying didactic text. In at least one crudely painted Pompeian exemplar, a text is actually present: *lente impelle*, "push in slowly." Its nice elision and Horatian echo (*lente festina*) might prove its saving grace for litterateurs.[15] In other words, the paintings of the *figurae veneris* were originally copied from an illustrated handbook on sexual positions, which Brendel assumes to be of Alexandrian-Egyptian origin. The Hellenistic vogue for didactic is as well documented as the native Roman taste for it (Effe 1977; Pöhlmann 1973). The vogue seems to culminate in Rome at the turn of the first century, and Ovid himself (*Tr.* 2.471–96, with Owen and Luck *ad loc.*) offers a list of didactic trivia poems by his contemporaries. Of erotic didactics or sex handbooks enumerating *figurae* of sexual intercourse, we know less, but traces of evidence are extant. The names of Elephantis and Philaenis, supposedly celebrated courtesans, keep cropping up as the most famous authors of such works, and women traditionally seem to be associated with this type of knowledge, a fact thought-provoking in itself (see Parker, Chapter 5 in this volume). Ovid's own *Ars* may trace its inspiration to one of these lost poems, however different the final product in conception and scope (Cataudella 1973, 1974; Kenney 1982: 121; Myerowitz 1985: 196 n. 65). Whatever the source—if there be any single source—for Ovid's *Ars* or the pictures, the *Ars* enables us to understand these Roman pictures better by compelling us to consider more deeply the implications of didactic on the way we think about ourselves.

Not only does didactic, more insistently than any other form of literary representation, mean that we must objectify ourselves, splitting ourselves into the role of both student and teacher as one part of us strives to follow the instruction that the other part assimilates and implements, but there is always a self-evident and necessary split *within* every didactic poem, since by definition a teacher is incomplete without a student. Within the context of every didactic poem, the presence not only of a *praeceptor* but also of a student must be assumed, even as the picture pictured on the wall within the context of lovers pictured in their bed visually represents that split *within* the single artistic representation. The external context, the invisible viewer, inhabitant of the bedroom, reader of the poem, internalizes the split represented in the work of art and inevitably experiences the schism within his or her self. The subject, whether it be the poet/painter, the text/picture, or the reader/viewer, is split into subject and object. Thus, didactic eliminates even the possibility of a pose of complete subjectivity (generally assumed in Roman love elegy). The audience is pulled into the picture or the poem and lives out the split it dramatizes and represents, not simply imitating art but experiencing it.

Didactic shatters the illusions of unity, harmony, and sameness—the conceits of decorum—imposing the alienation prefigured by a glimpse of the self in the mirror, in much the same way that in Greek myth the baby Dionysus after seeing his own reflection in a mirror experienced dismemberment by the Titans, or that Narcissus perished of the split between subject and object occasioned by his own image reflected in a pool of clear water. Paradoxically, the splitting engendered by didactic heals the breach between life and art, demanding *metamorphosis,* a fluid interaction between reality and representation, what is and what seems to be, a process of dispersion and reintegration which requires, as Vernant puts it, "that one travel in reverse the path of the mirror" (Vernant 1990: 476).

The model I propose for reading these paintings, then, is the model of *reflection* in which art becomes not simply a prism through which experience is filtered to be analyzed and understood *retro-spectively,* but a mirror that at every stage demands our attention, forcing us to objectify our activity, to think about what we are doing even as we do it, always with an eye to the way we appear. The mirror invites us to play against it, self-consciously, forcing us to be conscious of the self and at the same time alienated from the self, making a statement both metaphoric and metonymic, as we simultaneously perceive both identity and difference. One extreme case of this mirror effect is, of course, making love in front of a mirror or by a book, which, as anyone who has tried it can attest, is one sure way to lose subjectivity in the most subjective of activities. Students of the interiors of Augustan homes have long remarked the theatricality of these interiors (e.g., Picard 1968: 96; Allroggen-Bedel 1974)—possibly a Hellenistic heritage (Pollitt 1986: 4–7)—the publicness of even presumably private space (e.g., Thébert 1987: 321). Erotic *tabellae* within the domestic interiors of Roman villas are yet another expression, perhaps the most dramatic to modern sensibilities (as is the *Ars* itself), of the theatricality felt not only in Augustan homes but in the literature and social life of the period: life lived, to borrow Paul Veyne's analogy, in a puppet theater (Veyne 1987: 316). Like the *Ars Amatoria* itself, which transformed the subjectivity of passion into the objectivity of art, pictures of people making love confronting real-life lovers refract life against art and blur any clear-cut division between the two. Subjective experience is qualitatively objectified, magnified, and contextualized by these pictures which, because of their location, go beyond titillation, celebration, or didacticism in a limited sense to turn the bed into a stage and the lovers inexorably into self-conscious actors.

Mirrors themselves were known to have been used in the same context for exceptionally direct and jarring effects. The first-century philosopher Seneca the Younger, in an aside on mirrors, devotes a lengthy moralizing passage of his work on natural phenomena (*QNat.* 1.16.1–8) to the sexual antics of Hostius Quadra. This wealthy Roman (murdered, Augustus said deservedly, by his own slaves) used special mirrors not simply to reflect his own sexuality, "so that he might be the spectator of his own debaucheries" (*QNat.* 1.16.3), but literally to make it larger than life. By amending nature with the help of art, Hostius Quadra enables himself in full consciousness to "feast on a lie" (*QNat.* 1.16.9). Seneca rails against the man's perversions, but Hostius's quoted explanation for his use of mirrors—"so that nobody thinks that I don't know what I am doing" (*QNat.* 1.16.7)—parallels almost parodically the philosopher's own explanation for the reason for the invention of mirrors: "mirrors were invented so that man might know himself" (*QNat.* 1.17.4). In the Stoic philosopher's view, it is precisely the kind of self-knowledge that a mirror enables that leads to artistic and technological culture—for better or, as is usually the case with Seneca (to whom culture generally signifies moral decline), for worse (Lovejoy and Boas 1935: 260–86). Hostius's use of trick mirrors to reflect an aggrandized sexual self has its echo in Suetonius's (probably spurious) anecdote of the poet Horace's mirrors in the bedroom to reflect sex with prostitutes back to himself, "so that wherever he looked, there the image of copulation was returned to him" (Suetonius *Horatii Vita* ad fin., Roth 1893: 298; see Rostagni 1944: 19–20). Art itself is also seen as a kind of trick mirror for an enlarged self in the story of the emperor Nero's colossal self-portrait (120 feet high) which was ominously struck by lightning and burned (Pliny *HN* 35.51; cf. Suetonius *Nero* 31). So, too, Trimalchio's cycle of frescoes glorifying and enlarging his own upstart career is described for comic effect by Petronius (*Satyricon* 29).

In a later age, the Christian convert Clement of Alexandria (born ca. A.D. 150) rails against the pagans who "adorn their chambers with painted tablets hung on high . . . regarding licentiousness as piety; and while lying upon the bed, while still in the midst of their own embraces . . . fix their gaze upon that naked Aphrodite who lies bound in her adultery" (*Protreptikos* iv.53P, trans. Butterworth 1919: 137–39). Not only do the so-called mythological travesties draw the theologian's fire, but also those generic depictions of sexual positions to which Ovid alluded, first in his *Ars Amatoria* and later in *Tristia* 2: "You dedicate these monuments of shamelessness in your homes, and are as eager to procure paintings of the postures of Philaenis as of the labours of Heracles" (*Protreptikos* iv.53P, trans. Butterworth 1919: 139; Parker's text *N,* Chapter 5 above).

Clement is afraid of these pictures not merely because of their sexual content but because of his identification with the Judeo-Christian tradition that condemns all image making, ostensibly because the image substitutes a man-made divinity for a transcendent god, but more profoundly because in the process of making the image, man does not simply create an alternative object of worship but himself becomes the creator, and thus the true god (*Protreptikos* iv.54P). Ovid would probably agree with Clement's understanding of the process of representation, but would not join him in condemning it: "It is expedient that there be gods and as it is expedient, let us think that they exist" (*AA* 1.637). The pagan poet condones that which the Christian theologian reproves: the transformation of man from pure object to his own subject. For Ovid it is self-evident that people do and should decide whether gods exist and under what conditions such a belief is useful. All representation of humans in image and word splits us into subject and object, making man both his own god and acolyte. The type of representation found in didactic iconography and literature dramatizes this split most forcefully. The representation of lovemaking—or of anything—in picture and word acts like Seneca's mirror in imposing the element of self-awareness on the audience's consciousness, splitting sexual activity into oscillating subject and object, transforming and irrevocably acculturating subjective instinctual activity. Generic couples in *tabellae*, like Ovid's *Ars* with its generic student lover, point up this transformation precisely because they deal with non-specific couples (whose referent can only be ourselves and in no way the "other," as in scenes of mythological lovers); and (in the case of pictures) because, by their location, they insistently follow and reflect our own activity back to ourselves. Activity is immanent in both text and pictures; transcendence is held at bay.

Erotic *tabellae* from the Augustan age may have filled needs quite different from our own, which makes it difficult to apply contemporary feminist theories of pornography without risking anachronism. In a most general way, one should recall that sex, both in the ancient world and in contemporary traditional societies, is understood by both women and men primarily as "women's business" rather than men's, bound up with the exclusively feminine natural biological processes of pregnancy and birth. No wonder handbooks of instruction on sexual lore were attributed to females, or that the myth of the prophet Teiresias, blinded for revealing the supremacy of feminine sexuality, encodes a belief that sex is mostly for women. In ancient and traditional societies, a keen, often obsessive, feminine interest in the mechanics of desire is entirely compatible with the strictest social codes of premarital chastity and postmarital fidelity, and not relegated exclusively to professional prostitutes.

When sexuality is transformed from nature to culture and enters the realm of representation and construction—as in our pictures or Ovid's *Ars Amatoria*—it moves away from the feminine and toward the masculine realm. Here again, anachronism is a pitfall to be avoided in applying contemporary feminist judgments on pornography to these Roman representations. Located within the familial realm of the *domus*, usually within a *cubiculum*, rather than between the leaves of a clandestine publication, the anonymity of a darkened cinema, or even the occasionality of a home video, these *tabellae* and wall paintings cannot have served simply for the delectation of a voyeur, assumed in feminist antiporn literature to be exclusively male (Pally 1985).[16] Nor, since they were part and parcel of a domestic context, could they represent the innocuous substitution of fantasy for reality, à la Aristotle's *katharsis*, as argued by some contemporary porn apologists (Barrowclough 1982: 33–36; Stern 1982).

It is equally difficult to view these Roman scenes, often romantic and certainly nonviolent—a fact especially remarkable in light of the infamous Roman taste for cruelty and violence (Wiseman 1985: 5–10; and see Brown, Chapter 9 in this volume)—as fantastic preludes to realistic violent enactment, i.e. as evidence for the almost Platonic stance of the "pornography is the theory, rape is the practice" argument (Meese Commission 1987: 78; Brownmiller 1980: 32–33; Diamond 1980; Bart and Jozsa 1980; Russell 1980; Morgan 1980). Roman erotic paintings may have, as argued earlier, didactic implications, but they are not a didactic text for rape, and the sexuality depicted is remarkably free of the sadism characteristic of much modern pornography. Nor in the Roman world of the early first century, in which there was greater fluidity between public (the world of others) and private (the world of ourselves) than today, could these pictures primarily have satisfied voyeuristic curiosity about the private sexuality of *others* (Barrowclough 1982: 26–36; E. Kaplan 1983: 310–11). It is the *self* that these Roman pictures, located on the walls of rooms where real-life people cohabited, force us to see.

The notion of the self represented in art leads to one most theoretically interesting application of contemporary feminist writing on pornography to these Roman representations of sexuality. This is the argument, most clearly enunciated by Susanne Kappeler, regarding the sexism inherent in all cultural representation. In her book *The Pornography of Representation,* Kappeler refers to the mirror analogy, pointing out that a lot depends on "who is holding the mirror" and "at what angle." Pornography includes all sexist representation, thus vitiating the necessity for any fine-tuned distinctions between pornography and erotica in terms of low or high art, violent or nonviolent, or hard or soft content (Kappeler 1986: 2–3). Kappeler's arguments about the relationship of representation to reality—as well as other points relevant to discussions of pornography and representation—were raised in the first century A.D. by Seneca the Elder, uncle of the philosopher and an expert on rhetoric. Seneca's *Controversia* 10.5, one of his collection of hypothetical cases debated in schools of rhetoric, deals, perhaps significantly, with Parrhasius, the supposed *primus inventor* of erotic *tabellae* (although Rumpf 1951: 2 notes similar anecdotes told of Michelangelo and Rubens). Here Parrhasius stands trial for harming the state. He had bought an Olynthian slave and had him tortured to death in order to have a model for a realistic representation of the sufferings of Prometheus. The relation of representation to reality and its potential public harm is raised by Argentarius, one of the participants in the debate, who argues that Parrhasius has tortured the viewers as well as the model, since he has not simply painted a Prometheus but has created a Prometheus (*Hoc Promethea facere est, non pingere*). "He said to the torturers: Stretch him like that, flog him like that, keep his present expression just so—or I'll make a model of *you*" (10.5.3, trans. Winterbottom 1974: 453).

Arellius Fuscus Senior, another debater (and, incidentally, Ovid's teacher, 2.2.8–9), argues for socially positive principles of representation: "Paint Prometheus—but paint him creating man, paint him distributing fire; paint him, but amid his gifts rather than amid his agonies" (10.5.7). Latro, a third participant, reiterates the issue of the morality of certain types and means of representation. Constructing an imaginary dialogue between torturer and victim, he quips: "[the slave to Parrhasius]: 'Parrhasius, I am dying.' [Parrhasius] 'Hold it like that' " (10.5.26). These positions, in a *controversia,* are for the sake of argument only; still, such arguments were made.

In an identical vein, Kappeler ("Problem 1," 5–17) argues against certain types of representation, instancing the case of a white Namibian farmer who had a black worker tortured to death while his friends took pictures of the event. The farmer was convicted *because* of the pictures, which served as evidence. Kappeler argues, however, that the torture and killing done before the camera constituted *in toto* an artistic composition, that is, that the representation itself was integral to the crime. The torture and killing were part of the representation, and thus representation does not imitate reality but creates reality. Her arguments here reproduce the points raised in the Senecan passage: that it was wrong to torture the slave for a picture; that the production of the picture was the sole reason for the torture and not just the evidence for it; that both the picture and the torture taken together and individually were crimes against the state. The Parrhasian representation—like Kappeler's Namibian case—is both the occasion and cause of the (immoral) reality.

For Kappeler all representation constructs reality in this way. So sexist representation—pornography—constructs sexist reality as much as it is shaped by it. Furthermore, all representation is sexist. The mirror of culture is angled by men for a male gaze, which does not simply reify and objectify women but carries within it a power of objectification, possession, and destruction that is lacking in the female gaze (E. Kaplan 1983: 311).

Certainly, men were holding and angling the mirrors in the Roman world, however much tradition ascribes authorship of manuals on *figurae veneris* to ignominious female courtesans and despite traditional attributions of the invention of modeling to a woman and the record of several women as artists and subjects of art.[17] Certainly, women as well as men gazed at this erotica within the domestic context, and it is just as certain that the gaze of the Roman male held a power that the female gaze did not and could not share. The differential in power, however, is not a function of the sexual representation itself but of the social context in which the image exists. Paradoxically, explicit pictures of *figurae veneris* are probably most difficult to construe *in vacuo* as evidence of sexism or lack of it. In themselves, they do not appear to be constructing a sexist reality. One can argue, as Paul Veyne does, that in these pictures "the woman was a servant, and the lover sprawled on top of her as though she were a sofa," or for the converse pose, "The woman served her lord's pleasure and, if necessary, did all the work herself. If she straddled her passive lover, it was to serve him" (Veyne 1987: 204). But such conclusions are based on evidence and intuitions that go beyond the representations themselves. Sexism—indeed, outright sadism—toward women seems more characteristic of some literary sources (e.g., some of Horace's *Epodes,* Juvenal, Martial) than of these painted pictures, for which judgments such as Veyne's seem highly subjective and predetermined. As is clear from the extant *tabellae,* there are a fixed number of poses possible for humans in sexual intercourse, determined first and foremost by human anatomy. In fact, of the twenty-five scenes I have studied, almost half show the woman "on top," for whatever it is worth. If the significance of the man on top of the woman is read to be that he treats her "like a sofa," and the significance of the woman on top of the man is that "she caters to her passive lover," then virtually no sexual pose remains that can be read as an iconography of male-female equality. Reading sexual representations this way would mean that all heterosexual relations would have to be defined as involving an inequity of power, and as such all sex between men and women would have to be seen as pornographic, as indeed has been argued by some.[18]

There is nothing in the iconography of these Roman *tabellae* to suggest sexism as opposed to sexuality. None of the representations depicts or seems to have occasioned Promethean torture. In none of these pictures is the woman frontally on display for a voyeur/spectator/owner as in the European tradition of the nude described by John Berger in *Ways of Seeing* (1972: 45–64). If anything, they seem to conform to what Berger attempts to distinguish as a sexual rather than sexist iconography: "If . . . the theme is sexual it is likely to show active sexual love as between two people, the woman as active as the man, the actions of each absorbing the other" (Berger 1972: 53). Sex requires a text/context in order to be sexist. Sexism is an act of interpretation placed upon the inherently neutral act of sex, *pace* Andrea Dworkin. This is seen most clearly in the case of rape, which transforms sex into a sexist act of violent objectification, possession, and destruction. Unless there are words or signs of intent, consent, or dissent—that is, a context and/or system of signification—there is no way to define sex as rape (Ferguson 1987). Without a context, the system of signification can be read only in the painting itself, which Barthes describes as "the connection between the picture and the language inevitably used to read it" (Barthes 1985a: 150). But there are problems not only in the reading but in the writing of such pictures. This, it seems to me, is partly occasioned by the difficulty inherent in representing active female sexuality, of finding an iconography for a sexuality that is more internal and abstract than that of the male— even as the reverse holds true for fertility, in which maternity is concrete and easily represented while paternity must be imagined and its iconography by definition must be more remote and suggestive. Indeed, perhaps one key to a nonsexist iconography for human sexuality would be the representation of fertility as part of the sexual continuum, rather than apart from it.

What we see in Roman erotic paintings in the context of domestic interiors is the reflection of a sexual reality that includes two participants and that objectifies both. These paintings serve as a stylized frame that accomplishes and underlies the transformation of the biological into the cultural, a mirror for identification and alienation. Women are sex objects in these pictures, and so are men, even as they are in the *Ars Amatoria*. Only in the process of acculturation through objectification may men and women become bedfellows, fellow game players, as indeed occurs in Ovid's *Ars,* where sexist clichés and paradigms are turned into self-conscious rules for a game that requires two self-aware players (Myerowitz 1985). There is no going back. Like Abraham at Haran, one can break the old representations, but not without creating new ones or, alternatively, leaving for a new place where all representation is forbidden. Culture alone, the shimmering play of art's mirrors, enables the possibility of recognition of the kind of mutual subjectivity that Lacan has called intersubjectivity, describing its three-term structure as (1) I see the other; (2) I see the other seeing me; (3) the other knows that I see him or her. In the *Ars Amatoria,* Ovid constructed such a relationship for love, *pace* Barthes, who argues, in his discussion of Lacan's formulation of imaginary intersubjectivity (*Seminaire* I; Barthes 1985c: 240–41), that in the lover's relationship the gaze lacks the third of these trajectories. The lover sees the beloved and sees the beloved seeing himself, but is so panicked by the other's all-powerful gaze that he cannot recognize that the other knows that he is also being seen. Perhaps this is the reason so many readers feel that Ovid's *Ars* is *not* about love. In his three-book work, Ovid insists on all three trajectories of seeing as the *sine qua non* of a cultivated love affair.

Ovid would be the first to agree with Foucault (1978a) that all human sexuality is constructed, arguing, however, that construction is not only inevitable but desirable. If the Roman gaze was primarily male, so then is its object. If anything, it is the female object, rather than the female subject, that may be elided, in these pictures where men hold the mirrors (with the remarkable exception, I think, of the paintings from the Villa della Farnesina, which seem to me—and seemed to the "ragged imagination" of my Roman summer—to represent a female object for a female subject which might speak directly to women without male mediation). From the start, it had been the Roman male *self* (usually in a political or military role) that was the subject of Roman art. For the Roman male, it was perhaps more significant and noteworthy that in his erotic *tabellae* he gazed at, objectified, and took possession of himself, as he had been doing in other types of representation all along.

There may indeed be Roman pornography—those representations that speak a language of violence rather than sex, that construct a hierarchy of objectification, that equate female masochism with female sexuality, and that in themselves offer a sexist construction of reality—but I believe we will not find such pornography in these erotic paintings from first-century Rome.

Finally, as for the *parva tabella* Ovid claimed could be found in Augustus's own residence—for the reading *vestris, "your* houses," must certainly be correct—it would be nice to be able to report that Carettoni's excavations on the Palatine (Carettoni 1983) had turned up one such painting in the austere *cubiculum* to which the emperor reputedly retired for forty years, winter and summer, scorning the extravagance of fancy villas while transforming Rome from brick to marble, or perhaps in the ruins of the *technyphion,* his famed upper-story retreat (Suetonius *Augustus* 72.2–3). So far, no such picture has surfaced. But then, this would not be the first time that Ovid held a less than flattering mirror to the emperor's preferred image, and the digging on the Palatine is not done with yet.

NOTES

1. I am grateful to Professor Eleanor W. Leach, director of the 1986 NEH seminar on "Roman Art in Its Social Context" at the American Academy in Rome, for introducing me to the vital connection between the art and literature of the Romans and for providing the forum in which the ideas for this paper could be developed and tested. I should also like to express my thanks for the help I received from Professors Mariette de Vos, Jorgen Mejer, David Thompson, and Amy Richlin.

Ancient works cited by abbreviation throughout the text and notes are *HN* = Pliny *Historia Naturalis; Tr.* = Ovid *Tristia; AA* = Ovid *Ars Amatoria; QNat.* = Seneca *Quaestiones Naturales.*

2. *Vestris:* Crispinus (Lyons 1792), Reise (Leipzig 1874), Merkel (Teubner 1881), Guthling (Leipzig 1884), Owen (Oxford 1889), Ripert (Paris 1937), Luck (Heidelberg 1967). *Nostris:* Merkel (Teubner 1889, 1902, 1904), Owen (Oxford 1915, cf. 1924), Wheeler (Loeb 1924), André (Budé 1968). Note that Merkel (1881, cf. 1889/1902/1904) and Owen (1889, cf. 1915/1924) reverse their own earlier readings of *vestris* to *nostris.*

For the manuscript tradition of the *Tristia,* see S. G. Owen's introduction to his edition and commentary of *Tristia* 2 (1924) and more fully in the introduction to his 1892 Oxford edition of the complete *Tristia. Nostris* appears in B (Laurentianus 36.33) and S (Leidensis 191 d, a 13th-century manuscript at Leiden), both of which belong to Owen's class III, and in some of Heinsius's manuscripts. The Laurentian manuscript (once Marcianus 223, M in André edition, L in Owen and Wheeler), an eleventh-century manuscript, which though defective in parts does include *Tr.* 521 and which is classed by Owen as the best manuscript, reads *vestris* according to Owen, *nostris* according to André! *Vestris* may have been meant as a synonym for *tuis* in this passage, as it is in *Tr.* 2.65; see Owen *ad loc.* for discussion; cf. *Oxford Latin Dictionary* s.v. *"vester,"* 2c.

For a statement of the editor's quandary, see Owen 1924: 271. For an example of the tortuous argumentation necessitated by framing the dilemma in this way, see the commentary of Luck 1977: 153.

3. Propertius 2.6.27–36, with Enk 1962: 106–7; *contra* L. Richardson 1976: 228; Pliny *HN* 35.72; Suetonius *Tiberius* 43–44; Plutarch *Moralia* 18B; Athenaeus *Deipnosophistae* 13.567b; *Priapea* 4 in Baehrens 1879: 59; Ovid *AA* 2.679–80, with Brandt 1902: 120; *Tr.* 2.521–24.

4. For example, in his commentary on a line from the sixth-century *Latin Anthology*—*inque modos omnes, dulcis imitata tabellas,* "for all modes, imitating sweet pictures" (Riese and Bücheler 1894: poem 429)—the great eighteenth-century Dutch classicist Pieter Burman wrote: "He means those obscene pictures [*lascivas tabellas*] such as were made according to the instruction of Elephantis and Philaenis and were kept hung from the walls near the bed so that they might whet desire [*libidinem acuerent*] from gazing at them" (Burman 1759: 633). Note that the ancient text stresses didacticism, the modern commentator desire.

5. My translation here follows the text of the Loeb second edition of the *Ars* (Mozley 1979), reading *accipienda* for *aspicienda* in line 776, *modi* for *ioci* in line 787.

6. It is tempting to reread Roman love elegy's frequent allusions to Milanion and Atalanta (e.g., Prop. 1.1; Ov. *Am.* 3.2.29–32; *Her.* 4.99–100; *AA* 2.185, 3.775; *Met.* 8.317–23, 380–81, 426–36, 10.560–707; *Ib.* 371) as subtle allusions to the infamous picture by Parrhasius (which may have substituted Meleager for Milanion); for discussion of the Milanion-Atalanta erotic tradition, see Brandt 1911: 222 and 146–47 ad *Am.* 3.2.29–30, and Brandt 1902: 196; Bartholomé 1935: 49; Reinach 1921: vol. 1, 236 n. 1. On the precise pose of the pair in Parrhasius's painting, see Hallett 1978.

7. Pausias: Pliny *HN* 35.123–27, 137, cf. 21.4; Boardman and LaRocca 1975: 133–34. Nicophanes: Pliny *HN* 35.111, 137; Plutarch *Moralia* 18B with Reinach's (1921: vol. 1, 236 n. 1) note on the emendation of "Chairephanes, a painter of lewd scenes of sexual intercourse" to "Nicophanes." Aristeides: Pliny *HN* 35.98–100; cf. 35.110.

8. On Epicurus and Leontion, see Diogenes Laertius *Lives of Eminent Philosophers* 10.4–6, 23; Alciphron *Epistle* 4.17 [2.2]; Athenaeus *Deipnosophistae* 13.588b. Anecdotal tales of hetairai abound in the pages of Athenaeus, especially Book 13, and are used by Lucian for his *Dialogues of the Courtesans.* For discussion, see Licht 1932: 329–410; Flacelière 1962: 133–61; Henry, Chapter 12 in this volume.

9. Croisille 1982: 259 n. 102 gives a partial listing of generic sexual scenes in the *Raccolta Pornografica,* but without identifying their original location. Domestic *cubicula* account for a significant proportion of identified locations for extant erotic *tabellae,* and Suetonius (*Tib.* 43–44) states that erotic pictures were placed in the *cubiculum* of Tiberius. Thus, the evidence is sufficient to place the burden of proof on those who wish to locate these pictures in brothels. Furthermore, as argued above, there is no good reason to assume that sexually explicit *figurae veneris* would be restricted to brothels because of their content when the same scenes appear on Arretine pottery, lamps, mirror backs, and gems, all of which were in daily domestic use.

10. In fact, it is difficult to determine whether husbands and wives shared a common bedroom. The narrowness of the single beds and small size of the rooms seem to argue against a conjugal bedroom, however much smaller the ancient Romans may have been than we are. Although the erotic poetic tradition (e.g., *paraclausithura*, etc.) is predicated on the woman having her own room, it cannot be decisive, because of the Greek origins and undomestic nature of the topos, for a decision on the marital *cubiculum*. Some literary sources do represent married couples as sharing a room. The first-century poet Lucan, for example, indicates that Pompey and Cornelia habitually slept together in the same bed (*Pharsalia* 5.735–815; cf. Ovid *Heroides* 13.117–20; Juvenal *Satire* 6.116–32; Lucian *Lucius or the Ass* 12). On the other hand, at the turn of the first century, Calpurnia, wife of the wealthy senator Pliny, has her own sleeping quarters (Pliny *Epistle* 7.5.1). Mau (1902: 262) notes the presence of *cubicula* with alcoves for two beds in several houses at Pompeii. Veyne (1987: 73), on the contrary, implies that husbands and wives kept separate bedrooms, each guarded by domestic servants in the same room or at the door. My own guess would be that the poor shared a room but that the rich usually did not.

11. For the erotic poet's claim that his licentious writing does not reflect his irreproachable private life, see *Tr.* 2.345–56; elsewhere in Ovid, see *Tr.* 1.9.59–60; 3.2.5–6; 4.10.65–68; *Epistulae ex Ponto* 2.7.47–50; 4.8.19–20; cf. Catullus 16.5–6; Seneca *Controversiae* 6.8.265M; Martial 1.4.8; 11.15.13; Pliny *Epistulae* 4.14.3–5; 5.3.2–7; Apuleius *Apologia* 11; Ausonius *Cento Nuptialis* 130. On the conventionality of such *apologiae*, see Richlin 1983: 2–13.

12. On the relation of literature to life in Augustan poetry, see the now classic article of J. Griffin 1976, reprinted in J. Griffin 1985: 1–31.

13. On the *Ars* and Augustus's marriage legislation, see Stroh 1979; Della Corte 1982: 552; Frank 1982: 572–78.

14. For pottery medallions with *tabellae,* see Marcadé 1965: 83, 85C. For possible *tabellae* within *tabellae* in Pompeian paintings, see Figure 7.7 and Marcadé 1965: 126, both from the House of the Centenary (IX.viii.3.43) at Pompeii.

15. The Pompeian exemplar (R.P. 27690 = Helbig 1506; reproduced in Vorberg 1932: 234; Marcadé 1965: 30; Marini 1971: 75; Grant 1975: 161) dating from ca. A.D. 70 seems to be the work of a local unskilled artist and the writing probably a graffito scratched onto the painting, but such exhortations are common on relief-decorated medallions from Gallo-Roman pottery made in the Rhone valley during the late second century A.D. (Johns 1982: 137); e.g. Johns 1982: 138, fig. 114; Marcadé 1965: 83, 84A, 88C; Vorberg 1932: 658.

16. Soble (1986) argues that pornography offers men a fantasy of power as escape not only from real political and economic powerlessness but from the reality of sexuality itself. It is doubtful that this kind of escapism was relevant to the lives of the upper-class, rich, slave-owning Roman men who inhabited villas.

17. On the invention of modeling by a female, see Pliny *HN* 35.151; and Athenagoras, *Presbeia* 17, quoted in Jex-Blake 1896: 225–27. On women painters and women as subjects of art, see Pliny *HN* 35.147–48, with Jex-Blake *ad loc.;* cf. Pliny *HN* 34.31. For ancient paintings of female artists at work, see Helbig 1868: 1443 = Naples Museum Inventory #9018, reproduced in Picard 1968: fig. 39; and Helbig 1868: 1444 = Naples Museum Inventory #9017.

18. Following this argument to its logical conclusion would mean that the only kind of sex that then might be seen without the differential in power would be sex between people of whom neither owns a phallus, "noninvasive," perhaps some kinds of lesbian sex. This extreme position has been argued by Andrea Dworkin (1987). For an attempt to argue for coital positions as signifiers of ancient and modern cultural attitudes, see Marks 1978.

8

Reading Ovid's Rapes

Amy Richlin

You are the inspiration for a poet, he seemed to say. If you think you are being
spied on, tell your parents. They will think you are silly and hysterical. They
will tell you how great art is made.

—Laurie Colwin, "A Girl Skating" (1982)

He gives kisses to the wood; still the wood shrinks from his kisses.
To which Apollo said: "But since you will not be able to be my wife,
you will surely be my tree."

—Ovid, *Metamorphoses* 1.556–58 (Apollo and Daphne)

I don't particularly want to chop up women but it seems to work.

—Brian De Palma (quoted in Pally 1984)

A woman reading Ovid faces difficulties. In the tradition of Western literature his
influence has been great, yet even in his lifetime critics found his poetry disturbing
because of the way he applied his wit to unfunny circumstances. Is his style a virtue
or a flaw? Like an audience watching a magician saw a lady in half, they have stared
to see how it was done. I would like to draw attention to the lady.

Consider Ovid's *Metamorphoses,* cast as a mythic history of the world: more
than fifty tales of rape in its fifteen books (nineteen told at some length). Compare
his *Fasti,* a verse treatment of the Roman religious calendar: ten tales of rape in six
books. These vary in their treatment; some are comic. In general, critics have
ignored them, or traced their literary origins, or said they stood for something else
or evidenced the poet's sympathy with women.

But we must ask how we are to read texts, like those of Ovid, that take pleasure
in violence—a question that challenges not only the canon of Western literature but
all representations. If the pornographic is that which converts living beings into
objects, such texts are certainly pornographic. Why is it a lady in the magician's
box? Why do we watch a pretended evisceration?

Critical Orientation

Before beginning to analyze the text, I offer some cautions and a theoretical framework.

Problems in writing: (1) The text I am writing is metapornography and partakes of the same subject-object relationship, the same "gaze," that structures its object. (2) Similarly, criticism and theory have been tools of the patriarchy and may not be useful toward subversion (see Jehlen 1981; E. Kaplan 1983: 313; Lorde 1984). (3) To write about Ovid keeps the focus on the male writers of the canon. But this does not exclude ancient women (*pace* Culham 1990): the nature of Ovid's rapes surely bears on the lives of the women who heard his poems and live(d) in the sign system that produced the canon. And one option is to do the best we can with the tools and materials at hand.

My goals are to hold up the content of some canonical texts to a political scrutiny and to suggest a theoretical model that enables escape from the trap of representation in the hierarchy.

Axioms: Content is never arbitrary or trivial; content is not an accident of a text but an essential. A text about rape may also be about something else, but it is still a text of rape. A seductive treatment is standard equipment for any fantasy; stylistic analysis does not replace content analysis and, in fact, leaves us to explain what that style is doing on that content, like a bow on a slaughterhouse.

Moreover, there is a reciprocal relationship between the content of the text and the lives of the text's consumers. Stylistic beauties serve to expedite the absorption of content by the audience, though the narrative structure directs audiences even without the stylistic adornment of high-culture texts—tragedy is to weep at, comedy is to laugh at, and so on. To resist the direction of narrative because of content is to break the rules; but such a breakdown in the perpetual motion of text and life is possible. For example, here, even in the thick of metapornography.

Otherwise my theoretical framework is fourfold:

Rereading in the Classics

As its name suggests, Classics is not wide open to the idea of a re-formation of the canon. This has been true even for feminists in the field (see analysis in Skinner 1986, 1987a, 1987b). So even recent studies of Ovid by feminists (Myerowitz 1985; Verducci 1985) have kept their eyes focused on the magician rather than the lady; others have set out to absolve the poet of his apparent sexism, concentrating on the distinction between poet and persona and the effect this has on the message of the text (Cahoon 1985; Hemker 1985).

But these readings join the magician's act as he saws away. Erased from the field of vision: the price of admission, the place of male and female onstage, the experience of the magician's assistant, the voyeurism and gaze of the audience, the motivation of the magician himself, the blood that is not really dripping from the box. In order to confront the canon and explain what is going on in Ovid's act, we need other ways of reading.

Feminism For and Against Pornography

The feminist controversy over the nature and danger (or use) of pornography contributes a basis for a political critique of texts like Ovid's. The argument against
pornography holds that the common images of women contribute to the oppression
of women (e.g., S. Griffin 1981; Lederer 1980; see Echols 1983); the argument in
favor of pornography has highlighted sadomasochism, both in fantasy and in reality,
as a valid sexual mode, and/or claimed that violent images are cathartic and/or not
harmful. The nonjudgmental stance coincides with the anthropologist's and the
classicist's yearning for objectivity. But these arguments again elide some questions. Why should sexuality and violence be so commonly connected? Represented?
Can a person have a right to be physically abused? Is violence inevitable and
uncontrollable? Do cultural or historical differences excuse anything?

Fantasy and Representation

Theories of representation, starting with the formulation of the gaze as male, trace
the link between gender and violence (esp. Berger 1972; E. Kaplan 1983; de
Lauretis 1984). Studies sometimes claim that the explicit content of a fantasy is not
its meaning. Here, as E. Ann Kaplan has noted (1983: 320), there is a danger of
losing sight of content altogether: "If certain feminist groups (i.e., Women Against
Pornography) err on the side of eliding reality with fantasy . . . , feminist [literary]
critics err on the side of seeing a world constructed only of signifiers, of losing
contact with the 'referred' world of the social formulation."

Thus, analysis of Ovid's rapes as figures of the artist's predicament dodges the
questions of why rape is the figure of choice and what its effects might be on its
audience.

Questions of complicity and origin arise in any discussion of culturewide fantasy. What of the women in the audience? Is there a female gaze? Is gaze itself
gendered, in a way separate from social gender? Whose idea is it to saw a lady in
half? Can specifically female fantasies be isolated? (This critique dates back to
Mary Wollstonecraft.) It is possible to trace historical change (see, e.g., Thurston
1987); still, within the closed system of the patriarchy (Lorde's "master's house"),
women, as a muted group (Ardener 1975), can speak audibly only in the master's
language, whether or not their speaking transmutes the language (as claimed, e.g.,
by Maclean 1987; see Elsom, Montague, and Marsh in this volume).

Yet if, with the most radical critiques, we say "Art will have to go" (Kappeler
1986), where do we go? The problem here is the gap between our ability to analyze
the problem and our ability to realize a solution.

Gender and Reading

Feminist literary criticism endeavors, in part, to come to grips with problems of
gender and reading (so also Gubar 1987). Two of its strategies—canon reformation
and appropriation—are particularly pertinent to reading Ovid.

As Teresa de Lauretis says (1984: 107), "any radical critique [entails] a rereading of the sacred texts against the passionate urging of a different question, a different practice, and a different desire." Feminist critics advise readers to resist the text (Fetterley 1978), to read against the text, to misread or reread the text (Kolodny 1985), to reject the canon of Western literature and make a new one, or end canons altogether (Fetterley 1986; Kolodny 1985; Showalter 1985: 19–122). Three things to do with a lot of male-based texts: throw them out, take them apart, find female-based ones instead. (This critique goes back to *A Room of One's Own.*)

Another approach is of special interest; our prefeminist sisters had it as their only option (other than silence or co-optation). This is the appropriation of male-based texts; becoming, in Claudine Herrmann's phrase, *voleuses de langue,* "women thieves of language" (or "of the tongue"), taking myths and reseeing them (Ostriker 1985). As it happens, a myth of Ovid's has seemed important to steal: Philomela, raped, her tongue cut out, weaving her story to her sister who had thought her dead; Philomela, who may have become the nightingale. Her story has been claimed by a male critic as the voice of poetry and reclaimed by a feminist as a paradigm of woman writer and reader (Joplin 1985); claimed by Virginia Woolf in *Between the Acts* and reclaimed by her feminist reader (Marcus 1983, 1984). The misreading of texts here is deliberate, heroic; as Patricia Joplin says (1985), "we have a rescue to perform. Those who gave us the sad news that we had no sister lied to us." But we realize just how heroic an act the rescue of myths must be when we look at how Philomela and her sisters are known to us.

Gazing at the Text

Texts are inseparable from their cultures, and so, before looking at Ovid's rapes, we need a context. We know that Ovid was a popular writer; law students emulated his rhetorical tricks, schoolboys read his stories (Bonner 1949; 1977: 217). How might Ovid's rapes have fit in with the cultural experience of his audience?

We know that great numbers of people attended theatrical shows and wild beast "games" that exhibit some of the same traits as Ovid's writing: portrayal of sexual scenes from Greek myth, especially in the polymorphous theater of the pantomime (Beare 1955); savage and gruesome deaths (Hopkins 1983, Barton 1989). Wealthy people had representations of such scenes in their houses (see Myerowitz and Brown in this volume). The practice cases of the rhetorical schools where Ovid was trained often dealt with rape and violence (Bonner 1949). Roman humor is full of rape; a series of first-century jokes focuses on the god Priapus, who graphically threatens male and female thieves with rape (Richlin 1983). And from Pompeii have been recovered phallic wind chimes, birdbaths, statues of Priapus, phallic paving stones (Grant 1975). Roman law on rape was ill defined, real cases rarely attested, and the victim was blamed (Dixon 1982; Gardner 1986; see Joshel, Chapter 6 above). All slaves were, more or less, the sexual property of their owners; on the other hand, in Ovid's Rome the new emperor Augustus was attempting to reform family life among the aristocracy (Richlin 1981).

Ovid's rapes play a significant role in his work. He was the last great Augustan poet, having outlived his more conventional coevals, and he wrote prolifically; here

I will look at sections of only three of his works, though my analysis could well be extended. In the *Metamorphoses,* rape keeps company with twisted loves, macabre and bloody deaths, cruel gods, cataclysms of nature (the Flood, Phaethon's fire), wars, and, of course, grotesque transformations. Rapes (some Ovid's) fill Arachne's tapestry in Book 6, and, like threads in a tapestry, the themes in the poem run in and out of sight; sometimes a horror in a half-line, sometimes half a book, sometimes gone. The rapes in the *Fasti* adorn the etiologies of Roman religious festivals, while the two in the *Ars Amatoria* contrast with the normal suavity of the narrator's advice. But the poems overall share a certain point of view, and the rapes capture its essence.

The Metamorphoses*: Rapes and Transformations*

DAPHNE'S FEARFUL BEAUTY

The attempted rape of Daphne by Apollo, one of Ovid's best-known passages, is almost the first event in the poem after the Flood. At once the narrative directs the reader's gaze. Daphne begins the episode as a nymph and ends as a laurel tree; in between, she flees from the god, who appears ridiculous and fails to rape Daphne as a nymph (though he has his way with her as a tree). But look at Daphne in her flight (1.525–30):

> As he was about to say more, the daughter of Peneus, with timid pace,   525
> flees him, and leaves his uncompleted speech, along with him.
> Even then she looked [literally *visa (est)*, "was seen"] pretty; the winds laid
>   bare her body,
> and the breezes as she met them fluttered her clothing as it came against
>   them,
> and the light breeze made her locks go out behind her,
> and her beauty [*forma*] was increased by her flight.[1]   530

Indeed, your looking at her is the point. Does the fact that the narrator's voice is not identical with the voice of the historical Ovid undercut this? Is this the point of view only of the buffoonish god? Hardly; glazed thinly, if at all, by its literary mechanisms, there is Daphne's body. Ovid liked this trick; he says of Leucothoe during her rape, "fear itself became her" (*M.* 4.230); of Europa, "and fear itself was a cause of new beauty" (*Fasti* 5.608); of the Sabines, "and fear itself was able to adorn many of them" (*Ars Amatoria* 1.126); of Lucretia, spied on by her future rapist, "this itself was becoming: her chaste tears became her" (*Fasti* 2.757). And the display of the woman's body and fear to her rapist-to-be (and reader) often precedes her rape; Arethusa, who flees her rapist naked, is made to testify: "because I was naked, I looked readier for him" (5.603). Curran (1984) has argued that the narrator's consciousness of the victims' fear shows his empathy for them; but surely the narrator stresses how visually attractive the disarray of flight, and fear itself, made the victim (see Joshel, Chapter 6 above).

PHILOMELA'S TONGUE

Like R-rated movies, Ovid's rapes are not sexually explicit. But no such limits hamper the poem's use of violence, which sometimes stands in for the sexual, as most vividly in the story of Philomela (*M*. 6.424–674; see Galinsky 1975: 110–53).

Ovid begins the tale when Procne, daughter of the king of Athens, marries the barbarian Tereus. They go off to Thrace, and Procne duly bears a baby boy, Itys. Five years pass; then Procne wants to see her sister, Philomela. Tereus goes down to Athens to fetch her, gazes at her, and lusts after her; he wishes he were Philomela's father, so he could fondle her (475–82); and he fantasizes about the body that lies beneath her clothes (490–93). He then takes her back to Thrace, but not to her sister; in a hut in the woods, he rapes her. Here Philomela is a rabbit to Tereus's eagle (note esp. 518: "there is no flight for the one captured, the captor [*raptor*] watches his prize"). Moreover, she is grammatically passive, while Tereus is grammatically active. He is the subject of all the verbs, she is the object, except where the verbs signify fear (e.g., "she trembles," 527). The rape itself takes two and a half lines and is indeed inexplicit; though when Philomela is next compared to an animal, she is a lamb wounded by the wolf's mouth, a dove with feathers bloodied by greedy talons. We are reminded that she had been a virgin.

After the rape, Philomela makes a long and rhetorically polished speech, and Tereus's fear and anger at her threats are so strong that he cuts out her tongue (549–60):

> After the wrath of the wild tyrant was stirred up by such words,
> no less his fear, spurred on by either cause,   550
> he frees from its sheath the sword with which he was girt,
> and he forces her, having been grasped by the hair, with her arms bent
>   behind her back,
> to suffer bonds; Philomela was readying her throat
> and had conceived a hope of her own death once she had seen the sword;
> he, as [] was reproaching and calling out on the name of "father"   555
> and struggling to speak, having been grasped by the forceps,
> ripped out her tongue with wild sword; the utmost root of the tongue
>   flickers,
> []self [] lies and, trembling, mutters into the dark earth,
> and as the tail of a mutilated snake will jump,
> [] quivers, and, dying, seeks the trail of [] mistress.   560

Tereus's first action after the rape (551) is to remove his sword from its sheath; an action parallel to the rape is about to take place. But here we get details not given for the rape, with a list of further actions—by, as we gradually discover, three actors: Tereus, Philomela (who only bares her neck and hopes for death), and Philomela's tongue. All the verbs and participles from 555 on of which Tereus is the subject take a single object, heralded by a remarkable cluster of modifiers: "reproaching" (555), "calling out" (555), "struggling to speak" (556), "having been grasped by the forceps" (556). The surprise here is that the postponed object (indicated by [] in the text) is not Philomela, as the feminine modifiers lead the reader to expect, but *linguam*, "tongue" (556)—a feminine noun that here stands in for the feminine victim both grammatically and literally.

The point of view now switches vividly to that of the tongue itself: 558, *ipsa iacet*, "herself, she lies there" (like a person, a victim of violence); 558, *terraeque tremens inmurmurat atrae* (the tongue itself makes its own speech; note the effect of the repeated *t*'s and *r*'s, sounds made with the tongue); 560, "she quivers" (recalling, with "trembling" [558] the verbs of earlier clusters associated with Philomela [522–23, 527–30]). Finally, dying as Philomela cannot, the tongue like the snake's tail seeks the body of which it once had been a part.

What are we to make of "muttering into the dark earth" and the comparison to a snake? This image complex is more familiar from the *Eumenides*—a woman, the earth, darkness, the snake (often opposed as a sign to the eagle, here associated with Tereus). Earlier, Procne's marriage had been attended by the Furies; later, the two sisters turn into Fury-like creatures (esp. 595, 662). The "dark earth" tallies with the dark night within human beings (472–74, 652) and with the locus of the crimes committed in this tale—against Philomela in the hut in the deep forest, and soon against Itys in the depths of the house (638; cf. 646, "the innards of the house [*penetralia*] drip with gore"). The simile, so close to her mutilation, surprises us with a new view of Philomela—a snake rather than a lamb or dove. Is the text shifting its sympathies?

The end of the tale bears out this suggestion. Tereus keeps Philomela shut up in the hut, and rapes her occasionally, for a year. Philomela cleverly weaves an account of her experience and sends the weaving to her sister via a servant. Procne, reading Philomela's web as a "pitiable poem" about "her own" lot (see Gamel n.d.), rescues Philomela and plans a way to get back at Tereus: the two sisters will butcher Procne's son Itys, cook him, and serve him to Tereus for dinner. (When they seize Itys, the poet describes him with an object cluster [639–40] like the ones he used of Philomela, and her tongue, earlier.) When Tereus discovers what has happened, he calls on the *vipereas sorores,* the "snaky sisters" (i.e., the Furies; 662) and jumps at the two sisters before him with his sword: they turn into birds with marks of blood on their feathers, while he turns into a bird with a spearlike bill.

Ovid's story of Philomela has been construed as a sympathetic and accurate picture of a rape and its aftermath, and of a reading of one woman's plight by a sister woman (Curran 1984; Bergren 1983; cf. Gamel n.d.; Joplin 1985; Marcus 1983, 1984). But something else is going on here. Ovid has shifted the focus of dramatic attention in this tale forward off the rape and backward off the metamorphosis, onto the scene of the cutting out of Philomela's tongue. Is it decorum that makes the poet omit the details of the rape? If so, it is a decorum that allows him to show us what the inside of her mouth looks like with the tongue cut out of it. This is a conflation of violence with sex.

The cutting out of Philomela's tongue is the sort of set piece that was increasingly to characterize Latin literature in the first century A.D. (G. Williams 1978: 184–92). Her unexpectedly eloquent speech immediately after her rape, which seems to make the mutilation such a comment on speech and gender, is also the kind of anomaly Ovid plays with elsewhere; for example, Latona's speech to the farmers when she is too thirsty to speak (*M.* 6.349–59) or the speech of the satyr Marsyas as he is being flayed (*M.* 6.385–86). I echo the critics who quote Dryden's comment: "If this were Wit, was this a Time to be witty, when the poor wretch was in the Agony of Death?" (Galinsky 1975: 77n, 132–33; Gamel n.d.: n. 17). But the very source of this wit is the delighted incongruity of clever style with gruesome subject matter (cf. Verducci 1985).

The bodies of Philomela, Marsyas, and many others feed the magician's box.

This poetry depends for its elegant existence on the exposure of violence (the flaying of Marsyas, the opening of Philomela's mouth).

MYRRHA'S BODY

The cutting out of Philomela's tongue is a transformative point in the tale, turning her from object of violence to perpetrator; her literal metamorphosis at the end is abrupt and relatively unstressed. But Philomela's mutilation has much in common with the metamorphoses suffered by many victims in the poem (mostly female); for example, Daphne into laurel, Io into a cow, Callisto into a bear, Actaeon into a stag, Arachne into a spider, and many into trees (Phaethon's sisters, Dryope, Myrrha), pools (Cyane, Arethusa, Byblis), and statues (Phineus's men, Niobe). All lose the ability to speak with a human voice; if they have been turned into animals, their efforts to speak, resulting in grunts, and their horror at this, are recounted. A favorite tactic of the poet's is to trace the metamorphosis step by slow step, particularly horrible in the case of Myrrha, whose metamorphosis into a tree encases her pregnant belly in wood (10.489–513): roots burst through her toenails, her skin "hardens with bark" (494), she voluntarily sinks her face into the uprush of wood (497–98), but her pregnancy advances and the birth splits her open, nor has she a voice with which to cry out (503–13). In the similar transformations of Phaethon's sisters and Dryope, one mother tries to pull the tree off her daughters and can only mutilate them (2.345–63); another, having herself unwittingly enacted a like mutilation (9.344–45), feels her breasts harden to her nursing child (9.349–93).

So the metamorphosis of women can be something special. In some cases, their previous beauty is grotesquely disfigured, and just those details are given that drive this home in Roman terms (Callisto's hairy arms, Io's comic bovine grin). In many cases, illicit sexuality is the catalyst for metamorphosis, and whereas a rape is normally not explicitly described, the text makes up for this in the metamorphosis. It is as if there were an analogic or developmental relationship between rape and mutilation. Indeed, several women are transformed as a *punishment* for their rape (Io, Callisto, Medusa), and two are killed outright by their angry fathers (Leucothoe, Perimele).

The place of rape in Ovid's texts is thus one where pleasure and violence intersect. Fear is beautiful; violence against the body stands in for rape.

SALMACIS'S DESIRE

The only rape scene in the *Metamorphoses* that involves explicit physical contact also involves a major role reversal: the rape of Hermaphroditus, a beautiful boy of fifteen, by the naiad Salmacis (4.285–388). Her proposition to him makes him blush, "and to have blushed became him" (330)—fear again beautiful, here at some length (331–33). Salmacis then spies on the boy as he first dips his toes in her pool, then strips; her voyeurism here (340–55) rivals that of Tereus.

Bathing scenes recur as incitements to lust in the poem (see esp. Arethusa); they combine the innocence and tempting solitude of other favorite settings (picking flowers, sitting on the riverbank, wandering on the beach) with an opportunity to show the body naked. Here both raped and (female) rapist strip down. Indeed, the passage overdetermines Salmacis's desire and marks its abnormality: not only she but her *eyes* burn, and they burn like the sun (Phoebus, a familiar rapist in the poem) reflected in a mirror, *opposita . . . imagine* ("with opposed image," 349). She is a looking-glass rapist. The boy is compared (354–55) to an ivory statue or white lilies; her likenesses are not so nice. In a switch on the usual comparison of rapist to eagle or wolf, Salmacis is compared to a snake *attacking* an eagle and (unique in the poem) to an octopus (361–64, 366–67).

The result of this rape is twofold: Salmacis and Hermaphroditus, in response to a prayer of hers, become joined into one creature, a hermaphrodite, who speaks with the boy's (dismayed) consciousness; and he prays that the pool will henceforth turn any man who swims in it into a *semivir,* a "half-man" or eunuch (386), and gets his wish. Salmacis's consciousness is gone—the answer to her prayer?

Other women in the *Metamorphoses* pursue men out of excessive desire (the maenads, Byblis, Myrrha, Circe), never with good results. But here the poet experiments with a female who has all the trappings of the most forceful rapist, and the interchange of roles here results in a permanent and threatening confusion of gender. We will see male rapists who dress as women, even a male raped because he is dressed as a woman, and these events turn out well; when a female acts male, the result is the unmanning of all men, and the narrative makes it clear that this is a bad thing (e.g., 4.285–86). A character in Book 12 shows what is at stake: Caenis, raped by Neptune and given a wish in return, replies (12.201–3):

> This injury produces a great wish
> now to be able to suffer/take in [*pati*] no such thing; give that I not be a
>   woman—
> you will have given everything.

In the world of the *Metamorphoses,* a sensible request. As we will see, to *try on* a female role is important for Ovid; but that role, like the trying on, has its limits.

Rapes in the Ars Amatoria

It has been argued that the two scenes of rape in the light, witty *Ars* reflect Ovid's knowing use of an unreliable narrator, the *praeceptor amoris* ("teacher of love"), and that these scenes represent love that the *praeceptor* deplores (Myerowitz 1985: 66) or the poet rejects (Hemker 1985). If so, how is it that he has used the same voice in the *Metamorphoses* and the *Fasti* as well? At least it is safe to say the poet found this sensibility congenial.

The poem's attitude toward women has well been described as desirous of control (Myerowitz 1985; see Parker and Myerowitz in this volume). In this setting, we find the rape of the Sabines and the tale of Achilles and Deidamia, texts that share with the rapes of the *Metamorphoses* the content that lies between the brackets of narratorial persona.

THE RAPE OF THE SABINES (AA. 1.99–134)

At 1.99, the *praeceptor* sets up his account of the incident, so hallowed a part of Roman history, in terms of his own present and of the gaze. Women, he claims, now come to the theater to watch and be watched. The tale of the Sabines is adduced as an *aition* (origin story) for this putative phenomenon; the setting of the rape in the theater is Ovid's innovation and suggests he is not just telling a story but staging a scene here. At 109, the *praeceptor* begins his description of the mass kidnapping:

> [Romulus's men] look about, and each marks for himself with his eyes the
> girl
> whom he wants, and with silent breast they ponder many things.   110
> [And while the performance was going on onstage, as the audience began to
> applaud,]
> the king gave the awaited signal of booty to the people.
> At once they leap up, professing their intention by shouting,   115
> and they lay desirous hands on the maidens.
> As doves, a most timid throng, flee eagles,
> and as the little new lamb flees the wolves once seen,
> so they feared the men rushing without restraint;
> the same color that had been before remained in no one of them.   120
> For there was one fear, not one face of fear:
> some tear their hair, some sit without sense;
> one, sad, is silent, in vain another calls her mother;
> this one complains, that one is stupefied; one stays, another flees;
> the captured [*raptae*] girls are led, a marital booty,   125
> and fear itself was able to adorn many of them.
> If any of them had fought back too much and denied her companion,
> the man picked her up himself, held to his desirous breast,
> and thus he spoke: "Why do you ruin your tender little eyes with tears?
> What your father is to your mother, this I will be to you."   130
> Romulus, you alone knew how to give bonuses to your soldiers;
> if you give bonuses like that to me, I'll be a soldier.

As in the Philomela episode, the men are here subjects of action verbs, especially of the gaze (109); the women begin as objects of action. This situation is reversed from 117–26, but, like Philomela, they act only to show fear. The simile of doves and lambs is similarly familiar, and was in fact a commonplace; so for Lucretia in the *Fasti* (below), and in Horace, *Epodes* 12.25–26 (a cross-sex travesty) and *Odes* 1.23 (to "Chloe"; see Montague, Chapter 11 in this volume). In the climax of the scene (121–26), the narrator sketches the crowd of girls in a series of short subject-verb clauses. But the summary subject—"girls"—is in apposition with a concrete noun—"marital booty" (125)—and what actions these women perform again only mark their vulnerability.

These clauses are remarkable in the Latin for the neatness of their construction, one figure balanced against the next by parison, chiasmus, and asyndeton, in the smallest possible space—Ovidian prestidigitation. By their brevity they achieve the effect of a miniature, with little figures mouthing inaudible cries and stamping inaudible feet. But we do not have to rely on aesthetics for a reading of the passage; the narrator tells us: "And fear itself was able to adorn many of them" (126)—the voice of the *praeceptor*, but also, as we have seen, that of the *Metamorphoses* and the *Fasti*.

At 127, the possibility of fighting back is conceded, but the man's action and speech are indulgent, amatory, and paternalistic (128–30). He marks only her tears, annulling her resistance; carrying her off like a child, he talks of her "tender little eyes," as the poet Catullus did to his mistress in a poem where she weeps over a dead sparrow (c. 3).

Once again the narrator tells us how to read this, declaring that he would volunteer as a soldier himself if he could get such a reward (131–32)—recalling Ovid's beloved metaphor, *militat omnis amans,* "every lover is a soldier" (see Cahoon 1988). But metaphors often convey a literal perception, and a poet who sees love as comparable to battle might well see violence as part of love.

Remarkably, a recent critic sees this passage as a strong antirape statement by Ovid (Hemker 1985). The premise of the argument is that the *praeceptor* is so obviously wrongheaded that the reader sees the falsity of all he says, as if the whole poem were in quotation marks and the quotation marks nullified the content. Yet Hemker simultaneously argues that Ovid's description "sympathetically conveys the horror of the situation"; she singles out the climactic vignette of the women in flight as showing "the women's perspective" (45).

Such a reading blurs content; the women's fear is displayed only to make them more attractive. We have this myth, too, in comedies and action romances (squeaky voice: "Put me down!"); it is part of the plot. Likewise, for the Sabine women, there is really nothing to be worried about, because they are getting married. Their fears are cute (see Modleski 1982: 46), and the whole thing is a joke. Again the text uses women's fear as its substance (and see Myerowitz 1985 on the female as *materia* in the *Ars*). There are indeed quotation marks around the text, the marks that tell the reader "this is amusing"; but they act not to attack the content but to palm it off.

ACHILLES AND DEIDAMIA (*AA* 1.663–705)

Toward the end of Book 1 of the *Ars Amatoria,* the *praeceptor* illustrates his contention that no means yes (663–80) by telling the story of Achilles and De-idamia. He first suggests the lover should mix kisses with his wheedling words (663), whether or not the woman wishes to give them (664). If she fights and calls the lover "naughty" (665), nevertheless "she wants herself to be conquered in fighting" (666). A man who has taken kisses and not "other things" (669) was not worthy even to get the kisses (670). Once he got the kisses, how close he was to his "full desire" (671); such hesitance was not *pudor* ("modesty/chastity") but *rus-ticitas* ("country-bumpkin-ness"), the *praeceptor*'s bane (672). Then he generalizes (673–78):

> You may call it *vis* [rape/force]; that *vis* is pleasing to girls;
> "unwilling," they often wish to have given "what helps" [a euphemism].
> Whatever woman is violated by the sudden seizing of Venus [= sex],   675
>   rejoices, and "naughtiness" serves as a gift/does them a favor.
> But a woman who has departed untouched, when she could have been
>   forced,
>   though she simulates gladness with her face, will be sad.

Women's emotions are consistently unreal throughout this passage—"unwill-ing" (674) must describe a feigned emotion; "naughtiness" (676) must be feigned scolding as in 665; even their facial expressions are artificial (678). The pupil is to believe that women do have emotions with which to enjoy the experience, but there is apparently no way to tell for sure. What *does* a woman want? The deletion of women's voice here is even more thorough than in the tale of Philomela.

The *praeceptor,* skimming over the rape of the Leucippidae (see Sutton, Chapter 1 above), then launches into his illustrative set piece. Having delineated the beginning of the Trojan War in six lines, he takes the same time to show us the young Achilles in drag, disguised as a girl on the island of Skyros. And he is in drag when he becomes a rapist. He is put in to room with the royal princess, "by chance" (697), and—*voilà!*—*haec illum stupro comperit esse virum,* "she knew him to be a man by means of rape" (698), *stuprum* apparently the acid test. The *praeceptor* goes on to hint that it was no rape at all (699), saying that she desired it (700) and begged Achilles, now in armor and hurrying off to war, to stay (701–4). *Vis ubi nunc illa est?* he asks, smirking—"Where's that 'rape' now, eh?" (703). He concludes, "You see, as it's a matter of *pudor* for her to begin certain things first, thus it's pleasing to her to undergo them (*pati*) when another begins" (705–6). His point is that *pati*—"to suffer," "to be passive," "to be penetrated sexually"—is pleasing to women, and this is the mark of the woman, as *vis,* "force," is the mark of the man (see Parker, Chapter 5 above). When we want to know the gender of the adolescent hero dressed in women's clothing, the signifier of his maleness is his ability to commit rape. (Ovid was to repeat the idea of transvestite rape several times in the *Metamorphoses* [4.217–33, 11.310, 14.654–771]; see esp. 2.433, where Jupiter disguised as Diana embraces Callisto and *nec se sine crimine prodit—* "does not thrust out/reveal himself without crime"; gender revelation equals penetration.)

These two passages from the *Ars Amatoria* show both enjoyment of women's fear and objectification of women. Whereas *pati* is repugnant to men, here *pati* is women's nature, and they enjoy it (but contrast Caenis). As in New Comedy (Fantham 1975), the outcome of rape is happy. This idea also appears in the *Metamorphoses,* for example, for Orithyia and Boreas, immediately after Philomela; they marry, and Orithyia has twins (see Modleski 1982: 35). And it appears in the *Fasti* as well. But note again the intersection of pleasure with violence, now with fun in place of pain (Richlin 1983: 156–58). The erasure of female subjectivity is complete; the poem presents the female reader with no exit (Richlin 1984).

Rape in the Fasti: *Comic Relief*

The rapes in the *Fasti* are a mixed bag. Three (1.391–440, Priapus and Lotis; 2.303–58, Faunus and Omphale/Hercules; 6.319–48, Priapus and Vesta) are comic: a rustic and ithyphallic god attempts to rape a nymph/Amazon/goddess in her sleep and is interrupted in comic fashion before he succeeds. Three (5.193–206, Chloris and Zephyr; 5.603–20, Europa and Jupiter; 6.101–28, Crane and Janus) emphasize the fortunate outcome: Chloris marries Zephyr and becomes the goddess Flora, Europa gives her name to a continent, Janus gives Crane a goddess's power over all house boundaries. One (2.583–616, Mercury and Lara) stems from a punishment but also ends well, since Lara gives birth to twins. Finally, three are "historic": the stories of Lucretia (2.723–852), Rhea Silvia (3.11–48), and the Sabine women, part II (3.187–234). Rhea Silvia and Lucretia, like the comic victims, are asleep as their rapists approach (cf. in the *Metamorphoses* only Thetis—who, however, also has to be tied down—and Chione); Lara is mute, and Lucretia is repeatedly said to be dumbstruck. Crane and Lara gain through rape the guardianship of boundaries; Chloris/Flora gives Juno the power to bear a child without a father. Common elements are the powerlessness of the women and the potential for unlocking that results from their penetration; hence the catalytic function of the historical women (see Joshel, Chapter 6 above). Like the Virgin Mary, they are lowly creatures whose very humility and penetration foster the creation of power.

As in the *Metamorphoses,* these rapes probably have Hellenistic models; but the model is the poet's choice, and footnotes do not cancel content any more than narrative structures do. These rapes echo the rapes of the *Metamorphoses* and *Ars Amatoria* and provide us with a new element: a paradigmatic structure.

RAPE AS JOKE

The three comic rapes are peculiar in that they are almost identical and seem to be Ovid's invention (see Fantham 1983); Priapus's attempted rapes of Lotis in Book 1 and of Vesta in Book 6 are the same in all but name. The shared elements are summed up in Table 8.1.

The poet clearly marks these stories as jokes, with labels or narrative elements ("everyone laughed") or both. Note the element of visual stimulus in the two longer tales: the nymphs show their breasts, legs, and naked feet through openings in their clothing (1.405–10); Omphale's fancy clothes leave her "well worth looking at for her gilded bosom" (2.310). All three tales remark the gaze of the potential rapist. But more, the voice of these women is one that is "asking for it." The circumstances allow license; most curious is the intimate dinner in the cave (a location marked as both ritual and bucolic), with its cross-dressing (both traditional and ritual) which turns the rape of Omphale into the rape of Hercules (see now Loraux 1990). The poet gives a detailed description of Hercules in Omphale's clothing, bursting the seams with his huge body (2.318–24); we recall Achilles' transvestite rape of Deidamia.[2] The targeted woman goes to sleep, but attention is focused on the stealthy approach of the god. Slowly he comes, step by step . . . he pulls the covering up from the bottom . . . we hold our breath; this is the technique of the striptease (or of the horror story, or of the Hellenistic love charm; Winkler 1990: 71–98), highly erotic, and the reader is seduced into the scenario. Such scenes were common in Roman wall painting (Fantham 1983: 198–99). The explicit descriptions of the god's erection embody the source of the narrative's desire—Faunus here assimilated to Priapus (2.346). Alarm, discovery, everyone laughs; the sight of the tumescent god in mid-rape is the primal scene of comedy.

THE COMIC STRUCTURE DRESSED UP

This comic structure recurs, surprisingly, in tragic and historic rapes in the *Fasti,* notably those of Lucretia, Rhea Silvia, and Lara.

TABLE 8.1. Comic Rapes in Ovid's *Fasti*

Common features	Lotis (1.391–440)	Omphale (2.303–58)	Vesta (6.319–48)
Marked as comic tale.		*Antiqui fabula plena ioci* (304).	*Multi fabula parva ioci* (320).
Women provide visual stimuli.	Scantily clad naiads reveal bits of their bodies (405–10).	Omphale goes walking with Hercules, all dressed up— *aurato conspicienda sinu* (310).	
Rustic gods look and are excited.	Satyrs, Pan, and Silenus are aroused by the nymphs (411–14); Priapus wants Lotis.	Faunus sees Omphale and Hercules and falls for her at once.	Priapus, who has been chasing nymphs and goddesses, sees Vesta (335).
An idyllic party is in progress.	A Bacchic rout in a forest glade.	Hercules and Omphale go into a cave, switch clothes, feast, and go to sleep in separate beds to keep pure for a Bacchic festival the next day.	A party with Cybele as hostess, including drinking, dancing, and wandering the valleys of Ida.
The woman targeted goes to sleep.	Lotis, at the edge of the group.	Omphale, in her bed in the cave.	Vesta, in the grass.
The rustic god approaches stealthily.	Long description of silent approach on tiptoe.	Long description of Faunus searching through the cave at midnight.	Priapus approaches with careful steps (337–38).
Details of the rape attempt.	Priapus balances himself (429) and pulls off Lotis's covers from the feet up (431); his erection is described later (437).	Faunus climbs onto Hercules' bed (misled by cross-dressing), lies down; his erection described (346); pulls up Hercules' dress from the feet up; surprised at hairy legs; tried "other things" (345–50).	*Ibat, ut inciperet*—"He was going up to her to begin . . ."
Sudden alarm.	Silenus's ass brays.	Hercules wakes up and dumps Faunus.	Silenus's ass brays.
Discovery.	Lotis runs away; Priapus exposed.	Faunus exposed in light.	Vesta gets up; all gather; Priapus runs away.
Everybody laughs.	Everybody laughs at Priapus and his erection (437–38).	Hercules, onlookers, and Omphale laugh at Faunus (355–56).	

Ovid's version of the Lucretia story follows closely the account in Livy's history of Rome (1.57–59; see Joshel, Chapter 6 above) but changes the focus significantly. The men, and the reader, spy on Lucretia and overhear her as she weaves by her bedside (2.741–58); the narrator comments on her looks (763–66); and Tarquin gloats on them in his memory—like Tereus. The staging of the rape enacts its meaning. Tarquin enters—*hostis ut hospes init penetralia Collatini,* "enemy as guest, he goes into the house/innards of Collatinus" (787); en route to Lucretia's room (793), he "frees his sword from its sheath" (cf. *M*. 6.551, 10.475)—like Priapus.

The rape itself includes physical details unusual for Ovid except in the comic rapes (794–804). Tarquin presses her down on the bed; she feels his hands on her breast. Lucretia is compared to a lamb *lying under* a wolf (799–800). The narrative presents her mute thoughts, and her difficulties with speech continue in the scene that follows the rape (823–28). The physical details of her suicide are strikingly emphasized: she falls *sanguinulenta*, "bloody" (832), rather than simply *moribunda*, as in Livy; Brutus pulls the dagger from her "half-living" body (838); her corpse shows her approval by moving its eyes and hair; and, the last we see of her, her wound (not just her body) is being exhibited to arouse the populace—*volnus inane patet*, "her gaping wound lies open" (849). She ends as she began, as object of the gaze. As in the comic rapes, the viewer/voyeur sees, burns, and acts; in the tragic version, we get to see the woman die as well. We even get to see inside her wound, as inside Philomela's mouth. (Indeed, the poet moves from this episode to a brief allusion to Procne and Tereus, 853–56.)

Familiar elements recur in the rape of the Vestal Virgin, Rhea Silvia, by the god Mars (3.11–48), which resulted in the birth of Romulus, founder of Rome. We see her tripping down the path to fetch water; she sits on the riverbank; she opens the front of her dress (15–16) and pats her hair. And then she falls asleep in her idyllic surroundings. Mars sees her, desires her, and has her (21), and she wakes up pregnant (23)— "for, to be sure, the founder of the Roman city was within her guts" (*intra viscera*).

Lara's story involves, like Philomela's, not only rape but the punishment of sisterhood through silencing and mutilation. The story is given to explain who the *dea Muta* ("mute goddess") is (2.583), so presumably Lara is to be elevated to godhead; this is not narrated. What is told is that the naiad Lara has warned the nymph Juturna that Jupiter intends to rape her (603–4) and has also told Juno (605–6). To punish Lara, Jupiter rips out her tongue and gives her to Mercury, conductor of souls, to be taken down to live "with the ghosts in Hades, as the proper place for those who are silent" (609). En route they pass through a grove, where the mutilated Lara excites Mercury's lust: "she is said then to have pleased the god, her guide" (612). He "gets ready" for rape (613, *vim parat,* a recurrent phrase in the *Metamorphoses*). She tries to plead with him but cannot: *voltu pro verbis illa precatur,/et frustra muto nititur ore loqui,* "she begs with her face in place of words,/and in vain she struggles to speak with mute mouth" (613–14; the mimetic effect of 614 can be compared with that of *M*. 6.558, Philomela's tongue muttering into the ground). The instant result is that she becomes pregnant with twins who turn out to be minor gods (615–16)—end of story.

Familiar here is the incitement to lust inherent in the woman, the bucolic setting that serves as license, and the postponement of rape with compressed reference to male arousal (*vim parat,* both elliptical and insistent). In this case the postponement comes not from the tease of the rapist's stealthy approach but from the efforts of a woman who is both speaking and silent, like someone attempting to speak in a dream: terror made voluptuous. The muting and mutilation of Lara, like that of Philomela, propel stories not theirs.

Rape: The Insertion of Theory into the Text

To deal with these texts, I now present three theoretical models, in search of one that might offer a way out of the trap of representation.

The Pornographic Model: Rape Is Rape

Content analysis allows us to see past the legerdemain of style. As Laurie Colwin's poet points out in the first epigraph, "great art" partakes of the mechanisms of pornography. The episodic structure, the elision of the act of rape, and the physical cruelty of the *Metamorphoses* recall Angela Carter's analysis of Sade, especially of the scenarios of *Justine* (Carter 1978: 39, 44); indeed, Ovid's endless supply of innocent nymphs prefigures Justine's picaresque resilience, as the dissolution of bodies in metamorphosis prefigures the fantasies of the Freikorps men (Theweleit 1987: 171–204). When Susan Griffin says of the pornographer, "he gives woman a voice only to silence her" (S. Griffin 1981: 40), can we not apply this to Philomela? Lara? Lucretia?

The pornographic model, then, allows us to take Ovid's rapes literally; to realize that they are, if not the whole text, an important part of it, not to be ignored; and to consider what we want to do with a canon that includes many such texts, finally weighing their hurtfulness in with their beauty. We want a way out. But then we must keep faith with history. Maybe Sade should not get so much credit for initiating modern sensibility; maybe history provides no way out. The average inhabitant of Rome enjoyed spectacles in reality that Sade could only bear in his imagination. And we must recall that to a Roman of the literary class, a story about a raped woman with a Greek name would have a peculiar resonance, suggesting not only the abstract figures of Greek erudition but the looted marble figures in his garden, the enslaved (= sexually accessible) and living figure serving him dinner. Or serving her dinner.

The Cross-sex Fantasy Model: To Rape Is to Be Raped

> *Et qui spectavit vulnera vulnus habet.*
> [And a man who has seen wounds has a wound.]
>
> —Ovid *AA* 1.166

The question of the experience of Ovid's audience raises the possibility that the pornographic model is incomplete. If, as theorists of fantasy argue, subjectivity oscillates, could Ovid have provided, even enjoyed, a female subjectivity? Before I consider what good this would do the (female) reader, I need to establish how it might have been possible in Ovid's world.

The construction of Roman sexuality and textuality included two features of interest here. First, Roman men of the literary class often professed to be bisexual (Richlin 1983, esp. 220–26). Normative adult male sexuality, as expressed in love poetry, gossip, and political invective, took the form of attraction to both women and adolescent males. Freeborn adolescents, though in principle off limits, were at least conscious of their attractiveness to older men, and there was no lack of slave boys. Attraction of adult males to other adult males was, in these texts, the source of loathing. Being penetrated (*pati*) was seen as a staining of the body (which illuminates the claim, discussed above, that women enjoyed it; we recall Caenis).

Our sources on the construction of Roman women's sexuality are too indirect and fragmentary to tell us much; they were expected to marry, often before age fifteen, and might well divorce and remarry.

Second, the theater at Rome in Ovid's time (Lucian *On Dancing* 34) included an extremely popular form, pantomime, in which a male dancer was the central figure, often playing a woman. A line of musicians and singers sang the story in Greek, and a second actor played any necessary minor characters; but the first dancer was the star and danced all the main roles (hence *panto-mimus*) of the play (Beare 1955).

Pantomime sets Ovid's rapes in 3-D. That it was so popular testifies to a special ambivalence in Roman culture, which commonly stigmatized dancing as effeminate (Richlin 1983: 92–93, 98; cf. Pliny *Panegyric* 54.1). Meanwhile, the satirist Juvenal indicates that pantomimes sometimes depicted the sexual misadventures of mythic heroines: Leda (6.63), Pelopea (who bore Aegisthus to her father Thyestes), and Philomela (7.92).

Gossip records that dancers were lusted after by the rich and famous (so of Bathyllus and Maecenas; Tac. *Ann.* 1.54.3). Satire avers that women found the dance of rape sexually exciting (Juv. 6.63–66):

> When effeminate Bathyllus dances the pantomime Leda,
> Tuccia can't control her bladder, Apula squeals,
> as if in an embrace, suddenly and a wretched sostenuto.
> Thymele pays attention; then rustic Thymele learns.

"Leda" would be the rape of Leda by Zeus in the form of a swan. Is the male actor called effeminate because he is? Because he is dancing? Because he is playing a woman? Because he is dancing a rape? Because he is dancing a man/bird/god raping a woman? Does the women's purported reaction have an objective correlative? We think of Mick Jagger in drag. That such a spectacle would have been considered dangerous for a respectable young man is attested by a letter of Pliny (7.24), in which he describes the situation in the house of Ummidia Quadratilla: a racy old aristocrat, she considered her troupe of pantomime actors a good relaxation for herself, but she always sent her grandson away to study when they were about to perform.

Was this any more to Ovid than part of his social milieu? It seems so. The Elder Seneca's rhetorical memoirs include a sketch of Ovid, the star student, in his college days; Seneca ends by observing that "Ovid rarely declaimed *controversiae* [arguments], and only *ethicas* [ones involving character portrayal]; he much preferred *suasoriae*" (*Controversiae* 2.2.12). *Suasoriae* were speeches given in character, usually of a famous historical person; this penchant for dramatics pervades Ovid's poetry. Other writers wrote for the *pantomimi*, especially when they needed money: the son of one of Ovid's fellow students, who Seneca complains "polluted his talent" (*Suasoriae* 2:19); the first-century poets Statius, who Juvenal claims sold an *Agave* to the *pantomimus* Paris to make ends meet (7.82–92), and Lucan, who wrote fourteen *salticae fabulae,* "scripts for the dance" (*Lucani vita*). Ovid explicitly denies having done any such thing—even though his poems are appearing on the stage, "danced to a full house," during his exile (*Tristia* 2.519–20, 5.7.25–28; see Myerowitz, Chapter 7 above on this apologia).

The seriocomic dialogue *On Dancing,* by the Greek writer Lucian, composed at Antioch in Asia Minor between A.D. 162 and 165, testifies to the conservative view of pantomime as effeminate (1, 2, 3, 5), both in itself and in its effect on the audience; to the frenzy of the audience (2, 3, 5); and to the prominence in the performance of the man dancing the woman's role, especially a raped woman (2, 28). The crusty interlocutor describes being in the audience of the pantomime (2):

> Watching an effeminate man mincing vainly about with dainty clothing and unbridled songs and imitating sex-crazed dames, the lewdest of those in antiquity, Phaedras and Parthenopes and Rhodopes. [Parthenope was a Siren who yearned for Odysseus; Rhodope married her own brother.]

Lucian describes the dancer's flowing silk garb (29–30, 63, 66) and his masks—five for one performance would not be unusual. The mask was beautiful (unlike those of comedy and tragedy) and had a closed mouth.

But what most suggests a tie with Ovid is Lucian's list of the topics a good *pantomimus* must know by heart (37–61), which tallies closely in order, arrangement, and content with the *Metamorphoses* as a whole (Galinsky 1975: 68–69, 132, 139). It includes the tale of Procne and Philomela (40): "and the [daughters] of Pandion, both what they suffered in Thrace and what they did." Also the tale of Pelopea (43), which Juvenal mentioned as well—a father seduces a daughter. The *pantomimus* is to learn, in particular, transformations (57) and, most of all, the loves of the gods (59)—that is, their rapes of goddesses and women. This list mentions fifty-six women's roles, including two historical figures (Stratonice and Cleopatra), plus one for a man in drag: Achilles on Skyros. This recalls not only the tale of Achilles and Deidamia in the *Ars,* inset into the text like a dramatic interlude, but also the *Fasti* and the attempted rape of Hercules (which Fantham suggests came from pantomime; 1983: 200–201); the freeze-frame tableaux of the Sabines running (set in the archaic theater and forerunner of the experience of women at the theater); and the rapes by gods in drag in the *Metamorphoses.*

Describing a great dancer at the court of Nero, Lucian stresses the way he could tell a whole story in gesture. This might explain one curiosity of Ovid's style; look again at 6.551–57 (Philomela's rape). With one hand, Tereus unsheathes his sword; with the other, he grabs Philomela by the hair; with the other, he bends her arms behind her back; with the other, he chains her wrists; with the other, he grabs her tongue with a pair of forceps; and finally he uses the sword to cut out her tongue. And compare 6.338–68, in the comic tale of the goddess Latona and the Lycian farmers: throughout, Latona carries her newborn twins in her arms (338); they even play a part in the drama (359); at 368, the angry goddess dramatically raises her palms to the sky to curse the oafish farmers. What has happened to the babies? Perhaps this is not baroque illogic but cubist logic; perhaps this transformative poem derives its poetry from motion, the motion of the dance.

Lucian also draws a direct comparison between dancing and rhetoric (65), basing it explicitly on the shared art of impersonation, especially as found in rhetorical exercises, Ovid's old specialty.

The connection between Ovid's poetry and the pantomime accords well with the model of fantasy derived from psychoanalytic theory, in which the subject is said to oscillate among the terms of the fantasy (Fletcher 1986; C. Kaplan 1986, based on the work of Laplanche and Pontalis). Thus, in one of the basic schemas, "a father seduces a daughter," the subject can be in the place of "father," "daughter," or even of the verb "seduces." The interrelations among this concept, Ovid's poetry, and the pantomime are most striking. The model exactly describes the performance of the dancer—first one character, then another, with the essential need to enact the interaction between the characters; and not just any characters but, often, the father seducing a daughter (Pelopea) or an equivalent (Leda). Or vicariously: Tereus imagining himself in Pandion's place *so that* he could fondle Philomela. The poet's fascination with the reversal, whereby a [daughter] (Medea, Scylla, Byblis, Myrrha) seduces a [father], is delimited by the extreme anxiety of the Salmacis episode, where the female has become subject rather than object, and the male is forced not only to become but to remain female.

Roman poets generally published their works by giving readings, usually to circles of friends; and we recall the male Roman's experience of being the object of the male gaze, as an adolescent. So can it be said that Ovid empathizes with his rape victims? Certainly—as a great *pantomimus* might; but not with any but a delicious pity for them, a very temporary taking on of their experience, their bodies. How beautiful she looks in flight; one woman feels the hot breath of the rapist on her neck, another is caught bathing naked, a third taken by surprise on her way to visit her sister. For a few the rapist even first dresses as a woman, so that the phallus can be a surprise and teach its lesson about gender again. I imagine the poet himself (or the narrator, or both) "dancing" his characters one by one: a father, seduces, a daughter.

Ovid's special circumstances lend themselves to this imagination. The *Metamorphoses* was completed when Ovid was in exile, for offenses connected with his poetry (Goold 1983), to the cold wilderness of Tomis. The muted victims, the artists horribly punished by legalistic gods for bold expression—Marsyas, and especially Arachne—read like allegories of Ovid's experience. Philomela weaves a message to her sister; the unvoiced Cyane with her "inconsolable wound" (5.426) gives Proserpina's belt to Demeter as a sign. At this level it might be possible to argue for Ovid as metapornographer. But if the *Metamorphoses* lays bare a cruel cosmos, it does so voluptuously.

The pleasure of the style and the pleasure in the content are congruent. Moreover, the universe described horrifies and allures us precisely because it is out of kilter, as is the style with the content. Perhaps this is why rape is such a suitable scenario for the *Metamorphoses,* which comes to involve dissolution of the boundaries of body, genus, gender, and genre. (And not rape alone; the poem is full of incest, the mating of human with statue, cross-sex transformations.) Such a phenomenon has been taken into account for Greek literature (Bergren 1983; Zeitlin 1985a) but not for Latin. But perhaps Roman culture, so obsessed with boundaries, is precisely the place for it. Rape as a passport to death, or to dissolution of the body, may have made sense to Ovid and his audience.

Compare a story in Tacitus (*Annals* 5.9):

> It was then decided that the remaining children of Sejanus should be punished, though the rage of the mob was thinning out, and many were soothed by the executions already carried out. Therefore they are carried into the prison, the boy understanding what was about to take place, the girl still unaware, so that she was asking over and over, "For what misdeed, and where was she being taken? She would not do it again," and "she could be cautioned with the ordinary children's beating." The authors of that time say that because it was considered unheard-of for a virgin to be submitted to a capital execution, she was raped by the executioner with the noose lying next to her; then, with their necks squeezed, bodies so young were thrown out on the Gemonian steps.

The execution was, except for the rape, normal for political prisoners in those abnormal times (see G. Williams 1978: 184). The story appears again, generalized, in Suetonius (*Tiberius* 61.5); editors compare a case during the triumviral proscriptions (a time Ovid lived through), reported by the much later writer Dio (47.6), in which a young boy was put forward into the class of men—made to assume the *toga virilis*—so that he could legally be executed. The sixteenth-century classicist Lipsius comments that the same reasoning underlies the case of Sejanus's daughter—that once having been raped and deflowered, *mulier videretur*, "she would seem a woman."

The case of Sejanus's daughter comes from A.D. 31, the accounts of it from the early second century A.D.; but the logic of it, rape as a *rite de passage*, atrocity as it is to these two writers, informs their texts as it does Ovid's.

We begin to look for ways out; the model begins to feel like a trap.

First, what about the female members of Ovid's audience? Is it possible that this poetry includes a female subjectivity? But we have no evidence of any raised consciousness among Roman women; I think rather of Angela Carter's description of the women listening eagerly to a male speaker in Sade's *Philosophy in the Boudoir* (1978: 143): "Since he is good enough to class them with the masters, they, too, will be permitted to tyrannise as much as they please. Libido . . . is genderless." If women are invited to identify across gender boundaries, the process is not necessarily revolutionary (C. Kaplan 1986).

Isn't this just the pornographic again? In Sade, and commonly, the assumption of a female voice is a central technique (Kappeler 1986: 30; and see Parker, Henry, Joshel in this volume); even dominance by women, when written into the scenario, is just another thrill (Carter 1978: 20–21). Fantasy of movement within the system is not escape from the system.

But some argue that fantasies mean something completely different from what they say—for example, that fantasized violence provides an excuse for cuddling (Russ 1985), or that the mutilation of the love object is a covert expression of anger at the object's power (Modleski 1982: 24–25). The implication that the degree of the "covert" anger correlates directly with a real power is very disturbing when applied to fantasized violence against women (for a glaring example of this, see Auerbach 1982). Rather than congratulate ourselves, we must bear in mind the disparity between the reality of women's historical power and the size of the shackles historically placed upon it.

Like the pornographic model, the cross-sex fantasy model offers no exit from gender hierarchy. The female is still the site of violence, no matter what the location of the subject. Even if the magician and the lady change places, *he* is still taking *her* place.

A Political Model: Rape Is Rape, Resistance Is Possible

> *Proprium humani ingenii est odisse quem laeseris.*
> [It is proper to human nature to hate one whom you have hurt.]
> —Tacitus *Agricola* 42.3

We need a political model that will both describe the magician's act and suggest a way to end it. Let me postulate that the problem is not gender but hierarchy: within hierarchy, violence is a right, and the control of violence diminishes liberty. An anarchic system is thus a precondition for the deletion of the pornographic. Though escape from hierarchy has seemed impossible, I would postulate that there are some "open" discourses that permit it: theory, mathematics, nonrepresentational art, music. Other, "closed" systems—humor, fantasy, narratives, film, and representational art—all interrelated, form the bars around hierarchy.

The structure of these closed discourses is political, and they have four main characteristics: (1) They contain a cue that says any item is untrue, creating what I call the "Archie Bunker fallacy" ("It's just a joke!"). Ovid actually asserted this in his poems from exile (e.g., *Tristia* 2.491–96). (2) Content follows function and is not arbitrary. (3) The relation between each item and reality depends on the status of the users; these discourses maintain the status quo. (4) Historically, though perhaps not necessarily, the hierarchy has been gendered. The position at the bottom, so often a woman's, has never been pleasant; something in it "exposes the meatiness of human flesh" (Carter 1978: 140; see Kappeler 1986: 63–81; Rabinowitz, Parker, Brown in this volume).

Where does this leave us? On the one hand, history weighs heavy, and closed discourse is more comfortable than open. Revolutionary discourse is intrinsically unamusing. How ephemeral, how dry this essay is compared with Ovid's poetry! And insofar as it amuses, it fails. On the other hand, when we see problems of discourse as systemic, we can gauge our task. The female can no longer be by definition the site of violence—nothing can. What *happens* if we say, as Kappeler does (221), "Art will have to go"? Maybe there is something else. Meanwhile we must use what exists to show what is wrong.

Conclusion

How *can* women read? And why should we read Ovid? How badly do we need this history? I borrow an answer from Toni Morrison. We're stuck with Philomela; she's like Beloved, the dearly beloved ghost of grief, and to be blind to her is not to exorcise her. We need to know her and keep faith with history.

The battle for consciousness must go on (see de Lauretis 1984: 185) and focus on concrete political improvements in women's lives. As classicists, as scholars, as teachers, as women and men who speak to other people, we can fight in this battle. What can we do?

(1) We can speak and write about antiquity for other feminists and people outside the academy. We can remake our disciplines (Hallett 1985). We can move outside of Classics, and we can open up the boundaries of Classics itself; that's what this book is trying for.

(2) We can blow up the canon. Canons are part of social systems. We recognize the one we have as dysfunctional. It must and will change; we can surely critique the pleasure of the text without fear of breaking anything irreplaceable.

(3) We can claim our lack. We can ask, where am I in this text? What can it do for me? What did it do to its audience?

(4) We can appropriate; we can resist. The old stories await our retelling; they haunt our language anyway. And if the only names we have to speak in are names of blood, maybe we can speak the blood off them. History is what groups write as they come to power.

NOTES

Thanks to Marilyn Skinner and Susan Kapost for the bibliography that got me started; Terri Marsh for much help along the way; groups at Carleton University, UC Santa Cruz, Hamilton College, and Amherst College for critical listening; and the Lehigh Valley Feminist Research Group for jumping in. To the readers of the manuscript—Sandra Joshel, Molly Myerowitz, and Robert Sutton—I am more indebted than I can say.

Pro comite stuprata trucidata: postremo munere mortis.

1. All translations are my own and are as close to word-for-word as possible.

2. This tale bears a striking resemblance to a current joke: Batman sees Superman, who looks distressed. Batman asks why. Superman says he had flown down to the beach to look at women, when he saw Wonder Woman lying naked in an enclosed backyard, writhing and groaning sexily. So he zoomed down and . . . did it! Batman is horrified. But wasn't she *scared?* Did she *scream?* "Did *she* scream!" says Superman. "You should have heard the Invisible Man!" (Collected Norwich, Vermont, 1981.) There is the same transferral of the rape from female to male object (and from human to divine spheres). A similar flying-and-spying takes place in the tale of Mercury and Herse (*M.* 2.708ff).

9

Death as Decoration:
Scenes from the Arena
on Roman Domestic Mosaics

Shelby Brown

. . . the realism with which their anguish is portrayed is excruciating; and this
picture raises in a most acute form the problem of how householders could wish
to perpetrate such scenes of carnage on the floors of their homes.
> —Toynbee 1973: 83, on dying leopards in the Borghese Mosaic

. . . there are different cultural definitions of being human, being male, and
being civilized.
> —Marvin 1986: 135, on Spanish bullfighting

Bears and big cats prowl the bloodied sands of an arena, and leopards attack bound
seminude male captives. One cat balances itself on the staggering body of its victim
and bites directly into his unprotected face; blood streams from his wounds and
forms puddles on the sand (Figure 9.6, below). How is the modern viewer to
understand this scene on a Roman mosaic from Tunisia? To evaluate the violent acts
of another culture in an objective way is a difficult, perhaps impossible, task,
especially when the acts are completely unacceptable within one's own society. Too
great an appearance of objectivity or understanding may even bring upon a scholar
the opprobrium of his or her peers. Many modern authors who discuss the ancient
sources on Roman venatorial and gladiatorial combat have felt moved or obligated
to emphasize their personal distaste for the topic (i.e., to pass moral judgment on
the act). The authors' emotional responses are sometimes incorporated in the form
of pejorative adjectives into the body of facts or ideas presented. More rarely,
negative comments are relegated to introductory or concluding remarks. This judg-
mental approach, although understandable, is noteworthy; in the evaluation of more
socially acceptable topics, anthropologists (or archaeologists, or historians) have
often been expected to overcome their own cultural biases, sometimes to an unrealistic degree, and to empathize with the subject (Geertz 1974: 27; Hopkins 1983:
29). While it is hardly desirable to applaud the Roman system of death as entertain-

ment, and perhaps impossible or unnecessary truly to be objective about it, we nevertheless cannot simply assume that the Romans did react (or should have reacted) to the games of the arena according to our own personal values or the standards of our own society, especially when we ourselves find those standards difficult to identify or define.[1]

The problem with judging the violence of others is illustrated by the very terms that describe it. Even the word *violent*, used by one group or culture to designate activities performed in another, may carry with it connotations of illegitimate or inappropriate behavior entirely absent in the minds of most members of the other group (Ball-Rokeach 1972: 101; Riches 1986: 1). Physical hurt done to others is only considered violence in certain social contexts. "The physical force employed by the state is . . . government . . . and not violence" (Riches 1986: 3). Different governments and societies, and separate groups within one culture, often disagree about what force is legitimate and against whom it may be employed. In recent decades, although scholars of many disciplines (anthropology, ethnography, sociology, psychology, criminology, biology, medicine) have turned their attention to the problem of defining and explaining past and present violent behavior in a wide variety of (usually contemporary) contexts,[2] too little systematic effort has been made to identify those factors that legitimized the "violent" acts of the arena in their own time and context.[3]

One potentially very informative body of data about Roman attitudes toward the games of the arena is the art depicting the events. Gladiatorial and venatorial imagery was widespread and available to all social classes. It ranges from prefabricated, standardized representations in inexpensive media, intended for the lower levels of society, to individualized, carefully detailed, and expensive works commissioned by the very wealthy and powerful. Individual combatants as well as groups of gladiators, beast fighters, animals, and equipment were represented in figurines and illustrated on lamps, ceramics, gems, ivories, funerary reliefs, and—with more room for detail—architectural reliefs, wall paintings (rarely preserved), and floor mosaics.[4] Modern scholars tend to evaluate the art depicting the arena less negatively than they do the ancient literature on the topic. They sometimes discuss even very gruesome images matter-of-factly, solely in terms of the artist's technique or style and the limitations or potential of the medium employed. Some even evaluate violent scenes positively.[5] Most frequently, authors cite such depictions as evidence for the types of events that took place, the functions of various participants, the clothing worn and the props and equipment used, the kinds of animals exhibited and killed, and the "rules of the game." They also discuss the images as illustrations of chronological change in the nature of gladiatorial combat and in the development of artistic technique and design. Only rarely does an art historian like J. M. C. Toynbee consider the context of the images or question why and how they depict what they do—and Toynbee's presentation of "the problem" is itself an expression of horror rather than a search for an answer (Toynbee 1973: 83). Yet the art constitutes a valuable record of how a people viewed its own institutionalized violence. These images should be able to tell us more than just what acts were performed, and according to what conventions.

Of particular interest for their scope and attention to detail are polychrome mosaics, mostly of the second through fourth centuries A.D., which depict both standardized illustrations of the encounters of men and beasts in the arena and individualized recreations of particular events. Some of the best examples are preserved in North Africa and Gaul (centers of the mosaic industry), where they usually decorated the public areas, including receiving and dining rooms, of the private houses and villas of the wealthy (Dunbabin 1978: 25–26). These mosaic images, intended to please both hosts and guests, are not merely reflections of real life: "Representations are not just a matter of mirrors, reflections, keyholes. Somebody is making them, and somebody is looking at them, through a complex array of means and conventions" (Kappeler 1986: 3). Susanne Kappeler here considers representations in the context of current feminist debate on the nature of pornography, but understanding *who* the observers are, and not only how they see but how they transmit their views, in literature and in art, is of pressing interest in varied fields of study. Discussion ranges from identification of the viewers and their overt or hidden values to consideration of the ethical issues underlying their point of view. Roland Barthes evaluates various levels of meaning in so mundane an image as a French advertisement for Italian pasta (Barthes 1985b: 22–26). Raymond Williams, discussing literature, cites "material so laden with values that if we do not deal directly with them we have literally nothing to deal with" (R. Williams 1971: 6). Spencer Weart, author of *Nuclear Fear: A History of Images* (1988), wants the historian to ask "what psychological and social needs did the images meet? How might they have influenced decisions?" (Weart 1989: A44). Viewers (writers, artists) transmit information by a medium that incorporates the values of the group to which they belong, and their work will appeal to, and be most comprehensible to, those who share their values. This, of course, is true of both the artists creating texts or images and the scholars studying them. Clifford Geertz notes that anthropologists too cannot separate the "reality" of what they study from the way they choose to discuss or present it (by writing it, speaking it, or showing it in museum displays or films): "the line between mode of representation and substantive content is as undrawable in cultural analysis as it is in painting" (Geertz 1973: 16).

Many recent authors writing specifically about the ways in which certain members of society "see" less powerful people, especially in painting, have focused on women as the objects and victims of a male gaze and interpretation.[6] A male artist and audience create and view a female product that reflects their beliefs and fantasies, and which is posed and arranged within the two-dimensional image not only in relation to the other figures within the frame but also in reaction to the gaze of the three-dimensional viewer. Some conventions of representation entail the abuse of an object, often female, designated in its cultural context as appropriate to victimize. This provides a rationale for the depiction of violence against women in "slasher" films: "To me it's almost a genre convention at this point—like using violins when people look at each other or using women in situations where they are killed or sexually attacked. . . . Women, over the history of Western culture, seem to be more vulnerable than men. . . . I don't particularly want to chop up women but it seems to work" (Brian De Palma, quoted in Pally 1984: 17). Members of the audience, male and female, are expected to understand the implied social system and react favorably to the imagery, or at least not to respond with excessive pity or indignation. Conversely, Jeffrey Sammons records an example of the repression of "victim" imagery when the victim belongs to the wrong group. American fight films were banned after 1910, largely in response to the racially charged defeat of white fighter James Jeffries by black fighter Jack Johnson, so that viewers could not see a black man beating a white (Sammons 1988: 34–44; Wills 1988: 6). The spectator, assumed to be a white male or to share his values, could not be subjected to watching someone like himself lose, nor could the traditional victim be allowed to witness an inappropriate victory. Here the importance to the viewers of distancing themselves from—or accepting themselves as—victims is illustrated. Some theorists have even evaluated the degree of empathetic distance between human viewers and animal victims in different times and places. John Berger discusses ways in which modern, Western people view animals and distance them from themselves in zoos and art (J. Berger 1980: 1–26). Garry Marvin emphasizes, in contrast, the modern Anglo-Saxon "closing of the distance between animal and human worlds" which makes us disapprove of inflicting harm on animals for entertainment such as bullfighting (Marvin 1986: 134).

In the mosaic art depicting the arena, the object of a spectator's gaze is an animal or a human usually shown being killed or in a situation in which he may soon be killed. These mosaics can illuminate the cultural norms that encouraged people to enjoy or tolerate the games and influenced artists to select what they regarded as appropriate and appealing images for reproduction. The scenes depicted on the floors are varied, but they share, as Katherine Dunbabin has pointed out, "a love of exotic beasts and of scenes of violent, often bloody action for their own sake," and "a desire to commemorate the giving of spectacular displays to the community" (Dunbabin 1978: 85). The real events of the arena were interpreted and transformed by mosaicists into permanent records of "the (generic) arena" and of specific shows. The giver of the games (*editor*) and the audience are not usually shown in the mosaics, so the viewer of the scene replaces the crowd at ringside. The actors— men and beasts—fighting to the death in real life, under the eyes of an audience seated safely to the side, are summarized in vignettes placed on permanent display for another (even safer) showing. These images can contribute to our understanding of the ways in which the Romans viewed less powerful beings who could legitimately be killed. Which aspects of the games do artists commemorate? Is the complex relationship between *editores* and audiences and those they watched in the arena reflected in the mosaic reenactments, in which usually only the participants, and not the spectators, are shown? Does the art illustrate or encourage an emotional distance between the viewer and those viewed in the mosaic floor?[7] Since artists categorize encounters in the arena according to types of combatants, an examination of mosaic scenes by genre may help answer these questions and reveal more clearly the ancient attitude toward the events. Before turning to specific images, let us consider the role of the games in society and the context of the mosaics on the villa floor.

Background

The Nature of the Games

The killing of men and beasts in both private and official games played a significant role in Roman public life and politics from the third century B.C. into the fifth

century A.D. No brief overview can capture the complexities of and the chronological changes in the events of the arena (Balsdon 1969: 244–70, 288–313; Ville 1960,
1981). The most impressive games, such as those in 108–9 with which Trajan
celebrated his Dacian victories, involved slaughter on an almost unimaginable scale
(123 days of shows with 10,000 gladiators and 11,000 animals, Dio Cassius 68.15).
Despite the protests—or lack of interest—of some Romans, the literary sources, the
numerous representations in art, and the many preserved amphitheaters and circuses
illustrate that the games were not merely an entertainment but virtually a require-
ment of Imperial Roman social and political life. It is the Christian authors who
were most horrified by the events of the arena and by the audience response to
bloodshed (St. Augustine *Confessions* 6.8). Pagan authors, even those who saw the
games as a vulgar, cruel, or inappropriate entertainment, were nevertheless often
affected by how commonplace the killings were. Already in the late Republic,
Cicero could complain that it was not pleasurable to watch a puny human mangled
by a powerful beast—but even if it *was* supposed to be worth seeing, there was
nothing new in it (*Letters to Friends* 7.1.3). By the second century A.D., the
presentation of gladiatorial games and beast fights for entertaining people and
fulfilling official obligations had spread throughout the Empire. As the Romans saw
it, the *munus,* a display usually of both men and beasts pitted against one another, in
circus, forum, or amphitheater, served to fulfill an *editor's* civic and religious duties
and to illustrate his wealth and social status.

The crowd was tantalized with the unusual and the large in scale (elaborate sets,
exotic animals, dwarves or women, huge numbers of men or beasts fighting in pairs
or groups)[8] as well as by the violent and bloody. Animals were sometimes only
displayed (there were no public zoos) but more often were set against each other or
against armed men (*venatores,* skilled hunters, or *bestiarii,* less well-trained fighters), or they were incited to attack and maul unarmed prisoners or criminals (*damnati ad bestias*). The hunting of animals in the arena (*venatio*) was an extension of
the longstanding practice of hunting animals in the wild. The killing of criminals,
prisoners of war, and other social outcasts served the state as execution and taught a
public lesson in the results of criminal behavior (see Tertullian *De spectaculis* 19 for
a Christian reaction). The combat of gladiators supposedly taught the audience to
value courage: "the love of praise and desire for victory could be seen, even in the
bodies of slaves and criminals" (Pliny *Panegyric* 33).[9] While it is clear that not
every animal and man in a show was killed, the immediate purpose of a major
portion of many games was for a stronger opponent to overcome a weaker and to
stab, claw, gore, bite, or trample the loser to death for the enjoyment of spectators
protected from the fray—except in the reign of a few bad emperors who were
capable of throwing even members of the audience into the arena (Suetonius *Caligula* 35; *Domitian* 10; Dio Cassius 59.10.3). The audience was usually protected
from both the combatants in the ring and the *editor* in the stands with them, which
makes the throwing of a member of the crowd into the arena an especially disturbing
event. If the patron could ignore the boundaries between viewer and viewed, the
games ceased to function properly. Pliny (*Panegyric* 33) contrasts the good emperor
Trajan, who does not turn spectators into spectacles, with his evil predecessor
Domitian, who did.

The animals brought into the arena to kill other animals and condemned criminals might be saved to serve the same function on another day (Jennison 1937: 177–78). Certain valuable animals were specially trained and could become famous, like gladiators, for their behavior in the ring (Statius *Silvae* 2.5). Some arena animals were dear to their masters; *venatores,* like hunters, valued and even loved the dogs that worked with them for years (Toynbee 1973: 121; Martial *Epigrams* 11.69). These animals, however, were companions, trained to help their human masters capture or kill other animals or humans for whom people did not feel a similar empathy. Tertullian comments indirectly on the audience's usual lack of empathy when he questions ironically whether a member of the audience will be moved by pity at the sight of a biting bear or of the *retiarius*'s nets (*De spectaculis* 25). On one recorded occasion when the crowd did pity the animals in the arena, the show was a failure: in the games with which Pompey dedicated his theater in Rome in 55 B.C., some of the elephants that had been pitted against armed men ceased to fight and began to trumpet a lament that moved the viewers (Dio Cassius 39.38.1–4; Cicero *Letters to Friends* 7.1.3). Cicero attributed the crowd's compassion to a feeling that the elephants had a fellowship with the human race. The audience's feeling for the animals was specific to this occasion; the elephants in other shows did not elicit a similar reaction. Most beasts of the arena, and many people, did not warrant any fellow feeling.

Damnati ad bestias were criminals and other opponents of social or military order such as Christians and rebels (Ville 1981: 231, 235–38). These victims of the arena were, at least in theory, outcasts from Roman society, or people who not only had never belonged to it but actively opposed it. Those sent to be killed by wild beasts in Apuleius's *Metamorphoses* (4.13) are specified as having forfeited any chance for reprieve. One woman, condemned to the beasts by a local prefect but instead (or in addition) procured by the wealthy owner of an ass to mate with his animal in the arena, was a multiple murderess (*Metamorphoses* 10.23). Such people were considered too low to deserve a fighting chance and were sent unarmed, even completely bound and helpless, to die. Their deaths were public executions, occasions—in other times and places as well—for a public to witness, and by its approval to justify and participate in, the annihilation of opponents of the ruling powers and of the social good (Foucault 1979: 47–59; see Tacitus on the public's reaction when Nero punished Christians out of cruelty rather than for the public good, *Annals* 15.44).

Less heinous criminals, condemned not *ad bestias* but to combat with animals or with other men (*ad ludum venatorium* or *gladiatorium*), often had the opportunity to make a good showing. Part of the appeal of these combats was the potential for a "good fight." A gladiator who sensed his imminent defeat had the right to request the *editor* for *missio*—to be dismissed honorably from combat—unless he had been condemned to fight to the death, *sine missione* (Martial notes that an audience could sometimes even request *missio* for an animal: *Epigrams* 13.98; Ville 1981: 419–20). The *editor* had the power of life and death over the individual combatants who requested his intercession, but he responded to the judgments of the audience, which expressed its collective pleasure or displeasure with the loser (Ville 1981: 442–43). The crowd was also granted another power not normally familiar to its individual members: as a large, anonymous body, it was uniquely able to express its sentiments to the emperor or other officials even on topics unrelated to the arena (Hopkins 1983: 14–20). Emperors, even those who were not enthusiastic about the games, found it expedient to attend as well as provide them.[10] These aspects of the arena undoubtedly made the games even more popular; they also enhanced the distinction between empowered viewers and those they viewed, who could legitimately be killed for entertainment.

The most favored gladiators were those who voluntarily submitted to the harsh rules of the arena, and especially those who had been freed but had reenlisted, thereby exhibiting the "right attitude." At Trimalchio's dinner, one of the guests praises the upcoming show of an *editor* who will provide mostly freedmen as combatants (Petronius *Satyricon* 45.4–5). Such veterans were likely to enlist in the "best bands" (Apuleius *Metamorphoses* 4.13; Ville 1981: 251–52). Whether freed or free men, those who volunteered for the arena became slaves and took an oath (*auctoratio*) to hand themselves over to their master (an independent owner or, in the first century A.D. and later, an Imperial official) body and soul, and to submit to being beaten, burned, or put to the sword.[11] In this way, even volunteer gladiators were both symbolically and actually punished, and established as a separate class of people whose deaths were appropriate, if not always desirable (it was not in a master's best interest for all the experienced men to die).

The combatants' indifference to death is illustrated by the famous salutation to the emperor Claudius by men condemned to fight a naval battle: "They who are about to die salute you" (Suetonius *Claudius* 21; Dio Cassius 60.33). In this case, however, the men were merely paying lip service to the ideal and ultimately had to be threatened and cajoled into fighting. Such unwilling combatants are rarely attested. References to pleas for mercy or to the rebellion of vanquished gladiators who were denied *missio* are also unusual (Ville 1981: 417; Suetonius *Caligula* 30), perhaps because they were not effective (merely confirming that the losers deserved to lose). Victorious gladiators, although despised as a group for their low status and occupation, could, like charioteers (Humphrey 1986), as individuals nevertheless acquire honor, money, and fame (Tertullian *De spectaculis* 22). In a society that valued physical prowess and victory, gladiators who survived and pleased the crowd (and thereby their masters and trainers) were adulated, and could eventually win their freedom. It is indicative of the complex relationship of crowd and combatant that many freed gladiators voluntarily reenlisted and submitted themselves again as victims to a system in which they were also rewarded as victors (cf. Sammons 1988: 243, 251). The reasons for this voluntary system of self-enslavement, for the crowd's desire to see battles to the death, and for the ambiguous veneration of the victor are complicated and far beyond the scope of this paper. Carlin Barton cites the willing gladiator in the early years of the Empire as a paradigm for the man who nobly accepts the degradation of the human condition (Barton 1989). Hopkins equates gladiators with "culture heroes," like "pop stars and athletes," and notes the Roman "commitment to cruelty." He cites the effects of slavery, militarism, and all-powerful fathers, as well as the crowd's need to release "collective tensions," as reasons for the gladiatorial games (Hopkins 1983: 21, 28–29). These factors, which remain to be studied in depth, and many others still unstudied,[12] probably all contributed to the institutionalization of death as entertainment and to the polarization of people into viewers and viewed. It is the latter—the dichotomy between spectator of and participant in the arena—that the art in particular may illuminate.

The Mosaic Floors

Polychrome representational mosaics decorate the floors in both public and private rooms of Roman houses in the second century A.D. and later. Multicolored mosaic floors increased in popularity in the second century A.D., when new mosaic schools and workshops developed in the western Gallic provinces and in North Africa (Dunbabin 1978: 8–9, 18–19). In Gaul, the overall decorative effect came to dominate, sometimes at the expense of individual scenes. Representational panels were symmetrically arranged within a dense background pattern, creating a more rigid, less narrative overall picture. In North Africa, in contrast, the entire mosaic field became a vehicle for the depiction of events, such as hunts and gladiatorial games, taking place on varied terrain and even at different times. Their more flexible approach to the composition of mosaic floors meant that the African mosaicists could more easily mirror the stylistic changes occurring in other artistic media and could more readily incorporate into even a standardized scene an individual patron's requests (Dunbabin 1978: 9–11; Lavin 1963: 276–77). The arena is only one of many subjects depicted in these mosaics. Other themes include other entertainments such as hunting in nature and chariot racing in the circus, different scenes taken from real life, landscapes, still lifes, and a host of mythological topics and literary allusions.[13] The recurrence of single motifs, whole scenes, and patterns of composition in different mosaics, not only within one area but also across geographical and chronological boundaries, indicates the existence of workshops using stock repertories (Dunbabin 1978: 23–30; Ovadiah 1987: 181).

Special care was taken with certain mosaics, but a high quality of workmanship is not necessarily associated with a public rather than private location in a house. Certain subjects also do not seem to be confined to particular rooms, nor is there a marked difference in the themes depicted in public architecture (such as baths and basilicas) as opposed to private homes, although innovative or individualized scenes are more likely to appear in houses and to reflect a patron's special interests. Subjects within one room in a house or between rooms could be linked thematically (for example, the scenes in the dining room [Figure 9.1], thresholds, and even outside the doorways of the Maison des Autruches at Hadrumetum, discussed below, all involve the arena), and ceilings, walls, and floors could be planned as unified systems. In many instances, however, it is not possible to identify a clear thematic relationship between even the paintings or mosaics within one room (Brilliant 1974: 135–36). In too many cases, the provenience of mosaics within a house, or even within a city, is unknown (excavators removed the floors to museums without recording their location) or unpublished (the style and subject of mosaics are often evaluated with no regard for their original location and function within a house or within a broader decorative framework). Even when the mosaics of one house are fully published together, some of them may have been altered by repairs or may be replacements for earlier, perhaps originally more thematically coherent floors (Dunbabin 1978: 26–27). Many mosaics can only be dated on the basis of style, and there is sometimes considerable disagreement about their chronology; the dates given below are therefore not always secure.

Of the approximately forty extant arena mosaics (excluding hunting scenes that are not clearly *venationes*), the provenience of roughly two-thirds is known. Most decorated the public rooms of private houses, including peristyles, corridors, and (least explicably to the modern sensibility) the Roman reception-cum-dining rooms called *triclinia* or *oeci* (roughly half of those of known provenience),[14] in which the host fulfilled his social obligations by entertaining and impressing guests with his wealth, taste, and education.[15] In antiquity the terms *triclinium* and *oecus* could be used interchangeably, as they sometimes are today, especially if there is only one clear "dining room" in the house—often, but not always, indicated by the nature of the mosaic decoration itself, which may be T-shaped, as in Figure 9.1, or otherwise offset the appropriate spaces for couches along the walls (Dunbabin 1978: 27 n. 53). Some houses have both a large formal room opening onto a peristyle, which could be used for many purposes including dining, and a smaller, less centrally located room for more private dining. The diners reclining around the periphery of a room observing an arena mosaic in the center recreate in miniature the audience in the stands of an amphitheater viewing the spectacle on the sands. With this context of the games and the mosaics in mind, we can now turn to the specific events of the arena depicted in mosaic art.

The Events of the Arena

A *munus* normally included a variety of events and encounters between beasts and men, and arena mosaics sometimes provide an overview of many possible or actual events of a show. The combats therefore cannot always be neatly segregated into completely distinct categories, but artists do subdivide the events according to combatants: animals against animals, animals against men, men against men.

Animals are illustrated alone (or at least not directly interacting with humans, even if men are present) in four essentially different visual contexts, which sometimes overlap: (1) busts and full figures of inactive or calm animals, sitting, standing, or walking alone, fill medallions; (2) animals, alone or in groups, strike standardized, more active poses, usually charging or running, but not clearly attacking or fleeing from a specific opponent; (3) carnivores and other aggressive beasts, such as bulls, attack weaker herbivores; and (4) equally ferocious beasts attack one another.

In encounters between men and animals, either may be depicted as the weaker (the attacked): (1) animals are shown attacking unarmed, sometimes bound men (in which case a "handler" of the animals or men may be present) or men only poorly equipped to defend themselves, and men are depicted beating, whipping, or impaling relatively defenseless animals. A more equal form of combat between man and beast is (2) the confrontation of skilled huntsmen with dangerous animals, often big cats.

Gladiators are sometimes shown alone, in standard poses of combat, but usually

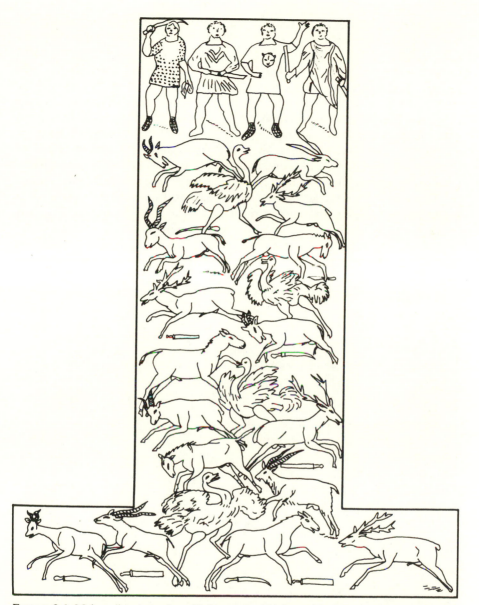

FIGURE 9.1 Maison des Autruches, Hadrumetum. Frightened herbivores flee under the gaze of four *venatores* (drawn from Foucher 1964b: fig. 7).

fight one-on-one in pairs. They are typically represented facing each other, preparing to fight; already engaged in battle, with the outcome uncertain; or at the end of the fight, when one man has lost his shield or weapon, staggered or fallen, or received a wound rendering him unable to fight effectively.

A mosaic of the mid-third century from a villa at modern Bad Kreuznach, West Germany (Guthmann 1965: 38), serves as a useful validation of this tripartite subdivision. It illustrates events of the arena arranged in decorative patterns and ranked thematically in importance (Figure 9.2). The roughly square mosaic (7.40 by 6.72 meters), centered within a geometric border, is dominated by a central medallion depicting a variety of beasts of the arena. The figures are oriented toward a niche (3.80 meters wide by 2.40 meters deep) in the middle of the eastern wall, which Guthmann interprets as the location of three dining couches (Guthmann 1965: 40). This niche is located on axis with the entrance to the room, which opens onto a peristyle courtyard. The images of two *venatores* standing in the center of the medallion are now almost entirely destroyed, but their activities are indicated by one bear with a broken spear in his snout (Parlasca 1959: pl. 88:3). Eight semicircular panels encircle the medallion, filling the square except for the corners, which are decorated with small, square representational panels. Within each semicircle a duel takes place, gladiatorial pairs alternating with men fighting beasts, while beasts kill beasts in the square corner panels. The gladiatorial duels are emphasized by their placement on the main, intersecting axes (the main axis through the door is west-to-east). The outcome of the gladiators' battles is the least certain of all the encounters; no man has yet fallen, although one man has lost his shield.[16]

In contrast, the outcome of the four venatorial combats centered on the diagonal

N
→

FIGURE 9.2 Villa, Kreuznach. Arena-mosaic illustrating three types of combat: animals against animals, animals against men, men against men (Guthmann 1965: 39). Courtesy of the Schloßparkmuseum, Bad Kreuznach.

axes of the room is not in doubt. In the semicircular panel in the southeastern corner of the floor, the *venator* turns away from a bull, fallen on its haunches, which he has impaled in the back with a spear. He looks to his right, outside the frame, toward the audience. In the other three panels, a *venator* is successfully impaling a springing animal in the chest (a boar, leopard, and bear, respectively), and blood runs from their wounds onto the ground (Figure 9.3). The victorious animals in the four small corner panels also dominate their opponents. These panels are oriented toward only two sides of the room (the two northern ones toward the northern wall, the two southern ones toward the southern wall). The two losers in the western panels, a bull and a boar, still struggle (Parlasca 1959: pl. 91:2, 3), while those in the eastern panels, an ass and a stag (prey rather than equal opponents), have been forced onto their haunches (Parlasca 1959: pl. 91:1, 4).

In this mosaic, the violent scenes of the arena are not only presented in all their diversity within a decorative framework, within which they themselves are made to serve as decorative patterns, but they are also thematically organized according to types of combat. A variety of animal victims is emphasized in the central medallion, while the hierarchy of scenes around it seems to illustrate the relative importance of different pairs of combatants: peripheral panels, animals against animals; diagonal panels, animals against men; main panels, men against men. A different moment or outcome of combat is also emphasized in each category of pairs. In the peripheral panels, predators overcome their wounded opponents: equally matched combatants still struggle as they fall, while prey inevitably lose. In the diagonal panels, men vanquish ferocious beasts, but at a bloody moment of great danger to themselves. In the main panels, gladiators still battle; the outcome of their combat, in contrast to that between beasts or men and beasts, remains uncertain. This tripartite subdivision according to types of combatants and representative moments in their combat recurs

FIGURE 9.3 Villa, Kreuznach. Detail from a scene in Figure 9.2: a *venator* fatally wounds a springing leopard (Guthmann 1965: 41 [bottom]). Courtesy of the Schloßparkmuseum, Bad Kreuznach.

in other venatorial and gladiatorial mosaics. Using these three categories, we turn now to an examination of specific mosaics that can help illuminate the interests of the spectator; the relationship of actor, *editor,* and crowd; and the emotional distance of the viewers from those they view.

Animals against Animals

Some mosaics serve as visual displays or "catalogues" of animals not clearly specified as appearing in an arena.[17] The numbers, diversity, or exotic nature of the beasts may indicate that their context is venatorial. More often, attack is implied or clearly specified. Some animals are "set pieces," however, and do not necessarily interact even if they are depicted in the same panel or shown in poses of aggression or flight. A mosaic from the *triclinium* of the Sollertiana Domus in modern El Djem, Tunisia (Foucher 1963: plan 1), probably of the third century, illustrates two ways to present the animals. The shaft of the T-shaped central panel is decorated with individual standing or walking beasts isolated within medallions (Foucher 1963: pl. 16). The decoration in the bar of the T more clearly indicates a location in the arena: a whole field of varied prowling and fleeing animals surrounds a shrine of Diana, a goddess associated with the games. Only the two beasts directly in front of her shrine, a bull and a lion, confront each other and prepare to fight (Foucher 1963; pl. 17); the other animals do not seem to see or react to each other. A mosaic panel of the third century from Carthage shows a literal "count" of animals of different types (boars, bears, bulls, cats, stags, rams, ostriches). The flanks or rumps of some of them are labeled with the letter *N* (*numero*) followed by a number indicating how many beasts of that type were displayed.[18] Despite the aggressive poses of some of the carnivores, only six cats to right of center seem to respond directly to one another (Poinssot and Quoniam 1952: 133–134). The emphasis here is on quantity and variety rather than on attack, which is nevertheless clearly intimated.

Other catalogues of animals document the nature of present or future violence in more specific ways. A mosaic of the third century, from the T-shaped *triclinium* of the Maison des Autruches at Hadrumetum (modern Sousse), Tunisia, illustrates a field of herbivores in flight, their frightened, rushing forms arranged in a decorative pattern (Figure 9.1). The reason for their panic is symbolized by the venatorial weapons strewn among them, and indicated in an even more direct fashion by the figures of four *venatores* at the base of the shaft of the T and further by the scene outside the entryway which illustrates a *venator* beside dying bears which he has impaled; his name and accomplishment are recorded: *Neoterius occidit,* "Neoterius has killed (them)."[19] Other, very damaged scenes of *venatores* and animals decorate the thresholds. An apsidal mosaic from modern Le Kef, Tunisia, of the late second or early third century (the function of the room and building is uncertain), shows a number of ostriches and deer enclosed within a net.[20] Their fate is indicated by the trainers who bring snarling dogs (elsewhere shown attacking, not herding—see Figure 9.5 below) through gaps in the enclosure. In these mosaics an attack is still not explicitly shown. In other mosaics different kinds of animals actively attack one another, or predators maul prey. On a mosaic of the fourth century from the Maison de Bacchus in El Djem, Dionysus is depicted in the center of a field of fighting bears, boars, and beribboned bulls, clearly not animals in the wild.[21] (A mosaic from modern Rades, Tunisia, apparently from an early Christian basilica, also illustrates a field of beasts prowling, attacking, and fleeing, but personalizes the scene by listing the animals' names over their heads.)[22] The third-century floor of the *triclinium* of the Maison Cour de la Ferme Hadj Ferjani Kacem of El Djem isolates animal combats into separate decorative motifs (Figure 9.4). The floor is inset with medallions showing the encounters of pairs of animals, mostly carnivores mauling herbivores. The variety of beasts depicted here is characteristic of the arena, as is the pairing in one medallion of a bear and a bull. The point of the encounters of unequally matched animal opponents was the killing of the weaker,

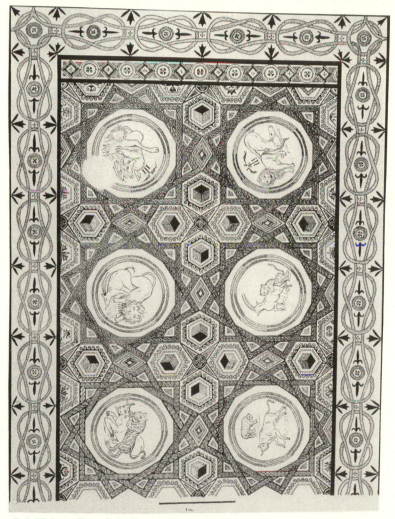

FIGURE 9.4 Maison Cour de la Ferme Hadj Ferjani Kacem, El Djem. Medallions depicting animal combat (Foucher 1963: pl. 45).

which may be clearly shown, whereas the element of uncertainty in the combat of different, equally ferocious animals (bears, bulls, cats, boars), not shown dying, provided the excitement.

Animals against Men: Stronger vs. Weaker

Unequal encounters between men and animals, as between predators and prey, resulted in the expected subjugation or death of the weaker. It was conventional to show the suffering, fear, or ferocity of an animal, especially in its encounters with men, through facial details and positions of the body. Animals such as bears, felines, and dogs are often shown afraid or enraged, with teeth bared and ears drawn back. Through their poses and expressions, ferocious animals may be shown still fierce, although mortally wounded. The fear or pain of young animals or of small, relatively defenseless creatures such as hares and rodents is sometimes emphasized. Lionesses defend crying cubs in hunting mosaics of the fourth and fifth centuries from Antioch (Morey 1938: pl. 20; Levi 1947: pl. 77a; Kitzinger 1965: fig. 4). In the "Small Hunt" from the villa at Piazza Armerina in Sicily, probably of the late third or early fourth century, a hare cowers in a thicket as a mounted hunter prepares to impale it with his spear (Gentili 1956: pl. 19). In contrast, human faces are usually serene, and vigor or effort is indicated only by a man's poses or gestures. This lack of facial expression is characteristic of *bestiarii, venatores,* and even *damnati ad bestias* in the arena, of hunters on horseback in rural settings capturing beasts for the arena or killing them for sport, and of gladiators whose faces were exposed. The faces of most gladiators were hidden behind the featureless visors of their helmets (as in Figure 9.11 below), which, like theater masks, made heads more visible from a distance but, unlike masks, eliminated rather than emphasized facial expressions. According to Suetonius, the emperor Claudius liked to watch *retiarii* (who did not wear helmets) die, because he could see their uncovered faces (*Claudius* 34).

A border mosaic from Zliten (modern Bar Duc Ammera) in Libya provides an unusually explicit and detailed visual definition of an entire *munus* (Figure 9.5), and links the attack of "prey" animals by men and predators with the attack of unarmed or bound men by big cats. The narrow, rectangular border friezes enclose a central panel composed of opus sectile and mosaic squares. Animal combats and the throwing of men to big cats (lions, leopards) are illustrated together in the western and eastern friezes. Charging dogs and men with whips, sticks, or spears attack herbivores: ostriches, gazelles, goats, stags, and a horse (for variety, a bull and a boar also fight, chained together and overseen by a handler with a hook, and a man confronts a bear), and big cats attack condemned men, all but one tied to stakes anchored in the ground or in moveable carts.[23] Men incite (whip) the cats to ferocity and push condemned men toward them (Aurigemma 1960: pls. 151–59). In these scenes, the major emphasis is on the variety of animals and the attacks upon and by them, rather than on specific one-on-one combats (missing here, for example, are the more difficult encounters of spearmen with big cats). The figures are grouped in twos and threes, sometimes overlapping or stacked one above the other. In contrast, the gladiators in the northern and southern friezes fight neatly in a row, in clearly delimited pairs sometimes overseen by an official.

N

FIGURE 9.5 Villa, Zliten. Border-mosaic illustrating the varied events of the arena (Aurigemma 1926: fig. 77).

The borders of the Zliten animal friezes are decoratively marked by a leaping animal in each corner: in the eastern frieze a leopard (northeast) and lion (southeast), in the western frieze a dog (each corner). The patterned repetition of violent images (as with other motifs) tends to diminish the impact of any one scene. Here the symmetry is not exact, since in the northeastern corner proper a man tied to a stake is mauled by a leopard clinging to his chest; it is the man to his right, also bound, at whom a leopard leaps. A comparable mosaic from El Djem illustrates more clearly how repetition diminishes the significance of violent images. Leopards attack men *damnati ad bestias* in the corners of the central floor panel of room 3 in the Sollertiana Domus, whose *triclinium* is also decorated with beasts of the arena. The mosaic is probably to be dated to the second century (Foucher 1963: 24–25; Dunbabin 1978: 66). The back (western) third of the mosaic is destroyed, but it presumably mirrored the scene preserved along the eastern entrance. Leopards and bears prowl an arena bloodied by earlier events; an empty raised stage, a *catasta* (oriented toward the northern long side), dominates the center of the arena and the mosaic floor, by its very emptiness emphasizing the activity in the corners of the mosaic (Foucher 1963: pls. 21a–b, 22a–b).

In each of the two eastern corners of the El Djem mosaic, a slightly different version of the same scene is repeated, each oriented toward the nearest long side (toward the south and north). To the southeast a shaggy-haired, reddish-skinned (Foucher 1963: 19) captive, usually assumed to be a rebellious "barbaric" local, his arms bound behind him, is held upright by two handlers (who are preserved only in outline) and forced to confront a leopard which springs, mouth open and snarling, toward his bare chest. To the northeast, a similar captive, also bound and manipulated by a handler standing behind him, falls backward under the assault of a leopard which clings to his body, its claws embedded in his thigh, chest, and shoulder as it bites directly into his face (Figure 9.6). Blood streams from his wounds and forms puddles beneath him similar to the other pools of blood irregularly covering the surface of the arena (for a literary description of the results of one bite of a leopard, see Musurillo 1972: 129–30; see also Bomgardner 1989: 88–91). This offer of men to the beasts is situated within a chronological framework: the *damnati* are clearly killed after a preliminary event has already taken place. The victims are also clearly specified as non-Romans. This mosaic may commemorate

Figure 9.6 Sollertiana Domus, El Djem. *Damnatio ad Bestias:* a leopard attacks a bound man held upright by an attendant (Foucher 1963: pl. 21b [top]).

an actual historical event, a *munus* for which the owner of the house obtained these public enemies and had them thrown to the beasts. At the same time, the image of a man ripped by a leopard is used as a decorative motif, presumably in all four corners. (If one considers the likelihood that a rich patron today would choose attractively arranged scenes of the slaughterhouse or repeated images of public execution to decorate the borders or central panel of a living room or dining room rug, one can indeed see that social context is crucial.) The doomed men, with their handlers and the animals who will kill them, balance the composition dominated by the central *catasta*. These prisoners, alien and threatening to Roman society, are appropriate victims; presumably, their role as repeated elements of decoration was not undermined by a viewer's empathy with any one man.

Animals against Men: Equally Matched Opponents

The skilled hunting of beasts in the arena is based on the animal hunts of the wealthy conducted in a natural setting, an aristocratic tradition also depicted in mosaics and other media.[24] Like the motif of predator overcoming prey, the theme of man hunting beast has a long history in both Greek and Roman art. In the former motif, the natural order is shown in which weaker succumbs to stronger; in the latter, a man proves himself by overcoming a valiant beast. (The emperor Commodus showed his skill, but not his courage, by spearing animals from above: Herodian 1.15.1–4.) In neither case was the usual point of the image to make the viewer identify with a wounded animal. Numbers of beasts, presence of exotic species, and variety in the animals available to be killed are more characteristic of the *venatio* in the arena than of the hunt in the wild (unless the hunt, too, is staged). General familiarity with the varied animals of the arena, however, led to their incorporation into hunts that were not necessarily venatorial, and into mythological scenes as well.[25] Mosaics also illustrate the capture of animals intended for the arena—like hunting, a difficult, dangerous, and costly operation worth commemorating.[26] The main floor of a dining hall with multiple apsidal niches from a large villa at Cuicul (modern Djemila), Algeria, probably of the third century, depicts the events of the hunt and the arena together within the same mosaic frame.[27] In the upper half of the scene (oriented toward the entrance on the eastern, short side of the room), a huntsman on horseback (the master of the house?) rides in front of an arcaded portico in an outdoor setting indicated by trees and vegetation. He is surrounded by wild animals (a boar, impaled and bleeding; a lion; a stag). To the upper left is a dog, and below it a second huntsman, on foot, carrying small game. The lower scene, separated from the upper only by thick ground lines, takes place in an arena filled with felines: four lions and a leopard. A *venator* has impaled a lion(ess?), emphasized by her position in the center of the lower frame; she has no strength in her front limbs, crumpled beneath her, but still tries to pull the spear from her bleeding wound. Her (presumed) attacker has already turned to face another lion. Below, a second *venator* apparently keeps a lion at bay with a commanding gesture and perhaps some magical assistance.[28] In such encounters between *venatores* and animals, the goal was for the men to win, as in hunting. The instant of fatal wounding of the animal— or the moment afterward, before the beast had completely lost its strength—was the time of maximum danger and excitement. The mosaics show the beast with the spear protruding from its body or emphasize the actual thrust of the spear. In either case, wounds are emphasized by dripping blood, which forms puddles on the ground (see Figures 9.3, 9.6, 9.7, 9.8).[29]

The victory of skilled hunter over ferocious beast, as well as the relationship among *editor,* audience, and combatants, is illuminated by an inscribed mosaic from modern Smirat, Tunisia, probably of the third century (Figure 9.7; Dunbabin 1978: 67–70). In this mosaic, the positioning of figures within the scene and the direction of the gaze of the actors—toward other participants within the frame or directly out at the real viewer—emphasize a hierarchy of actors within the mosaic and invite the viewer's participation in their relationship. An inscription conveniently summarizes the verbal exchange between participants in the arena and the audience in the stands. Although it is unclear where in the house the mosaic (6.80 by 5.30 meters) was found, it is such a blatant piece of propaganda that it was probably intended for a *triclinium* or *oecus.* Two parallel columns of inscription are roughly centered in a panel within the larger floor and can be read from only one of the long sides, but representational scenes are arranged around the text so that observers from either long side will see the closest figures right side up. Looking from one direction they can read about the show provided by Magerius, while from the other their gaze is rewarded by the portrait (presumably) of this very Magerius, who probably both owned the house and commissioned the mosaic.

FIGURE 9.7 Smirat: Mosaic of Magerius. Venatorial combat against leopards. In the center an agent of the *editor* displays the money owed to the men (Mahjoubi 1968?: pl. 1).

Magerius is not, as one might have expected, the central figure of the mosaic. Instead, a well-dressed male figure with long hair (a boy?) stands facing forward between the two columns of text (emphasizing the "main view" as the one from which the inscription is legible), holding a tray with four bags, each labeled *1,000 denarii*. The inscription to his left records an announcement by a herald asking the audience to pay the Telegenii, a venatorial family, 500 *denarii* for each leopard. To the right is recorded the *adclamatio* of the crowd, perhaps also recorded on a more public monument, thanking Magerius for providing the show (he probably intended to do so all along and did not rise to the occasion unexpectedly) and praising him for his generosity with his money. Magerius's name is also inscribed alone in the vocative ("Mageri") to either side of the main text, the two acclamations facing in opposite directions to ensure legibility from both long sides. Beside the left acclamation stands a figure that has reasonably been interpreted as the goddess Diana, who looks toward the bearer of Magerius's money. Beside the right acclamation stands a heroically nude Dionysus (or Mercury), wearing only sandals and a cloak, gesturing (with a garland?) toward the man with short hair and beard standing (presumably; only his head, his left shoulder, and a staff held in his right hand are actually preserved) immediately beneath his name.[30] This scene recalls a similar work of art described in literature: an inscribed painting in the entryway to Trimalchio's house illustrated his entry into Rome and his personal successes under the similar patronage of Mercury and Minerva (Petronius *Satyricon* 29.3–5).

The events of the arena—four combats of men and leopards—are represented above and below the central inscription. Three leopards still struggle on the spears of *venatores;* the fourth has been defeated and hangs its head weakly as it bleeds to death. Its *venator* has departed for the opposite side of the mosaic to help a comrade impale another leopard. The name of each *venator* and leopard is inscribed over his head (these are the single, capricious names of slaves and animals: Spittara, Bullarius, Hilarinus, Mamertinus, Victor, Crispinus, Romanus, Luxurius).[31] Such names were sometimes cited in advertisements and announcements of events, in which the famous names of survivors and victors might serve as special attractions (Tumolesi 1980: 116–19, 139–41, 147–50). Sometimes mosaicists and other artists borrowed famous or standard names without reference to a specific event (Ville 1964), but on this mosaic the names are probably actually those of the *venatores* and the animals they killed on an occasion carefully recorded by the *editor* of the *munus.*

Magerius has chosen to emphasize his money (the bags of coins are at the heart of the mosaic) and the crowd's response to his spending it for their benefit (the central inscription: *de re tua munus edes . . . hoc est habere, hoc est posse,* "you will give the show at your own expense . . . this is what it means to be rich, to be powerful"; Beschaouch 1966: 139). Of all the actors in the scene, only Magerius and the boy holding the money look directly out of the mosaic at the viewer, the audience, emphasizing the relationship and bond between them. Magerius assumes for himself the patronage of two divinities elsewhere also associated with the animals and venatorial events of the arena, who are subordinated to his moment of glory (Foucher 1963: 18; Foucher 1964b: 101–4; Tertullian *De spectaculis* 12.7). Like the audience, they gaze toward him and his agent. Finally, he identifies for us the highlight of the event for which he paid: the final struggle of mortally wounded but still spirited leopards, impaled on spears, gushing blood which spreads in puddles beneath them. The combatants, man and beast, the objects of the viewer's gaze, there to "be seen" in real life, are here also confined to the two-dimensional arena; they look only at each other or down. Magerius has provided their names, which personalize them and allow them to be exhorted or discussed by members of the crowd at ringside or by those reclining comfortably at home.

Other details of the composition are more subtle. Hilarinus and Bullarius are perhaps not shown joining forces to kill the leopard Crispinus because they really did so in the arena, but because the removal of the gladiator from the "top" of the scene roughly balances the two halves of the composition: from either long side the viewer sees, flanking or below the central figure plus inscription, one divinity, one cry of "Mageri," two upright men, two downed leopards, and one lunging *venator* impaling a leaping leopard in the chest; along each long side, man also alternates with beast. Although Magerius is located metaphorically "in a corner of the amphitheater itself, almost on top of the nearest leopard" (Dunbabin 1978: 68), he is shielded from the action in the arena by the body of the defeated, quietly dying Luxurius (which turns its back to him) and by Dionysus. The boy holding Magerius's money is also isolated from the men and beasts around him by the text which encloses, almost encapsulates, him, following the outline of his body and the tray he holds. The images and text are carefully manipulated to establish the relationship and relative importance of figures in the scene.

There is a tendency to assume that realistic portrayals of suffering beasts, like the leopards in Magerius's mosaic, indicate an artist's or patron's sympathy with the animals. Henri Frankfort, describing Late Assyrian reliefs of royal lion hunts from Kuyunjik, concludes that "the love and care expended on the rendering of the dead and dying animals turn these scenes, intended as a pictorial epic, into a tragedy in which the victims, not the victor, play the chief part" (Frankfort 1970: 190); yet it is certain that Assyrian rulers did not intend such reliefs as moving tributes to the lions (Bersani and Dutoit 1985: 14, 39). J. M. C. Toynbee is moved by the "anguish" of dying cats in the Borghese Mosaic, from the corridor of a villa in Rome probably of the fourth century. She also describes "moving" scenes of leonine agony on eastern Romano-Christian ivory diptychs depicting government officials presiding over venatorial events of the fifth and sixth centuries A.D. (Toynbee 1973: 63, 83). On these reliefs, representations of the *editores* can fill as much as three-quarters of the frame.[32] The goal is to invite, not sympathy for the animals, but respect and gratitude for the *editor,* who looms over the event for which he claims credit.

The Roman ability to see something cute or humorous in the killing of animals and men is documented in several mosaics depicting children as *venatores,* gladiators, or *damnati ad bestias.* The *oecus* of the Maison des Chevaux at Carthage, probably of the early fourth century (Salomonson 1965: figs. 2–3), like room D from the villa at Zliten, has an opus sectile and mosaic floor bordered by scenes of the arena oriented toward the center of the room. The house gets its name from the horses depicted in the mosaic squares, which probably indicate the owner's fondness for circus racing; his interest in the arena, here relegated to a "joke" and subordinated in a border, is secondary to his interest in the circus. Children function as tiny beast fighters, lassoing and impaling small animals: various cats, hares, deer, goats, birds, and rodents (Salomonson 1965: fig. 4A–C, pls. 22–24). The kicking and squealing of some of the impaled and bleeding animals are vividly depicted. Although it is possible that real children sometimes fought in the arena (Dunbabin 1978: 87), the presence of two *erotes* in the border frieze and the parallels with other scenes of children and *erotes* inappropriately engaged in the affairs of adult mortals or gods make it likely that this mosaic is intended in the same humorous vein, despite its sometimes graphic violence. A very similar series of vignettes of probably the late third or early fourth century appears as the main decoration, in registers, in room 37 in the villa at Piazza Armerina in Sicily (Figure 9.8), where children are also shown, in another room, as charioteers of bird-drawn chariots (Kähler 1973: fig. 4). In one register, two boys flank a hare, one impaling it in the chest, the other raising his right arm in a gesture of excitement which contrasts with both boys' placid faces. The hare, bleeding profusely as so many wounded animals in mosaics tend to do, wears an expression that it is hard to imagine is not intentional: its mouth is parted and its profile eye is fully round, giving an impression of astonishment or fear as it meets the spear in mid-leap. To their right, another boy drags (strangles?) a flapping duck by the neck. In the next register, in a further twist on the joke of child *venatores* and their inappropriate victims, the small animals seek revenge and turn on their tormenters, chasing and biting them. A damaged mosaic of approximately the same date from the *triclinium* of a Roman house located north of the ports of Carthage illustrates a similar scene of

FIGURE 9.8 Villa, Piazza Armerina. Children combat small animals in a mosaic intended as a humorous play on standard venatorial imagery. In the lower register the animals turn on their attackers (Gentili 1956: pl. 42). From G. V. Gentile, *La Villa Imperiale di Piazza Armerina*, 1956, Instituto Poligrafico e Zecca dello Stato. Courtesy of Instituto Poligrafico e Zecca dello Stato.

child *venatores* (Salomonson 1965: 35). The patterns from Carthage and Sicily may conceivably stem from the same workshop (Dunbabin 1978: 86; Wilson 1983: 53–59, 67). Whether they do or not, this theme was not one patron's special request but a standardized humorous motif.[33]

Gladiators

The victory of man over beast illustrated on Magerius's mosaic is typical of Roman venatorial scenes. In contrast, the mortal wounding of gladiators is not usually illustrated, even in other media. Gladiators are depicted preparing to fight, fighting, and losing much more often than receiving a death blow or already dead. George Ville has called the moment of defeat the "most pitiful" (Ville 1981: 410); yet pity is perhaps not the emotion (at least, by no means the only emotion) the mosaicist or his patron wanted to elicit from a viewer, any more than it is the response an *editor* wanted from a crowd watching animals die on spears, whether in the arena or on a dining-room floor. (Tertullian implies that the branding of corpses in the arena to ensure that they really were dead was humorous: *Apology* 15.5.) There was no automatically preferred human victor, since both combatants were men. The excitement of the encounter was at its peak when victory was still undecided, or at the time of a loser's request for *missio,* the moment that occasioned the maximum participation of the viewers. The excited commentaries and exhortations of the crowd, which expected bravery from even the lowliest of condemned men, are described by Seneca (*Letters* 7.5). It was the courage rather than the pathos of a fighter that won him *missio.*

The participation of an unseen *editor* and audience in a gladiatorial duel may be indicated by the presence of the official who intercedes when one fighter requests *missio.* A gladiatorial scene dominates the floor of the centrally located *triclinium* (roughly 10 by 15 meters) of a long, rectangular villa from Nennig, West Germany, probably of the late second or early third century (Figure 9.9). Along the long axis of the room, inset into a complex geometric background pattern, are two square panels separated by a smaller, octagonal panel and surrounded by a further six octagons, two on each long side and one at each end. The main, tripartite entrance to the room is on the western, short end, where, unfortunately, the octagonal panel is damaged. The square panel east of it contains a marble basin and fountain (apparently part of the original design; Parlasca 1959: 36). The vignettes illustrated in the octagonal panels reveal the presence of the personnel in the background of the violence (a lion handler, musicians), the subsidiary figures (stopgap, still un-bloodied stick fighters), and the "second string" attractions (men killing big cats, and big cats mauling asses).

The centerpiece of the floor—and, presumably, the main attraction of the show—is depicted in the large, square representational panel on the central axis of the room. The scene dominates the eastern half of the floor and is oriented toward the central, most important couch or seat at the back of the room. (The water basin dominates the western half.) A *retiarius* and his more heavily armed opponent face each other in combat stance under the eyes of an official standing between them, holding a staff in his left hand. The official draws back his right arm, apparently

N →

FIGURE 9.9 Villa, Nennig. Octagonal medallions illustrating representative combats in the arena (Parlasca 1959: pl. 36). Courtesy of Deutsches Archäologisches Institute Zentrale, Berlin.

preparing to give the signal to start. This unarmed man with short hair and neat white tunic is sharply contrasted with the seminude fighting men who stand before him in their specialized protective clothing, the *retiarius* sporting long, shaggy hair, his opponent wearing a helmet. Into the heroic moment preceding battle to the death is intruded the watchful figure who symbolizes the real agents of the event: the man who paid for it, and the people who watch it, without whom neither the show nor the mosaic would be meaningful. The outcome of combat is still undecided, inviting the viewer's curiosity and participation in the event.

The relationship of *editor,* audience, and gladiators fighting to the death is more clearly illustrated in an inscribed mosaic panel, originally from Rome (exact context unknown) but now removed from its floor and exhibited in the National Archaeological Museum in Spain (Figure 9.10). It is paired with a similar panel, apparently from the same floor, but inscribed in less detail. The first panel (0.58 meter square) is divided into two registers by figured scenes meant to be "read" chronologically from bottom to top. In the lower register, two armed gladiators face each other with short swords raised. Behind each stands an unarmed official in a tunic, the one on the right carrying a staff. These men watch the gladiators, who watch each other. The gladiators are named: Maternus on the left, whose name is followed by the symbol ∅, indicating his death (Watson 1952; Friggeri and Pelli 1980), and Habilis on the right. The officials are unnamed; the audience does not need to know their

FIGURE 9.10 Rome: Mosaic of Symmachius. Two stages in the combat of Maternus and Habilis: in the lower register the men prepare to fight; above, Maternus is killed (Freijeiro 1950: fig. 9). Courtesy of Museo Arquelógico Nacional, Madrid.

names, since they are not the objects of attention. An inscription running between the registers tells us that while the gladiators were fighting (*quibus pugnantibus*), Symmachius *ferrum misit*—presumably "thrust the sword." This inscription caused some confusion when the scene was first interpreted, since Symmachius was assumed to be the victorious gladiator (Ashby 1914: 17). Yet he cannot possibly be one of the gladiators, who are clearly identified. The meaning of the inscription is clarified by the later scene in the upper register, where Habilis leans over the prostrate, bleeding body of Maternus (whose name is again followed by the ∅), apparently about to kill him. To Habilis's left stands the official with the staff, his head turned toward the two gladiators but his body and eyes turned to the left, toward someone outside the frame of the mosaic. This someone must be the *editor*, Symmachius, whose role it was to decide whether Habilis could in fact kill Maternus. The inscription *neco* above the official is probably to be interpreted as "I kill [him]," and is perhaps Symmachius's own statement that he himself kills Maternus. The crowd answers with a cry of verification and agreement, "We see" (*haec videmus*), and calls Symmachius, in the vocative, a happy man (*Symmachi, homo felix*), presumably because he has put on such a good show and made such appropriate life-and-death decisions.

The companion piece (Freijeiro 1950: fig. 8) similarly illustrates in two registers the combat of a *retiarius* (net fighter), Kalendio (his name followed in both registers by the ∅), and a more heavily armed gladiator, Astyanax. In the lower scene, Kalendio has thrown his net over Astyanax and menaces him with his trident. He is overseen by an unnamed official with a staff. In the upper register, "Astyanax has won" (*Astyanax vicit*) is inscribed over the head of the victor, who looks down at his defeated opponent, sitting on the ground below him. In this register, an official appears behind each fighter. Kalendio and the official standing behind him look to their right, to the left of the mosaic, and gesture with their right hands toward the unseen *editor*. The official behind Astyanax turns his face toward the combatants but twists his body and slews his eyes toward the *editor* while also gesturing to him with his right hand. We, the audience, watch the gladiators at the moment of decision (life or death?); the victor watches the loser; the loser and the officials watch the *editor* (and the *editor* presumably watches us). The presence of *editor* and waiting audience is clearly implied even in the absence of explanatory inscriptions.

In the mosaic from Zliten discussed above, scenes of bloody gladiatorial and venatorial combat are relegated to a position as decorative motifs in a border (Figure 9.5). The mosaic decorates the end room (room D) of a long row of rooms opening onto a portico to the north (Aurigemma 1926: figs. 10, 11). Room D also opens, unlike the other rooms in its row, onto a southern corridor parallel to the portico. It is the largest room, with the possible exception of one other, in the row (some of the rooms are damaged, however, and the villa is not fully excavated). The date of the mosaic is debated but it is usually ascribed either to the late first or early second century A.D. or to the early third.[34] The central part of the floor is composed of opus sectile squares alternating with mosaic panels depicting fish and marine life. The scenes of the arena border this central square, oriented inward in a continuous frieze (central square plus border roughly 3.50 meters square; frieze approximately 0.59 meter high). Since the figures are not oriented toward the wall, room D perhaps did not function regularly as a dining room. Gladiatorial combats are confined to the northern and southern friezes, while the western and eastern friezes illustrate animal hunts and the throwing of men to the beasts. Each gladiatorial frieze is introduced on the left by a herm and by musicians playing organ, trumpet, and horns. A hint of spatial depth—as well as an informal border—is provided in the form of death carts (for corpses) placed with their heads angled inward at both ends of each frieze (the bed in the southwestern corner has been destroyed). The gladiators fight one-on-one in a row between the death carts.

The presence of the unseen *editor* is clearly indicated here, as elsewhere, by the officials who oversee several of the gladiatorial fights and by the requests of the gladiators themselves for the *editor*'s intercession in a fight (Robert 1946: 132). The emphasis is on individual combat and on the moment of decision rather than on the deaths of gladiators. In two vignettes from the northern frieze, an official intercedes between two fighters, one of whom requests *missio*. (In the western half of the southern frieze, largely destroyed, at least one other official is represented.) To the northwest, next to the musicians, one man is down, lying on his back and raising his left arm in the air; his right arm, still clutching a dagger, has been forced to the ground by his opponent (Figure 9.11). The victor leans toward him with right arm raised but is restrained from striking by an official who holds the victor's raised arm in both hands. Both victor and official look to the left of the frieze (to their right) at an unseen *editor* outside the frame. In the eastern half of the same frieze, the eyes of official and combatants seek the *editor* to the right (their left; Aurigemma 1960: pl. 146). A lance fighter leans in a relaxed pose on his spear, as his opponent,

FIGURE 9.11 Villa, Zliten. Detail from a scene in Figure 9.5: a defeated gladiator, knocked to the ground, requests *missio* with raised left arm; his victorious opponent is restrained by an official (Aurigemma 1960: pl. 144).

bleeding from a shoulder wound, raises the index finger of his left hand toward the official and the *editor* to his left (Figure 9.5). The official raises his staff in the air between (although it appears behind) the two gladiators and looks over his left shoulder out of the frame to the right. The *editor* is not imagined in a fixed spot but merely outside the mosaic, beyond the frame, and those inside it look toward—and beyond—the nearest border. In contrast with the less organized, more varied chasings and attacks in the animal friezes, the neat arrangement of the gladiators in twos, the watchful officials, the gestures for *missio,* and the participants' eye contact with the *editor* outside the scene all emphasize the importance of one-on-one combat carefully observed and judged by a viewer.

Conclusion

In this essay I have suggested that the mosaic art depicting the Roman arena can reveal more than just which events took place. The images of the legitimate victims of institutionalized violence can help the modern viewer understand the Roman attitude toward the games. The scenes on these Roman floor mosaics do document the interests of spectators and *editores* and inform us about the relationship of watchers and actors. The function of the events of the arena was to be exciting; the action—and the crowd's reaction to the events—was the point. The viewers remembered large numbers and different kinds of beasts, and appreciated seeing a variety of killings—the routine, expected subjugation of weaker by stronger and the less certain domination of one of two different but equal opponents. In the combat of animal predators and helpless prey, including bound men, artists emphasize the panicky flight or bloody wounds of the inevitable losers. In the more equal encounters of skilled hunters and fierce animals, the wounds of the animals are dramatically illustrated gushing blood, but at the moment of maximum danger to their human opponents. In the combats of equally matched men, in contrast, imminent death is not usually depicted, although bloody wounds may be. The uncertain outcome of battle, the gestures of gladiators for *missio,* and participants' glances outside the mosaic frame instead invite the viewer's involvement in a life-or-death drama produced by the *editor.* Similarly, Roman mythological wall paintings invite the spectator to enter into "suspended moments" before violent action, like those before a rape (Leach 1988: 396–402).

Some of these mosaics seem merely to have evoked the memory of pleasant pastimes; others can reasonably be interpreted as commemorating the specific beneficence of an individual to the public, and the honor and favor that were his reward. We cannot be sure that individualizing elements in a scene (such as the names or numbers of men or animals, the symbols of wins and losses, the acclamations of the audience, and the illustrations of special events that highlighted a particular show, such as the mauling of prisoners by leopards) necessarily signify the commemoration of one particular show by its *editor,* but they do indicate a desire on the part of the homeowner to identify or simulate specific games. Petronius, in his satiric description of Trimalchio's house, notes that a scene from a *munus* provided by someone else was painted on the wall of the peristyle (*Satyricon*

29.9). Presumably such individualized scenes depicted in the homes of their actual *editores* elicited from observant guests the same kinds of questions and positive comments that result today from the display of trophies, signed letters from the president, or records of civic honors.

Toynbee wonders how the Romans could illustrate violent scenes from the arena on their floors. If we ask "How could they?" about gladiatorial and venatorial themes, it is because we cannot imagine today enjoying what the scenes represent, or focusing our own private living or dining rooms on permanently displayed, fixed images that either specifically depict graphic (and still ongoing, rather than mythological or historical) violence, or at least imply that the violence will occur— although we can permit the fugitive violence of the television screen into these rooms.[35] We are more likely to accept the display of mounted heads (or antlers, or other parts) of killed animals, from which we distance ourselves perhaps partly because they are disembodied. We are also not disturbed by the images of typical arena beasts depicted alone in medallions in a mosaic floor, in which no aggression is even implied. It is the graphic illustration of animals' fear or pain and of the terrible wounds inflicted on man and beast that provoke the question "How could they?" The simple answer to the question is that the Romans did not typically see the images that bother us—or the practices behind them—the same way we do: with empathy for the victim. The mosaics instead emphasize the distance of patron and audience from those whose deaths they enforced or delayed; scenes of attack and suffering may be funny, they may be diminished in importance by subordinate locations and small scale, and they may be reduced to decorative patterns.

In this essay I have considered only the mosaics of the relatively wealthy. Depictions in other media may illustrate different aspects of the games and suggest other interests or reactions of lower social classes. For example, in art on a smaller scale with less scope for narrative and detail, such as that on terra-cotta lamps (probably intended for less wealthy spectators who could not themselves afford to give shows), the emphasis on blood and on requests for *missio* does not seem to be as strong. But on the richly detailed floors of the wealthy, scenes of panic, blood, and fatal moments were indeed decoration, celebrating the social structure that both permitted the games and admired appropriate reproductions of them. The cooperation or approval of viewers of the art who were themselves potential victims of the arena, such as slaves or non-Roman visitors, is assumed in the mosaics and in the homes that display them. These gladiatorial and venatorial images were surely observed by visitors and diners who responded with praise for their hosts; the violence they saw was essential to the games, commonplace in its context, and directed against legitimate victims.

NOTES

I would like to thank Amy Richlin for interesting me in this topic in the first place and for inviting me to contribute to this book. She and Robert Sutton have been kind and helpful critics. I am especially grateful to my colleagues Jeremy Rutter and James Tatum for their enthusiastic support and suggestions, and for generously sharing with me their own archaeological and literary research on Roman sports and gladiatorial games. Thanks also to Kathleen Corrigan, Jeanne O'Neill, and Laurie Talalay for their useful criticisms, Gail Vernazza for typing, and Jennifer Kochman and Lorie Berger for their assistance with a variety of tedious tasks. Dean Richard Sheldon of Dartmouth College was especially helpful in securing funding for my research.

1. James Clifford's introduction to *Writing Culture: The Poetics and Politics of Ethnography* (Clifford and Marcus 1986) provides a useful overview of the history of anthropologists' attitudes toward their own subjectivity (Clifford 1986: 1–26). See also Williams (1971: 6) on the "pursuit of the falsely objective" in literary and social studies. Elvin Hatch's history of ethical relativism (1983) is also relevant here.

2. Titles of potential interest to the student of gladiatorial violence include Ball-Rokeach 1972; Bernard, Ottenberg, and Redl 1971; Dunning 1986; Duster 1971; Hopkins 1983; Kelman 1973; Lintott 1968; Marvin 1986; Sammons 1988. Collections including essays on the general topic of violence include Elias and Dunning 1986; Henry and Sanford 1971; Parkin 1985; Riches 1986; Short and Wolfgang 1972.

3. Many modern authors have, of course, attempted to draw general conclusions about the reasons for the violence: Auguet 1972: 184–89; Barton 1989; Hopkins 1983: 27–30; Wells 1984: 277–78. Ville 1981 does so not explicitly but by virtue of presenting a wide variety of ancient opinions and statements about the arena.

4. For general overviews and illustrations, see Auguet 1972; Bailey 1980: 51–56; Berger and Joos 1971; Daremberg and Saglio 1896: 1563–99; Dunbabin 1978: 65–78; Faccenna 1956–1958; Ghislanzoni 1908; Grant 1967; Jennison 1937; Pearson 1973; Robert 1940, 1946, 1948, 1949; Toynbee 1973; Ville 1981 (who discusses but does not illustrate depictions in art); Wollmann 1917.

5. D. von Wilmowsky interprets the mosaic scenes of the arena from a villa at Nennig, West Germany (Figure 9.9, discussed below), as intentionally minimizing the violence of the arena: the mosaic avoids "wounding the eye" and the sensibilities, thereby surpassing other arena mosaics (Wilmowsky 1864, I: 3, 14). It is doubtful that the average Roman eye, used to more explicit scenes of carnage in real life and on mosaic floors, needed protection; nor is it entirely clear how the violence is minimized. While there is indeed not an emphasis on human blood in this mosaic, these scenes are hardly nonviolent; only the musicians to the far east of the floor are not directly associated with the theme of attack. G. V. Gentili calls a mosaic from Piazza Armerina in Sicily (Figure 9.8, discussed below) "gay and humorous," while R. J. A. Wilson dubs it a "charming mosaic of boys hunting"; it shows children, dressed as tiny beast fighters, lassoing and impaling small, struggling, and bleeding animals (Gentili 1956: 42; Wilson 1983: 56).

6. Berger 1972: 45–64; Betterton 1987; Cropper 1986; Dijkstra 1986; Duncan 1982; Ferguson, Quilligan, and Vickers 1986; Garrard 1982; Goldberg 1986; Gordon 1984; Hess and Nochlin 1972; E. Kaplan 1983; Kappeler 1986; Kent and Morreau 1985; Roberts 1972; Vicinus 1972. See, in contrast, Ffolliott 1986, on the iconographic solutions of a woman, Catherine de Medici, to the problem of creating her own political art once her husband had died; see also Garrard 1989 on a seventeenth-century female painter's untraditional depiction of women.

7. Katherine Dunbabin addresses some of these questions, although not in detail, in her book *The Mosaics of North Africa* (Dunbabin 1978: 65–87).

8. See Ville 1981: 155, 263–64, on dwarves and women.

9. Sammons 1988: 251–52 discusses the similar need in American society to justify boxing and see in it a redeeming social value (it proves manhood, builds character, purges the audience of its aggressions).

10. Suetonius *Claudius* 21; Dio Cassius 60.13, 66.25; Fronto *Ad Lucium Verum* 17 (*Loeb Classical Library* vol. 2); Scriptores Historiae Augustae *Hadrian* 18–19; Herodian 3.8.9.

11. Petronius *Satyricon* 117.5; Horace *Satires* 2.7.58–59; Seneca *Letters* 37; Juvenal 11.5–8; Ville 1981: 246–49. See Matz 1977: 135–37, on the hierarchical structure of the gladiatorial establishment.

12. The possibility that the deadly games of the arena functioned as a literary metaphor, or that they influenced literary depictions of violence, has only begun to be explored (Saylor 1987; Barton 1989; Tatum 1989). Eleanor Leach concludes that perceptions shaped by landscape painting and literature describing landscape could be transferred by the spectator (viewer or reader) from one medium to the other (Leach 1988: 24, 409). The real games of the arena (or the artistic interpretations of arena events) could similarly have affected literary authors and audiences. Christine Kondoleon argues that enactments of mythological episodes in the arena "conditioned the way the public 'saw' myths" (Kondoleon 1986).

13. See D. Smith 1983 and Dunbabin 1978: 1–37, for a general discussion of mosaics, and Brendel 1979: 155 on the subjects generally depicted in private as opposed to public art.

14. Vitruvius 6.3.8–10; Ward-Perkins 1981: 240–44, 402–4, 494 (*oecus*), 496 (*triclinium*).

15. See Petronius *Satyricon* 31 ff.; Apuleius *Metamorphoses* 2.19. Thébert 1987: 364–78 provides a useful overview of the appearance and function of receiving and dining rooms in North African houses of the second century A.D. and later. M. Smith 1975: 66 illuminates the "social stratigraphy" of Trimalchio's dining room by diagramming the "good seats."

16. Plates 89:2 and 3 are confused in Parlasca's text.

17. Carandini, Ricci, and de Vos 1982: pls. 7–14, 45; Pace 1955: figs. 12–17; Foucher 1963: pl. 16.

18. Poinssot and Quoniam 1952: figs. 1–6; Dunbabin 1978: pl. 24:57.

19. Foucher 1964b: figs. 6–7, pls. 12–15, 17:1; Dunbabin 1978: pl. 25:60–62, 64.

20. Poinssot and Quoniam 1952: figs. 12–15; Dunbabin 1978: pl. 22:54.

21. Merlin and Poinssot 1934: figs. 5–6, pl. 9:1; Dunbabin 1978: pl. 27:68.

22. Gauckler 1910: pl. 511; Poinssot and Quoniam 1952: 129 n. 2; Dunbabin 1978: pl. 24:58.

23. Some *damnati ad bestias* have been restored on the basis of these stakes: Aurigemma 1926: figs. 112, 120, 124. Aurigemma and others have interpreted the *damnati,* who have dark skin, as Garamantes (inhabitants of the area around Tripoli) captured during their incursion into the area of Lepcis Magna in A.D. 70 (Tacitus *Histories* 4.50; Dunbabin 1978: 235).

24. See Aymard 1951, Dunbabin 1978: 46–64, and Jennison 1937 on hunts in general; Mahjoubi 1967 on a hunting mosaic from Carthage; and Lassus 1950 on hunts depicted on mosaics from Antioch. Kondoleon 1986 suggests that standard hunting motifs in the mosaic pattern books of the east could be affected by the *venationes* viewed in the arena (venatorial events rather than gladiatorial games were the popular spectacles in the east).

25. Orpheus charming the animals: Gauckler 1910: pl. 32; and Carandini, Ricci, and de Vos 1982: pl. 15. The triumph of Bacchus: Gauckler 1910: pl. 67. Ganymede and the eagle in a central scene surrounded by medallions containing a variety of animals: Foucher 1960: pl. 20.

26. See Carandini, Ricci, and de Vos 1982; Gentili 1956; Kähler 1973; L'Orange 1973; Pace 1955; and Wilson 1983 on the Great Hunt (for animals to display in the arena) from Piazza Armerina.

27. Dunbabin 1978: pls. 19:45, E; Lassus 1971: figs. 4, 6; Lavin 1963: fig. 87; Leschi 1953: fig. 7; Kitzinger 1965: fig. 8.

28. For a discussion of possible magical elements depicted in, and prophylactic effects of, scenes from the arena, see Aymard 1962: 171; Dunbabin 1978: 76–78, 85; Merlin and Poinssot 1934.

29. The emphasis on dripping blood in many venatorial and gladiatorial scenes is in noteworthy contrast to the usual absence of blood in Roman sacrificial art, in which the moment of communication with a god (the prayer), rather than the kill, is most frequently shown (see the plates in Ryberg 1955). In the supposed original context of gladiatorial combats as funerary games in the third and second centuries B.C. (Valerius Maximus 2.4.7; Livy 23.30.15, 28.21, 31.50.4, 39.46.2, 41.28.11; Polybius 31.28; Tertullian *De spectaculis* 12), blood seeping into the ground might really have served a religious function. Blood is also sometimes strongly emphasized in scenes of hunts outside the arena (Veyne 1987, color plate).

30. On Magerius's floor, Diana and Dionysus hold emblems elsewhere indicative of specific venatorial families, although only the Telegenii are mentioned here (Dunbabin 1978: 67, 83). Mercury and Dionysus are both depicted in the center of the floor of the *triclinium* in the Sollertiana Domus at El Djem (Foucher 1963: pls. 15, 18a,c), surrounded by beasts of the arena.

31. Toynbee 1973: 83–84, 96–97, 177–83; A. Gordon 1983: 17–27; Matz 1977: 112. See also the similar names of men and animals on the fourth-century Borghese Mosaic (Rocchetti 1961).

32. Delbrück 1929: pls. 9–12, 20–21, 37, 58; Volbach 1976: pls. 4–5, 8; 9:20–21, 31, 32:59.

33. For *erotes* as gladiators and *damnati ad bestias*, see Johnson 1984: fig. 3; Walters 1926: pl. 20:1500; Wuilleumier and Audin 1952: pl. 3:40; Lancha 1984: fig. 8, color plate following p. 460. Children and *erotes* also drive chariots pulled by a variety of animals and fish (some explicitly shown in an arena, some not; Dunbabin 1978: 91–92, 105–6).

34. Earlier date: Aurigemma 1926: 278; Aurigemma 1960: 56; Foucher 1964a: 9; Ville 1965: 147–48; Dunbabin 1978: 235–37; Parrish 1985: 137 n.1. Later date: Azevedo 1962: 376; Parrish 1985: 137–58.

35. It is startling to find the walls of the Rothschilds' television room at Ferrières covered with a large seventeenth-century tapestry showing a desperate boar pursued by a pack of snarling hounds, one of which clings to the boar and bites it (Boodro 1988: 404). The antiquity of the tapestry and its value as an artifact presumably mitigate the violence of this scene, which would be an unlikely one (except perhaps in a hunting lodge) for a modern hanging or mural, even in a television room. The seventeenth-century artist and patron were more "Roman" than we are.

10

Callirhoe:
Displaying the Phallic Woman

Helen E. Elsom

The ancient romances were written during the last century before the common era and in the first three or four centuries of this era. A precise chronology cannot be established because (like most popular texts) the romances do not place themselves in a historical context; instead, they recycle familiar elements of high culture and plot, ringing the changes on well-received formulas. Although only five of the Greek boy-and-girl romances survive, along with papyrus fragments and citations from a number of others, they have been highly influential in Western literature. They form the model for later romances, particularly after the rediscovery of Heliodorus in the Renaissance, idealized as the modern epic (Forcione 1972: 16–19); and they are significant in the development of the modern novel, which also, as feminist critics have noted (Brownstein 1982: 32; DuPlessis 1985) regularly ends in marriage. Thus, the romance plot offers a guide to the historical vicissitudes of gender.

The same questions can be asked of romance as are regularly asked of pornography. Can women read it usefully, and is it worthwhile for us to try? Or does it invariably exclude female subjectivity? These questions have been widely debated with regard to pornography, modern mass-market romances, and the latter's predecessors in the European novel.

The ancient romances have not yet been interrogated in this way. Until recently, they were widely held to be written for women on the grounds that, according to male establishment critics, they are not great literature. As a result of recent changes in academic politics, the romances are now recognized as masterpieces of literary subtlety for an educated (male) elite. In fact, the emphasis of modern readings is academic *stricto sensu,* since they invoke a skeptical outlook which was associated in antiquity with Plato's boys' club, the Academy. But the epistemology of the romances is already explicitly gendered: their narratives work to authorize (putatively to teach) the difference between the sexes. Their plots always consist of the adventures and ultimate reunion in marriage of a boy-girl couple. Traditionally each text is named after this couple—surviving works include *Chaireas and Callirhoe* and *Daphnis and Chloe.*

My aim here is to show that the ancient romances embody a structure common to romance and pornography, that of the exposure of a woman to the public gaze. Nevertheless, they cannot be labeled either male pornography or "pornography for women" (Snitow 1983). Rather than defining a gendered reader, they present an open epistemology which is nevertheless typically read as male-centered because modern scholarship makes male-centered assumptions. Ancient readers of the texts are likely to have done the same, of course, since the dominant culture was patriarchal then as now. But I shall argue that these texts do not assume an ideology of gender. Each text constructs its own, and by exposing the process by which gender is constructed offers a critical reader the choice of passive consent or active criticism.

My inspiration in this project is Jack Winkler's reading of Apuleius's *Golden Ass,* in particular his observation that the reading of any text depends on what you know as a reader (Winkler 1985a: 1–22). In the Greek romances, however, the problem does not exist at the level of the text. Except in Heliodorus (Winkler 1982), there is no real question—as there is in the *Golden Ass* or in modern high literature—of unreliable narrators, arbitrary sources of authority, or simple authorial mendacity. In the romances, the reader accepts what is said. The problem is what to do with what is shown.

The situation is comparable in many ways to that of the Hollywood film, and I shall make considerable use of theorizing about film in what follows, in particular the work of Kaja Silverman and Teresa de Lauretis (Silverman 1988: 1–42; de Lauretis 1984: 103–57; 1987: 1–30). Events are shown, and we react to them; we do not systematically doubt them or investigate their means of production. Moreover, much of what is shown, both in romances and in films, is precisely shown without reality. Objects are presented to be desired which are not available to the reader or viewer except vicariously, via a substitute in the text. In particular, of course, what is shown in the romance is the heroine, suffering and being desired.

Making a woman the center of the narrative in a patriarchal culture is, of course, both conformist and transgressive. The heroine is exposed to the gaze of the hero, of other people in the narrative, and of the reader. The sight of her is marked as supernatural, miraculous, or divine, although it is generated within a plot that has an economy metaphorically—it is organized and coherent—but also literally. The heroine's display is an element in what Gayle Rubin has called the "traffic in women" (1975). Rubin offers a synthesis of Freud, Marx, and Lévi-Straussian kinship to show that women function in culture as the phallus, the sign of male sexuality. Women always serve as a sign, as something unreal which can be passed around in place of the intangible real—wealth, the phallus, or power. Callirhoe is always on sale in order to preserve the balance of power between men; she passes from man to man in return for power in order to preserve the status quo which is disrupted by desire for her. Her display is both essential to the economy and superfluous, since it is enjoyed by everyone, not only potential buyers.

To illustrate and explore this point, I shall discuss briefly some scenes that enact this relationship between display and power, and then examine in more detail the structure of Chariton's *Chaireas and Callirhoe* to show how the "political economy of sex" operates at all levels of the text. The questions that frame my discussion— "Does this text have space for female subjectivity?" "Is the ideal reader male or female?"—cannot be answered conclusively, because the answer depends on what we know, on the frame within which we read; but we can attempt to define the frame offered by the text by taking the text itself seriously, as well as by historical research.

The first of these projects is substantially easier than the second. Scholars have, however, determined some facts about the text, even when they have not done anything with them. With regard to the historical circumstances of its production, our knowledge is tenuous, although our ignorance is being remedied to some extent by scholarly work on the papyri, in particular by Winkler and Stevens in their forthcoming edition of romance fragments. Scholars cannot agree on who read the romances (men or women, privileged or underclass), and do not even on the whole see that this is a different question from that of how they were read. Discussion of the readership and reception of the romances is also heavily colored by perceptions of their place in the institution of modern classical scholarship. The major work on the romances since World War II is premised on the view that they are not much good, that their various literary designs are inherently flawed by the subject matter of their narratives (heterosexual love), and that their readership is (therefore) basically female, juvenile, or both (Perry 1967: 36–42). Other scholars contest this view: the romances are quite good to read, in fact "enjoyable"; moreover, a part of the pleasure they offer derives from their literary qualities, from the fact that a scholar familiar with the classical canon can see allusions to it, and philological research can reveal more (Bowie 1985: 683; Levin 1977). These scholars, who are literate and generally male, argue that the romances were read by a literate and (therefore) possibly male audience.

This situation replicates the current debate about pornography: different scholars read the romances on their own scholarly terms and come out pro or con. Perry does not enjoy modern stuff like the romances and infers that his ancient equivalents never could have either. Scholars closer to the margins of the institution discover that they can read these texts within the institution, and so claim to extend the canon and make a place for their own expertise within it. A further twist occurs when scholars, Arthur Heiserman for example, take Perry's conclusions as given and offer a "feminist" reading of the romances as a reflection of what ancient women really wanted to read.

The reception of the romances in antiquity is a little less obscure. A major historical reason to link romance with pornography is the fact that romance was subjected to a cognitive blackout in the literary canon similar to that which porn suffers (or enjoys) in sociology and literary scholarship today. Macrobius (*Commentary on the Somnium Scipionis* 1.2.6–12), tells us that fiction is bad for the soul and names the two surviving Latin romances as examples; the emperor Julian (*Epist.* 89(301b), ed. Bedez and Cumont, p. 141) forbade his priests to read *erôtikai hupotheseis* for similar reasons. According to Plutarch (*Life of Crassus* 32), the Parthian leader Surena found a copy of the *Milesiaca* of Aristides in the luggage of Roscius after the defeat of Crassus's army, and included this book in an obscene mock triumph over the dead Crassus. Plutarch or his source remarks that while the rest of Surena's triumph was a mockery—a Roman resembling Crassus was dressed in women's clothes—Surena's scorn of the dirty book was justified. This comment confirms a popular view which accords with Macrobius's and Julian's ethical judgment.

A doctor, Theodorus Priscianus, has an even more interesting line on fiction. He lists a number of therapies for impotence, and concludes with the prescription: "Meanwhile, the services should be procured [*servitium procurandum est*] of pretty girls and likewise boys. Of course, make use of reading which lures the mind to sexual pleasures [*ad delicias*], for example, the works of Philip of Amphipolis, Herodian, and above all of the Syrian Iamblichus, and of other works which recount tales of love in an agreeable manner" (2.11, p. 133 Rose). The doctor links both looking at attractive bodies and reading texts about sexual activity with achieving an erection. The text that is most likely to succeed in this (*certe,* "above all") is the novel of Iamblichus, which we know from the epitome of Photius to be a boy-girl love and adventure story with rivals and false deaths, not unlike the romances we are discussing. In antiquity, a medical man, permitted by his medical "disinterest" to talk about such things, clearly identifies the function of romance as pornographic, as the generation of an erection for a male reader.

The transmission of the texts of romance reflects their exclusion from canonical literary discourse: a small selection (four complete texts plus one substantial epitome) survives in the manuscript tradition; a further selection survived into Byzantine libraries, where the patriarch Photius read some of them before they were lost; and an indeterminate but substantially larger number were "lost" in antiquity and are known to us from papyrus fragments contemporary or a little later than their original production (Bowie 1985: 684). It is worth noting that the texts that survive in the tradition are at the more literary end of the spectrum; they take seriously their status as the new epic or as pseudo-cult narrative. Those we know from papyrus, in contrast, seem to constitute the sleazier side of fiction; in fact, they sometimes seem to be nonparodic Greek versions of the *Satyrica,* the Roman novel notorious in more recent times for its "degeneracy." These texts offer quite explicit and unmediated sex and violence in a criminal rather than epic or religious context (Parsons 1971; Haslam 1981).

Nevertheless, as with modern porn and romance, the dividing line between "literature" in the canon and "popular" texts is transgressed from either side. Although porn defends itself by pretending to be art, art also appropriates the countercultural claims of porn and romance (Suleiman 1986). This is a tricky subject. Because the number of texts we have is so small, we cannot say what "real" romance looked like in antiquity. It is likely that the privileged readers and reproducers of romance texts selected the more "acceptable" ones and left aside those where sex and sensation were less "justified" by literary form. But the romances that survive in the tradition contain elements that are shocking and taste-less to us, and which seem to have only a minimal defense in literary form.

This point is well illustrated by some episodes in Achilles Tatius's *Clitophon and Leucippe* that might be at home in a snuff movie. It is worth looking at these passages because they show clearly how the play between literary form and subjec-tivity operates. The first of these scenes occurs when Leucippe is captured by bandits in Egypt, and Clitophon joins a military expedition to rescue her. The soldiers close in on the villains:

> We saw the robbers standing armed in full force on the other side of the trench. They had improvised a mud altar, and there was a coffin beside it. Two of them led the girl forward with her hands tied behind her back; I did not know who the men were, as they were in full armor, but I recognized the girl as Leucippe. They poured a libation on her head and led her around the altar. Flute music played as the priest intoned an Egyptian hymn—the shape of his mouth and the movements of his face showed that this is what it was. At a given sign all withdrew to a distance from the altar. One of the attendants laid Leucippe on her back and tied her down using pegs fixed in the ground, just like the clay statuettes of Marsyas hanging from the tree. Then he took a sword and plunged it into her heart; drawing it down to the lower part of her belly, he split her open. Her guts poured out, and the robbers gathered them up in their hands and put them on the altar. Once they were cooked, they shared them out and ate them. When they saw this, the soldiers and their general cried out at each action and averted their gaze from the sight, but I watched transfixed with amazement. I was thunderstruck: the immeasurable evil paralyzed me. Perhaps the tale of Niobe is not false; perhaps she too had a similar experience after the deaths of her children, looking to the world as if she had become a rock, because she did not move. (3.15)

This scene highlights the subjectivity of the narrator by increasing his suffering. He does not have the possibility of looking away like the rest because Leucippe is his beloved; he is personally engaged in this scene of woman murder. But he also cannot look away because if he did there would be no scene, no narrative; his looking itself makes this horrible scene happen. The immutability of Clitophon's subjectivity is marked by the reference to the two statues, of Marsyas always being flayed in effigy and Niobe always mourning. The reversal of gender in the images, however, reveals a problem. Clitophon frozen and rigid in mourning identifies with Niobe the bereaved mother; it is his loss—his symbolic castration—that enhances his sense of self. Leucippe, cruelly killed, conversely becomes valorized and male: she *is* his manhood, his phallus, precisely at the moment she is violently lost.

Why read or watch such a scene? The Freudian answer, suggested in the pre-vious paragraph, is that the murder of Leucippe displaces the threat of loss from the male viewer to the female victim. Clitophon's loss in fact does not harm him, even though he suffers the anxiety attendant on the threat of castration. His subjectivity not only remains intact but is confirmed by the violence done to his beloved (Silverman 1988: 27–32). Moreover, the image of Marsyas, the satyr flayed by Apollo for competing with him in music, highlights the point that whereas Clitophon, the narrator, is constituted by his own discourse—the narrative voice is his—Leucippe is constituted of a messy, bloody body. "Inside" Leucippe is blood and guts; "inside" Clitophon is a subjective self. Notice also, though, that while the genders of the "statues" that comment on the respective positions of the lovers are reversed, each statue preserves qualities appropriate to the subject's present situation. Clitophon expresses his sense of loss in terms of the female Niobe; he describes the valorized, phallic Leucippe in terms of the male Marsyas. When Leucippe explicitly and violently becomes that which he fears to lose, she becomes identified with a male figure who in fact also symbolizes the discontinuity of physical appearance with subjectivity. In a famous and familiar passage in Plato's *Symposium* (215a6–c6), Alcibiades compares Socrates first to the clay sileni which have a golden god inside, and then to Marsyas, the ugly satyr who produces beautiful music. This image conflates the two ideas (using a word for a maker of clay statues found only once elsewhere, also in Plato) to suggest that Leucippe as the object of Clitophon's desire is both like him (valuable inside) and not like him (bloody inside). On the one hand, her death is a threat to him; on the other, it does not affect him, as his voice and subjectivity are not constituted as her body is. Thus, this scene can be seen as an attempt to use the display of a woman's body to cover over the threat of castration.

It seems, then, that the reader of this passage is already gendered as male, and as far as the scene itself is concerned, that is the case. But readers of Achilles Tatius's novel will know (and others familiar with the conventional happy ending in marriage of the romances may well guess) that Leucippe does not die in this way in this scene. The outpouring of guts is a theatrical trick, engineered by two friends who turn out to be the attendants Clitophon did not recognize in the passage cited above. We can, and are probably meant to, laugh at his extreme and melodramatic reaction, at least after the event. When, two books later, he again sees Leucippe die, this time beheaded and thrown overboard off a pirate ship while he watches from a pursuing boat, his speech of lamentation over her headless body is inherently absurd: "Now you are really dead to me, Leucippe; now you have died a double death, on land and on sea! I have the relic of your corpse, but I have lost you yourself! The division of you between land and sea is unfair. For the smaller part of you is left to me, though it seems to be the greater part, while the sea in having the smaller part of you has you all! Since fate has begrudged me kisses on your face, let me kiss your severed neck" (5.7). Even as he proclaims his wretchedness in watching his beloved die not once but twice, we are reminded that the first death was a hoax. His argument about the equity between land and sea is not merely tasteless; by denying Leucippe's real presence (represented by her head and face), he makes it clear that his address is not to her but for himself. Once again her death provides material to reinforce his subjectivity, his voice. It comes as no surprise to discover that in this case, too, Leucippe has not died. A prostitute has appropriately enough suffered in the place of the heroine; a woman who guarantees no man's individuality is murdered within the narrative to conserve the hero's subjectivity, which is also protected by the survival of his beloved.

So Leucippe's scenes of violent death are typical violent pornography if they are taken separately, and there is nothing to stop a misogynist reading them in this way. They are both, after all, scenes of violence against women, and one is a real murder of a woman whose value is not guaranteed by the dominant ideology. But the text also gives us grounds for laughter at the self-importance of the narrator, and at the absurdity of his phallic subjectivity.

This account of romance as a series of acts of looking recalls the case made by J. P. Sullivan in his ground-breaking study of the *Satyrica* (1968). Sullivan concludes: "Petronius has chosen as the main element of his realism various sexual motifs, and has concentrated on such perversions of the sexual instinct as are related to scopophilia and its polarity exhibitionism" (1968: 251). We have already noted, however, that "scopophilia," the sexual act of looking, is not a "perversion" but the regular activity of a reader. Let us look at some of the scenes in which Sullivan diagnoses perverse looking and see whether they represent anything different from the scenes in Achilles Tatius already discussed.

Sullivan notes several kinds of scopophilic interest in the surviving sections of the *Satyrica*. The most obvious are scenes in which the narrator and other characters spy on people having sex. When Giton deflowers the seven-year-old Pannychis, Encolpius and Quartilla watch through a peephole (26.4–5); when Eumolpus plays a complicated sex game with two children, the children's brother watches through a peephole and willingly accepts Encolpius's proposition (140–51). In both of these scenes, people are sexually aroused by watching others. But the second example illustrates a point we have already observed: the narrator is always a scopophile in any case. Although the brother is explicitly the person who is watching—whom the narrator shows us watching—the narrator also "sees" the scene with Eumolpus and the children, in order to narrate it, and is himself aroused. Thus, he exposes himself and his arousal to us. It is not merely the "original" sex act (that of Eumolpus) but the whole act of Encolpius's narrating which is a display, and the reader is the ultimate voyeur. This is equally true of other scenes in which the characters expose their penises to each other's (and our) gaze (Sullivan 1968: 240–42).

Sullivan also claims that there is scopophilic interest in other scenes in which secrets are revealed, and things that should not be seen are seen (1968: 246–49). In general, scenes of witchcraft and the supernatural can be described in terms of the uncanny, of displaced recognition (Silverman 1988: 16–18), and so can be accounted for in this text in the same way as all other scenes of voyeurism—as a defense against castration anxiety, an assertion of the reader's subjectivity. Sullivan's assertion that these scenes are disguised scenes of scopophilia is, of course, correct, although they are not particularly disguised, occurring as they do at Trimalchio's exhibitionist dinner.

Sullivan's discussion leads to the conclusion that the particular choice of material reflects Petronius's own sexual tastes, and that these tastes in turn reflect his Neronian background (1968: 251–3). This may well be the case, but we can draw a more general conclusion, namely that narrative always involves exposure and revelation, which is inherently transgressive and violent (de Lauretis 1984: 103–57). The significant choice the author of the *Satyrica* made was not what material to include in his "satyric tales" but what text, what genre, to write in the first place, and whether to write at all. Tacitus suggests that Petronius's writing was a subversive gesture: "In his will he did not do as most compulsory suicides did and flatter Nero, Tigellinus or some other powerful man: he listed the perverted acts of the emperor under the headings of various catamites and women, and outlined the sexual innovations in each case. Then he sealed the document and sent it to Nero" (*Annales* 16.19). If we can identify this Petronius with the author of the *Satyrica,* we might be able to identify the novel as a similar gesture and account for its systematic inversions of the conventions of romance as satire—exposure of the inversions of traditional ideology in Neronian circles.

This hypothesis, however, must remain completely open, although its economy is appealing. It is equally possible that a later scholar searching for an author for the *Satyrica* came upon the passage in Tacitus and thought he had found one. But we must ask one further question. In the other works of fiction we are examining, the gaze constitutes sexual difference; in the *Satyrica,* the (sexual) relationships that structure the narrative and the scenes it generates are generally between men. Can we describe the relationship between this narrative structure and that of the romances in terms of parody, subversion, or some other literary transformation? Sullivan is persuasive that, at the level of style and incident, the text is a skillful rhetorical synthesis. Is he also right when he claims that the particular sexual relations depicted in the *Satyrica* represent an idiosyncratic act of exhibitionism on the part of the author?

It could be argued that the *Satyrica* simply inverts the main convention of romance and replaces heterosexual love with male homosexual lust. It is certainly possible to read its main episodes this way: Encolpius and Giton, the lovers with whom we seem to begin, are not merely unfaithful to each other; they do not constitute a couple at all, as far as we can tell, since Giton drops out of sight before the end and leaves Encolpius and Eumolpus, who are not lovers, traveling together. In fact, the episodic nature of the narrative leaves open the question of whether the novel ever reaches a closure at all. The narrator may be part of a series of unfaithful couples as an inversion of romance convention. An inversion of this kind can be seen when Encolpius laments the infidelity of his beloved Giton in a comparable mode to the heroes of Greek romance. One such lament takes place in an art gallery, recalling the openings of Achilles Tatius and *Daphnis and Chloe.* Encolpius stands before a set of pictures by Apelles:

> In one, an eagle was carrying Ganymede high up to heaven; in another the fair Hylas was fending off the importunate Naiad. Apollo cursed his bloody hands and decorated his unstrung lyre with the newly transformed flower. In the midst of all these portraits of lovers I cried out as if I were alone: "Love touches even the gods. Jupiter did not find a beloved in heaven, but when he set off to sin on earth he harmed no one. The nymph who ravished Hylas would have controlled her passion if she had known that Hercules would come and dispute the matter. Apollo recalled the spirit of the dead boy in the flower, and all the stories tell of love without rivals. But I have taken into my company a guest more cruel than Lycurgus." (83)

Encolpius's mythology is skewed, of course: the rape of Ganymede may have had no ill consequences for Jupiter, but Hylas was ravished by the nymphs, and Apollo's love for the dead Hyacinth cannot be called happy. But this is clearly a variation on the situation at the start of Achilles Tatius, where Clitophon comes upon the narrator as he sighs over the picture of Europa and the bull and comments on the power of love.

Encolpius may, however, be simply the narrator of a discontinuous series of episodes with parodic sexual content. In this case, the first-person narrator does not represent the possibility of closure in his present (male) subjectivity, but merely the aesthetic of realism. The first person, like Richardson's use of the letter form, seems to guarantee the "reality" of the narrative, and so stresses that all these (sordid) events reflect the way the world (really) is.

Both of these views (as always) are possible, as is a more sophisticated view that the *Satyrica,* like Sade's novels, is not just a parody but an exposé of the conventions of romance as being based on sexual display, and display of the phallus in particular. We could see the narrator simply as a phallus, embodied in a penis, made into an agent. The name of the novel, *Satyrica,* means "satyric acts," acts of an erect penis; and the narrator's name, Encolpius, means "the thing in your lap," more or less. Many of Encolpius's adventures represent the only adventure a phallus can really have: failure. Although he displays his enormous equipment when there is no occasion for penetration (92.12–14, 140.6–10), when he comes to use it he almost predictably fails—in the second scene of scopophilia discussed above, for example, the peeping Tom brother is aroused, but Encolpius turns out to be impotent; and his impotence leads to an elaborate adventure in the Circe episode (126–40), in the course of which he is subjected by wise women to a fantastic cure and attempts suicide because he cannot please Giton. Thus, the narrator himself embodies both the display of the phallus and its lack, which are represented by the heroine in the romances. The threat of castration is made more immediate by its presence in the narrator, who is exposed directly to the reader. The reader is thereby confirmed more forcefully in his own subjectivity by his awareness of the narrator's lack.

The main problem with all of these accounts is the fact that the text we have of the *Satyrica* is fragmentary, and the fragments have obviously been selected for two major reasons. The first of these criteria is rhetorical and literary: many of the fragments are purple patches or discussions of rhetorical theory, including the preamble to the *cena;* or they are parodies of literary topoi, notably the *cena* itself, the description of the dinner given by the millionaire freedman Trimalchio, which is a literary tour de force. But the second criterion seems to be precisely phallic display—a monkish or other hand has selected passages for their sexual explicitness and included none of the narrative context. We cannot determine whether these scenes in fact include a frame that allows for defense in their reading.

In addition, there is some evidence that there were Greek novels similar to the *Satyrica* which consisted mainly of sexual and violent episodes in a criminal context. A reader approaching the text with expectations from this genre would presumably find similarities enough; a reader expecting a romance text (but why should he or she?) might find the parody but might also give up reading in disgust. And a "scholarly" reader would be in the same uncertain position as a modern scholarly reader: the desire for a literary reading might override the libidinal potential of the text, but enjoyment or revulsion might override understanding of the literary aspects of the text.

While it is striking that there is a coincidence of structure in the constituents of at least some of the episodes in the Greek romances and in the *Satyrica,* our information about the latter is possibly even more incomplete than that about the former. The particular problem is that while individual scenes can be suggestive, they are inevitably only parts of the novel that gives them their full significance. As I suggested above with regard to the passages from Achilles Tatius, while the scene alone provides a libidinal offering which is potentially transgressive, the plot in which the scene is contained ultimately offers conformity. The "traffic in women" requires a display of the commodity, the woman as phallus, which is always superfluous to the economy; the economy itself, the confirmation of the balance of power between men, always enforces order and suppresses the free play of desire.

This can be illustrated with a text that survives complete and represents a complex and sophisticated piece of writing, Chariton's *Chaireas and Callirhoe.* This is generally regarded as the oldest complete novel we have, and also as typical of Hellenistic and Greco-Roman fiction (Perry 1967: 96–98; Reardon 1982: 14, 18– 24). Scholars today date it to within a century around A.D. 50 on papyrological and literary historical grounds (Plepelits 1977: 4–9; Reardon 1982: 1; Lesky 1971: 957, 963).

The discourse of kinship and offspring that contains the traffic in women is established from the start. The narrative begins: "Hermocrates, the Syracusan general who defeated the Athenians, had a daughter, Callirhoe by name, an amazing young woman [*parthenos*] and an adornment [*agalma*] of the whole of Sicily" (1.1.1). Callirhoe is presented as a work of art; her "divine" beauty is described as "not that of a Nereid or mountain nymph, but of Aphrodite the Virgin herself" (1.1.2). This unlikely attribute of the goddess introduces the central paradox of the novel: Callirhoe is both desirable and chaste (Heiserman 1977: 77). That is, she presents the occasion for transgressive desire but not for actual transgression. Callirhoe as an object of desire *is* Aphrodite, a work of art for enjoyment separate from any hierarchical ordering; but it is her father who initially controls her appearance in public in accordance with his status in the world. Her beauty and chastity are of concern precisely because of her noble birth. This opening reveals the initial structure of desire in the novel: Callirhoe is who she is, and is desirable, both per se and as her father's daughter. There are, of course, other "scenes" in the novel that display Callirhoe without a male viewer as a stand-in for the reader, but these can be seen to co-opt women observers as both male-identified viewers and rival objects. An obviously "artistic" scene occurs immediately after Callirhoe, wounded by her young husband Chaireas, believed dead, and laid in a tomb, has been carried off by pirates and sold as a slave in Miletus. The other slave women (we are sneaking a look in the women's quarters, as in much pornography) undress and bathe her: "They went into the house, and oiled her and carefully rubbed her skin; they were even more awed by her beauty after she was undressed—when she was dressed they had thought that they were looking at the face of a goddess. Her skin shone white, glowing with a kind of sparkle; her flesh was soft, and they were afraid lest the touch of their fingers damage it in some way" (2.2.2).

She is, of course, being prepared as a slave by slave women who accept their own objectivity, and who also serve as secondary objects for the male viewer granted this look in the women's bathhouse. The narrative relates her as a construct of skin and flesh, normally hidden under clothes and, once exposed, in danger of damage (literally, wounding, *trauma,* with its etymological overtones of penetration). This view asserts a hierarchy: Callirhoe is a more desirable chattel or object than the other slave women. Once again, she has the "choice" of being a more desirable and therefore less subjective object, or of being treated as one slave among many. In this case, before she knows that she is carrying her husband's child, she tries to choose the latter. But the exposure she has had in the narrative tells us that is not possible.

When soon afterward she finds herself pregnant, her role as the carrier of status for her father and husband comes to the fore. She chooses to pass off Chaireas's child as the son of Dionysius, the tyrant of Miletus, whom she agrees to marry to give status to her unborn child. Callirhoe's pregnancy stands at the center both of the plot and of her status as an object of desire. This is perhaps the element in the novel that has caused the most concern to critics (Reardon 1982: 23; Hägg 1983: 11; Perry 1967: 138 sees the episode as unrealistic but attributes all to the demands of pseudo-historicity). They are distressed that Callirhoe can "cynically" pass off Chaireas's child as Dionysius's, in the interests of getting him brought up in the style to which she is accustomed; and they are even more concerned that Chaireas in the end thinks it is to his credit that his son and Hermocrates' grandson is being brought up by a stranger of high rank and wealth in Asia. Heiserman, who otherwise has many perceptive things to say about this text, goes so far as to censor the story in his summary: "she [Callirhoe] never tells Chaireas he had begotten a son in the womb he had kicked" (Heiserman 1977: 86). He notes the violence against Callirhoe but suppresses the evidence of the system in which it takes place: the jealousy that caused Chaireas to kick Callirhoe in the first place, so as to make her faint as if dead, is part of the same system of male propriety over women as Chaireas's pride in the fortune of his (wife's) child. Callirhoe herself endorses this view, as can be seen from her reasoning to Dionysius when she agrees to marry him: "I wish to be a mother so that the family of Hermocrates may have a descendant" (3.1.6; Anderson 1984: 106–8). It is this ordering of kinship, and in particular of nobility, that forms the "real," that is ideological, framework for the display of Callirhoe as an object of desire.

It is not only Callirhoe who sees herself in this way. The critical series of scenes begins when her guardian and confidante, the steward's wife Plangon, tries to persuade her to marry Dionysius for the sake of her unborn child, who can then be passed off as his and have the aristocratic upbringing he deserves. Plangon knows that Callirhoe would never assent to this as a positive proposition, so she pretends to argue the opposite case, for an abortion: "Let's do this. It's less dangerous than deceiving the master. Cut yourself off completely from all memories of your noble birth [*eugeneia*], and don't hope any more for your native land. Give in to the fate at hand, and become a slave well and truly" (2.8.6–7). Plangon, in fact, has chosen to describe the abortion precisely in terms of the things by which Callirhoe defines herself: nobility and country. At the same time, her rejection of her family is identified with slavery: paradoxically, if she asserts her subjectivity outside of the patriarchal system that defines her, she offers herself as a slave and presents her body for the physical abuse of an abortion. She is shown as having a choice: she can be an object either willingly or unwillingly.

In a subsequent scene, Callirhoe with her child is presented as an object of desire, wonder, and admiration with only a hint of self-regard. She presents herself as a mother to the people of Miletus and to her husband, and the text stresses her silence about her real place in the order of things as she perceives it. The tension between the reality of Callirhoe's marriage to Chaireas and her mute acceptance of the role of mother and Dionysius's beloved is heightened by our knowledge (and hers) that Chaireas has recently left a trace of himself in Miletus, since he has been seen in the temple of Aphrodite, where this scene occurs. She has married Dionysius and accepted the possibility of a substitution of the object of desire for the sake of another substitute, the child who is an image of his father. Her true position is a mystery (*aporrhêton,* 3.8.1) not to be revealed, and she is operating in terms of appearance, not of ordered reality; yet we are given the appearance as an object of desire, to enjoy for its own sake. Callirhoe assents to Dionysius's wish to give thanks to Plangon, who has acted as his pander, and to Aphrodite "in whose temple we first saw each other" (3.8.2). She reminds him that she has just given birth but gets up quickly, and, we are told, "she became fairer and taller, increasing with the maturity of a woman, no longer merely of a girl" (3.8.3). Callirhoe's transition from girl (*parthenos*) to woman happens not when she first has sex, but when she gives birth and actually becomes a token in the kinship system. Both her womanhood and her motherhood, however, are embodied in her physical appearance, her availability to an audience (consisting at least of the readers of the novel) as an object. The actual situation (she is pregnant by Chaireas, married to Dionysius) shows that one man is not responsible for both: her passage into status, like the paternity of her child, depends on an arbitrarily chosen man, and potentially any man.

Dionysius, believing his position as this man to be more than arbitrary, plays his role as master of all he surveys and leads a public sacrifice at the temple of Aphrodite. He offers thanks to the goddess in a speech full of double meaning for the readers of the text: "Lady Aphrodite, you are the cause of all my good fortune; because of you I possess Callirhoe and my son, and I am a husband and father because of you" (3.8.3–4). Aphrodite really is the cause and origin of Dionysius's good fortune since it is Callirhoe's love for Chaireas that has persuaded her to marry him.

This scene is explicitly one of erotic enjoyment. Its separation from the rational development of the narrative is marked, as often before, by reference to a work of art: "Dionysius uttered his prayer in the hearing of everybody; but Callirhoe wished to talk to Aphrodite alone. So first she placed her son in her arms, and a most beautiful sight was seen, the like of which no artist has drawn, nor sculptor has carved, nor poet has recounted up to the present day. For not one of them has depicted Artemis or Athena carrying an infant in her arms. Dionysius wept for pleasure as he looked, and silently supplicated Nemesis" (3.8.5–6). Callirhoe holds the infant before the goddess Aphrodite, but herself resembles one of the virgin goddesses Artemis and Athena; she is chaste, but infinitely desirable, and all the more so because she is a mother. Yet she also still resembles Aphrodite, as we are reminded by a difficulty in the text: the words translated "she placed her son in her arms" are unnatural in Greek as well. The verb *anethêke* usually refers to setting something up, often as a dedication, and our first thought might be that Callirhoe places the child as a dedication to the goddess. The subsequent words specify that the child is placed in her own arms, but the resulting picture is not of a mother who has scooped up a child in the normal way. Callirhoe is posing, and standing in for Aphrodite, to whom Dionysius has just given thanks for his child.

Callirhoe sets herself up as a work of art, a painting or sculpture. As before, she is a willing but unwilling object. She is like the people in porn photos and peepshows, who perform "voluntarily," without visible coercion, but in fact under economic coercion: they are available to the "disinterested" viewer as pure objects (Kappeler 1986: 53–62). The invisible strings of the commercial transaction which is involved in both kinds of display locate the power game in a wider context. Patty M., who worked as a peepshow dancer, told Henry Schipper, "I do this for only one reason—to put clothes on my kids' backs" (Schipper 1980: 33). The models and performers need the money, and the punters are willing to pay; the entrepreneurs who bring the two together manage to carry off the bulk of the payment (Schipper 1980: 60–62).

Callirhoe's motherhood is culturally incompatible with such display, but her status as Dionysius's wife/possession requires it. She is his object of desire as a mother as well as a woman. Although we use categories such as chastity, fecundity, and maternity to place women's bodies in an ordered world, we are not explicitly told to use these categories here. We can read such categories into the choice of goddesses, but we do not have to. There is, indeed, no connective between the image of the goddesses and the sentence relating Dionysius's pleasure: the pleasure is at the whole composition, woman and child. This is the point at which Callirhoe's status as an object of desire is displayed as most transgressive, because it is the point at which she is most explicitly phallic. The fact that she is a mother "confirms" Dionysius's possession of the phallus; but the pleasure comes when she accepts her status as an object.

We might infer at this point that the action of the romance is in some way subordinate to the scenes that interrupt it (Hägg 1971: 82, 89–97, summarized by Reardon 1982: 3, 11–12), that Callirhoe as erotic subject and object is more important in this text than the patriarchal order. On the other hand, Callirhoe's desirability is also an element in the economy of the plot: she is also the object of desire that motivates all the actors and determines their choice of action. Whenever the text seems to give way to a scene of open desire, there is always a residue or foreshadowing of the plot; and there are always traces of desire in the orderly development of the plot.

As the narrative passes its midpoint, the balance between desire and order shifts, although desire is never totally displaced from the text. Callirhoe's marriage to Dionysius is impossible, both in terms of the plot, since we know she loves Chaireas, and in terms of the patriarchal order. A woman simply cannot marry anyone she chooses for the sake of convenience, especially when she is already married to someone else. The narrative offers to resolve this situation with Chaireas's arrival in Asia, but it takes its time and sets up several more scenes before a resolution is even suggested. Callirhoe, believing Chaireas to be dead, arranges a mock funeral at which she is again the object of a desiring gaze. Mithridates, the satrap of Caria, falls in love with her (4.1.9), and this leads to another entanglement of the plot.

We expect that all will be resolved when the Great King orders a trial at Babylon (5.8.2–8), but this too leads to further complications and scenes. The crowd in Babylon gathers to see Callirhoe. She appears still more beautiful (5.5.8), entering the courtroom like Helen on the battlements of Troy. All who see her are amazed and silent, especially Mithridates. Dionysius and Mithridates construct legal arguments about propriety over her, but these arguments are purely rhetorical display: we know that Chaireas has been brought along by Mithridates as his ace in the hole (Dionysius has accused Mithridates of writing letters to Callirhoe which Chaireas himself has written). But the revelation that Chaireas is alive and present does not close the traffic of desire that centers on Callirhoe; he himself does not yet have full propriety over her. Instead, his appearance leads to a battle between Callirhoe's lovers, where the crowd knows where everybody stands except Callirhoe herself. Her appearance as a subject is always also an appearance observed by others—if not an audience within the text, then the audience of the text, the reader.

The description of the effect of Chaireas's appearance brings out this complexity:

> Callirhoe saw him and cried, "Chaireas, you are alive?"; she made to run toward him, but Dionysius held her back and, placing himself in the middle, prevented them from approaching each other. Who could adequately describe the scene in the courtroom? What poet has put such an amazing plot on the stage? It was like being in a theater full of a thousand emotions, all mixed together: tears, joy, shock, pity, disbelief, prayers. People said that Chaireas was a happy man, they shared Mithridates' joy, they grieved for Dionysius, and they didn't know what to think about Callirhoe. She was in a state of shock and stood fixed and voiceless, doing nothing but look at Chaireas with trembling eyes. Even the King, I think, would have wished to be Chaireas at that moment. (5.8.1–3)

While the two rivals fight it out to everyone else's glee, "Callirhoe stood weeping with downcast eyes, in love with Chaireas but ashamed before Dionysius" (5.8.6). The scene ends when the King arbitrarily breaks off the trial, leaving an impression of a comic, parodically rational debate between the two men juxtaposed with the affectively complex and irreducible scene of Callirhoe's reaction. Her relationships with the two men cannot be reconciled in an orderly story. She loves Chaireas; that is, she sees him as her only love and in some sense her equal. But this leaves her exposed before Dionysius, whom she has treated as a lover, and puts him in a position of dominance even while he is rejected. She has slept with another man after all, and her relationship with Chaireas has to be revised. She has now had erotic experiences of which he is not a part, and her self-awareness is not centered on him exclusively. Yet her (and our) reaction to Chaireas's appearance attempts to reconstitute her original single-minded desire for him, which would be the happy ending of a plot.

Chaireas cannot now claim Callirhoe and go home, because the traffic of desire she has initiated by her marriage to Dionysius has moved where he cannot follow. The King himself, whom we expect to resolve the case, has seen and desired Callirhoe at the trial. He delays the decision he might have made and consigns Callirhoe to the royal harem, where she is again exposed to the gaze of other women, who are in turn exposed to the reader's gaze.

All of the adventure and danger that generates these scenes of Callirhoe as the phallic woman serves to postpone the moment when gender is finally constituted—when all is revealed, so to speak. Guile and strategy, on the part of the author and the characters, are necessary in order to avoid a premature exposure which would wreck the enjoyment of the text based in the display of Callirhoe as phallus. The novel approaches its happy ending with an act of deceit, Chaireas's trick in entering the harbor at Syracuse (8.6.1–7). He has been reunited with Callirhoe, and is returning in triumph with his three hundred Greek heroes and loyal Egyptians. The trick is minimally motivated because the Syracusans are circumspect about letting in a foreign fleet, but Chaireas's obvious lie when he says that he is a merchant from Egypt (merchants do not sail triremes) only highlights the absurdity of his deceit (8.6.4). The payoff comes, however, when the ship ties up in harbor with what looks like a tent full of treasure on deck. The people of Syracuse, and Callirhoe's father, see the drape at the front suddenly drop to reveal a tableau: Callirhoe reclines on a couch, decked in Tyrian purple; Chaireas stands beside her in his general's uniform.

This tableau, with Chaireas and Callirhoe together but in contrasting poses, reveals the contrast in the roles assigned to the sexes in the ordering to which the novel seems to be moving. Callirhoe reclines, wearing rich clothes, a passive carrier of value (as she was in the tomb). Chaireas stands, and bears the insignia of a *stratêgos* (even though his military service has not been for any city); he carries himself as an agent of the state and deviser of stratagems, one of Chariton's preferred words for the double dealings that advance the action (see, for example, the complex of military imagery used in the account of Plangon's "campaign" against Callirhoe's resolve on Dionysius's behalf, 2.7.6; Gerschmann 1975: 55–56). In itself, this depiction of difference is fragile. Callirhoe moves and speaks, and destroys it. But her "voluntary" move actually serves to reinforce the hierarchy of the tableau. She greets her father, the (real) *stratêgos*, with the words "I am alive, father; I am truly alive now I see that you are alive" (8.6.8). Throughout the novel, as we have seen, although Callirhoe's emotions have focused on her husband, her abilities and self-esteem have derived from her awareness that she is her father's daughter. Her husband the general owes his wife's survival to the qualities she has inherited from her father the general. Chaireas is revealed as a copy or substitute for Hermocrates in Callirhoe's life. His pose as *stratêgos* marks him as a stand-in for her father, who observes the scene. Callirhoe, the carrier of Chaireas's wealth within the scene, stands up and acknowledges herself as the carrier of her father's phallus.

The novel ends with Chaireas narrating his heroic deeds, asserting an end of the narrative of his becoming truly Callirhoe's husband, Hermocrates' son-in-law, Ariston's son, an ally of the Great King, and a leading citizen in Syracuse—and, incidentally, the father of his own child, now being reared by Dionysius in Miletus.

All of these identities confirm his subjectivity, and make him a stand-in for the male-identified reader. Before Chaireas begins his narrative, Callirhoe leaves the assembly to go home ("as is appropriate for a woman recently welcomed home from a sea voyage and adventures," 8.7.3). She is not present during his narrative; having conveyed the phallus to him, she is now superfluous. In the very last paragraph, though, we learn that she is not at home either. She has gone to Aphrodite's temple to address the goddess, to thank her for her marriage to Chaireas and tell her that she does not blame her for the sufferings she was fated to undergo (8.8.15). Finally, she prays that she and Chaireas may never be separated again but may live a happy life together. Callirhoe knows that she is still desirable—she has regularly been mistaken for Aphrodite—and that the accidents that have separated her from Chaireas may recur as long as she is so. Her union with Chaireas, which depends on him desiring her, is therefore based on something that can still destroy or endanger it. Chaireas the general may be in a better position to hold on to Callirhoe than Chaireas the wimp who married her at the start of the narrative; but as long as she is desirable, he faces competition.

Callirhoe's resistance to objectification, which derives directly from her awareness that she is carrying the phallus, remains. The story of her subordination can potentially be repeated. Her final pose purports to leave open even while it closes the possibility of future desire. It recalls previous scenes in which she is desired and claimed as property. If the text represents Callirhoe as a subject, it does so under two conditions. First, it reminds us that Callirhoe *is* represented, that there is an artist's hand behind her presence—she is brought into being by an author and put in her place in the narrative by both the author (manipulating "chance" and narrative conventions) and her husband. Second, she is most a subject when her status as the carrier of the phallus is highlighted, when she is the mother of her father's grandchild and her husband's son, and when she is her husband's wife and guarantor of his status. Her subjectivity allows her willingly to make herself available as a woman to bestow the phallus on men.

The structure of romance, and of Chariton's romance in particular, then, is essentially the display of women as objects and as the carriers of male value, but this structure is not hermetically closed. Where does this leave us? Can this observation be transferred to pornography?

Winkler's insight about reading narrative—that it all depends on what you know—helps with pornography as well. In romance, what libidinal use we make of what we see depends at least partly on who we are and what we know. Compare the case with pornography. Scholars and readers disagree irreducibly on their own reactions to it, and on what the correct reaction should be. Angela Carter (1978) argues that pornography exposes the system, not just its objects, and is therefore philosophically useful. Other radical feminists have tried with some vigor to defend pornography, and more sporadically romance, on the grounds precisely that these genres reject the ideological order of things. It is possible, they argue, to ignore or dispense with the literary defense altogether, and to lie back and enjoy the infantile pleasures of unmediated sensation and danger that pornography and romance both offer. (Rich 1986 offers a recent critical survey of the debate.) Others (most familiarly Steinem 1980) reject pornography as making women into objects, while advocating eroticism as liberating. Finally, of course, many feminists, notably Mac-Kinnon (1985), Dworkin (1981), and Kappeler (1986), reject this distinction and argue that pornography is inherently anti-woman.

This diversity of views is at first bewildering. How can essentially the same bodies of material be seen as unacceptable objectification of women, acceptable diagnosis of (for example) the commodification of sex, an unacceptable false consciousness for women (a view often offered of romance), or an acceptable opening up of women's sexual subjectivity? I suggest that part of the answer is that there is a dialectic between the language and the material constituents of the text, which always invoke closure and conformity, and the referent of the language, which invokes the reader as a desiring subject; the reader is never completely constructed by the text, and the reader's own subjectivity is never totally effaced in the process of reading. Thus, Carter's account of the intellectual uses of Sade's pornographic writings is accurate—for feminists. But MacKinnon's evidence that pornography creates the conditions for violence against women is a valid basis on which to demand legislation. Carter's intended readers have a desire of their own, for an understanding of how the dominant ideology works, whereas the majority of (male) readers of Sadeian pornography probably already desire to abuse women and accept the representation of violence in the text as authorization to do so. They are, of course, helped by the fact that much else in modern culture authorizes their desires, often by the very means society takes to frustrate such desires—another major point in MacKinnon's case.

Since a sign has to be seen, this traffic requires the display of the woman as a possession or a commodity. Such display offers "pleasure" which is apparently in conflict with the economic order. Any woman looked at as a woman is the phallus, and so is possessed by any man, in the dominant ordering of things, since when a man looks at a woman her lack of the phallus guarantees his possession of it. Yet arbitrary value is placed on the possession of particular women by particular men in the system of kinship: a particular woman confirms not only a man's phallus but also his individuality, and his particular status in the world. So the act of looking at a woman both confirms the manhood of the looker and the value of another man's possession, and also transgresses against the other man's propriety over the woman.

Where do women fit in as readers and viewers in this scheme? Ann Snitow calls modern mass-market romance "pornography for women" (Snitow 1983) and rightly observes that the plots of romance are somewhat different from commercial pornography. But there is an important point of resemblance. What the women whose stories are related in romance want, are prepared to suffer for, is marriage or "true love"; and there is an economic necessity which appears at most only obliquely in the narrative but which the readers of romance themselves cannot ignore. The reward for a woman who "chooses" to be a heroine of romance is marriage, social status, economic security and then some (Snitow 1978: 247–50). Her husband is desirable because of his wealth and professional skills as well as because of his rugged looks and callousness to her (Modleski 1982: 39–48). Modern romance fiction is also inscribed in a commercial system, of course. Women "choose" to buy low-cost books marketed in supermarkets and drugstores because the producers of these books realize that there is money to be made by selling them there (Radway 1984: 134–45). The depiction of women as passive objects of male brutality and subsequent desire is marketed as what women want. The ways in which they choose to tell their own stories reflect acceptance of the images of themselves which they have purchased, as Sharon Thompson's interviews with teenage girls show (Thompson 1984). Although we cannot comment with comparable knowledge on the production of the ancient romances, the economic and social determination of the careers of Callirhoe and other heroines is clearly similar.

The play between conformity and transgression observed above is always present in texts: reading requires assent to a set of conventions but also gives play to the reader's own subjectivity. It is possible, however, to be more precise about the situation of the readers of pornography and romance. The reader of pornography or romance always seems to be transgressing—to be looking at what should not be seen—but he or she is in fact performing an act that is quite commonplace and economically determined, reading a novel or looking at pictures that have been produced to make money. If the reader chooses to regard the commodity purchased as infinitely valuable, he or she has sold out to the system that values male subjectivity above all else; if he or she assesses it as a commodity, it has been studied and not enjoyed. But it is also perhaps possible to accept the pleasure on offer, or to reinvent it, without buying the whole system. Although the production of visual pornography is harmful when the people in it are exploited economically and doing things likely to damage them psychically and physically, the same is not necessarily true of prose. Susan Rubin Suleiman, for example, has argued that intertextual play can make "pornographic" texts self-referential and literary (Suleiman 1986).

The converse is also true: a literary text can be read as pornography by people with evil minds, or possibly with misapplied intertextual assumptions. Carter's or MacKinnon's scholarly discussions could be read as compendiums of pornography by unsympathetic readers. Such misreading is still easier with fictional texts. Peter Rabinowitz (1987: 193–208) shows how Chandler's *The Big Sleep* is read not quite as pornography but as an anti-woman diatribe because contemporary readers assume that the nymphomaniac Carmen must be the "real" villain, since she is punished. No one unprompted by Chandler's letters seems to have noticed that the successful racketeer Eddie Mars, who escapes unpunished, is in fact responsible for the systematic slaughter in the novel. Because the text is never determinate, because it can never completely foresee the subjectivity of the reader, it is always potentially a cue for transgression; and in this case again, the transgression—the violence against women in the punishment of Carmen and the hatred she arouses in many readers—is in fact licensed by the dominant ideology.

This, then, is what makes the doctor recommend reading romances to generate an erection. Callirhoe and the other heroines of romance offer themselves willingly to confirm the phallus, the male subjectivity, of men who feel insecure. For women readers, they offer themselves as models of strength and subjectivity who nevertheless willingly take their place in the patriarchal order. For us as scholarly readers, they offer an exposé of the political economy of sex: Callirhoe suffers unwillingly because of the violence the system does to her, even when (like Sade's Justine [Carter 1978]) she tries to conform.

The ancient romances function as pornography by invoking a play of transgression and conformity which is inherent in the contemplation of a visual image. Like pornography, romance exposes woman *as* an object. In both senses it is possible to look at the heroine, or to look at the heroine being exposed. The choice between libidinal and intellectual, between enjoyment and diagnosis, is in the eye of the beholder.

NOTE

Thanks to Mary Beard for introducing me to this area of thought; to Simon Goldhill, Jack Winkler, Piero Pucci, John Henderson, Paul Glendinning, and Eve Samson for help and discussion; and above all to Amy Richlin and Terri Marsh for invaluable and radical comments and editorial work on a very rough original manuscript.

11

Sweet and Pleasant Passion: Female and Male Fantasy in Ancient Romance Novels

Holly Montague

She saw him again in her mind's eye, tall and large with a physique that wouldn't tolerate an ounce of fat, and she couldn't help but think that a woman would have to be more than pretty to gain his notice. Only beautiful women would get a second look from the virile-looking Grant Harrington, she felt sure. She was tempted to get out of bed and take stock of her fine boned face. Then she remembered tomorrow, and wondered why she should have a sudden yen to be beautiful.

—Jessica Steele, *Tomorrow—Come Soon* (1984)

Standing before the spring, he washed his hair and his body. His hair was dark and luxuriant, and his complexion sunburned. . . . As she watched him, Chloe realized for the first time how handsome he was. . . . She washed his back for him and felt how soft his skin was; stealthily, she touched her own several times, testing to see whether it was softer. . . . Young country girl that she was, she did not understand what was happening to her.

—Longus, *Daphnis and Chloe* (A.D. 200?)[1]

Nearly two millennia separate these descriptions of innocent female sensuality. In each, love lays a gentle hand on a young girl, who remains but vaguely conscious of her own emotions. Next we find, in each case, a series of episodes arranged to frustrate and confound the nascent desire. Each story ends with the heroine's full erotic initiation—after the wedding, of course.

During the early centuries A.D., a few Greek writers produced what may be viewed as prototypes of the modern romance novel. Of these works, it is Longus's *Daphnis and Chloe* that most nearly anticipates those present-day romances often called "Harlequins." I, too, will use this convenient term, although Harlequins are only the most notorious of a genre which admits much variation in quality and which, by one account (Thurston 1987), has developed greatly over the decades. Books in this group have recently drawn attention from feminist critics who see in

231

them a remarkable form of female erotica or, as some say, pornography (Modleski 1982; Snitow 1983).

In what follows I will explore some of the parallels between ancient and contemporary romances. My main concern will be with the representations of female sensibilities so important in romantic novels. What roles do these elaborate fictional constructs have in the fantasies promoted by the various authors? This question will lead me, finally, to touch upon more general matters. Analysis of characters in novels has always had a place in feminist thought. Beauvoir (1953), Ellmann (1968), and Heilbrun (1979) all build theories in part on the basis of comparisons among fictional women, some of them created by female authors. Recent debate has settled on increasingly abstract issues. Critics wonder whether any genuinely female experience or means of expression can occur in a world where literary forms (among other kinds of language) have themselves been articulated by men. Further, is it even a legitimate project to look for a distinctly female mode of writing or of being? I will try in the course of my argument to treat such issues directly, but I am aware that for some this essay will remain a document of the manner in which yet another reader has been seduced.

Pamela's Grandmother

Many of the connections to be drawn between ancient and contemporary romances could also be made among novels from the intervening centuries. We are, after all, as concerns the whole modern era, dealing with a family resemblance. The membership of *Daphnis and Chloe* in the same family, however, comes as a surprise. I am speaking not so much of the medieval romance tradition, whose links to classical literature are well known (Beer 1970: 2, 33–34), but of the romance novel, which is usually considered a separate development. The fullest scholarly discussion of the sentimental romance and of the romantic heroine begins for practical purposes in the eighteenth century and proclaims its range with the title *Pamela's Daughters* (Utter and Needham 1936). Yet much that is considered original in Richardson's *Pamela* can be found also in *Daphnis and Chloe*. For example, Utter and Needham remark in *Pamela's Daughters* (19): "The typical plot of the English novel has love for the starting-post and marriage for the finish-line. It is always an obstacle-race—if the course were smooth there would be no story—and almost always the obstacles are economic." Utter and Needham describe this emphasis on economics as a result of the growth of capitalism (20). Similarly (4), they attribute the appeal of *Pamela's* coy modesty to "the rising tide of middle-class morality of the time." Yet marriage, finance, and prudery all play large roles in Longus's plot as well.[2]

Most strikingly (and more than any other ancient novel), *Daphnis and Chloe* resembles the later romances in the extent to which it focuses upon the interior life of a young woman. Chloe lives and breathes a convincing version of the same sensibility that so impresses critics of Richardson. Some of the tender verisimilitude of *Pamela* and novels following it may well be traced to direct contribution to the genre by women authors. As Utter and Needham (humorously, of course) explain it (20): "In the eighteenth century in England women wrote most of the novels, the men wrote only the best ones. Naturally the women gave leading roles to the heroines, and wrote much from experience."

Thus, the modern tradition may be said to result from a fusion of female and male voices. Today's supermarket romance, on the other hand, seems almost entirely the province of women. Harlequin romances are nearly all signed with female names. Some few authors turn out to be male, but readers reject books that are obviously written by men (Thurston 1987: 66 n.4, 171). We know far less about the writers of ancient romance than about those of Harlequins. Longus leaves only a novel and a name, which, like those of his colleagues, is masculine. The maleness of all the ancient romancers has in hypothetical terms been doubted: it has been suggested that some may be women using pseudonyms (Hägg 1983: 95–96). In any case, we have no concrete evidence for female authorship in the ancient period.

On the question of audiences, we find once more a disparity of sources. Both scholars and market researchers have gathered information about the readership of contemporary romance. Male consumers are all but unknown. In fact, men claim to be unable to read the books (Thurston 1987: vii–viii; but see Radway 1984: 55). The women who do read them have often been categorized as "middle-class housewives," but a recent survey (Thurston 1987: 115–21) suggests that they are far more socially and economically diverse than was previously thought. Nor is there any real basis for the slighting remarks commonly made about the readers' intellectual abilities. One informant compares her own reading of romances to a man's interest in football (Thurston 1987: 131). Like football, romance has an appeal that, however frivolous some may consider it, is wide and democratic.

The original audience for Longus's writing can only be deduced from a few general principles and from the apparent orientation of the text. The ancient novel, as one critic has explained it, emerged from the later Hellenistic period, with its growing multiplicity of interests and social groups (Hägg 1983: 89, citing Perry 1967). By this account, the novel will have drawn its audience partly from people who had recently become literate, including the "middle classes" and women (Hägg 1983: 90–91). Cues within the text of *Daphnis and Chloe* do not contradict these suggestions, even though Longus is, in terms both of dates and of influences, a writer of the Roman empire: if the emerging novel met a new demand, that demand proved long-lasting. Some appeal to socially curious "middle classes" could possibly be detected in Longus's fabulous depictions of both rich and poor, which I will discuss further below.

A theory that romances were directed toward a female audience (for that matter, like the idea of women authors concealed behind male pseudonyms) is intuitively appealing, but it may depend on a projection of modern values onto the themes of the ancient novel. It is argued (Hägg 1983: 95–96) that the ancient romance gives special prominence to women's concerns and thus speaks to women as a distinct group. We must ask, however, whether marriage (invariably the goal of romance) has always been a women's concern in the same sense that it is now. Modern women have been persuaded to believe that a wedding is in the most intimately subjective sense the happiest day of a girl's life. Such an expectation would be less likely to apply to a twelve-year-old girl entering an arranged marriage, often the case in the Roman empire (Pomeroy 1975: 165; for Athens, see Sutton, Chapter 1 above).

More generally, self-fulfillment through heterosexual love leading to marriage was, as Winkler notes (1988: 1570–71), not a familiar notion in classical times; to Longus's readers it might have seemed as far-fetched as kidnapping by freebooters or the recognition of lost offspring. Not that either the Harlequin or *Daphnis and Chloe* is firmly grounded in everyday existence. We might say that where marriage is concerned, Longus spins a fantasy while Harlequins fantastically transform reality, creating an exaggerated picture of marriage as a means of filling emotional needs which in our culture have been considered specific to women. The full extent of the difference between Longus and Harlequins may be impossible for modern readers to grasp. Our ideas of love and marriage are in all likelihood so deeply fixed that we cannot avoid sometimes reading Longus's novel as if it were a modern love story.

To differences of social context we must add a few considerations about the reading of contemporary and ancient novels. Harlequins (like other novels) are today used for purposes that ancient readers would be hard put to imagine: for deep identification with characters, for the greater understanding of personal problems, and for vicarious self-realization (see, e.g., Thurston 1987: 130–35). The emotional issues raised in modern romances are taken seriously by the readers, who, although they read acutely and retentively, profess little interest in the technical aspects of style and composition (Radway 1984: 189–91). In contrast, *Daphnis and Chloe* often strives for emotional effects, but it is also largely concerned with witty and humorous treatment of poetic traditions, above all the pastoral, and of rhetorical techniques. The primary intended reader of *Daphnis and Chloe* is probably at least a would-be literary sophisticate who would read (as he or she might claim) only incidentally for less academic gratification. The polymorphous adaptability of novels may be peculiar to the genre (see Bakhtin 1981a; Elsom, Chapter 10 above); this would account not only for the many ways a novel might be read within its culture but for the way in which we can adopt *Daphnis and Chloe*.

Other ambiguities of reading and interpretation, however, are found more particularly in romance novels and create special problems for any analysis that attempts to take gender into account. The issue of gender in the reading of romances arises explicitly as early as the seventeenth century. Thornley, Longus's original English translator (whose rendering is often quoted here), subtitles his edition of 1657 *A Most Sweet and Pleasant Pastoral Romance for Young Ladies*. To be sure, the subtitle may be intended mainly, in the manner of the time, to pigeonhole *Daphnis and Chloe* as a trivial work. Yet Thornley also correctly identifies a part of his market. His categorization of the work hints at a versatility inherent in the romance novel. Utter and Needham (1936: 4–6) discuss the readers of *Pamela*: ". . . ladies flourished their copies at one another in public places. . . . There is no such direct evidence that it was popular with the rakes, but it might well have been so. . . . *Pamela* is the study of an adolescent girl kept for months on the verge of sexual experience." The appeal of the romance in this way differs according to whether the reader identifies with the young woman or with the imagined "rake." For readers in the first group, the text would provide a chance to experience (again) the drama of sexual initiation. For those in the second group, it would afford (again) the thrill of ravishing a virgin. This bivalent effect might be explained in the eighteenth-century romance by the genuine combination of female and male voices. Nevertheless, Richardson's novel draws its double appeal from subject matter it shares with *Daphnis and Chloe.*

Bivalent appeal does not disappear when we turn to the contemporary romance—surprisingly so, in view of the fact that Harlequins aim for a female audience and at least present the author as a sympathetic woman. As it turns out, however, this fiction involves contradictory points of view. Modleski (1982: 41) has described the peculiar status of the Harlequin protagonist. Although the story is told from her perspective, she is often objectified, even belittled, by the narrative. What is more, she cooperates in her own objectification. Even in my first epigraph, the heroine turns away from viewing the man to a contemplation of herself, in such a way as to give the reader a picture of her, and an erotically charged picture at that. The character is excited by the idea of herself as an object of desire. (Berger [1972] gives the definitive account of this process.)

The circumstance that "women's fiction" should itself make this use of the female character is part of a problem that recurs whenever a woman's perspective in fiction is sought. One cannot simply choose to read as a "lady" or a "rake." A dislocation of the woman's identity takes place wherever women's sexuality is seen as not just subordinate to but a reflex of men's. It is this consideration above all that renders difficult the search for a female fantasy in any erotic text.

Seduction through Packaging

As an entrance to the texts, let us survey some of the means romance authors use to draw readers into the realm of fantasy. Settings are chosen and described with care. Often the main action takes place somewhere removed from geographical and chronological reality (Snitow 1983: 251). *Interlude in Arcady* (1969; vaguely bucolic but plainly not inspired by Longus) is set in an old-fashioned English country house; others use exotic tourist locations (Snitow 1983: 248). Always, too, there is an element of class fantasy: the heroine is poor but genteel, socially advanced by her marriage to the rich and powerful hero (Modleski 1982: 48). Daphnis and Chloe inhabit a version of Greek Lesbos rendered mythic by the literary stereotypes of the pastoral (but see Hunter 1983: 21–22). A fantasia of class advancement is not lacking: the two lovers are finally revealed as offspring of the Lesbos elite. But Longus adds an element of comedy always latent in the pastoral mode. His characters are picturesque bumpkins who smell like goats. When the hero and heroine rise socially, they move from one fantastic world to another—in the terms of mass folklore, from Dogpatch to "Dynasty." A blend of irony and artificiality allows the reader to enjoy the story in comfortable complicity with the narrator.

Fantasy is encouraged still further by the delicious packagings of romances. Ancient books were sold without benefit of glossy covers, but *Daphnis and Chloe,* at any rate, attracts the reader with a colorful advertisement (Proem 1–2):

> When I was hunting in Lesbos, I saw in the grove of the nymphs a spectacle the most beauteous and pleasing of any that ever yet I cast my eyes upon. It was a

painted picture, reporting a history of love. . . . There were figured in it young
women, in the posture, some of teeming, others of swaddling, little children; babes
exposed, and ewes giving them suck; shepherds taking up foundlings, young persons plighting their troth; an incursion of thieves, an inroad of armed men. . . .
When I had seen with admiration these and many other things, but all belonging to
the affairs of love [lit. *erôtika*, "erotic matters"], I had a mighty instigation to write
something as to answer that picture. . . . [This book] will cure him that is sick, and
rouse him that is in the dumps. . . . For there was never any yet that wholly could
escape love, and never shall there be any, never so long as beauty shall be, never so
long as eyes can see.

Longus adapts here the classical ecphrasis, or description of visual art within a
literary work. Traditionally such a digression breaks up the narrative; in this case, it
forms an opening. It encourages from the first a sensual approach to reading, with
vivid visualization of the narrative. The claimed mood-altering effect of this story is
to be seen again in the testimony of modern romance readers (Radway 1984: 87–
96): "I read to forget my troubles, to feel good."

However, where Longus's ecphrasis awakens the visual imagination and pro-
motes a sensuous attitude in the reader, Harlequins visually advertise themselves in
what cannot but be regarded as a frankly pornographic manner. The technique used
on many recent covers seems incongruous with the status of the books as women's
literature. That of *Tomorrow—Come Soon,* for example, shows a man, whose
features are mostly hidden, embracing a young woman dressed in loud pink with a
generous decolletage. Her expression is troubled. The viewer's eye is directed from
above the lovers, who sit on the floor, much as if one were looking through a
window. If the reader is invited to identify with the heroine, she is also encouraged,
even before opening the book, to regard her as a desirable object (see Modleski
1982: 54, citing Berger 1972). Covers of this kind are especially startling given the
current theory that women, unlike men, are excited less by visual stimulation than
by subtler forms of verbal erotica that allow more imaginative work on the part of
the reader (Thurston 1987: 1–57). *Tomorrow—Come Soon* has adopted the technique of male pornography to appeal not to men but to women looking for a way to
present themselves to men—and to themselves. Modern illustrators of Longus have
produced pictures wonderfully like Harlequin covers: Hägg (1983: 218) reprints an
etching of 1890, in which Chloe appears standing naked, playing a shepherd's pipe,
her eyes studiously downcast, while Daphnis embraces her from behind, his profile
cast in shadow.

Narrative Acrobatics

Part of all romance's psychological appeal derives from a careful balance of episodes which allows erotic tensions to be maintained at length. Sexual intrigue is
often interrupted by some external crisis. A condensed plot summary will show how
the process works in *Daphnis and Chloe.*

Books 1 and 2 (roughly the first half of the novel) tell a story of emerging love.

Two children, foundlings raised by shepherds, are sent out by the divine machinations of Eros to pasture flocks side by side. A relationship develops by fits and starts: romantic idylls of growing intensity alternate with episodes of adventure and peril which also escalate, lending to the narrative a constant sense of imminent crisis. Daphnis falls into a pit and is rescued; Chloe falls in love. A rival (Dorcon) sues for Chloe's attention; Daphnis falls in love. Dorcon tries to rape Chloe; Daphnis and Chloe discover their mutual love. Daphnis and Chloe both survive kidnapping attempts; Chloe exacts a vow of fidelity from Daphnis.

In Books 3 and 4 the development is more complex, less linear. In the first two books, significant events are mainly private and emotional, with interferences from the outside world. Now that world begins to exert a greater influence over the lovers. Daphnis and Chloe are separated when each returns home for the winter; Daphnis visits Chloe; spring comes and they are reunited. Daphnis and Chloe try but fail to accomplish sexual intercourse. A woman shows Daphnis the technique; he will not, however, share it with Chloe until they are married. Chloe is approached by a number of suitors who threaten to displace Daphnis. Daphnis miraculously finds a store of money, which qualifies him to marry Chloe.

Almost on the eve of the wedding (Book 4), a wild assortment of complications flourishes. A disappointed rival destroys a garden owned by the absent landlords, and in which Daphnis's adoptive father has worked. A man tries to rape Daphnis. Daphnis is next revealed as the son of the landlord; in the ensuing confusion, Chloe is once more kidnapped. Chloe, too, emerges as the daughter of a rich and prominent man. At last the marriage takes place.

Such, then, is the romantic "obstacle course." The pleasurable effect of this sort of delayed resolution is so often noted that, for instance, reading is parodically described by a character in David Lodge's *Small World* (1984) as "masturbatory" or like a "striptease dancer" (30). The analogy does no gross injustice to Longus's narrative technique. The reader knows that fully achieved love is the inevitable outcome, since it is Eros who has put Daphnis and Chloe together. By the midpoint, the reader is accustomed to a pattern of foiled climaxes.

Although Lodge's comparison suggests a stereotypically male avenue to pleasure, a similar technique, likewise attributed to erotic appeal, prevails in Harlequins and is in fact looked upon as an essential part of the genre. Often a delay is achieved through some practical difficulty that seems insoluble. *Interlude in Arcady* revolves around a scheme whereby the two main characters, for painstakingly contrived reasons, must live in a house together under the pretext of having a love affair. Actually to have one would, by the logic of the story, spoil the pretense. In this manner the consummation to follow can be enjoyed again and again in anticipation, highlighted by suggestive problems (e.g., early on, the eventual lovers are forced to share a bedroom). The teasing postponement of sexual fulfillment has been claimed to reflect something essential about women's attitude toward love: rather than seeking active and immediate completion, it thrives on waiting, that is, on passivity (Snitow 1983: 250). A less derogatory account might hold that female sexuality, and female fantasy, simply goes on and on (Modleski 1982: 98, on soap operas).

Again we confront the problem of the disturbingly bivalent text: female sexuality (if this label is valid) is so constructed as to fit altogether too well into the striptease effect. The woman's innocence falls away charmingly. Techniques that contribute to this pattern are extremely common. In the Harlequin series great emphasis is placed on the heroine's lack of awareness. Modleski (1982: 54–56) notes that frequent statements such as "she was unaware of how beautiful she looked" create a "schizophrenic" effect in a narration that purports to convey unmediated the thoughts of a woman with whom the reader is expected to identify. Womanly sexuality appears in the romance actually to depend on a high degree of ignorance in the female. In *Daphnis and Chloe,* too, we see an apparent focus on female sexuality. The entire novel presents an account of Chloe's erotic development. Yet Chloe also is often presented as unaware, even sympathetic because of her lack of awareness.

Violence, Passion, and Pleasure

Not only, however, does Longus's narrative sometimes patronize Chloe; it often treats her in a manner that contradicts the ostentatiously sweet tone found overall. The strong undertones of violence in *Daphnis and Chloe* have recently been examined by Winkler (1990) in a study that brings out especially well the complexity of the narrative stance toward the female character.[3] I propose now to examine the tension in Longus's narrative (between its sweetness and its sometimes violent sexuality) as a source of reading pleasure. Great emphasis on Chloe's innocence makes more delectable the numerous threats to it. Longus incorporates sexual fantasy into a generally high-minded discourse through a subtext formed of vivid imagery and subordinated narratives. Much of the suggested material has the quality of private thought or fantasy which may be loosely construed as associated with one individual or another, creating an appearance of psychological depth the greater for being ambiguous.

In the opening sequences of the novel, for instance, metaphorical associations become literal. Throughout Longus's story, the realms of beasts and humans often interact in a form of pathetic fallacy. At first, when Daphnis and Chloe remain in a childish state, nature and animal life appear benevolent (1.9: "Now was there humming of bees, and chanting of melodious birds, and skipping of newborn lambs"). The first sign of a romantic crisis comes when this harmony is disrupted (1.11): "Afterward Love in good earnest kindled up this fire. A wolf that had a kennel of whelps was come often ravenous upon the neighboring fields." Daphnis falls into a trap set for the wolf. It is in the aftermath of this accident that Chloe discovers her longing for Daphnis, when she sees him naked as he bathes. Longus shows her dawning awareness (1.13):

> . . . to Chloe's eye he seemed of a sweet and beautiful aspect, and when she wondered that she had not deemed him such before, she thought it must be the washing that was the cause of it . . . and that night there was but one thing in Chloe's mind, and that the wish that she might see Daphnis at his washing again. . . . [The next morning, playing his shepherd's pipe,] he seemed again to her goodly and beautiful to look to, and wondering again, she thought the cause

must be the music; and so, when he was done, took the pipe from him and played, if haply she herself might be as beautiful. Then she asked him if he would come again to the bath, and when she persuaded him, watched him at it; and as she watched, put out her hand and touched him; and before she went home had praised his beauty; and that praise was the beginning of her love.

Chloe appears suddenly as an inexperienced but vigorous and resourceful lover. She goes on to manifest the full pathology of romantic love. She complains of obscure pain, of illness and burning (1.14), and even tries to reason her way through her dilemma: "I feel pain, and there is no wound. . . . I burn, and here I sit in the deepest shade." But Longus draws this engaging picture of a girl in love only to turn love into a dangerous practical joke. A rude cowherd named Dorcon blazes with desire after overhearing, along with the reader, Chloe's innocent soliloquy (1.15). (The locus classicus for this situation is the story of Lucretia, spied on at her weaving [see Chapters 6 and 8 herein]; so, too, is Richardson's Pamela overheard "prattling" by Mr. B. [Modleski 1982: 53].) One fine day, dressed as a wolf, Dorcon hides next to a spring which he knows Chloe will visit (1.20). The violence of what he intends is made obvious by the animal costume. One thinks of Horace's poem addressed to another Chloe (*Odes* 1.23): "Chloe, you run from me like a young fawn . . . but I am not chasing you, like a savage tiger or lion, with intent to crush you." (A colorfully evoked possibility is here too elaborately discarded. "Don't worry, my dear, I won't hurt you . . . much!" The girl's fear entices; see Richlin, Chapter 8 above.) Daphnis and Chloe are too naive to see Dorcon's evil intent; when in the course of his rape attempt he is attacked by dogs, they rescue him. In this early cycle of events, then, Longus suggests a range of possibilities for the functioning of a female character: first he displays Chloe as an energetic lover; then he gives the reader an intimate view of her complex emotional state; finally, he shows her up as vulnerable and absurdly unaware—the source of her erotic appeal.

It might be useful to pause here and ask what place threats of aggression have in male or female fantasies. The prolonged harassment of Chloe by a figure in an absurd costume suggests a spectacle familiar in slasher films (see Clover 1987). But, as so often, startling parallels can be found in women's narratives. Harlequins often show violence between the sexes, in one case with a strange acknowledgment that such behavior has sexual implications. The following exchange is taken from *Love's Sweet Revenge* by Mary Wibberly (1979: 106–7): " 'I would like to beat you—' His voice shook with anger. 'I'll bet you would too. Is that how you get your kicks?' " And so on. The purpose of this conversation may, of course, be to reassure the reader that no real enjoyment of violence is present; if it were, the heroine would not refer to the possibility so flippantly. Needless to say, these two characters marry. It would be easy to label such fantasy sadomasochistic. According to a more optimistic view, violent material can give readers a chance to come to terms vicariously with sexual threats (Modleski 1982: 29–30, 37–39; cf. Radway 1984: 41, 75). The meaning of violent elements in a romance, by this account, depends to a large extent upon the attitudes of the reader. Violence in the text may be seen as serving up the helplessness of the female as a source of pleasure for a male or male-identified reader, with or without token sympathy; or it may be taken to represent realistic fears in such a way as to promote constructive understanding.

Longus's subordinated narratives are full of visual detail. Vulnerability is made a source of excitement through graphic use of myths. These tales of metamorphosis and suffering, narrated by the characters themselves, contain ever greater amounts of violence.[4] In Book 1, Daphnis tells Chloe of the transformation of a shepherd girl into a dove. He compares Chloe to this young woman in his opening (1.27): "Once upon a time, young maiden, there was a beautiful young maiden . . ." The metamorphosis occurs after the girl gets into a musical competition with a neighbor boy ("himself handsome") who charms away some of her flock. The girl's grief prompts the gods to turn her into a bird.

In Book 2, a mythical tale is first recounted and then dramatized. The double narration presents sexual vulnerability as an incitement to desire, but covers erotic danger with a layer of reticence. At a rustic party (2.32), Lamon, the adoptive father of Daphnis, sings the ballad of Pan and Syrinx (a tale known from Ovid's *Metamorphoses*, 1.689). Pan here appears in a sinister aspect, trying to seduce a nymph. She spurns him, and a chase ensues (2.34): "Pan follows her with violence and thinks to force her." Syrinx disappears into a bed of reeds and becomes Pan's pipe. Now (2.37) our young lovers are inspired to act out the same story: "Therefore they two, rising quickly, fell to dancing Lamon's tale. Daphnis played Pan, and Chloe Syrinx." At the critical moment Chloe mimes falling into the rushes. The shepherds enjoy the innocent charm of this enactment. Chloe, however, grows troubled after the performance. Reflecting on the faithlessness of Pan, she feels moved to try to exact a vow of fidelity from Daphnis. He complies, but the narrator knowingly remarks that Chloe believes him thanks to her rustic naivety (2.39). This incident gives one of the earliest explicit clues that the relation between the sexes may be treacherous. As often, the narrator combines ironic distance with sympathy, indirectly suggesting the way in which a playful enactment has worked more darkly on Chloe's mind.

The gruesome death of Echo is narrated in Book 3 (3.23), once again by Daphnis to a Chloe who appears as an eager pupil, buying her tuition with kisses. Echo tries to preserve her virginity until Pan becomes frustrated and has her torn to bits by the shepherds and their dogs. Just shortly before, the narrator has compared Chloe to Echo because of her beautiful performance in a love duet with Daphnis (3.11). Echo, indeed, may be said to stand as the most perfect mythical emblem of this narrative's presentation of sexuality. A brief, completely innocuous allusion to her story is followed by an extremely violent retelling. Then, too, she embodies in a symbolic fashion Longus's treatment of his characters. On the significance of the Echo myth, Zeitlin (1981: 147) has commented: "Echo, as the embodiment (or, better, the disembodied voice) of mimesis, is also the focal point for the concept of the feminine as the one who can never be grasped as primary and original but can only be the one who is imitated or the one who imitates; yet as such, she is therefore empowered as the mistress of mimesis."

Mimesis across gender boundaries amounts to a theme in *Daphnis and Chloe*. The relations between the genders are (as Zeitlin's account allows) more variable than any direct equation of the feminine with the imitative might suggest. In many respects Daphnis is an imitation of Chloe. Longus creates a structural symmetry wherein events are repeated even to minute details. The lovers become mirror images of each other. When Daphnis is first smitten with Chloe, for instance, he voices a complaint sounding much like the one she has made earlier (1.18). Near the end of the novel, a man called Gnathon makes advances to Daphnis (4.12), first ambushing him, as Dorcon did Chloe. Then Gnathon asks Daphnis to assume the position of a nanny goat being mounted by a billy goat, recalling an incident in which Daphnis clumsily tries to mount Chloe goat-fashion (3.14). Thus, Daphnis becomes an object of erotic interest in much the same way that Chloe does. Such treatment of a young male fits easily into the pastoral tradition where (in keeping with Greek and Roman sexual customs) women and young men function similarly as love objects for adult males. Yet Daphnis and Chloe are not quite interchangeable; Daphnis's experience imitates or parodies that of Chloe, which is more fully elaborated.

The Powers of the Female

Both lovers are also kidnapped. Here again, the narration of Chloe's kidnapping exploits more fully the erotic possibilities of the situation. The paired incidents also establish Chloe in a special role. Her innocence and purity are magnified in both stories to supernatural proportions. First Daphnis is carried off by pirates, who also kill Dorcon and take some of his cattle. In a touching death scene, Dorcon, the rude rapist of former times, exhibits a new sentimentality and begs Chloe for a final kiss (1.29). Has this change been worked by the inspiring influence of his love object? Then, playing upon a flute given to her by Dorcon, Chloe miraculously effects the restoration of Daphnis. Her own later abduction by a group of adventurers contains an element of degradation not inflicted on Daphnis. Her captors treat her in an especially insulting way; "[They] drove away her flocks and her before them, thumping her along with their battons as if she had been a sheep or a goat" (2.20). But if Chloe is humiliated more cruelly than Daphnis, she is also rescued with much more fanfare. Pan charms the boat on which she is carried and causes a series of divine portents: the horns of Daphnis's goats are decorated with ivy; Chloe's sheep howl like wolves; Chloe herself appears garlanded with pine, the tree sacred to Pan (2.26).

While the innocence and virtue of both lovers are constantly emphasized, Chloe's purity is more an essential feature of her character and exerts a special force. A telling scene occurs in Book 1 (1.25–26). Daphnis spies on the sleeping Chloe "completely shamelessly" (*mêden aidoumenos*). His speech is only mildly erotic, but once again references to animals add a suggestion of something more, even something subconscious: "What sweet eyes are those that sleep. . . . How sweetly breathes that rosy mouth! But I am afraid to kiss it. . . . Oh the prating grasshoppers! They make a noise to break her sleep. And the goats are fighting, and they clatter with their horns. Oh the wolves, worse dastards than the foxes, that they have not ravished them away!" Chloe dispels the erotic tension when she wakes up, a grasshopper having flown down the front of her dress, and the two children laugh harmlessly. In such circumstances Chloe has a transformative influence on the narration: her innocence acts as a check on the sexual undertow. Her more reticent, girlish attitudes in this fashion give her a moral ascendancy which controls the course of events. Thurston (1987: 61) notices a related phenomenon in Harlequins: the "fantasy of the woman as transcendentally powerful." This similarity renders the effect only more remarkable in Longus. In fiction written for women, after all, the projection of the woman's desires onto the outside world elevates in fantasy the members of a group whose wishes are all too often discounted in reality. It may be that in *Daphnis and Chloe* as well, the vision of female purity as a transfiguring force is a compensatory feature: certainly no spiritual transformation can prevail over events as they finally occur.

The Broken Jug

The second half of the novel brings a marked turn in the plot. Love, at first a private matter, now becomes the subject of contracts and obligations. Families appear more extensively than before; so, too, do economic considerations. We have already seen how Chloe, troubled by the wanton sexuality of Pan in the Syrinx myth, exacts an oath of fidelity from Daphnis, to the tolerant amusement of the narrator (2.39). It is shortly after this incident that the topics of marriage and full adult sexuality begin to emerge in earnest. Gender now becomes a more explicit issue. During their early courtship, Daphnis and Chloe avoid sexual intercourse because "that was too daring a thing not only for maidens but also for young goatherds" (2.9). Now, at the same time that Chloe's adoptive mother begins to speak to her of marriage (3.4), Longus hastens the end of the lovers' shared innocence. Daphnis meets the femme fatale Lykainion, a neighbor's wife; attracted by his obtuseness, she offers to instruct him (3.17). When Daphnis plans to tell Chloe what he has learned, Lykainion (perhaps selfishly) discourages him with a cynical piece of advice (3.19). A virgin, she says, will cry out in pain and bleed profusely: "she will lie there in a great deal of blood, as if slaughtered." Thus, Daphnis should deflower her in a secluded place. This grisly warning frightens Daphnis off completely for the time being. It not only prolongs the "obstacle course" but also encourages the reader to picture repeatedly the loss of Chloe's virginity. We hear that Daphnis shrinks in his imagination from a scene where Chloe will "cry out as if at an enemy, weep as if in pain, and be covered with blood" (3.20). Again, Daphnis and Chloe sleep together naked, "And Chloe would easily have become a woman, if Daphnis had not been afraid of the blood" (3.24). But identify with Chloe as he will, Daphnis cannot share her greater investment in virginity and the greater risk (even of physical damage) she runs by losing it. After the initiation of Daphnis, as Winkler (1990: 122) has observed, "Daphnis and Chloe continue their relation as more and more distinctly unequal partners, like Abraham and Isaac journeying up the mountain."

How is the reader to react to the growing suspicion that something not altogether sweet or pleasant is about to befall Chloe? An incident that occurs in the last book suggests one possibility. Lampis, a disappointed suitor of Chloe, maliciously lays waste a garden that has been tended by Lamon, the foster father of Daphnis. The whole violation is described in a suggestive manner (4.7–8): "Waiting until night and going over the wall he uprooted some of the flowers and broke off others, and trampled still more like a wild pig . . . the whole garden had had its appearance spoiled and all that was left was mud. But whatever had escaped the violence [*hubris*] still bloomed and shone forth and was lovely although it lay low." (See Bartsch 1989: 50–55, on the identification of heroine with garden.) The erotic potential of all this ruin would be well appreciated by a certain type of nineteenth-century reader. Utter and Needham (1936: 6) aptly note the perverse attraction of paintings such as a work by Greuze in which a very young girl in revealingly disordered clothes holds a broken vessel: "he who had broken such jugs would know that proverbially they cannot be mended."

This image of violated beauty contributes to the chain of associations that leads to the marriage of Daphnis and Chloe. For both lovers the wedding is part of a Cinderella-type transformation occasioned by the discovery of their noble birth. Chloe (after Daphnis has vouched for her virginity) takes a bath and gets her hair done; the narrator tactlessly claims that Daphnis can hardly recognize her in her new state of cleanliness (4.32). And so they celebrate what turns out to be a mock rustic wedding, returning to the country now as a charade (4.37). The narrator forecasts that they will live happily ever after (4.39). The very close of the novel, however, focuses on the moment when Chloe loses her virginity, with a reminder of the precepts of the neighbor woman (4.40): "And Daphnis now profited by Lykainion's lesson [lit. "did what Lykainion had taught him"]; and Chloe then first knew that those things that were done in the wood were only the sweet sports of children." Meanwhile, the guests sing uncouthly outside the bedroom door. Longus's description of the wedding is supremely ambivalent. All the other characters enjoy what is, for Chloe, the traumatic end of a blissful innocence.

The narrative's stance toward the heroine is thus puzzling. On the one hand, her inner life is depicted with sympathetic care. On the other hand, the text creates erotic fantasy from the prospect, and then from the reality, of her suffering. Her state of vulnerability seems all the more extreme in the midst of general celebration. There is, then, more than one way of reading the ending. The entertainment value of this wedding between children can perhaps be seen at its most crude by analogy to the show of child pornography arranged by Petronius's lascivious Quartilla. As a prelude to seducing Encolpius, she stages the "wedding" of the young Giton to a girl of seven (*Satyricon* 25). That ceremony seems to pass painlessly enough for those involved. In our text, however, pain and celebration are intimately intertwined. So might it have happened sometimes in actuality; witness the heart-rendingly matter-of-fact explanation of the wedding song by one ancient scholar: "Maidens sing the epithalamion outside the bridal-chamber, so that the voice of the maiden being violated [*biazomenê*] will not be heard" (translated from Wendel 1914: 331). How many times would a girl have participated in this ceremony before she became the central figure?

A Honeymoon in Hell

Brutality has to be discovered in *Daphnis and Chloe* amidst the charm; let us turn for brief comparison to another ancient novel in which we can see tension between chastity and violence presented in a much more obvious fashion.

The *Leucippe and Clitophon* of Achilles Tatius shows youthful love not in a pastoral setting but in the format of an international thriller. Just as in Longus, we find simultaneously a strong insistence on purity and an abundance of vivid erotic material. Unlike *Daphnis and Chloe,* this novel has been considered shocking because of the sexual behavior of the heroine (see Bakhtin 1981b: 66n). More arresting than any explicit statement is the system of imagery which, far outdoing Longus, is violent and suggestive of deep uncanny fears. In this sense, *Leucippe and Clitophon* bears greater resemblance to a modern Gothic than to a Harlequin (see Modleski 1982: 69, 71). Also unlike Longus, with his universal narrative irony, Achilles Tatius describes the action from Clitophon's point of view.

An equation between sex and force is established from the beginning. This novel also opens with an ecphrasis: rather than an illustration of the story itself, it presents a famous mythical rape scene. Europa is shown being carried off by a bull (1.1): "On the upper part of her body [lit. "her breasts"] she wore a tunic down to her middle [lit. "as far as her shameful place"], and then a robe covered the lower part of her body . . . her figure could be traced under the clothes—the deep-set navel, the long slight curve of the belly, the narrow waist, broadening down to the loins, the breasts gently swelling from her bosom." Europa is described with no reference to her feelings, even to her expression. But this picture is preceded by a description of her companions, left behind on the shore (1.1):

> The painter had put the girls at one end of the meadow where the land jutted out into the sea. Their look was compounded of joy and fear: garlands were bound about their brows; their hair had been allowed to float loose on their shoulders; their legs were bare, covered neither by their tunics above nor their sandals below, a girdle holding up their skirts as far as the knee; their faces were pale and their features distorted [the language actually describes a kind of grimace]; their eyes were fixed wide open upon the sea, and their lips were slightly parted, as if they were about to utter a cry of fear; their hands were stretched out in the direction of the bull . . . they seemed to be anxious to run after the bull, but to be afraid of entering the water.

The girls betray a combination of fear and desire that has for no clear reason made their clothes fall off. This tableau suggests to the reader, by showing the response of a supplied audience, a way to interpret what follows. Events proceed according to the expectations thus aroused (see Bartsch 1989: 49).

Something like sublimation can be detected in an early experience of Clitophon (cf. Bartsch 1989: 85–89). Promised in marriage to his half sister Calligone, he has a chilling dream (1.3):

> I seemed to have grown into one with Calligone from the belly [the navel] down-wards, while above we had two separate bodies: then there stood over me a tall woman of fearful appearance; she had a savage countenance, blood-shot eyes, grim, rough cheeks, and snakes for hair; in her right hand she held a sickle, in her left a torch. She advanced angrily upon me, bearing the sickle: and then struck with it at my waist, where the two bodies joined, and so cut the maiden away from me. In mortal fear I jumped up, terrified: I told nobody the dream, but revolved in-wardly the most gloomy forebodings.

Images of rape and castration are handily combined by this scene along with, perhaps, a certain ambivalence toward women. Soon after the dream, Leucippe appears with her mother as a visitor in the house of Clitophon's father. At the very sight of her, he falls in love (1.4), comparing her with the image of Europa in the opening ecphrasis. Clitophon and Leucippe arrange a tryst. Just as they retire to bed, Leucippe's mother, asleep in her own room, has the following dream (2.23): "She saw a robber with a naked sword snatch her daughter from her, throw her down on her back, and then rip her up the middle of the belly with a blade, starting from below [lit. 'from the shameful part']." She rushes into Leucippe's room, forcing Clitophon to flee, and berates her daughter. This intervention preserves the lovers' chastity for the moment.

The pair goes into exile and suffers much ill fortune until we leave them on the eve of their marriage. Early in the narrative we see yet another ecphrasis, this time a diptych of Prometheus and Andromeda, both in chains (3.6). Only Andromeda is described at length. She is "charmingly adorned by fear," like a "bride for Hades."[5] Great play is made of the elaborate sword of Perseus, who is coming to rescue her: "It began below as one, but halfway up it split; half was pointed, and that half remained a sword . . . the other half was curved, thus becoming like a sickle, so that in a single blow it might with one portion kill by piercing and with the other by cutting." The weapon (for use, of course, against the sea monster) reminds us of Clitophon's early dream, evoking the woman with her sharp implement and the divided body of her androgynous victim. Soon Leucippe finds herself in a plight similar to Andromeda's. Captured by pirates, she is doomed to become a virgin sacrifice (3.15–18). Any doubt about the sexual connotations of such an idea vanishes in the light of the ruse prepared by her friends to save her (see Elsom, Chapter 10 above). They fit her out with a false belly which when slit with a trick sword (lovingly described) spills animal viscera. We recall the dream Leucippe's mother had when the girl was in bed with Clitophon. The false sacrifice is described not just once but twice, the first time when the friends put on a surprise demonstration for the horrified Clitophon. Real challenges to Leucippe's purity are embellished with equally exciting special effects: tied up, she struggles and reveals "such things as a woman does not like to be seen" (4.9). All the more delightful, surely, for the viewer.

Readings and Rereadings

Leucippe and Clitophon is much more openly violent and misogynistic than *Daphnis and Chloe;* nevertheless, some similarities are obvious. In each novel the woman is portrayed with a show of sympathy, yet her pain and bloodshed are repeatedly either suggested in some way to the reader or imagined by a fearful yet desirous male. How, in any such context, can a fictional female subjectivity be said to represent a truly feminine point of view? Is it not rather the case that these depictions of women's inner lives are no more than a touch of the (spuriously) personal, intended to make an imagined violation of privacy still more delicious, like the biographies printed next to pictures of naked women in magazines? Perhaps a certain type of reader would even find *Daphnis and Chloe* not a weak novelty version of the hoped-for form but actually superior to a book like *Leucippe and Clitophon* by reason of its overtly high moral tone. Yet is it necessary for us to read this way? Does the text, in fact, require that we do so?

As Winkler has pointed out, it is hard to determine Longus's true sympathies, even if we assume that the narrator is at least partly coextensive with the author. Does this difficulty simply proclaim the complexities and multiple subjectivities of the book? Winkler observes (1990: 126): "The ambiguities [in *Daphnis and Chloe*] afford us an opportunity to become resisting readers." Rather, a work like *Daphnis and Chloe* obliges us to become resisting readers, to retrieve the positive elements of a female characterization from a context that constructs the female experience in such negative terms.

Such rescue missions have, it must be acknowledged, invited criticism. An argument against essentialism holds that the notion of a "female" way of being reinforces the division between the sexes (Echols 1983). This argument in turn, however, rests upon a set of alternatives—self-awareness or structural change— which may not really exclude each other. It also assumes that without a project of self-definition feminists can adopt an immediately available stance of genuine neutrality—a precarious assumption at best. By claiming this "neutral" view where the study of literature is concerned, one runs the risk of ignoring the power literature has over its readers, to call upon and to reinforce categories of thought too deeply inscribed to be adjusted by means of a mere determination to do away with prejudice.

Judith Fetterley, inventor of the term *resisting reader,* shows how American fiction not only places women in a subordinate role but prompts the reader to identify with a point of view that is actively derogatory to women (1978). In her own readings, women characters emerge as newly sympathetic and even on occasion powerful. In Harlequins as well as in *Daphnis and Chloe,* the female reader is (to put it in Fetterley's language) forced to "identify against herself" (1978: xiii). Nor can these works be read coherently by choosing simply to ignore gender or to cross gender boundaries and identify with a male figure (cf. Heilbrun 1979: 151). A rereading must take up the issue of gender explicitly.

The suggestions that follow are aimed toward romance novels in particular. First, how can we understand *Daphnis and Chloe?* This book presents a female figure substantial enough to awaken the reader's interest, but it encourages the reader to derive pleasure from her constant victimization. In an attempt to come to terms with this dilemma, I wish to expand on the idea that the romance contains within itself the possibility of more than one reading. Feminist theory has developed the idea of "women's fiction" as a "double-edged discourse," which contains both a "dominant" and "muted" text (Showalter 1982). Possibly *Daphnis and Chloe,* in many ways a male-centered text, also has a women's text which is there for the recovery. It is not necessary to claim that the author himself has any certifiable "feminist" sympathies; to choose one analogy, the strong female characters in Greek tragedy hardly attest to the authors' proto-feminism (Foley 1988: 1309), yet readers may still value Hecuba.

We might start, in the case of Longus's novel, by recalling Chloe. She appeals to the reader's sympathy first of all by her relative independence of thought and action.

She desires Daphnis; she seduces him. This show of autonomy, it is true, may not mean much in the light of the story overall. At the end, in fact, Chloe is left making a strong pathetic appeal to the reader. Pathos of this sort has indeed been taken as a source of feminist inspiration. I would compare the youthful characters in Colette's novels, so often cited by Beauvoir as depictions (both positive and negative) of female existence (1953: 329, 330, 339–41; cf. Carter 1982: 178). Longus's novel offers a similar potential.

Daphnis and Chloe may also be read as a form of commentary not only on the circumstances it describes but also on the later tradition. As Winkler (1990) has remarked, an interplay of "nature and culture" dictates that Chloe be subordinated to Daphnis. This observation is revealing: Chloe's inferiority seems in some degree externally imposed. In modern romances, by way of contrast, male domination has become a necessary value, the very heart of the erotic appeal. If (as often happens) it is challenged by an independent heroine, the challenge only leads to a more resounding affirmation (Modleski 1982: 39–45; Snitow 1983: 250). Longus, on the other hand, provides an aporetic ending, one that emphasizes the pain of initiation. These are, to be sure, slight enough differences, but they offer at least a corrective to the pattern that seems so inevitable in some women's fictions: oppression becomes regression. Longus does not lead us through an exercise in which doubts are raised only to have them explained away. *Daphnis and Chloe* implies the possibility that the relations between the sexes which we see today are not inevitably or by definition fixed.

A number of suggestions for more extensive rereading are put forward by the critics of contemporary romances. Modleski (1982) adopts the most abstractly theoretical approach, suggesting some aspects of female-oriented mass culture which may offer models of female expression. She settles particularly upon soap operas, with their "open-ended, multi-climactic" (90; 125n) narrative technique. This technique she indirectly compares (105) to Irigaray's description of the female consciousness as "a sort of universe in expansion for which no limits could be fixed and which, for all that, would not be incoherent." This essentialist account, in fact largely negative, recalls Echols's critique, though we have seen that this model jibes with Longus's narrative technique. But there are more pragmatic approaches.

Thurston (1987; see Butler 1988) and Radway (1984) each suggest that modern romances have already partly fulfilled the possibilities of rereading and rewriting. In Thurston's view, women's romances have undergone real changes reflecting the evolved position of women in society. As she admits, however, countertrends are visible (59, 160). Some publishers indeed seem to have moved backward. The cover blurb of *Tomorrow—Come Soon* gets in the heroine's "years as a cripple" and her "horror" at the threat of sex with her father's boss. The heroine of *See Only Me* (Shirley Larson, 1986) is (reversibly) blind. A tendency to put the heroine at a physical disadvantage has emerged only recently and is, I think, a means of preserving artificially a relation between the sexes that was accepted as natural when the earlier romances were written.

What of the works cited as more forward-looking? Some, to be sure, offer an improvement over *See Only Me;* nevertheless, the feminist content strikes me as superficial. One novel cited by Thurston (1987: 162–63) is called *Male Chauvinist*

(Alexandra Sellers, Silhouette, 1985). The title character's up-to-date politics result in this: ". . . a lot of men think that women have a rape fantasy, and it's just not true. And if last night gave you that idea about me, well, it shouldn't have." (Sorry; my mistake.) And the cover of the volume (Thurston 1987: 30) is hard to distinguish from that of any other romance.

Radway (1984) examines not changes in the texts but uses of the stories by women readers. She shows how much progress is made by her informants' critical readings of romances. Through active explorations of problems occurring in everyday life these readers, by their own account, achieve heightened awareness, if not independence. Their reading, it is suggested, helps them come to terms with daily oppression; it does not (as some analyses might suggest) celebrate it (e.g., 141). It is, finally, Radway's approach that seems to me most promising as a way of looking at romance novels. A number of objections can, of course, be raised. How much is the reading described by a Radway informant simply an illusion? Can it not be the case that the reading of romances is, far from an eye-opening activity, a flight into a world of dreams? The testimonies cited by Radway suggest that some of these criticisms may hold an element of truth without entirely compromising her thesis. The readers freely admit to seemingly contrary effects from reading. By their own explanations they seek out books largely as sources of escapist entertainment (e.g., 60). Yet they also overwhelmingly feel that the novels have taught them greater self-awareness which has had a marked effect on their lives (101–3). This account, with all its admitted limitations, contains a great deal that is persuasive. Romances, after all, present social relations in an ordered, mythologized form that allows readers to explore them (cf. Radway 1984: 198–99). Need we assume that these explorations can be done only to the exclusion of more complete recalculations?

The ancient romances certainly invite reading as exploration; a reader sympathetic to Chloe and those like her can achieve a vantage point from which to survey the confusing, perilous sexual landscapes of the novels. Still further, these works occasionally contain statements that might form the material of more radical re-vision. For example, the goddess-like Chariclea of Heliodorus's *Ethiopian Tales* is sometimes acutely conscious of her own situation. In one episode, her mother tries to make her confess her love for Theagenes (10.29; Smith 251):

> "Open your mind with freedom and confidence, and recollect that you are speaking to a mother . . . a parent knows how to excuse the failings of a daughter; and a woman can throw a cloak over the frailties of her sex."
> "This too is my additional misfortune," replied Chariclea; "I am speaking to those of understanding, yet I am not understood."

Chariclea could be speaking for all of her type when she deplores the difficulty of making herself understood. In our reading of such characters, we too often register the familiar negative stereotypes but fail to recognize anything more positive on the grounds that these ancient figures are products of male imaginations, or caught in the toils of male fantasy. In subjecting fictional characters to this double jeopardy we are mistaken. There is something to be learned from Chloe and her sisters. If we are to find it we need an exercise not only of the critical faculties but of the imagination as well.

NOTES

My sincerest thanks go to Amy Richlin and Sandra Joshel for many helpful comments on an early draft of this chapter. My colleague Rebecca Hague has kindly given me the benefit of her knowledge of ancient weddings; I am especially grateful to her for bringing to my attention the remarks of the scholiast on Theocritus 18. The late John Winkler kindly allowed me to see his article on *Daphnis and Chloe* before publication (in Winkler 1990).

Texts used in this essay are as follows. For the Greek text of Longus, I have reference to the edition of Reeve (1986); for Achilles Tatius, Vilborg (1955); for Heliodorus, Bekker (1855). Translations used in quotations include those of Thornley (1657, edited by Edmonds) for Longus, Gaselee (1917) for Achilles Tatius, and Smith (1901) for Heliodorus. Page numbers have been given only for Smith, who (unlike the others) does not follow the divisions of the Greek edition. In many cases the translation has been altered to represent the Greek more closely. For a concise survey of ancient romance novels, see Winkler 1988; for all the novels in translation, see now Reardon 1989. I regret that Bartsch 1989 appeared too late for me to make use of it here as I would have wished.

1. Jessica Steele, *Tomorrow—Come Soon* (Toronto: Harlequin Books, 1984). The passage from Longus is my own rather loose, excerpted translation (from 1.13) into language closer to that of the Harlequin, for the obvious purpose of emphasizing the comparison.

2. On the exaggeration by critics generally of the originality of eighteenth-century novels as compared to the ancient works, see Winkler 1988: 1563.

3. In what follows I will discuss an aspect of *Daphnis and Chloe* that is scarcely recognized by critics, with the exception of Winkler (1990). Winkler summarizes the subject of his discussion as follows (103): "My central topic . . . is the inherent violence of the cultural system discovered by Daphnis and Chloe . . . and the unequal impact of that violence." In this major respect Winkler anticipates my argument: he demonstrates that to some extent gender is a theme in *Daphnis and Chloe*. He also describes the novel as "a tale specifically of rape repeatedly escaped and yet continually and disturbingly re-surfacing." Winkler's analysis of episodes in Longus is several times in accordance with mine, but more detailed. I am especially indebted to him for his treatments of the Lykainion episode and of the actual wedding scene; but compare also his discussions of the attack by Dorcon, the Syrinx fable, and the ravishing of the garden. See also Zeitlin 1990.

4. I am indebted to Amy Richlin for this observation.

5. For the "charming" effects of girlish fear, see above on Dorcon's attempted rape of Chloe, and Richlin, Chapter 8 in this volume.

12

The Edible Woman:
Athenaeus's Concept
of the Pornographic

Madeleine M. Henry

Now she had a blank white body. It looked slightly obscene, lying there soft and sugary and featureless on the platter. She set about clothing it, filling the cake-decorator with bright pink icing. . . . Her creation gazed up at her, its face doll-like and vacant except for the small silver glitter of intelligence in each green eye. While making it she had been almost gleeful, but now, contemplating it, she was pensive. All that work had gone into the lady and now what would happen to her?

"You look delicious," she told her. "Very appetizing. And that's what will happen to you; that's what you get for being food."

—Margaret Atwood, *The Edible Woman* (1983)

Athenaeus the rhetorician (*Athenaeus sophistês*) is an author more often consulted than read. His extravagant work *Sophists at Dinner* discusses the minutiae of the classical symposium (drinking party) in nearly unreadable detail, giving recommendations for correct arrangement (*taxis*). In the last 150 years, almost no attention has been paid to investigating Athenaeus's thought, with the exception of Barry Baldwin, who considers that Athenaeus's intent was at least partly satirical.[1] While other scholars have acknowledged Athenaeus's contribution to our knowledge of the lost texts of classical Greek comedy and to cookery and other *Realien,* they generally have failed to find any unity of thought in his work. Gulick, the Loeb Library editor-translator through whom most readers of English come to know the *Deipnosophistae,* does little more than apologize for the object of his scholarly labor, claiming that the work is too long and that its author's powers can't sustain it (I, x, xii); he also holds that Athenaeus did not appreciate the literary merits of the works he quotes (I, xv). His remarks largely echo and rephrase the remarks of other classical scholars of the last two centuries.[2] Nor has Athenaeus fared better under the scrutiny of nonclassicists. Michel Foucault, one of the most provocative and influential recent historians of Western thought, makes virtually no use of Athenaeus. This is puzzling because much of Athenaeus's source material is drawn from the period Foucault examines in Volume Two of his *History of Sexuality,* namely the Greek classical period, and because Athenaeus himself lived and wrote during the historical period Foucault examines in Volume Three, namely the heyday of the Roman Empire. In fact, although Foucault is aware of the importance of *taxis* in the constitution of the "techniques of the self" and the "arts of existence," and understands two of those "arts" as erotics and dietetics, he has omitted an author whose work not only supports some of his own theses but is vital to understanding the way in which sexuality was constructed in the Greek world.[3]

Both Gulick the philologist and Foucault the historian of sexual discourse have ignored or erased important parts of Athenaeus's perspective. Gulick's blind spot is most evident in the apology with which he introduces the infamous Book 13, *Peri Gynaikôn* ("About Women"): "In an essay written in 1867 James Russell Lowell took occasion to say: 'The somewhat greasy heap of a literary rag-and-bone-picker, like Athenaeus, is turned to gold by time.' In this volume the reader will find that Athenaeus goes further, and presents 'a rag and bone and a hank o' hair' with embarrassing frankness" (VI, vii). Foucault goes beyond embarrassment to silence. He is aware that the "self" whose "techniques" and "arts of existence" he describes is a male "self":

> It was an ethics for men: an ethics thought, written, and taught by men, and addressed to men—to free men, obviously. A male ethics, consequently, in which women figured only as objects or, at most, as partners that one had best train. . . . This is doubtless one of the most remarkable aspects of that moral reflection: . . . it was an elaboration of masculine conduct carried out from the viewpoint of men in order to give form to *their* behavior. (1985: 22–23)

But he goes on to reproduce that one-sidedness in his own critique, which only rarely bothers to deduce the experience (or existence) of a female subject. His discussions of marriage (1985: 143–84; 1986: 147–85) constitute most of his treatment of women's experience, and both are written almost entirely from the husband's point of view; his section on prostitution in the Greek world mentions only boys. The absence of women rings through the pages.

Thus, Athenaeus's translator apologizes for the fact that Athenaeus mentions prostitutes in the *Deipnosophistae,* and the historian of sexual discourse finds an investigation of female sexuality irrelevant to his project, possibly because a discussion of women would be necessary to such a project. Foucault clearly understands that the pederastic erotic ideal is problematic but does not consider what problematics exist for heterosexual eroticism.[4]

Foucault's conceptualization and naming of the "arts of existence," however, do indirectly illuminate Athenaeus's representation of women. In the *Deipnosophistae,* references to and descriptions of women, and men's sexual relations with them, are largely subsumable beneath a Foucaultian "dietetics" rather than beneath an "erotics" of existence. That is to say, food and women perform analogous functions for the discussants of the dinner party. In contrast, Foucault's term "erotics" would be best used to describe the dialogue's representation of sexual relations between males.

I hope here to demonstrate how, and in what context, Athenaeus constructs an object of the sort that Margaret Atwood called the "edible woman" in her novel of that name. The fictitious and historical women whom Athenaeus's characters discuss and quote are women trained, in the Foucaultian sense, to gratify men. I shall argue that this construction on Athenaeus's part offers us a sophisticated though implicit concept of the pornographic, and that Athenaeus is a pornographer of the first water. I leave open the important question of how much of a "comic" view Athenaeus may have imposed on his subject matter. The possibility that the work was intended to satirize the symposiasts need not vitiate the points I make here; humor is a conservative strategy, not a visionary one.

The work and thought of Catharine A. MacKinnon, Mary Daly, and Susanne Kappeler inform my definition of pornography. Kappeler argues, "Pornography is not a special case of sexuality; it is a form of representation" (1986: 2). For her, pornography is always the gaze of the white male at women (or blacks or Jews), whose subordination to them is sexualized; because "the gaze is male," women (or blacks or Jews or homosexuals) do not look back. Their only choice is the degree to which they acquiesce in the pornographic scenario. In Kappeler's analysis, pornographic representation is a cultural practice that constructs, valorizes, genderizes, replicates, and perpetuates the subject/object dichotomy. Also instructive in forming a definition of pornography is Mary Daly's observation that pornography constructs woman as the mute but touchable caste (1984: 232). MacKinnon further specifies that

> pornography, in the feminist view, is a form of forced sex, a practice of sexual politics, an institution of gender inequality. In this perspective, pornography is not harmless fantasy or a corrupt and confused misrepresentation of an otherwise natural and healthy sexuality. Along with the rape and prostitution in which it participates, pornography institutionalizes the sexuality of male supremacy, which fuses the erotization of dominance and submission with the social construction of male and female. . . . To understand this, one does not have to notice that pornography models are real women to whom something real is being done, nor does one have to inquire into the systematic infliction of pornographic sexuality upon women, although it helps. (1987: 148–49)

I hope to show that attitudes expressed in the *Deipnosophistae* are perfectly congruent with a concept of pornographic representation as defined by current radical feminist theory. Such theory has greatly helped us define and analyze pornography and the pornographic worldview as it operates in the West today and as it has operated in the recent past. Yet many feminist theorists, seeming unaware of pornography's long history, go no further back than de Sade when discussing the origins and permutations of that worldview; as Lerner has said of de Beauvoir, they ignore history (1985: 221).

Kappeler, while offering a profound and thought-provoking analysis of pornographic representation, neither pursues nor suggests that we pursue our analysis of such representation past a point earlier than de Sade. In fact, we might say that de Sade is the "ur-pornographer" for Kappeler, Carter, Griffin, and others. Nor does Susan Griffin, a liberal analyst of pornographic representation, seek the connections that can be made between what she calls the nineteenth- and twentieth-century Western pornographic worldview and that of a pornographic worldview in classical antiquity. Griffin's work is not a history, yet there are obvious points of contact between the nineteenth- and twentieth-century "encyclopedic" pornographic novels, memoirs, and pseudoscientific treatises on sexuality that she analyzes and Athenaeus's "encyclopedic," "catalogue," or "overkill" approach to his topics, one of which is the human female (see Parker, Chapter 5).[5] The apparently seamless sameness of outlook between Athenaeus's characters and the literary passages they quote, which are often seven hundred to eight hundred years earlier than the date of the *Deipnosophistae,* argues for the persistence of a pornographic perspective in classical antiquity. And one might profitably investigate the later popularity and influence of the *Deipnosophistae* in the West; one suspects that there is no clear separation between it and *The Pearl.* Rabelais's Gargantua, for example, knows and mentions Athenaeus as an antiquarian of rank equal to Pausanias.

Where feminist analysts omit history, many historians of sexuality (e.g., Foucault, as seen above) ignore gender. By this act, their own works become part of the pornography of representation; Foucault, for example, denies self and subjectivity to the female and thus replicates the reality he claims to critique.[6]

We may critique his replication of an exclusively male subjectivity by reference to Kappeler:

> The most notorious methodological ruse exonerating both artist and critic is the technique of "showing up" or laying bare, derived apparently from the secular notion of realism, but going back to the medieval understanding of art as "showing forth God's creation." . . . Under the imperative of realism it seems natural that representations reflect the salient features of reality, and in the face of the natural existence of works of art, no question is asked why we should want such representations or reflections, no question is asked why someone produces them, and least of all, how these works themselves are engaged in shaping the reality they are said to reflect. . . . Werner Herzog, celebrated cineast of the cultured avant-garde, produces *Fitzcarraldo,* a film about the massive mega-ego of a colonialist who wants to build an operahouse in the middle of the Peruvian jungle and who, in order to carry out his plan, makes a crowd of native Indians carry a steam boat over a hill. . . . the massively inflated mega-ego of a western cineast repeats this self-same act of colonial imperialism and arrogance, carrying the production of his film into the jungle like the opera of *Fitzcarraldo,* and making, in the process of his venture, a crowd of native Indians carry a steam boat over the self-same hill. (1986: 112–13)

Foucault likewise continues to traverse the same path, by replicating the ancients' erasure of a female self in his "history" of "sexuality."

Here I hope to show that radical feminist theory gives us a way to see how Athenaeus constructs women and food as usable, consumable, and to be enjoyed by men in nearly identical terms. Females in the *Deipnosophistae* are usually silent; they speak only to the extent that they participate in their own commodification and when they themselves reinforce their status as objects. I shall also attempt to show how Athenaeus uses the term *pornographos* ("pornographer"), which appears here apparently for the first time in Greek. Examination and analysis of the first use of a word that has come to denote an important aspect of Western culture not only has intrinsic value but also helps us see the relationship of pornography to pornographers, past and present.

The *Deipnosophistae* is an account in dialogue form of the speeches given at a symposium or symposia, wherein are discussed the acquisition and enjoyment of those material comforts which are part of every such dinner party. The guests discuss wines, waters, fishes, breads and cakes, fruits, vegetables, couches, pillows, wine cups, and women. Athenaeus probably wrote in the late second or early third century A.D., a period termed the Second Sophistic. This cultural epoch of the Greco-Roman world saw a renaissance of interest in the classical Greek literature of the fifth and fourth centuries B.C. The *Deipnosophistae* is a valuable source of quotations from otherwise lost portions of Greek literature, particularly of Athenian comedy.[7] Athenian Old Comedy (which flourished in the fifth century B.C.) and Middle and New Comedy (which flourished in the fourth and later centuries) were characterized by their interest in food and sexual revelry (see Zweig, Chapter 4 above), the former more explicitly in regard to sexuality. By Athenaeus's own day, Greek comedy had long ceased to be a living art.[8] Little is known of Athenaeus's life and his other works, but, interestingly, he himself tells us (7.329c6–d2) that he wrote a treatise on Archippus's *Fishes* or *Thrattai*—a play of the Old Comedy in which fishes formed the chorus and women in the guise of fishes were objects of a debate.[9] In the *Deipnosophistae*, Athenaeus quotes extensively from comic writers in regard to both food and women. It is generally acknowledged that the work has not survived entire; the first three books are excerpts by a pre-tenth-century epitomizer, and the total number of books may have been twice the text's present length.[10] Thus, the incomplete state of the text forbids an extended structural or formalist analysis but rather forces the investigator to examine the ideas and habits of mind that the work's characters display.

Athenaeus grounds the *Deipnosophistae* in the tradition of symposium literature by setting the scene (see 6.224b6–9; 7.275b11–18; 9.366a1–5)—and by occasionally breaking the narrative to remind his addressee, Timocrates, that he is, in fact, recounting conversations that took place at a dinner (13.555a1–b8). But unlike the exposition of Plato's and Xenophon's symposium dialogues, Athenaeus's dinner party takes place over an indefinite number of days.[11] The discussants' preoccupation with correctness (of terminology, preparation, amount and order of the consumption of food) contrasts most curiously with the author-narrator's apparent disinterest in framing its record more precisely. This focus on etiquette I take to be an interest in *taxis* as discussed above.

The unexamined premise of the work is that Athenaeus and company have had the leisure and resources to engage in extended banqueting and conversation, that Athenaeus has had the time to recount the conversations (or to dictate his recollections to slaves à la Pliny the Elder, in Pliny *Letters* 3.5.14–15), and that Timocrates will have the time to read it. The deipnosophists, served by the unnamed and numberless slaves who introduce and remove the courses, are aristocratic, intellectual men, who discuss their world in much the same self-important way that Wally and André discuss life and art while being served elegant food in the film *My Dinner with André* (Shawn and Gregory 1981).

The amount of information given about the accoutrements of a symposium is simply staggering. As the epitomizer says, the conversation itself is an imitation of a feast: "In short, the plan of the discourse reflects the rich bounty of a feast, and the arrangement of the book the courses of the dinner. Such is the delightful feast of reason [*logodeipnon*] which this wonderful steward, Athenaeus, introduces" (1.1b7–c2, Gulick's translation). The *Deipnosophistae* contains both elements of the literary symposium and elements of the encyclopedia or catalogue. Different kinds of wine cups (11.461e3–504b11) and cakes (14.643e5–649a11), for example, are discussed, and in the discussion of women Myrtilus refers to his speech on them as a "catalogue": "Companions, I think in all of these things I've made this erotic catalogue, not without care, for you" (13.599e1–2; at 13.590a12, Myrtilus refers to his speech as a catalogue of women, *katalogon gynaikôn*). Because the proper way of using, obtaining, and consuming the objects under discussion is constantly in the foreground, the *Deipnosophistae* also participates in what Foucault has called the literature of "normalization"; we may qualify this definition by specifying that such literature contributes to our understanding of the economy and etiquette of upper-class *men's* existence.

Despite its truncated state, Book 1 provides an overview of the intellectual tenor of the entire *Deipnosophistae*. The authorial voice is explicitly male; the author arrogates to himself (or the epitomizer arrogates on his behalf) the biological aspect of creativity: Athenaeus is the father of this book (1.a1).[12]

It is not necessary to argue the literary merits or disadvantages of combining so many topics into a work that Gulick has rightly called "diffuse in style" and "heterogeneous in subject" (I, ix); the important point here is to see how women are specifically equated with food in the *Deipnosophistae*. The pervasiveness of this equation of women with food is what makes Athenaeus a pornographer. Although the various books concentrate on different items obtainable at the symposium, the pornographic likening of women to food is evident throughout. Of course, it does not surprise that food is a frequent topic of conversation at the table. What surprises is the persistent association of food with women and the likening of women to food.

The equation of women with food and prescriptions for the correct uses of each are given many times in the first book and are repeated frequently in subsequent books. Characteristic prescriptions are: it is important for men to be able to obtain food and women and to enjoy them masterfully; there is a correct manner in which to obtain and enjoy food/women; communal consumption of food/women by men is important. Communal consumption, of course, is a major premise of the dialogue; it is what the discussants do. Moderation in one's consumption of food/women is important, with Homer's male characters as particular models of moderation. Additionally, food/women are sometimes "prepared," "disguised," or otherwise falsely represented; it is important to be able to detect the "real" food/woman beneath the culinary or cosmetic deception. Lastly, there should be a similar distancing from the realities of the life of food/women. Little or no attention is paid to the arduous cultivation of food or to anyone involved in its preparation except the oft-quoted chefs of comedy, who themselves are quite removed from the actual cultivation of food. Similarly, little to no attention is paid to the physical realities of the lives of prostitutes; women in Athenaeus do not become pregnant and are never malnourished or ill.

Women can be described with culinary metaphors, or they can simply be likened to food outright. Not only is the frequency of the equation significant, but so are the contexts in which such remarks are made. When women are likened to food, the equation is usually made in connection with a discussion of food. In other words, food is the primary topic of a conversation and women are adduced in order to further and more fully understand and enjoy food. It must also be noted that the "art" of this dialogue, wherein food and women are almost constantly discussed as being implicitly like each other and are discussed in analogous ways, has an actual referent in "life"; sexual relations with hired women were as much a part of the classical symposium as was food. In Book 4, for example, not only does the long quotation from Matro's mock-epic account of a symposium begin with a catalogue of foods and end with the introduction of whores (4.134d3–137c5), but the conversational account of Karanos's elegant symposium—supposedly a historical event—also relates the introduction of both food and whores (4.128a8–130d11). Thus, in the symposiasts' little world, it is quite "natural" that food and women are as one. Both are part of the outlay.

Women and food are found in a list of the products of different *poleis* (1.27d7–e1). Women and food may simply be listed together (14.642a6–9), and women can be compared to fish in discussions of fish (3.106a1–3). Fish can also be described metaphorically as women (4.135a7–8, 4.135c2–d5). A devotee of Epicurus calls an eel "Helen" and rips it apart: "When an eel was served, a follower of Epicurus who was among the diners said, 'The Helen of dinners is here; and so I shall be Paris.' And before anybody had yet stretched out his hands for the eel, he fell upon it and stripped off the sides, reducing it to just its backbone" (7.298d5–e1). In a discussion of relishes, women and dalliances with them are compared to relishes (9.367c4–d8); in a discussion of rose casserole, its scent is compared to that of Hera anointing her body (9.406a1–b8); in a quotation from Aristophanes' comedy *Old Age,* courtesans' bodies are likened to olives (4.133a2–6). These examples could easily be multiplied. The commodification of women as food is implicit in a quotation from the fourth-century comic poet Diphilus: "No occupation is more abominable than the pimp's! I'd prefer to walk up and down the streets selling roses, radishes, lupines, olive cakes—anything rather than keep these women" (2.55d8–e1). A quotation from Epicurus removes the association of women with food from the context of the symposium to a philosophical *taxis* of the chief goods in life; food and *ta aphrodisia* ("sexual activity") are called the greatest goods (7.278f2–6; this is repeated with slight variation at 7.280a4–b4 and 12.546e1–11). The tendency to legitimize one's use of women by citing cultural authorities will be discussed later.

Perhaps the most telling proof that women and food are interchangeable is found in the following anecdote; if a woman, or a statue of her, cannot satisfy a man, he can copulate with a piece of meat like Cleisophus the Selymbrian. For he fell in love with the marble statue at Samos and locked himself up in the temple, in the belief that he would be able to have intercourse with it. When he was unable, on account of the chilliness and inelasticity of the stone, he thenceforth desisted from his desire. He set out a small piece of meat and had intercourse with that (13.605f4–10; see Sutton, Chapter 1 above, on a similar tale from Knidos).

Just as the discussants have commodified women as sexual "food," they take concomitant, though lesser, interest in the aphrodisiac and other sexually charged properties of food and in the sexual habits of animals. Thus, one can speak not only of women's definition as sexual "food" in the dialogue but also of the sexualization of food itself. The discussants display no little interest in the aphrodisiac properties of foods, as well as in the sexual behavior of certain other creatures, not all of which are commonly eaten. Certain foods have desirable or undesirable aphrodisiac properties. *Bolboi* (edible wild bulbs) produce desired effects (1.5c2–3), and the aroma from a cook shop is like the song of the Sirens (7.290d1–10). But one must not make excessive attempts to achieve and maintain multiple erections; some aphrodisiacs cause bizarre and unsightly erections—like those of birds (1.18c7–e6). Still other foods, such as lettuce, are soporific, reduce the sex drive, and induce impotence (1.69b4–f5).

More interesting than this frequent mention of the physiological effects (which are not only sexual but also digestive and circulatory) of certain foods upon the human body is the interest the discussants display in the feminized sexuality of food itself. Bread is described by a character in Antiphanes' *Omphale* as one might describe the body of a young girl: *leukosômatous* ("white-bodied," 3.112c8–d5); the copulation behaviors of the partridge and other birds are discussed at length (9.389b5–f11, 391d6–f4, 394b10–d7) even though it is not clear why this information is necessary. The author of the *Ornithogony* is quoted as saying that all birds had once been human beings (393e3–f7) and gives several examples of the sexual peccadilloes that had caused them to be metamorphosed. Similar interest is taken in the sexual behaviors and copulation postures of fish and shellfish, including that of the aphrodisiac crayfish (3.105c4–11).

Three passages show the specifically feminized sexualization of food. The courtesan Metaneira compares herself to food: "Further, to show that livers were customarily wrapped in the omentum, Hegesander of Delphi says . . . in regard to the custom, that the hetaira Metaneira received a lung among the wrapped livers, discovering it when she took off the fat. She cried out, 'I am undone! The folds of my garments have destroyed me' " (3.107e2–7). In a long quotation from Matro, an anchovy is called the hetaira of the sea god Triton (4.135a7), and "the white-armed goddess-fish, the eel, who boasted that she had lain in Zeus's embrace" (4.135c8–d1) is mentioned. Thus, the acts of beholding and eating food can become acts of seduction, rape, dismemberment, and murder; one also can recall the anecdote wherein a male diner, as Paris, dismembers an eel, as Helen, before he eats it/her.

The *Deipnosophistae* gives the implicit understanding that men have the right to obtain and consume food/women, but that this consumption ought to be moderate and ought to take place in a communal setting. While communal consumption is not openly praised, solitary dining is jocularly upbraided (1.8e3–6). As noted earlier, communal consumption by males is the unspoken premise of the dialogue, and men's ability to remember and recount what they have consumed is in fact proof of their moderation or of what has sometimes been called "sexual rationalism." A corollary assumption underpins this male sexual rationalism: a mark of women's difference and inferiority is that women do not understand the meaning of moderate consumption (see Foucault 1985: 82–86).

Moderation is to be practiced not in an absolute but in a rational sense, and with particular reference to food, drink, and heterosexual *aphrodisia*. The fundamentally excessive nature of the consumption of food/women is rarely questioned. For example, the questions of why scores of different kinds of drinking cups exist, why an entire book is devoted to a discussion of prostitutes and yet another book to a disquisition on gluttony, are questions never raised within the dialogue; the topics proposed by the host Larensis are those "worthy of inquiry" (1.2b3–c1). Furthermore, the numerous cautionary tales regarding sexual overindulgence overwhelmingly refer to heterosexual, not homosexual, activity. Even if we allow for the loss of books through accident and censorship and for the possibility that the *Deipnosophistae* once contained many more references to homosexual *erôs* than it now does, the amount of caution advised in relation to men's sexual activities with women is quite startling. Drunkenness can lead to *gynaikomania* ("madness for women"); thus, a man's immoderacy is betrayed by his excessive interest in wine and women (10.444e2–4; see also 10.433f2–435a8, 11.464c1–d10). The fact that Athenaeus often offers examples of immoderacy in the consumption of food together with immoderacy in the consumption of women again marks the connectedness of women with food.

Athenaeus's symposiasts tell anecdotes that illustrate this point. Though he consumes too much wine and is unable (unlike the exemplary Nestor and Phoenix of 13.556c11–d8) to have intercourse with a hetaira in his old age, the philosopher Dionysius of Heraclea recognizes the fact and offers her to someone who can. At another time, in a remarkable display of rationalism coupled with excess (and reminiscent of Gay Talese), Dionysius demonstrates his fine memory by paying his bill at the brothel in the company of his friends:

> Antigonus of Carystus, in his work *On the Life of Dionysius* . . . says that Dionysius was once feasting with his servants at the festival of the Pitchers. Because of his age he was unable to have intercourse with the hetaira whom they had called in, so he turned and told his fellow-diners, "I cannot stretch the bow, let another take it" [= *Odyssey* 21.152]. Now Dionysius . . . was sex crazed [*pros ta aphrodisia ekmanês*] since his boyhood, and frequented whores indiscriminately. Once when with some acquaintances he came upon the brothel where he had gone the previous day and where he owed some money. By chance he had the money at that time, and he stretched out his hand in the sight of all and paid up (10.437e2–f5; Gulick's translation).

This passage, which is found in a part of Book 10 that contains anecdotes about men who are both intemperate and prone to sexual overindulgence, is of interest because it shows not only Dionysius's lack of moderation but the communal nature of the consumption of women. Dionysius is unable to enjoy the woman, and so he offers her to a companion who can; furthermore, he pays his debt *pantôn horôntôn,* in the sight of all.[13]

The deipnosophists eagerly discuss just how much indulgence in a pleasurable life-style—*to tryphân*—constitutes abuse, how close one can come to crossing that border, where that border is, and why one should not cross it. In Book 12, Athenaeus provides numerous cautionary tales of men who have transgressed the border. Too much *hêdonê* (pleasure), particularly sexual, weakens the reasoning power (12.511d, e) and will culminate in the worst consequences of all—either *hybris,* violence against others, or the loss of one's ability to feel anything at all, whether by becoming unsexed or even by falling into a state of *anaisthêsia.*

Excessive luxury and self-indulgence beget *hybris,* as we see when the hybristic Lydians rape the wives and daughters of other men (12.515f1–4); similar stories are told of the Tarentines (12.522d3–e8) and of the violent deaths of the rivals Straton and Nicocles (12.531a5–e2). The tales crescendo to ever more shocking consequences: Cotys cuts up his wife alive, starting with her genitals (12.531e8–532a9; cf. 10.415c8–d3); the most horrific example is that of another Dionysius, of Syracuse. After he rapes the Locrian virgins, the victims' fathers wreak upon Dionysius's own wife and children a hideous vengeance of rape, murder, and defilement (12.541c4–e11); Dionysius himself ends his life as a mendicant priest of Cybele. One cannot be quite certain if one is supposed to sympathize with the victims of this *hybris* or whether one is to heap moral indignation upon the perpetrator. Certainly the tale of Dionysius, along with many others in the *Deipnosophistae,* legalistically emphasizes the perpetrator's *akrasia* (lack of self-control) rather than the injustice done to his victim.

Women, on the other hand, categorically demonstrate that they neither understand nor practice the principle of moderation. Sometimes women reveal their lack of moderation in their own actions and words. Hecuba attempts to deflect Hector with food and drink from his mission of going out to fight (1.10b7–c5); the placement of this allusion in Book 1 may be deliberately programmatic. Again and again women reveal themselves as bibulous.[14] One woman is described as being "a wine-filled receptacle" (10.441d8–9), and another is singled out because she can drink more than men (10.440d7–e1).

More frequently, men describe or address women as immoderate. In Alexis's comedy *The Dancing Girl* a character remarks that if women have enough wine to drink, they are satisfied (10.441c9–d2). The poet Semonides is said to have observed that women, unlike Homeric heroes, even gobble sacrificial offerings before they are consecrated (5.179b7–d9; cf. 4.161d6–e4 and 3.97b1–c2). Even other creatures have better control over women than do women themselves; in a discussion of various birds, it is said that the porphyrion watches over women lest they commit adultery (9.388b12–c7). And the Massilians and Milesians are said to have prohibited women from drinking (10.429a11–b2).

Food may be sexually seductive, and women may be consumable, but it is not entirely proper to approach either of these things too closely in their natural state. Men of the leisure class can enjoy the end product, the beautiful meal; they need not participate in its preparation. The epitomizer of Book 1 notes, "Athenaeus says that those whose property is secure do not earn their bread with their hands" (1.4d9). The symposiasts in the *Deipnosophistae* are interested in culinary "deceptions" and delight in obtaining rare or out-of-season foods under arduous circumstances. Apicius packs oysters for shipment to Trajan when the latter is in Parthia (1.7d1–4). When the real item is unobtainable, the skillful cook can feign a dish, as one diner reminds his fellows:

> At any rate, the cook in Euphron, the comic poet, says: "I was a student of Soterides. When Nicomedes [king of Bithynia] was twelve days' journey from the sea in midwinter, he wanted an anchovy. Soterides served it to him, by Zeus! so that everyone cried out in astonishment. . . . Taking a tender turnip, Soterides cut it into thin, long strips, making it look just like the anchovy. Then he boiled it, poured oil on it, salted it nicely, sprinkled on exactly forty black poppyseeds, and satisfied Nicomedes' desire in Scythia. . . . The cook is no different than the poet: each man's art lies in his brain." (1.7d8–f4)[15]

Food can not only be prepared elegantly but can also be cultivated with the finest ingredients. Aristoxenus the hedonist waters his lettuces with wine and honey and announces that the earth had especially prepared them as "cakes" for him; earth herself has become a cook who tempts his palate (1.7c4–11). Cooks know how to deceive the diners into thinking, for a little while, that they are eating cucumbers in January (8.372d4–8). The deception is seen as a clever one once the diners have unmasked it. The cook's magic can make food violate its very nature.

The alimentary and the sexual are fused in other, more fantastic corners of the Greek male literary imagination. Several classical comedies had Golden Age, utopian, or underworld focuses. Comic characters quoted by the deipnosophists imagine that one happy characteristic of these other worlds had been the ubiquitous and constant presence of good food.

A quote from Pherecrates' *Metalleis* (*The Miners*) gives a pointed example of this utopian vision: "Pubescent girls in silken shawls, shorn of their pubic hair, drew full cups of fragrant dark wine through a funnel for those who wished to drink" (6.269b7–c2). Females participate in the Golden Age in the same manner as does food. Both are for men's consumption and enjoyment.

Women's attempts to disguise themselves (or brothel keepers' attempts to disguise them) in order to make themselves more attractive to men, however, are not looked upon with like favor. Cynulcus decries as unsightly those married women who use cosmetics (13.557e10–558a1; cf. Ischomachus to his wife in Xen. *Oeconomicus* and Horace *Satire* 1.2). Harlots and the brothel keepers who give them wigs, false bosoms, and other cosmetic adornments are also castigated by the Cynic (13.568a1–d6). It is better, says Cynulcus, to hire as cheaply as possible a woman whose qualities are evident and undisguised, lest one pay more than is necessary or lest one risk the charge of adultery:

> On this account I advise you . . . to cleave only to the women in brothels and not consume unprofitably the wealth of your sons. . . . Or . . . to quote Eubulus's

[comedy] *The Vigil,* "decoy-birds, Aphrodite's trained fillies, naked and arrayed in battle-line, stand in finely woven scarves. . . . Safely and securely, you cheaply buy your pleasure from them." Again, in *Nannion,* . . . Eubulus says, "Isn't he who mates stealthily and in the dark the wretchedest of all men? For he can, in broad daylight, gaze at naked girls . . . he can cheaply buy his pleasure, and not pursue a clandestine lust." . . . Xenarchus also, in *The Pentathlon,* censures those who live as you do and who are eager for highly paid hetairai and freeborn married women ". . . for there are very pretty girls in the brothels here, whom youths can see basking in the sun, bare-breasted and arrayed in battle-line; of these one may choose the one that pleases him, thin, fat, rounded, lanky, shrivelled, young, old, middle-aged, overripe. . . . For the women themselves use force and drag the men in, calling the older ones 'Daddy' and the younger 'Dearie.' And you can see any one of them easily, cheaply, by day, at evening, and in any way you want." . . . And Philemon, too, in *The Brothers,* tells that Solon, on account of the *krisis* [turning point][16] which comes to young men, bought and situated females in brothels . . .: "You, Solon, bought and stationed women in various neighborhoods, ready and available for all. They stand naked, lest you be deceived; look at everything. Perhaps you're not feeling quite yourself; perhaps you're worried about something. The door is open; the price, one obol! Jump right in, and there isn't any dissembling or nonsense. She doesn't snatch herself away; but straightaway, [take her] as you wish and in whatever way you wish. You exit, and you can tell her to go to hell. She's a stranger to you." (13.568d7–569f6)

While the discussants' speech creates a pornographic world, casual references made in the dialogue also make plain that they inhabit a society in which real women were similarly commodified. For example, in a discussion of beauty, it is noted that the Spartans strip young girls to be looked at by *xenoi* ("guest-friends"; 13.566e3–5). Pursuit of and proper attention to such references may someday correct the surprisingly persistent tendency to idealize women's—particularly prostitutes'—lives in classical antiquity (see Zweig, Chapter 4, and Sutton, Chapter 1, above).[17]

Book 13, which is almost entirely taken up with a discussion of the erotic and things erotic, is a final and focal point of my discussion. Here the Cynic Cynulcus and the grammarian Myrtilus argue—the latter good-humoredly and the former contentiously—about the merits of *ta aphrodisia* with women. Several elements distinguish this section of the *Deipnosophistae.* First, the content of Book 13 provides a concentrated reiteration of the pornographic representation seen elsewhere in the work. Next, it is the only section of the work as we have it to contain an invocation to a Muse. Erato, the Muse of love poetry, is invoked at the beginning of the book (one is reminded of the reinvocation in *Aeneid* 7, and of the invocation at the beginning of *The Voyage of the Argo*). Third, in Book 13 is found the first attested use of the word *pornographos* (literally "pornographer"). It is necessary, if one is to understand the meaning of the term *pornographos,* to examine the nature of the debate between the two men in this section of the dialogue.

The characterizations of Cynulcus and Myrtilus are consistent with their portrayal in the other books. In general, Cynulcus advocates that one minister to the body's needs as seldom, as inexpensively, and as efficiently as possible; in Book 13, he staunchly advocates that one find the best possible sexual bargain. (Cynulcus resembles Diogenes the Cynic as described by Diogenes Laertius, the third-century A.D. biographer of the philosophers.) Myrtilus, on the other hand, here advocates a cultured enjoyment of elegant foods and of kindly hetairai, just as he had prescribed the informed and moderate enjoyment of food and drink in other books. The remarks of other characters who discuss women in Book 13 are introductory to and transitional between Cynulcus's and Myrtilus's protracted argument.

Before the centerpiece debate between Cynulcus and Myrtilus takes place, the host Larensis begins by mentioning the marriage customs of yore. Larensis's speech is mostly about men's heterosexual erotic exploits and the bestial destructiveness of harlots (13.555b9–558e4). The guest Leonidas continues by deriding marriage; he criticizes the dowry system, possibly because that system gives a wife some bargaining power in a marriage:

> Dowries are bitter, and filled with woman's bile. Compared with hers, a husband's bile is honey; when wronged, men grant pardon, but these females, however, both wrong their husbands and then blame them besides! They rule whom they should not, and neglect what they should rule. They don't keep their promises, and though they haven't a care in the world, they say they are ill each and every time. (13.558f3–9)

Leonidas next quotes other comic verses that provide a solution to the problem of nagging, insubordinate wives—namely that one patronize hetairai. The hetaira is more kindly than a wife, because she has to be; a wife's legal rights protect her, but since a prostitute has none, she must get and keep a man by being amenable. A quotation from Amphis's comedy *Athamas* makes this clear: "Well then, isn't a hetaira better-natured than a wife? Certainly, and fittingly so, because a wife, with the law's protection, stays haughtily at home, but a hetaira knows that she obtains a lover with a nice manner, or else she must go find another" (13.559a9–b3). In the rest of his speech (to 13.560a10), Leonidas cites numerous other sentiments decrying marriage. That prostitutes please men because they must is here a fundamental part of any argument in favor of having them.

A general discussion on the nature of *erôs* ensues. Myrtilus, the last to speak (13.563d6–13.566e8), praises erotic beauty and cites many passages from the philosophers and poets, only to be castigated roundly by Cynulcus for associating not with male friends but with prostitutes and bawds in wine shops (13.566e9–567b3). Myrtilus's attempt to justify his sexual tastes by referring them to literary and philosophical texts matches the contemporary practice, noted by Kappeler in regard to critical reception of the novel *The White Hotel*, of invoking "the category of the literary . . . to salvage the pornographic, where the literary is said to neutralize or redeem the pornographic" (Kappeler 1986: 85).

Cynulcus, however, does not accept his dinner companion's attempt to legitimize his sexual values and tastes via culturally respectable forms of representation. The Cynic promptly calls Myrtilus a *pornographos:* "So you're no different than Amasis of Elis. Theophrastus says, in his treatise *On Love,* that Amasis was skilled in love affairs. Nor would one be wrong to call you a *pornographos* also, like the painters Aristeides, Pausias, and also Nicophanes" (13.567b3–8). It is evident that the Cynic philosopher objects not to hiring prostitutes per se but rather to consorting with expensive prostitutes often and publicly. He advises Myrtilus to hire prostitutes cheaply at brothels so as to conserve his estate.

What does Cynulcus mean by *pornographos?* Though he professes indignation at Myrtilus's life-style, Cynulcus, like Myrtilus, approves of the institution of prostitution and, in a manner surprisingly like his supposed foe's, justifies his own preference for cheap brothel women by reference to the by-now-antique comic poet Philemon and Philemon's character's justification of *his* preference for brothel women by reference to the hoary sage Solon (quoted above). Thus, an objectionable and defining characteristic of the pornographer, to Cynulcus, is not that the pornographer consorts with prostitutes but that he represents them in speech or in pictorial form, that he admits knowledge of prostitutes and shares it publicly (compare Parker, Chapter 5, and Myerowitz, Chapter 7, above). These remarks by Cynulcus indicate that he believes pictorial and verbal representation to be analogous, and that he wishes less to censor pornographers and pornography than merely to restrict or "contain" their venues. Moderns who take similar stands on pornography might be said to adopt the Cynulcan stance when they advocate zoning laws that restrict prostitution, "obscene" movies, and sex shops to particular neighborhoods. (This stance is discussed by Kappeler 1986: 22.)

Myrtilus begins to answer the philosopher's rebukes (at 13.571a4). He claims that he had praised not prostitutes whose services were expensive but rather those who are "truly companions" (13.671c1, *peri tôn ontôs hetairôn*), those who can keep "a friendship undeceitful" (13.571c2). A prostitute demonstrates undeceitful friendship by flattering a man and cheering him up when he arrives downcast, kissing him, having nice table manners, and giving away her sexual favors on occasion (13.571e4–572b7). Such behaviors render a woman a hetaira (whose literal meaning is "female companion"), not a *pornê* (whose literal meaning is "buyable female").

By being sexually and emotionally available to a man on demand, then, a woman earns the appellation "companion." Stories of heroinic prostitutes, who give not only their bodies and money but occasionally their lives as well to various men's causes (13.572d1 ff.), and the clever sayings of witty prostitutes, take up much of the rest of Myrtilus's lengthy speech. An egregious example of heroinism is found in Myrtilus's account of Leaina, mistress of Harmodius the tyrannicide. When tortured by agents of Hippias, she died without revealing what she knew about the plot (13.596f1–5).

The numerous anecdotes concerning those witty women who appear to be "acting subjects" in their world are more instructive for the topic at hand. Analysis of their remarks and of the contexts in which these remarks are made shows the women to be not "acting subjects" but instead participants in a pornographic scenario (see Parker, Chapter 5 above, on the ascription of female authorship). Kappeler provides the means to understand the nature of women's participation, as "Sadeian women," in this scenario:

> The assumption of the female point of view and narrative voice—the assumption of linguistic and narrative female "subjectivity" . . . goes one step further in the total objectification of woman. It is indeed one of the well-tried pornographic devices to

fake the female's, the victim's, point of view. . . . The so-called female point of view is a male construction of the passive victim in his own scenario, the necessary counterpart to his active aggressor. . . . The [female's] options are strictly defined within the one imperative that it *will* happen to her; "she" can choose an attitude. As Roland Barthes defines it with characteristic oblique strokes: "The scream is the victim's mark; she makes herself a victim because she chooses to scream; if, under the same vexation she were to ejaculate [sic], she would cease to be a victim, would be transformed into a libertine: *to scream/to discharge,* this paradigm is the beginning of choice, i.e. Sadian meaning." (1986: 90–91)

Thus, witty prostitutes are witty insofar as they offer themselves to men. We can compare here the fragments of Golden Age/nostalgic comedy wherein foods vie with one another to be eaten, with stories of hetairai offering themselves, in ways implicitly like food, to men. The very language these women use confines them. Let us recall Metaneira, the courtesan who likened the liver wrapped in its caul to herself in an enfolding garment, which she says has "been her undoing." She, like the lung, will be unwrapped, unfolded, consumed, destroyed. The wrapping of the lung in the omentum and the clothing with which the woman is concealed are parallel. The covering exists in order that it might be removed and the contents enjoyed and consumed. The woman and the food are present at the symposium for the same purpose: to be unwrapped and eaten. Metaneira reportedly understands all too well the purpose for which she has been invited to the symposium, and she speaks accordingly, basing "her" speech on that understanding. And just as Cynulcus, Myrtilus, the diner who compared himself to Paris, and Dionysius refer to or quote literature, Metaneira, too, when declaiming paratragically, "I am undone!" refers the scenario to a culturally approved form of expression.

Metaneira, like her sisters Gnathaina, Nannion, Lais, and others, is a "Sadeian woman" who acts out the pornographic scenario within the *Deipnosophistae.* Additional anecdotes about historical courtesans illustrate how such women constructed themselves—or are here depicted as having constructed themselves—as willing, self-denigrating participants in the scenario: "The comic poet Machon, in the work called *Witticisms,* says the following: '[they say] that the posture of Leaina as she finished off Demetrius was wonderfully skilled; they say that Lamia also once rode the king gracefully and was praised for it. And she replied: 'Well then, take Leaina as well if you wish' " (13.577d1–8). Heath's 1986 study of the verb *kelêtizô* ("to ride," sens. obsc.) has shown that this sexual position was one considered degrading to women and that prostitutes often refused to perform it. Yet the high-priced Lamia skillfully performs the act and invites the king to hire another woman to do the same.

One more pertinent anecdote depends on the fact that the classical Greek word *graus* can mean both "the scum on the top of boiled milk" and "old woman": "Thus once the comic poet Menander, upon visiting the courtesan Glykera [Sweetie], was offered some boiled milk. He refused it because of the *graus* and she said, 'blow it off and use [*chrô*, which means "use" and "have intercourse with"] it' " (13.585c5–9). Menander visits his mistress. She offers him *graus.* Despite its repulsiveness to him, she jokes that he can enjoy it.

It should be noted that prostitutes in classical Athens often bore nicknames that described them as foods or animals. The mention of such nicknames is not unique to Athenaeus. But it is significant in the present context, because the fact that such names were in frequent use indicates that "life"—the real life of the prostitute—has its reflection in "art," that is, the repeated likening of women to food in the context of this symposium dialogue.[18]

Despite their eloquence and bravado, the courtesans Myrtilus praises speak only as the self-defined objects of men's sexual pleasure. They speak of their own bodies as if these are not attached to them; their remarks are confined to sexual and monetary allusions and puns. The speech patterns of the slave prostitute Habrotonon in Menander's comedy *The Arbitrants* (not quoted in the extant text of the *Deipnosophistae*) show that Athenian comedy could and did use dialogue to characterize prostitutes as "Sadeian women" (Henry 1985: 57–60). Moreover, numerous anecdotes (like that of Leaina) show courtesans inviting men to use other women as they are being used.

It is interesting to note that Athenaeus does not quote any passages from comedy that show the grimmer realities of prostitutes' lives. For example, Menander's fourth-century comedy *The Woman from Samos* offers a poignant counterbalance to the speech of these "Sadeian women." The widower Demeas, about to cast out his live-in mistress Chrysis on suspicion of infidelity, reminds her of the life she had led as a free agent before he took her in and forecasts the life she will lead without him:

> And you came to me, Chrysis, you know, in just one linen dress. Then I was your all-in-all, when you were impoverished [lines 377–79]. . . . Out in the big city you'll soon know exactly what sort you are—others like you, Chrysis, run to dinner parties for just ten drachmas, and drink neat wine until they die, or starve, if they don't perform readily and quickly. [lines 390–96]

In contrast to Menander's portrait of Chrysis, Athenaeus's women—both characters in comedy and historical figures such as Lais, Gnathaina, Glykera, and Nannion—are acting out or, rather, are shown by Athenaeus and the authors he quotes and paraphrases to be acting out, a pornographic scenario. Most of the anecdotes discussed here are found in Myrtilus's long speech in defense of courtesans. In no way are courtesans represented, nor do they represent themselves, as other than objects of men's pleasure. They exist for men.

After his defense, Cynulcus attempts to rebut Myrtilus. He claims that though Myrtilus's speech was learned and indicative of a good memory, it was nonetheless empty of thought (13.601b3–c3), thus acknowledging the finesse but disparaging the content of his fellow symposiast's remarks. The discussion of women fades off into an exchange of one-upmanship, quotations, and counterquotations, with Myrtilus speaking last (13.612f9).

The last two extant books of the *Deipnosophistae* range widely in subject matter from wine, jesters, jugglers, jokes, musical instruments, music, dance, and cakes (Book 14) to drinking games, wreaths, perfumes, lamps, drinking songs, and parodies (Book 15). Other accoutrements take the place of women in the discussants' lively and learned classification and enumeration.

Conclusion

The *Deipnosophistae* clearly exemplifies pornographic representation as defined by current feminist theory. This is so even though the work is not only incomplete but also is by no means wholly pornographic. We must now ask what light Athenaeus's work sheds on the history of women in classical antiquity, and how we might evaluate his contributions to our knowledge of Greek comedy.

Athenaeus can be of positive assistance to the historian of female prostitution. What he does and does not say about the lives of historical prostitutes should invite further feminist study. It is now time to coordinate his work, which constitutes an important literary source for prostitution in classical antiquity, with other written accounts and with the emerging archaeological record.[19] That, then, is the first use to which Athenaeus's testimony can be put by feminist scholarship.

The fact that Athenaeus's work preserves so many quotations from Greek comedy and derivative literature within a largely pornographic context has significant implications for our perception of Greek comedy. Aristophanes' comedy often represents prostitutes and other women as sexual food (see Zweig, Chapter 4 above); Aristophanes' contemporaries seem to depict prostitutes in like fashion. But while prostitutes are so depicted by Aristophanes, they are not major characters in any of his known plays. Nor does the evidence suggest that other fifth-century comedies that feature female prostitutes—for example, the *Putinê* and the *Kosannô*—represented these characters as "edible women." To what extent was Athenian comedy pornographic? Did the pornographic sensibility recede, advance, or change between Old Comedy and Middle/New Comedy, a period in which the genre of comedy underwent a decline in openly "obscene" language and situations at about the same time that it witnessed the rise of the stock character of hetaira?

Finally, studies such as this one might help us begin to investigate on a larger scale than previously the history of pornography and pornographers in the West. Is the West as indebted to Greco-Roman civilization for its concepts of pornography and the pornographer as it is for other equally important concepts?[20]

NOTES

Thanks to the Graduate College of Iowa State University for the salary and research grants that made it possible to begin this essay, and to Mary Lee Nitschke, R. Dixon Smith, and Tina Sparrow for inspiration. Special thanks to Amy Richlin and Marilyn Skinner for many helpful suggestions.

1. Baldwin's fine essays (1976, 1977) clearly reveal the chronological and prosopographical problems that beset the serious student of Athenaeus. Given that Athenaeus's other known work was a treatise on a play of the Old Comedy and that he frequently quotes from the comic writers, Baldwin's suggestion is in my view quite likely correct. I have used the Loeb text of the *Deipnosophistae;* unless otherwise stated, all translations are my own. Translations of works other than Athenaeus's are made from the Oxford texts.

2. Gulick's editorial remarks will be cited according to the Loeb volume and page number in which they appear. The general attitude to the work has been that its value lies in

what it has preserved; the characters lack differentiation, and any attempt to see them either as invented but internally consistent personae or as actual historical figures is vain. The remarks of Kaibel (1887: introduction, vi–vii), Desrousseaux (1956, following Kaibel's views in the introduction to the Budé text, I, xii), and Lesky (1966: 854), are typical.

3. Foucault (1985, 1986). See now the critique of Foucault in duBois (1988: 2, 189–191).

4. Foucault (1985: 214–17, 222).

5. Works discussed by S. Griffin (1981) and in many ways comparable to the *Deipnosophistae* in their construction of female sexuality are *The Pearl, My Life and Loves,* and *Thy Neighbor's Wife.*

6. Foucault (1985: 7) on connections between classical antiquity and the modern world. The "modern individual" whose sexual identity formation as subject Foucault limns is (curiously like the classical subject) unselfconsciously male; see also Foucault 1978b: 5–8; 1982; 1985: 5–6, 12; 1986: 7, 42.

7. Baldwin (1976) is helpful for the problems of Athenaeus's date. For discussion of the Second Sophistic, see Bowersock (1969) and Lesky (1966: 829–97).

8. For good general surveys of Attic Comedy (excepting some of Menander), see Norwood (1931) and Lever (1956). Henderson (1975) gives a full account of obscenity in Attic Comedy, making plain the metaphoric fusion of the sexual and the alimentary.

9. The surviving fragments of this play are found as numbers 718–24 in Kock's edition (1880–88) of the remains of Attic Comedy.

10. Kaibel (1887: I, xv); Lesky (1966: 854); Gulick (1927: I, xvii; VII, 175). For an opposing view on the state of the text, see Düring 1936, who thinks that Athenaeus's text essentially resembled the text that we have.

11. See Baldwin (1977: 41) for brief discussion of other elements of the literary symposium.

12. Lerner (1985: 180) discusses the importance to patriarchal thought of assignment of responsibility for the creation of life and for creativity in general to a male god.

13. As the Grateful Dead sing, "We can share the women, we can share the wine."

14. The notion that women were naturally inclined to drunkenness seems to have been an idée fixe among male writers in classical antiquity; see Richlin 1984.

15. Note that Encolpius, in Petronius's *Satyricon,* mocks both culinary sleights-of-hand and diners who admire them.

16. The term *krisis* has the medical connotation in Hippocrates and Galen of "the turning point of a disease," which supports the view that the alimentary and sexual are fused in both Athenaeus and Philemon.

17. Compare, for example, the naive and idealized view of the life-style of classical-age prostitutes as given in Delacoste and Alexander (1987: 233–35) with the less attractive realities of daily lives of prostitutes in the more recent past as documented in historical surveys by Rosen (1982) and Walkowitz (1980) and in the memoirs of sometime prostitute Maimie Pinzer (1977).

18. Other examples of women nicknamed as foods: the sisters Stagonion and Anthis were called the Anchovies, as was a woman named Nicostratis, because they had large eyes and were thin (13.586b2–6). Compare the observations made by "Jane Jones," a former pornography model (Lederer 1980: 63): "when I grew up, I found that I was a marketable commodity. . . . One of the porn series I was in used food names for the women, like Taffy, Candy, Cookie."

19. Until recently, histories of the city in classical antiquity ignored prostitution; Boardman (1980) is typical. But some attention has been drawn to prostitution and prostitutes in recent studies of the commercial centers of Naukratis (Coulson and Leonard 1981), the

Peiraeus (Garland 1987), and Corinth (Salmon 1984). Herter (1960) has a fairly full discussion of the ancient literary evidence for prostitution.

20. Even today, questions about what pornography is and whether or not to do something about it are framed in Platonic and Aristotelian terms: does pornography provide a harmless (and possibly helpful) catharsis, or does it encourage violent acts? But, as mentioned above, such thinkers as MacKinnon and Kappeler, who lucidly outline and analyze modern versions of these questions, do not recognize their long history.

EPILOGUE

The (Other) Maiden's Tale

Terri Marsh

It now occurred to him that through his decisive act [the sacrifice of . . . a redheaded, petite, talkative, freckle-faced woman] he had entered the realm of tragedy.

—Milan Kundera, *Life Is Elsewhere*

The Athens this paper imagines lies to the side of the images of Athens invented initially by Athenian men and secondarily by (virtually only male) classical scholars. It cannot be otherwise, not only because the cities they construct lie to the side of the cities familiar to Athenian women, but also because my interrogations are geared to create alternative spaces where we may begin to rebuild ourselves as we ponder the central question of this essay: are there tools besides the master's with us inside his house, or (even better) is there another house we inhabit simultaneously which will allow us to dismantle gently an order that is established by domination?

Prologue

A curtain rises. The stage is split into two rooms. In the first room men are seated on couches, watching as a woman kneels before an armchair. Standing nearby are men, ready to whip her. The men in the room tell her she is evil and insist that she consent to her own degradation. As she begins to give in, she recalls images she has seen of women in scenes like this one.[1] As the men in the room remind her of her (albeit enforced) consent, she accepts a guilt she cannot own. And like the women in the images, she becomes the victim of a desire (and gaze) she does and does not own. Her bondage, her cries, and her degradation gratify the men who whip her and those who watch; seduced by their power and her complicitous surrender, they believe momentarily in their own images of themselves as the masters of everything, including, of course, her.

269

In the adjacent room, women and men are burning effigies of the producers and consumers of the first scenario. Their self-righteous madness moves them to speak. And despite the differences in their words, the message is always the same. They demand that the perpetrators of scenarios *they* define as pornographic be silenced. They claim that these producers and consumers are deviant, that their images are perverse, that their desires are sick, that they are the enemy who must be purged to purify the state. And because of a manic need to name and blame an enemy, the censors in the adjacent room (perhaps inadvertently) replicate the strategies deployed by those they condemn.[2]

But since, as Audre Lorde observes, the master's tools will not dismantle the master's house, I propose a different tactic: to bend the master's tools, by bending the usage of two words, *pornographic* and *erotic*. Imagine with me two ways of constituting oneself in relation to others. The first orientation requires that we rigidly define ourselves in opposition to other selves. While this orientation does allow for identifications among individual selves, these unifying identities are themselves defined by the boundaries they share, a divide that separates "them" from "us," which is both the meeting place of hostile forces and the condition of identity itself (Carse 1986: 69). The second orientation is more difficult to describe precisely because it resists identification or any closure. Nor is it for that reason amorphous; it also allows for boundaries, separations, and alliances, but does not require that we define ourselves or anyone else by whatever impermanent boundaries we construct. This orientation allows us to move with and without others without needing a limit or label to tell us who we are. As a consequence, here differences may be mediated by partial connections rather than by antagonistic oppositions.[3]

While the first orientation is grounded in materialist patriarchies, the second orientation is a kind of hybrid—grounded both in the patriarchy and also in the strategies of its changelings (Haraway 1985). By allowing the terms *pornographic* and *erotic* to describe these two orientations, which are inscribed not only in our political behavior but in the stories we tell, I propose to problematize the erotic. Can we respond erotically to pornographic representation, or are our reactions controlled by the sadomasochistic pleasures and desires such scenarios and our own political histories invite?[4]

Monologue

Orthos, Aitiatike, Aitiatiklea, Orthophilia, Atheneia, and Orthokles are characters I have invented to tell my tale. The names of Orthos and Aitiatike are derived from words used by Stoic philosophers to designate the grammatical subject and object of a sentence. Aitiatiklea, Orthophilia, and Atheneia are female characters whose names signify "she who is known as the object (e.g., of another's desires)," "she who loves the subject (and master of herself)," and "she who resembles the goddess Athena." Orthokles is a male character whose name signifies "he who is known as the subject (and master of others)."

Euripides' *Hecuba* plays a prominent role in our tale. The play opens on the shore of the Thracian Chersonese, where Hecuba, the wife of the now dead Trojan king; her daughter, Polyxena; and a chorus of Trojan women are the captive slaves of their Greek enemies. The ghost of Polydorus, the son of Hecuba, tells the audience (1) of his own death at the hands of the Thracian king, Polymestor, to whom he had been sent by his parents when the city of Troy still stood; and (2) of the imminent sacrifice of his sister, Polyxena, at the tomb of the Greek warrior Achilles. As Hecuba gradually learns of and reacts to these horrors, the play reveals (esp. 218–95, 726–863) the moral monstrosity of the Greek army. Overcome with grief and rage, she retaliates by enticing Polymestor and his sons to her tent, where the women kill his children and blind him. As the anguished mother and blinded king present their cases to the Greek king, Agamemnon, Hecuba and the audience learn of her fate from her son's murderer. She will be changed to a dog, "a bitch with blazing eyes" (1265).

The curtain rises on Euripides' *Hecuba* around 425 B.C. Seated between the audience and the performers are two characters, Orthos and Aitiatike. Orthos is (among other things) the subject who knows himself through the other; the self who masters the other; the strength that consumes the other; the owner of the gaze, voice, and desire that limit and define everything—including Aitiatike, who has learned instead to see herself as she is seen. The gaze she both does and does not own is his. She is the contingent that grounds his autonomy, the appearance that grounds his reality, the part that grounds his totality, the resource that allows him his agency, the projection that allows him his identity.[5] She is the product, object, mirror, and so necessarily victim of his desire. But is she a woman, and is he a man? No. These characters are positions. More specifically, they are a variety of subject/object orientations that historically en-gendered spectators have learned to adopt by their engagement in signification—including (as de Lauretis observes in words not unlike these) the technologies and techno-practices of sex, ethnos, and class. This is not to suggest that an Athenian spectator was not constituted by gender relations, but that he or she was also en-gendered by her or his experiences as citizen or metic, hoplite or ephebe, rich or poor. For, as de Lauretis says (1984: 145):

> each person goes to the [theater] with a semiotic history, personal and social, a series of identifications by which she or he has been somehow en-gendered. And because she and he are historical subjects, continuously engaged in a multiplicity of signifying practices . . . the [film's] images for them are not neutral objects of pure perceptions but . . . significant by virtue of their relation to the viewer's subjectivity.

The spectator, then, is not unitary but multiple. And even before the performance begins, he or she has the potential for various kinds of identifications which themselves may be elicited differently by different types of scenario—including, for example, the sexy sacrifice of Polyxena in Euripides' *Hecuba* (485–628).

This episode begins when Talthybius the herald, who stood nearby and witnessed the maiden's sacrifice, returns to Hecuba's tent to give his report. This elicits Hecuba's second, no less weighty, revisionist account. The audience is thus invited to envision the spectacle from either or both of these two perspectives—that of the herald and/or that of the maiden's mother. Although each establishes different terms of identification by the different ways it positions the spectator in relation to the maiden, the responses each invites are equally pornographic. The look of the herald, Talthybius, allows the audience to see her as he and perhaps the whole army looking on (521–24) view her: the potable resource that grounds the Greek army's agency; the noble victim whose captive plight, though courageously accepted, is nonetheless required to unbind the ships; the sexualized product and aesthetized object of a desire she does not own but nonetheless elicits as she "exposes her naked breasts, bare and lovely like those of a sculptured goddess" (559–61). Her fall, graceful and modest, hiding what should be hidden from men's eyes, further sexualizes and aesthetizes her surrender to the blade that slashes her throat.

Unlike the gaze of Talthybius (in whom class and gender differences and hence distance provoke aesthetization), the mother's perspective is intimate and empathetic, but not for this reason erotic (585–628). Hecuba's bond with her daughter is predicated upon the plight they share as instruments of the Greek male army. Their identities as victims are themselves defined by the barriers that separate them from their oppressors—the enemy whose evil in Hecuba's view "stays itself, evil to the end" (593–98). Thus, while the mother's look does invite a similarly intimate bond between spectator and maiden, the spectator who adopts her gaze is drawn into an empathetic relationship with the maiden as a victim of those who force and witness her surrender. Nor, as the play progresses, is the barrier that separates Hecuba and the Greek army effaced; on the contrary, it is sustained as the mother turns her oppressors into the instruments of her own equally sadistic machinations.

Although the gazes of Talthybius and Hecuba are different, both are grounded in a barrier that excludes the Other, and which, as a consequence, invites rigidly oppositional and hence pornographic responses from the spectators seated in the theater. Orthokles, because of his gender, ethnic pride, and recent stint as a hoplite in the series of wars with Sparta and its allies, imagines the sacrifice as portrayed by Talthybius. Because of the distanced gaze of the herald and his own historically engendered distance from the maiden, he derives a voyeuristic pleasure from his own aesthetization and sexualization of Polyxena's acquiescence to a plight he views as expedient. The man seated beside him is more troubled by the spectacle. Something about the maiden reminds him of himself. Perhaps it is the way she courageously confronts her death; or perhaps her objectification reminds him of his own youthful experiences as the object of the gazes of elder men. As he begins to see glimmers of her in him, he becomes nervous. He's not a victim, he reminds himself, but a man; nor is he a Trojan. And because Hecuba's maternal gaze invites a similarly empathetic response, he projects his reactions onto her—she *and not he* resembles the maiden, helpless, pitiful, and enslaved. He begins to dislike the mother who now embodies the weakness he despises in himself; and, as she gradually comes to resemble her enemies, his own feelings are confirmed. And so, by the play's conclusion, he, too, has been entertained by his sado-participation in the sexy sacrifice of Polyxena.

Seated somewhere in the back of the theater are the women. En-gendered by her own Oedipal past, Aitiatiklea is drawn into an identification with the maiden as object of the male gaze within the play. Desiring to be desired, she enjoys imaging herself as the object of male desire. The maiden's nobility, modesty, and helplessness remind her of her own images of herself. Absorbed in her own objectification, she does not notice that the gaze she adopts is not her own. Seated beside her is Orthophilia. Unlike Aitiatiklea, this woman is torn between her sexuality and individuality. As a woman, she, too, desires to be desired; she, too, has imaged herself as an object, product, and mirror of a desire she cannot own. But, as has been observed, all is not well in Thebes:[6] "The story of femininity . . . and the riddle of the Sphinx have a single answer, one and the same meaning, one term of reference: man, Oedipus, the human male person" (de Lauretis 1984: 133). Unlike Aitiatiklea, this woman knows that her story is the story of his desire, that Oedipal desire requires an object, and that no one, not even a woman, can be utterly reduced to the status of an object. Caught between her desire to be desired and her desire for autonomy, she is drawn into an identification with the maiden as the object of both gazes—the herald's and the maiden's mother's. As she moves back and forth between these positions, her conflict is intensified by the dissatisfaction both identifications evoke. Because of her frustration, Orthophilia distances herself from the maiden and identifies instead with Hecuba, whose desire for mastery she confuses with agency. And so, seduced by her own desire to master the desire she cannot own, she reconstitutes herself as the object, product, mirror, and victim of her own ill-plotted response. Other spectators react differently. Another woman, Atheneia, adopts the gaze of the herald as she envisions the play in purely political terms. Her male-identified pose allows her to deny her own similarities to the maiden and, like Orthokles, to project whatever similarity she cannot efface onto both maiden and mother. As the spectators react, each in her or his own way, another character enters the theater.

She seats herself behind Orthos and to the left of Aitiatike. Her sex is indeterminate, and she is nameless. As she watches the play, she notes how the characters represent her own pornographic poses. She moves with the tragic characters whose identities are predicated upon barriers that separate them from others. But she also recalls moments when she stepped to the side of the representational system and moved with those who, like her, longed to craft a different kind of world. These experiences are also part of her consciousness and enable her to feel with the characters without becoming absolutely like any one of them; she is able to adopt their gazes and simultaneously see the fissures in the looks she does and does not own. And, by positioning herself in the deepest fissure she can envision, she imagines that the other spectators can move no less erotically, that everyone can and perhaps . . . And she smiles. And her smile invites us to move with her and them . . . so that together . . .

Another fiction interrupts this fiction. An assertive voice declares, "She has no name because she is not. She is not a person, nor a position. She is a dream, a fantasy, the vision of a utopian ideal which can never be realized." Another voice, less assertive, disagrees: "She is a woman. Like all women, she has lived only part of her life in Thebes. Jocasta is and is not her mother. Her other mother is nameless, but not for this reason unreal. Her experiences in the elsewhere she also calls her home are nameless, but not for this reason unreal. Because of her gender, she knows both worlds, the well-worded world of men and her no less real experiences as a woman." A third voice interjects: "There are no natural matrices of unity. Anyone can see the gaps. Anyone sufficiently weary of colonialism and patriarchy can craft alliances without relying on the logic of domination and exclusion.[7] She is not necessarily a woman, but like Orthos and Aitiatike, a position available to all historically engendered spectators. And thus perhaps she is and was many women and men."

Dialogue

Unlike the characters in the preceding section, the characters in this section—Aspasia, Xanthippe, Diotima—are already familiar to us from a variety of male-produced texts about Classical Athens. Aspasia occasionally appears in the texts of Aristophanes, Plato, Aristotle, Xenophon, Plutarch, and others. According to this all-male tradition, she lived with Pericles as his mistress from about 445 B.C., after he had divorced his wife, until his death in 429 B.C. She is perhaps best known for her inordinate influence on Pericles and for her association with Socrates. Neither her birth nor her death has been recorded; she may or may not have lived as long as my fictions presume (about 404 B.C.). Xanthippe was Socrates' wife. In the (male) tradition of Xenophon, Plato, Plutarch, and others, she is usually presented as a foil to her husband's "better" qualities. Diotima appears only in Plato's *Symposium*—as the legendary priestess at Mantinea and teacher of Socrates. It is impossible to know whether his fiction is based on a historical figure, because there are no other extant accounts of her. The setting is (and is not) Classical Athens (about 475–380 B.C.).

Three versions of the sacrifice of Iphigenia (Aeschylus's *Oresteia,* Euripides' *Iphigenia among the Taurians,* and Euripides' *Iphigenia in Aulis*) play a prominent role in the stories these characters tell. In all three accounts, the maiden is to be sacrificed to appease Artemis and enable the Greek fleet to sail to Troy and return Helen to her husband. In Aeschylus's version, the maiden is sacrificed by her father Agamemnon; the sacrifice is avenged by her mother, who guilefully kills Agamemnon; but at the end of the trilogy she, too, is dead and both murders of women judged unimportant. In Euripides' *Iphigenia among the Taurians,* the maiden, having been saved at the last moment by Artemis at Aulis, serves the goddess by her participation in the bloody sacrifice of strangers in Tauris. When her brother Orestes is captured to be sacrificed at the deity's altar, Iphigenia betrays Artemis and facilitates her brother's heroic ventures by enabling him to leave the island with the cult statue. Finally, in Euripides' *Iphigenia in Aulis,* the maiden volunteers to be sacrificed so that Troy may be conquered and Greeks rule barbarians and not barbarians Greeks.

Scene: twenty years later. The curtain rises on a dimly lit stage. Three figures are seated on the stage. It is dark, and while I am tempted to identify them as Aspasia, Xanthippe, and Diotima, I can't be sure. The one who most resembles Xanthippe (voice 2) has been complaining about her husband for some time—accusing him of misreading her female-centered vision and, even worse, of rendering her voices as an assortment of *daimones* who have chosen him as the instrument through which to enunciate their truths. By her privileging of what she calls a "female-centered perspective," she elicits the following dialogue.

Voice 3 (Diotima?): You willingly surrender the power they refuse you when you theorize the "erotic" as a position especially available to women. Even worse, you speak within the terms of the existing (pornographic) system by the emphasis you place on the specificity of women—the elsewhere you call our home is "there" precisely because it is not "here." But what separates here and there is precisely what separates self and other. Must we replicate the strategies inscribed in their master plots? Your utopian visions worry me and especially the homage you pay to their goddesses—Artemis, who feeds our sexual repressions with the blood of maidens and goats; Athena, who wears our sexuality on the weapon she uses to fight their battles; and Aphrodite, whose obsession with their libidinal economy is not only unhealthy but boring. Must we idealize our mothers and their mothers, who, like all the daughters of patriarchy, wear the scars of complicity? There are no natural matrices of unity. Anyone can connect—the erotic is a position available to anyone sufficiently weary of an economy of domination.[8]

Voice 1 (Aspasia?): The erotic is a fantasy created by those who would have us dream away the world that engenders us as male or female, prostitute or wife, free or unfree. Unlike the Athenian male elite, who enjoy the dual statuses of speaking and spoken subjects, the rest of us, excluded from their public discursive fellowships, cannot participate in the production of meaning.[9] Sometimes they represent us as subjects, but our "subjecthood" is still the fabrication of those who speak not with but for us. Yes, of course we speak, but only as spoken subjects. I have tried to convince myself it is otherwise—that we can speak and write our own bodies. But the "I" who speaks not only speaks from their sites but is herself encoded with a semiotic history of their making. There are no sites elsewhere where we may write, and so read, our own bodies. We are all constituted by those discourses, institutions, and practices that compel us to desire and hence facilitate the "othering" of ourselves and/or someone else. Sometimes I speak of women as "passive surfaces upon which meaning is inscribed"—"the greatest glory of a woman is to be least talked about by men."[10] Other times I remain silent and bespeak myself as that passive surface. But even when I critique their discourses, the "I" who speaks is nonetheless spoken. In this respect, I am like Iphigenia: like hers, my life has always been inscribed by those who have needed me—to play the resource that allows them their agency. Like Iphigenia, I, too, have played the Other—perhaps less theatrically but no less tragically.[11]

Young, foreign-born, and endowed with more than my share of charm, wit, and sexual appeal, how was I to know I'd been constituted by a series of pornographic discursive operations? As object of the desires of the most powerful men in the state, I considered myself deserving of what others called my good fortune. My life was exciting, and since I'd not begun to theorize myself (as the subject or object of a gaze I mistook for my own), I couldn't have known that I'd been excluded from their production of meaning and that, as a consequence, my subjectivity was constituted by those whose speaking spoke against me. If someone had suggested that I, like the maiden, "with guards against the lips' sweet edge" was also branded—by a representational system, I would have laughed like one who knew better.[12]

Unaware of my own semiotic history and the pornographic postures it implied, at the performance of Aeschylus's *Oresteia* in 458 B.C. I was drawn into a disturbing identification with the maiden as the object of the combined gaze of the male characters, poet, and audience.[13] Inscribed by those who read her for me, I saw glimmers of a self I barely knew in their images of her as helpless (because she could not cry out in response to the pain caused by the silencing bit); pitiful (as she "struck the sacrificers with the eyes' arrows of pity," *Ag.* 239–40); lovely ("as in a painted scene," *Ag.* 242), and for that reason appealing. As the saffron robe, traditionally dedicated to Artemis at Brauron by maidens "like" herself, fell from her body, this sole mark of her personhood further sexualized the plight I began to image as my own.

Immersed as I was in my own objectification, I was startled by the wail of the woman seated to my right. Standing upright, she began to cry out in terror: "their sadism requires this story . . . they who lifted upon the altar my child, like a goat, my child . . . they who must recoup in fantasy what is denied to them in reality . . ." As male guards gagged and dragged her from the theater, I knew in one horrific instant that we'd all been silenced by their discursive incisions.

Determined to escape our lot, I distanced myself from both the maiden and the woman who had been seated to my right; and, distanced from both sites, I witnessed the enactment of a second no less horrific sacrificial act: the gradual disfiguration of all female characters who dared to write and read their own bodies. Clytemnestra, the maiden's mother, was created and branded by the same kind of discursive incisions—an invented challenger to the Athenian male's privileges to "other" us. Then, as punishment, she was disfigured and read as the monstrous whore whose unbridled sexuality had disrupted the state. Unlike her, the Erinyes were literally disfigured. Like her, they were invented as posing a retrospective challenge to the pornographic underpinnings of the Athenian democratic state; but they appeared onstage as monstrosities—as "black and utterly repulsive . . . [from whose] eyes drip the foul ooze" (*Eum.* 52–58). And because of their disfiguring, the audience was invited to read any woman's attempt to write her own body as a monstrous and hideous form of bestiality. Aeschylus's pornographic gaze invited those of us situated on the Other side to inscribe ourselves as discursively paralyzed objects of male desire or (even worse) as the disfigured spoken speaking subjects of a female desire we may and may not own.

And so (once again) I chose to resemble neither. And distanced from womankind, I was engaged instead by the stance of (Aeschylus's) Athena, who seemed to escape what I then regarded as the sole sites of female oppression.[14] Like her, I began to speak masterfully from their sites, and before long I was illustrious, well regarded, and politically influential. I composed not only the famous lines delivered by Pericles to remind women that they, too, have a kind of glory and that "the greatest glory of a woman is to be least talked about by men," but also the lines he delivered to persuade the male populace to equate manliness, courage, and heroism with war, conflict, and self-immolation. Had it not been for my discursive incisions, Pericles would never have attained the status he did. No, I didn't realize then that I'd become a different kind of victim as I "othered" so as not to be "othered" myself—sacrificing those who, because of their naive desire to be inscribed eternally as heroes, bespoke themselves as active surfaces upon which our political meanings could be reinscribed. I was obsessed with the power I formerly lacked, and as my inscriptive remarks became public policy, I was dazzled with my own success. I could make a difference, and so I did.[15]

Assured that I'd escaped their grammatical operations, I was surprised when I was prosecuted by Pericles' enemies for crimes I didn't commit. I'd been attacked before (by poets and comic writers) and publicly insulted at the theater, but I'd always attributed it to malice tinged with envy.[16] But this was different. Something about this experience stayed with me. I knew I was innocent of their charges, but, all the same, I began to feel sorry for something I couldn't quite name. Still, it wasn't until I'd seen Euripides' *Iphigenia among the Taurians* that I knew (finally) that my adoption of their male-identified gaze, voice, and posture was itself a gesture within the existing system; that I, like all the other women I knew, had played a part in a story I couldn't call my own. I can still recall my initial surprise as I was drawn into an identification with the maiden as she was reinscribed by Euripides' equally pornographic incisions; as Euripides' revisions of Aeschylus adumbrated my own semiotic past, I saw in the maiden's posture the women I'd been.

Like the maiden imaged by Euripides, "I possessed a memory of my own [unhappy sacrifice]" . . . (*IT* 852–54). Like her, I was saved at the last moment by a goddess. No, not Artemis, who at the last moment substituted a goat in her place (20–42) and then compelled her to reenact her own salvation by the sacrificial murder of other victims. No, I was saved by Athena, whose masculine postures invited me to move masterfully with her into ever greater positions of prestige. But still, like the maiden's, my service to a male-identified deity perpetuated an economy predicated upon appropriation, domination, sacrifice, and all that they entail; like her, I'd used my powers to serve not my own projects but the discursive fellowships that have excluded my voice from their production of meaning; her complicity in her brother's ventures (1055–1435) recalled to me my own career.

But, unlike me, she felt sorry for her victims (224–27, 380–91). And in her sorrow, I read my guilt—the guilt I tried to evade by my adoption of postures traditionally reserved for men, a guilt (I finally realized) we cannot efface. I knew that all our bodies are charted and marked with their readings, their incisive inscriptions, and thus well equipped with memories of the sacrifice of maidens like ourselves and the wretched guilt such scenarios entail. To speak and chart ourselves, *all* women must have access to public discourse and thus participate in the production of meaning.

I left the play enraged; and because of my inability to induce Socrates and the other members of our circle to invite their wives, sisters, daughters, nieces, aunts, and other female acquaintances to our meetings, I dropped out.[17] When, a few years later, Euripides' *Iphigenia in Aulis* was performed, my rage and frustration got the better of me. As the maiden read her own masochistic desires as a form of noble heroism (in words similar to these: "to Greece I give this body of mine. Slay it in sacrifice and conquer Troy. For in war it is far better that many women go to their death, if this keep only one man alive," *IA* 1390–95), I heard myself cry out: their sadism requires a story, and so our story is the story of their desire and of our own masochism. And, like the elderly woman I now resembled, I was gagged and they dragged me from the theater.

And so it was we began to meet in private—those of us who wanted to understand the underpinnings of a system that by its rape of our minds has so censored our imaginations that self-immolation became a necessary form of (complicitous) survival. Despite our different classes, social roles, and statuses, we all agreed that their manliness required our masquerade. And that tragedy was geared not only to obtain our consent to our own masked objectification but also to celebrate the divide that separated the "hero" from women, other men, nature, and those (other) realms of experience he cannot bear. And that its pleasure "like the pleasure of narrative itself lies in killing what lives." We spent years trying to theorize what we began to call the sacrificial "plot." But nothing we said or did had any impact. Still, we decided to craft our own revision of the maiden's telling tale.

Imagine, if you will. The curtain rises, and a maiden is seated in a room. She is told that she must die at the altar like a goat. No, she's not surprised. It has happened before, and she imagines it will happen again. Does she desire it? The question makes her squirm. Of course, she longs to enact and reenact her aesthetized objectification; it's the only pleasure they allow her. But still something about the spectacle has always bothered her—perhaps the swords and manacles remind her of other kinds of punishment, the "sacrifice" of criminals, deviants, animals, and similarly marked Others. Perhaps she is thinking of other maidens similarly sacrificed—Philaenis, Iole, Callirhoe, Nico, Diallage, Persephone, Cassandra, Andromeda, Polyxena, Philomela, Chloe, Verginia, Sejanus's daughter . . . Perhaps she is thinking of the objectification of the other women she knows. As she ponders such questions, she knows something is wrong. And instead of blaming the system that requires the sacrifice of maidens, she blames the criminals, the deviants, the animals, and the other women who must suffer a similarly shameful fate. But most of all she blames herself, and as she succumbs to a guilt foisted upon her by their fellowships, she recalls her own involvement in other scenarios of female guilt— including her short stay on Tauris, where by her own sado-sacrifices of foreign young men, she'd assumed a position traditionally assigned to men. Bound to a fate she does and does not own through a guilt and desire she mistakes for her own, she voluntarily submits her neck to a blade whose incisive operations simultaneously signal and facilitate her inability to write or read herself.[18] She awakens, mutilated *but aware.* Her wounds oozing blood disclose her resemblance to the Erinyes, but still she calls herself Iphigenia. And she speaks, in words much like my own. But it doesn't matter what she says. In fact, the more truthfully she speaks, the more disfigured she appears, because we are all Iphigenia. Her story is our story. "It is the history of the female subject—of the territorialization and inscription of a body whose involuntary internalization of a corresponding set of desires facilitates its complex exploitation" (Silverman 1984: 346).

Voice 2 (Xanthippe?): You move about the city freely, but I can see how unfree you are. You have become like them, the men whose gaze you service. Have you genuinely lost touch with our female-centered look, a look that enables us to live and love erotically in the spaces women share with one another? Yes, we write ourselves as they read (and write) us, but we are not determined by their discursive structure. Prior to our entry into language, we forge bonds with our mothers whose erotic relations to our bodies shape the way we constitute ourselves as speaking and spoken subjects. Like men's, our entry into language subjects us to the kinds of grammatical and ideological strictures that inscribe us as male and female; but because of our initial bonds, we can also reject their currency of oppositions and domination.[19] Like men, we live in the master's house. But unlike men, we also inhabit another house, where we can speak I/you as both the same and different, as separate and connected, as self and other. We can speak differently, and so can create erotic moments—where "I love you: body shared, undivided. Neither you nor I severed" (Irigaray 1985: 206). And these moments speak with us always in the private domain, where we reconstitute our erotic bonds with our daughters and our daughters' daughters; where we valorize the body, reproductive time, fertility, and experience; where we think with our bodies, emotions, and experiences; where we weave the songs of Sappho and her daughters (our mothers) on the tapestries we craft. And because their representational systems define our shared (public) spaces as private, the elsewhere we call our home necessarily bridges public and private spheres. And because, like our mothers, we think with our experience, we think differently—inclusively, fluidly, and metamorphically. Like the baskets we weave in unbounded yet finite rings, returning to the beginning each time we come to an end, our thoughts weave worlds where "we are [not] afraid of not speaking well" (Irigaray 1985: 213). And because the worlds our words create are themselves fluid and metamorphic, we are less prone to reducing a multiplicity of experiences to some one thing. We see the gap between their images (some of us are "vile-tempered," "savage," and "recalcitrant,"[20] others dazzling and beguiling) and the erotic moments we enjoy; so we can see the way a look shapes what is seen. Thus, some of us also acknowledge the biases our (female) gaze engenders.

Men, on the other hand, confuse their biased gazes with the world itself; so (unlike us) they rigidly assert their historically en-gendered truths. I include here the certain uncertainty of Socrates, whose riddling questions baffle those who, like him, construe the questions he does ask (What is X?) as more important that the ones he doesn't ask (In whose interest is the asking?). Because they read our behaviors in their terms and interest, they reduce our lives to anecdotes geared to serve their ends, and because they cannot see beyond their own master narratives, they believe in the stories they tell about us. They call our strategy Metis.[21] They say that Zeus swallowed Metis. But I say that they can't swallow us, not even when Socrates appropriates our strategy, dazzling those whose need for a master logic matches his own.

Oh, I've tried to tell him, but he's obsessed (with those inane questions of his: Is it better to wrong or to be wronged?). He can't think outside of his own master logic and so disavows any logic that falls to the side of the inquiries he poses again and again. I've tried in vain to convince him that there is something in us that falls outside their master law; that "if we submit to their reasoning, we are guilty; [that] their strategy, intentional or not, is calculated to make us guilty" (Irigaray 1985: 211). But we will not be contained, we who live always in both worlds; and because we move back and forth, we can respond without guilt to their pornographic scenarios. Perhaps you will listen.

As I listened to your reactions to Aeschylus's (poetic?) sacrifice of Iphigenia, I was drawn into the same pornographic identifications. But I also saw the spaces between the tragic shadows they call life. I saw glimmers of my younger selves in the maiden; but I also noted the differences between the visions our (female) gaze engenders and the images of us their look creates. Unlike you, I imaged a mother who felt with and for the death of her daughter but for that reason did not violate the lives of others. I know such women. We are all the mothers of sacrificed daughters and the daughters of mothers disfigured by the grammatical scars we bear. We are all oozing with the blood of wounds inflicted by their pornographic gaze, but still our beauty remains to us. We possess an/other gaze that speaks our beauty even as they inscribe us as fanged, blood-oozing monstrosities, as submissive complicitous objects, as subjects who embrace our own objectivity. We are engendered by their look *and also* by our own. And it is from this vantage that I read their stories of maidens "bound" to guilt they/we can unbind if they/we learn to trust our (female-centered) look from the other side.

Imagine with me, if you will, the looking glass, from the other side (Irigaray 1985: 9–22). She closes her eyes and images once again the roles she must play as the object of a look she cannot own. In the spaces their looks allow her, she adheres complicitously to the structures that bind her to a reenactment of roles she can't erase. Sometimes, in her attempt to escape a fate she sees as hers alone, she searches in vain for a different plot. Mistaking bondage for freedom, she moves from one enthralling tale to the next. But in the looking glass from the other side, "behind the screen of Representation. In the house or garden" (Irigaray 1985: 9) where she opens her eyes, she sees differently. But still *they* speak of her as spoken. As an object of the pornographic gaze, she seems to them to mirror the only selves they know. She tries to explain. She tells of the other maiden—bound to live in two worlds, to enter the play of the tales she does not write as she beckons others to move with her into the looking glass. But still they image her as spoken. And so, she retells their tale in words not unlike these: "Oedipus, old and blinded, walked the roads. He smelled a familiar smell. It was the Sphinx. Oedipus said, 'I want to ask one question. Why didn't I recognize my mother?' 'You gave the wrong answer,' said the Sphinx . . . . 'When I asked what walks on four legs in the morning, two at noon, and three in the evening, you answered, Man. You didn't say anything about woman.' 'When you say Man,' said Oedipus, 'you include women too. Everyone knows that.' She said, 'That's what you think.' " (Rukeyser 1978). Although the women and men before the glass still read the Sphinx as she is written— as monstrous—the maiden, bound to live in both worlds, tells her other tale.

Voice 3 (Diotima?): Your stories remind me of my own. [Turning more directly to voice 1, she continues.] Like you, I live inside the master's house. I, too, have been seduced (by economic coercion, ideologies, and my Oedipal past) to consent to my objectification. Let's face it, submission is not only degrading, it's also safe. Paternalism provides us with economic support and partial protection in exchange for our service. As you yourself discovered, the cost of freedom is steep. There are no alternative networks to catch us if we speak the truths we live. It's still a man's world, and they still give preferential treatment to those who conform; they still punish, by ridicule or ostracism, any woman who interprets her own role or—even worse—tries to rewrite the script (Lerner 1986: 13). Even I have had to keep silent about some matters (including the lies contained in Plato's images of me in his

Symposium). When I have been courageous enough to speak my experiences, I, too, have been ostracized and silenced by their discursive incisions.

Yes, we are all Iphigenia. Her story is our story. We are all the mothers of sacrificed daughters and the daughters of mothers disfigured by the grammatical scars we wear. But as our friend here has suggested, we also possess a gaze that may allow us someday to craft a different world, by looking critically at the order of man's discourse, by distinguishing between the image their looks effect and those experiences that fall to the side of their gaze.

You, Aspasia, are yourself so aware of our bondage to their representational system that you either can't or won't explore the way signs can effect changes in behavior patterns. Through social practice, we can radically transform those signs that are geared to preserve the status quo (the bonds are breakable, the broken shackle cracks the mirror). You ignore the way your own "look" was modified by your interactions with their encoded stories (see de Lauretis 1984: 158–86). And while the practices you effected by your initial interactions with their discursive systems were predicated upon the pornographic strategy you tried to evade, this was not always the case.

Perhaps you don't see the radical potential of your reading of the Erinyes as wise and aware. Of course, from within their pornographic frame, the Erinyes and other speaking female subjects are spoken (as disfigured monstrosities). But from the site created by your group of outsiders, the Erinyes signify (among other things) our potentially radical female gaze. To borrow a phrase from our friend here, they live in the looking glass, from both sides. And, I might add, by your own illegitimate practices, you have initiated a movement that places you both inside and outside their representational system. If only you were conscious of it—of this twofold pull and the vision it effects. But you're not, and so you inadvertently efface the erotic potential in women (and men).

Turning to voice 2, Diotima continues: You have given us much, you who know how to write our bodies and recoup for us our own moves from "the space represented by/in a representation, by/in a discourse . . . to a space not represented yet implied (unseen) in them" (de Lauretis 1987: 26). Were it not for your creative texts and courageous acts, I'd be unaware of the creative and courageous potentials in humankind. Your looking glass, from the other side, has sustained me in times of difficulty. But you and I are similar. All women are not like us. We can all see ourselves in a looking glass, from the other side, but we see *differently*. Your look does not include the gaze that moves to the side of the visions *your* words effect. And your omission worries me because we need a feminist "interrogation of ethnocentrism; a poetics of identity that engages with the 'other woman.' "[22]

I am also troubled by our tendency as women to identify the spaces *we* share with the erotic. Do we really intend to relinquish the radical potential in men to move with us? Do you really believe their pornographic postures are innate? Are they (unlike us) doomed to tell the same stories, replete with the same barriers, wounds, and lies? Must they sacrifice maidens to feed a mastery they may never attain? Can't we persuade them to move with us to build an alternative house? If we can't, our options are limited: we can exclude and (so) "other" them, or move erotically with them. But can we love those who still confuse erotic love with their painful master love? I believe we can persuade them to step to the side of the representational system and, by their and our illegitimate practices, move erotically with us. The erotic is not a privileged site; it is a position available to anyone. For there is something in everyone that falls to the side of representation.

Like Diotima, I am assuming that history is not destiny, that despite what Spivak means by her term [masculine] "regulative psychobiography," men can move past their privileged access to legitimate forms of power and move with us erotically. However, the voice that speaks these words resembles Diotima's, a fictional character whose dreams may (or may not) become reality. The efficacy of our dreams lies not simply in our narratives but in the political choices we make every day—to live out the same dreary (master) dreams or to try to live the alternative dreams we envision.

Epilogue

Scene: two thousand years later. The curtain rises. Aitiatiklea, Orthophilia, and Atheneia are seated on a stage, discussing their own reactions to Euripides' *Hecuba*. They speak at great length. Their speaking is both like and unlike that of voices 1, 2, and 3. As I listen, I long to begin again, to craft (an)Other maiden's tale. I begin to imagine Aitiatiklea as more rebellious and considerably more self-aware. Orthophilia is still torn between her desire to be desired and her desire for autonomy, but she's a lesbian. The subject/object positions that draw her belong not to men but to women. Atheneia is perhaps the most difficult to resketch. She's married and in some ways resembles voice 2. She has a daughter whom she calls Metis, after her own mother. Her male-identified surface is a shield she has erected for protection. She is wise and adept at moving in and out of the gaps that link male public and female private (and public) spaces. Perhaps she weaves her tales on tapestries she crafts for us. Perhaps her incessant weaving wearies her and she longs instead to craft a song, about the reactions of the men she knows to the sacrifice of goats and maidens, about the reactions of Orthokles and the man seated to his right. A curtain rises, and a story is told. But why this story? Why these characters? And, as I ponder such questions, I imagine myself the object of the gaze of my characters. Their look reminds me of the inherently dialogical nature of my account; for I cannot see how my look (shaped, among other things, by the documents I have examined and the methods I deploy) refracts the gaze of others who see me. I can see to the side of my own historically en-gendered look, but I cannot see from within or to the side of the historically en-gendered gaze of others. But if, as I believe, it is possible to live erotically in a pornographic world, then it was possible then and it is still possible now. Perhaps.

Classics is one of the master's oldest houses and hard to break out of. But I have learned to trust my need to speak in a style that falls to the side of its master methods. This book, to me, constitutes an alternative house based on collaboration, friendship, and trust and productive of energy, love, and hope.

NOTES

1. See the episode in *Story of O* discussed in Silverman 1984: 341; de Lauretis 1984: 150.

2. The position I have adopted here follows Haraway 1985 but speaks with the voices of many others, including E. Kaplan 1983, Kappeler 1986, de Lauretis 1984, Rubin 1984, Silverman 1984. The positions being critiqued are those of the antipornography movement and anyone else who ignores her or his own patriarchal origins.

3. This position is especially well articulated by Haraway 1985. It is also implied in the analyses of Carse 1986 and de Lauretis 1986 and *resembles* the positions of Cixous 1986 and Irigaray 1985. By theorizing a genderless subject, I do not mean to imply that our political projects as men and women are identical or even similar. As Nancy Miller argues (1986), the postmodernist dislocation and dispersal of the author does not work for women because we have been "juridically excluded from the polis, and hence decentered, 'disoriginated,' deinstitutionalized, etc. [and as a consequence our] relation to integrity and textuality, desire and authority is structurally different from men's."

4. I am using these terms in their lay sense. The term *sadistic* is intended to describe anyone who derives pleasure in and from the degradation of others; *masochistic* alternatively describes those who derive pleasure from (and through their guilt facilitate) their own degradation.

5. My reading here is a fictionalized rereading of the cyborg manifesto (Haraway 1985).

6. De Lauretis 1984: 133; while the primary signification of these words in her account is somewhat different (in its immediate focus on the ways "fucking" does not work for men), the conclusions she draws (that it is and is not working for us) are the same.

7. As Haraway (also) observes (1985: 75), "White women, including socialist feminists, discovered . . . the non-innocence of the category 'woman.' That consciousness changes the geography of all previous categories. . . . In the fraying of identities and in the reflexive strategies for constructing them, the possibility opens for weaving something other than a shroud for the day after the apocalypse that so prophetically ends salvation history."

8. Voice 3 owes much to the writings of Donna Haraway and Teresa de Lauretis. I have named her Diotima to counter the erotic tales about love attributed by Plato to the Diotima he invents.

9. Voice 1 speaks for herself. However, she sounds like Lacan, Kaja Silverman (esp. Silverman 1984), and anyone else who, like them, situates our subjectivity within the parameters of the "grammar," "morphology," and "syntax" of (male-produced) language and representation. Voice 1 also speaks from within the male-produced fictions of and about Aspasia. Because of her epistemological "faith" in the power of discourse to define and delimit our subject status, I have (to some extent) written her as she has been read by Aristophanes (*Ach.* 515–29), Plato (*Menex.* 235e), Aristotle (*Ath. Pol.* 26.4), Plutarch (*Per.* 24.6, 25.1, 37.5), Xenophon (*Mem.* 2.6.36; *Oec.* 3.14), Eupolis (frg. 274 K), and others.

10. This line, from Pericles' Funeral Oration (Thucydides 2.45.2), was attributed to Aspasia by Socrates in Plato (*Menex.* 236b).

11. See Zeitlin 1986.

12. "Aspasia's" foreign birth, status, beauty, and seductive charm figure in most of the male-produced accounts of her—including Aristophanes (*Ach.* 515–29), Plato (*Menex.* 235e), Athenaeus (*Deip.* 13.589d), Plutarch (*Per.* 24.6).

13. Others have illustrated how tragic discourse and the spectacles it effected served the Athenian male state; thus, as Winkler observes (1985b), the tragic gaze is male, as is the self at stake (Zeitlin 1985a: 66).

14. See *Eum.*, especially lines 734–43, where she becomes the mouthpiece for the

prevalent masculinist ideology which includes (among other things) the male's appropriation of the womb, fertility, and women's (historically en-gendered) reproductive role.

15. Her political influence as the live-in mistress of Pericles and as a teacher of rhetoric are cited by Aristophanes (*Ach.* 515–39), Plutarch (*Per.* 24.6, 25.1), Athenaeus (*Deip.* 13.589d), Plato (*Menex.* 235e), and others.

16. Plutarch, who had access to a tradition no longer accessible to us, tells us (*Per.* 24.6) that she was attacked by the comic poet Cratinus and by Eupolis and (32.1) that she was put on trial for impiety.

17. According to Athenaeus (*Deip.* 13.570a), Aspasia belonged to the Socratic circle. I have invented her decision to leave Socrates' discursive fellowship, her reactions to the plays of Aeschylus and Euripides, her decision to form a women's group, and the play they perform.

18. This tale is modeled on Silverman's reading of *The Story of O* (1984: 320–49). The main character is Iphigenia, the maiden constructed in and through the three male-produced readings of her life.

19. Voice 2 sounds like those who tend to privilege the "erotic" as an exclusively feminine orientation—Cixous 1976, Lorde 1984, S. Griffin 1978, Irigaray 1985, and others. Like Irigaray, however, she argues from within and against the Lacanian frame presented by voice 1. She also resembles Xanthippe. However, because of her epistemological stance, I have paid less attention to the male-produced traditions about her as a shrew and instead invented an image of an Other Xanthippe, Socrates' speaking wife. More particularly, I have focused on her as the daughter of a mother and a mother herself to represent the focus on motherhood that characterizes feminist thought (Schor 1986: 26; Chodorow 1978; Gilligan 1982). See J. Davies (1981) for a synopsis of the male tradition which includes such authors as Xenophon (*Mem.* 2.2; *Symp.* 2.10), Plato (*Phaid.* 60A), Plutarch (*De Cohibenda Ira, Mor.* 13.461e), Aelian (*Var. Hist.* 11.12), Arrian/Epictetus (4.5.33), Diogenes Laertius (2.36), and so on.

20. The first two adjectives are from Xenophon's *Memorabilia* (2.2.7), a mock discussion between Socrates and his son about Xanthippe. In response to her son's description of his mother as "vile-tempered," Socrates exclaims, "Which, think you . . . is the harder to bear, a wild beast's brutality or a mother's?" The third adjective is from the same author's *Symposium* (2.10), in which Socrates is asked why he married a wife "who is the hardest to get along with of all the women there are—yes, or all that ever were, I suspect, or ever will be." The response attributed to him is no less telling: "Because I observe that men who wish to become expert horsemen do not get the most docile horses but rather those that are high-mettled, believing that if they can manage this kind, they will easily handle any other."

21. See Detienne and Vernant 1978 for a more detailed analysis of the role and functions of *mêtis* in Greek thought.

22. A. Rich 1986, but similar sentiments have been expressed by many, such as Spivak 1981; de Lauretis 1986, 1987.

BIBLIOGRAPHY

Abbreviations of titles of ancient works are as listed in the *Oxford Classical Dictionary,* 2nd ed. (Oxford: Clarendon Press). Abbreviations in Chapter 1 are as recommended by *American Journal of Archaeology* 90 (1986): 384–94; also:

ABV = Beazley 1956.
*ARV*² = Beazley 1963.
Paralipomena = Beazley 1971.
*Beazley Addenda*² = Carpenter 1989.

Abel, Elizabeth, ed. 1982. *Writing and Sexual Difference.* Chicago: University of Chicago Press.
Abramson, P. R., and H. Hayashi. 1984. "Pornography in Japan." In Malamuth and Donnerstein 1984, 173–83.
Allroggen-Bedel, Agnes. 1974. *Maskendarstellungen in der römische-kampanische Wandmalerei.* Munich: Wilhelm Fink.
Anderson, Graham. 1984. *Ancient Fiction: The Novel in the Graeco-Roman World.* London: Croom Helm.
Archer, W. C. 1981. "The Paintings of the 'Casa dei Vettii' in Pompeii." Diss., University of Virginia.
Ardener, Edwin. 1975. "Belief and the Problem of Women." In Shirley Ardener, ed., *Perceiving Women,* 1–17. London: J. M. Dent.
Arias, P. E. 1961. *A History of 1000 Years of Greek Vase Painting.* Trans. and rev. by B. Shefton. New York: Abrams.
Arieti, J. A. 1975. "Nudity in Greek Athletics." *Classical World* 68: 431–36.
Arslan, E., ed. 1950. *Arte del primo millennio. Atti del II° convegno per lo studio dell'arte*

dell' alto medioevo tenuto presso l'Università di Pavia nel settembre, 1950. Torino: Andrea Viglongo.

Arthur, Marylin B. 1984. "Early Greece: The Origins of the Western Attitude toward Women." In J. Peradotto and J. P. Sullivan, eds., *Women and the Ancient World: The Arethusa Papers,* 7–58. Buffalo: SUNY Press.

———. 1983. "The Dream of a World without Women: Poetics and the Circles of Order in the *Theogony* Prooemium." *Arethusa* 16: 97–116.

———. 1981. "The Divided World of *Iliad* VI." In H. Foley, ed., *Reflections of Women in Antiquity,* 19–44. New York, London, Paris: Gordon and Breach.

Ashby, T. 1914. "Drawings of Ancient Paintings in English Collections. Part I: The Eton Drawings." *Papers of the British School at Rome* 7: 1–62. London: Macmillan.

Atwood, Margaret. 1985. *The Handmaid's Tale.* New York: Fawcett Crest.

———. 1983. *The Edible Woman.* New York: Warner Books.

Auerbach, Nina. 1982. *Woman and the Demon.* Cambridge, Mass.: Harvard University Press.

Auguet, R. 1972. *Cruelty and Civilization: The Roman Games.* London: George Allen and Unwin.

Aurigemma, S. 1960. *L'Italia in Africa. Le scoperte archeologiche (1911–1943). Tripolitania I. I monumenti d'arte decorativa. Parte prima. I mosaici.* Rome: Istituto Poligrafico dello Stato.

———. 1926. *I mosaici di Zliten ("Africa italiana." Collezione di monografie a cura del ministero delle colonie).* Rome: Società Editrice d'Arte Illustrata.

Austin, Norman. 1975. *Archery at the Dark of the Moon.* Berkeley: University of California Press.

Aymard, J. 1962. "Notes sur une mosaïque de Westenhofen." In Renard 1962, 165–72.

———. 1951. *Essai sur les chasses romaines des origines à la fin des Antonins (Cynegetica).* Paris: E. de Boccard.

Azevedo, M. Cagiano de. 1962. "La data dei mosaici di Zliten." In Renard 1962, 374–80.

Baehrens, E. 1879. *Poetae Latini Minores.* Vol. 1. Leipzig: Teubner.

Bailey, D. M. 1980. *A Catalogue of the Lamps in the British Museum II: Roman Lamps Made in Italy.* London: British Museum Publications.

Bakhtin, Mikhail. 1981a. "Epic and Novel: Toward a Methodology for the Study of the Novel." In *The Dialogic Imagination,* trans. C. Emerson and M. Holquist, 3–40. Austin: University of Texas Press.

———. 1981b. "Forms of Time and Chronotope in the Novel." In *The Dialogic Imagination,* 84–258.

Baldwin, B. 1977. "The Minor Characters in Athenaeus." *Acta Classica* 20: 37–48.

———. 1976. "Athenaeus and His Work." *Acta Classica* 19: 21–42.

Ball-Rokeach, S. 1972. "The Legitimation of Violence." In Short and Wolfgang 1972, 100–111.

Balsdon, J. P. V. D. 1969. *Life and Leisure in Ancient Rome.* New York: McGraw-Hill.

Barré, M. L. 1877. *Herculaneum et Pompéi, Recueil Général des Peintures, Bronzes, Mosaïques, etc. découverts jusqu'à ce jour et reproduits d'après Le Antichità di Ercolano, Il Museo Borbonico et tous les ouvrages analogues.* Vol. 8: 'Musée Secret.' Paris: Firmin Didot Frères.

Barrowclough, Susan. 1982. " 'Not a Love Story': Susan Barrowclough Examines the Film and Its Assumptions." *Screen* 23: 26–36.

Barry, Kathleen. 1979. *Female Sexual Slavery.* New York: New York University Press.

Bart, Pauline B., and Margaret Jozsa. 1980. "Dirty Books, Dirty Films, and Dirty Data." In Lederer 1980, 204–17.

Barthes, Roland. 1985a. "Is Painting a Language?" In *The Responsibility of Forms*, 149–52.

———. 1985b. *The Responsibility of Forms: Critical Essays on Music, Art, and Representation*. Trans. by R. Howard. New York: Hill and Wang.

———. 1985c. "Right in the Eyes." In *The Responsibility of Forms*, 237–42.

———. 1976. *Sade, Fourier, Loyola*. Trans. by R. Miller. New York: Hill and Wang.

Bartholomé, H. 1935. *Ovid und die antike Kunst*. Leipzig.

Barton, Carlin. 1989. "The Scandal of the Arena." *Representations* 27: 1–36.

Bartsch, Shadi. 1989. *Decoding the Ancient Novel: The Reader and the Role of Description in Heliodorus and Achilles Tatius*. Princeton: Princeton University Press.

Beare, W. 1955. *The Roman Stage*, 2d ed. Methuen: London.

Beauvoir, Simone de. 1953. *The Second Sex*. Paris: Gallimard. Trans. and rep. 1961, Bantam Books.

Beazley, J. D. 1989. "Potter and Painter in Ancient Athens." In D. C. Kurtz, ed., *Greek Vases: lectures by J. D. Beazley*, 39–58. Rep. 1944 edition. Oxford: Clarendon.

———. 1971. *Paralipomena: Additions to Attic Black-figure Vase-painters and Attic Red-figure Vase-painters*, 2d ed. Oxford: Clarendon.

———. 1963. *Attic Red-figure Vase-painters*, 2d ed. Oxford: Oxford University Press.

———. 1956. *Attic Black-figure Vase-painters*. Oxford: Oxford University Press.

———. 1947. "Some Attic Vases in the Cyprus Museum." *Proceedings of the British Academy* 33: 195–242.

Beer, Gillian. 1970. *The Romance*. London: Methuen.

Bekker, Immanuele. 1855. *Heliodori Aethiopicorum Libri Decem*. Leipzig: Teubner.

Beneke, Timothy. 1982. *Men on Rape*. New York: St. Martin's Press.

Benjamin, Jessica. 1983. "Master and Slave: The Fantasy of Erotic Domination." In Snitow et al. 1983, 280–99.

Bérard, C. 1989. "The Order of Women." In C. Bérard et al., *A City of Images: Iconography and Society in Ancient Greece*, trans. D. Lyons, 85–103. Princeton: Princeton University Press.

Berger, John. 1980. *About Looking*. New York: Pantheon Books.

———. 1972. *Ways of Seeing*. Harmondsworth and London: British Broadcasting Company and Penguin Books.

Berger, L., and J. Joos. 1971. *Das Augster Gladiatorenmosaik*. Augst: Römerhaus und Museum.

Bergren, Ann L. T. 1983. "Language and the Female in Early Greek Thought." *Arethusa* 16: 69–95.

Bernard, V., P. Ottenberg, and F. Redl. 1971. "Dehumanization." In Henry and Sanford 1971, 102–24.

Bersani, L., and U. Dutoit. 1985. *The Forms of Violence: Narrative in Assyrian Art and Modern Culture*. New York: Schocken Books.

Beschaouch, M. A. 1966. "La mosaïque de chasse à l'amphithéâtre découverte à Smirat en Tunisie." *Comptes rendus de l'académie des inscriptions et belles-lettres:* 134–58. Paris: Librairie C. Klincksieck.

Betterton, R., ed. 1987. *Looking On: Images of Femininity in the Visual Arts and Media*. New York: Pandora Press.

Blake, W. E. 1939. *Chariton's Chaireas and Callirhoe*. Ann Arbor: University of Michigan Press.

Blakely, Mary Kay. 1985. "Is One Woman's Sexuality Another Woman's Pornography?" *Ms.* 10, no. 13 (April): 37–47, 120–23.

Bloch, Raymond. 1965. *Tite-Live et les premiers siècles de Rome*. Paris: Société d'Édition "Les Belles Lettres."

Blok, J. 1987. "Sexual Asymmetry." In J. Blok and P. Mason, eds., *Sexual Asymmetry: Studies in Ancient Society*, 1–57. Amsterdam: Gieben.

Boardman, John. 1989. *Athenian Red-figure Vases: The Classical Period*. London and New York: Thames and Hudson.

———. 1985. *Greek Sculpture: The Classical Period*. New York: Thames and Hudson.

———. 1980. *The Greeks Overseas: The Early Colonies and Trade*, rev. ed. London: Thames and Hudson.

———. 1979. "The Athenian Pottery Trade." *Expedition* 21.4: 33–39.

———. 1976. "A Curious Eye-cup." *Archaeologischer Anzeiger*: 281–91.

———. 1975. *Athenian Red Figure Vases: The Archaic Period*. London: Thames and Hudson.

———. 1974. *Athenian Black Figure Vases*. London: Thames and Hudson.

Boardman, John, and Eugenio LaRocca. 1975. *Eros in Greece*. New York: Erotic Art Book Society.

Bomgardner, D. L. 1989. "The Carthage Amphitheater: A Reappraisal." *American Journal of Archaeology* 93: 85–103.

Bonfante, Larissa. 1989. "Nudity as a Costume in Classical Art." *American Journal of Archaeology* 93: 543–70.

———. 1981. "Etruscan Couples and Their Aristocratic Society." In H. P. Foley, ed., *Reflections of Women in Antiquity*, 323–41. London and New York: Gordon and Breach.

Bonner, S. F. 1977. *Education in Ancient Rome*. Berkeley and Los Angeles: University of California Press.

———. 1949. *Roman Declamation in the Late Republic and Early Empire*. Berkeley and Los Angeles: University of California Press.

Boodro, M. 1988. "The Rothschild Style." *Vogue* (November): 404–13.

Bothmer, D. von. 1985. *The Amasis Painter and His World*. New York and Malibu: Thames and Hudson, J. Paul Getty Museum.

———. 1961. *Ancient Art from New York Private Collections*. New York: Metropolitan Museum of Art.

Bowersock, Glen. 1969. *Greek Sophists in the Roman Empire*. Oxford: Clarendon Press.

Bowie, E. L. 1985. "The Greek Novel." In P. E. Easterling and B. M. W. Knox, eds., *Cambridge History of Classical Literature*, Vol. I: *Greek Literature*, 683–98. Cambridge: Cambridge University Press.

Bradley, A. 1909. "Hegel's Theory of Tragedy." In *Oxford Lectures on Poetry*, 69–95. London: Macmillan.

Bragantini, I., and M. de Vos. 1982. *Le decorazioni della villa romana della Farnesina. Le Pitture II.1*. Rome: De Luca Editore.

Brandt, P. [pseud. Hans Licht]. 1925–28. *Sittengeschichte Griechenlands*. Dresden and Zurich: Paul Aretz.

———. 1911. (rept. 1977.) *P. Ovidi Nasonis Amorum Libri Tres*. Leipzig (1911). Hildesheim: Georg Olms.

———. 1902. (rept. 1963.) *P. Ovidi Nasonis De Arte Amandi Libri Tres*. Leipzig (1902). Hildesheim: Georg Olms.

Brannigan, A., and S. Goldenberg. 1987. "The Study of Aggressive Pornography: The Vicissitudes of Relevance." *Critical Studies in Mass Communication* 4: 262–83.

Brendel, Otto. 1979. *Prolegomena to the Study of Roman Art*. New Haven: Yale University Press.

———. 1970. "The Scope and Temperament of Erotic Art in the Graeco-Roman World." In Theodore Bowie and C. V. Christenson, eds., *Studies in Erotic Art*, 3–108. New York: Basic Books.

Brilliant, R. 1974. *Roman Art from the Republic to Constantine*. London: Phaidon Press.

Bron, C., and F. Lissarague. 1989. "Looking at the Vase." In C. Bérard et al., *A City of Images: Iconography and Society in Ancient Greece*, trans. D. Lyons, 7–17. Princeton: Princeton University Press.

Broude, N., and M. Garrard, eds. 1982. *Feminism and Art History: Questioning the Litany*. New York: Harper and Row.

Brown, Beverly. 1981. "A Feminist Interest in Pornography—Some Modest Proposals." *m/f* 5/6: 5–18.

Brownmiller, Susan. 1982. *Against Our Will: Men, Women, and Rape*. New York: Simon and Schuster.

———. 1980. "Excerpt on Pornography from *Against Our Will: Men, Women, and Rape*." In Lederer 1980, 30–39.

Brownstein, R. M. 1982. *Becoming a Heroine*. New York: Viking.

Bryson, Norman. 1986. "Two Narratives of Rape in the Visual Arts: Lucretia and the Sabine Women." In Sylvana Tomaselli and Roy Porter, eds., *Rape*, 152–73. Oxford: Blackwell.

Burguière, P., D. Gourevitch and Y. Malinas. 1988. *Soranos d'Éphèse. Maladies des Femmes*. Tome I, livre I. Paris: Les Belles Lettres.

Burman, Secundus P. 1759. *Anthologia Veterum Latinorum Epigrammatum et Poematum sive Catalecta Poetarum Latinorum*, Vol. I. Amsterdam.

Burn, L. 1987. *The Meidias Painter*. Oxford: Clarendon.

Butler, Marilyn. 1988. "Feminist Criticism, Late-80's Style." *Times Literary Supplement*, March 11–17, 283–85.

Butterworth, G. W. 1919 (rept. 1960). *Clement of Alexandria with an English Translation*. Loeb Classical Library 92. Cambridge, Mass., and London: Harvard University Press, Heinemenn.

Byrne, D., and K. Kelley. 1984. "Pornography and Sex Research." In Malamuth and Donnerstein 1984, 1–15.

Cahoon, Leslie. 1988. "The Bed as Battlefield: Erotic Conquest and Military Metaphor in Ovid's *Amores*." *TAPA* 118: 293–307.

———. 1985. "A Program for Betrayal: Ovidian *Nequitia* in *Amores* 1.1, 2.1 and 3.1." *Helios* 12: 29–39.

Campanati, R. F. 1984. *III colloquio internazionale sul mosaico antico. Ravenna, 6–10 settembre 1980*. Ravenna: Edizioni del Girasole.

Cantarella, Eva. 1987. *Pandora's Daughters: The Role and Status of Women in Greek and Roman Antiquity*. Trans. by M. Fant. Baltimore: Johns Hopkins University Press.

Carandini, A., A. Ricci, and M. de Vos. 1982. *Filosofiana. The Villa of Piazza Armerina. The Image of a Roman Aristocrat at the Time of Constantine*. Palermo: S. F. Flaccovio.

Carettoni, Gianfilippo. 1983. *Das Haus des Augustus auf dem Palatin*. Mainz am Rhein: Philipp von Zabern.

Carpenter, T. H. 1989. *Beazley Addenda. Additional References to ABV, ARV², and Paralipomena (Second Edition)*. Oxford: Oxford University Press for the British Academy.

———. 1986. *Dionysian Imagery in Archaic Greek Art*. Oxford: Clarendon.

———. 1984. "The Tyrrhenian Group: Problems of Provenance." *Oxford Journal of Archaeology* 3: 45–56.

———. 1983. "On the Dating of the Tyrrhenian Group." *Oxford Journal of Archaeology* 2: 279–93.

Carse, James P. 1986. *Finite and Infinite Games: A Vision of Life as Play and Possibility*. New York: Ballantine Books.

Carson, Anne. 1990. "Putting Her in Her Place: Woman as Dirt in Ancient Society." In D. Halperin et al. 1990, 135–69.

Carter, Angela. 1982. "Colette." In *Nothing Sacred,* 169–80. London: Virago.

———. 1978. *The Sadeian Woman and the Ideology of Pornography.* New York: Harper and Row, Pantheon.

Cataudella, Q. 1974. "Initiamenta Amoris." *Latomus* 33: 847–57.

———. 1973. "Recupero di un' antica scrittrice greca." *Giornale Italiano di Filologia* 4[25].3: 253–63.

Chodorow, Nancy. 1978. *The Reproduction of Mothering.* Berkeley: University of California Press.

La cité des images: Religion et société en Grèce antique. 1984. Paris and Lausanne: Fernand Nathan. English translation 1989, Princeton University Press.

Cixous, Hélène. 1986. "Sorties." In H. Cixous and C. Clément, eds., 1986, 63–132.

———. 1976. "The Laugh of the Medusa." *Signs: A Journal of Women in Culture and Society* 1.4: 875–99.

———, and Catherine Clément. 1986. *The Newly Born Woman.* Trans. by Betsy Wing. Minneapolis: University of Minnesota Press.

Clark, Stephen R. L. 1982. "Aristotle's Woman." *History of Political Thought* 3: 177–91.

———. 1975. *Aristotle's Man.* Oxford: Oxford University Press.

Clifford, J. 1986. "Introduction: Partial Truths." In Clifford and Marcus 1986, 1–26.

Clifford, J. and G. E. Marcus, eds. 1986. *Writing Culture: The Poetics and Politics of Ethnography.* Berkeley: University of California Press.

Clover, Carol. 1987. "Her Body, Himself: Gender in the Slasher Film." *Representations* 20: 187–228.

Colwin, Laurie. 1982. "A Girl Skating." In *The Lone Pilgrim.* New York: Washington Square Press.

Cook, R. M. 1960. *Greek Painted Pottery.* London: Methuen.

Cornell, T. J. 1986. "The Value of the Literary Tradition concerning Archaic Rome." In K. A. Raaflaub, ed., *Social Struggles in Archaic Rome,* 52–76. Berkeley: University of California Press.

Coulson, W. D. E., and Albert Leonard Jr. 1981. *Cities of the Delta, I. Naukratis.* American Research Center in Egypt Reports IV. Malibu: Undena.

Croisille, J.-M. 1982. *Poésie et art figuré de Neron aux Flaviens: Récherches sur l'iconographie et la correspondance des arts à l'époque impériale.* Collection Latomus 197. Brussels: Latomus.

Crome, J. F. 1966. "Spinnende Hetären?" *Gymnasium* 73: 245–47.

Cropper, E. 1986. "The Beauty of Woman: Problems in the Rhetoric of Renaissance Portraiture." In Ferguson et al. 1986, 175–90.

Culham, Phyllis. 1990. "Decentering the Text: The Case of Ovid." *Helios* 17.2: 161–70.

———. 1986. "Ten Years after Pomeroy: Studies of the Image and Reality of Women in Antiquity." *Helios* 13.2: 9–30.

Culler, Jonathan. 1975. *Structuralist Poetics: Structuralism, Linguistics and the Study of Literature.* Ithaca: Cornell University Press.

Curran, Leo C. 1984. "Rape and Rape Victims in the *Metamorphoses.*" In J. Peradotto and J. P. Sullivan, eds., *Women in the Ancient World: The Arethusa Papers,* 263–86. Albany: SUNY Press.

Curtius, L. 1929. *Die Wandmalerei Pompejes.* Leipzig: E. A. Seemann.

Daly, Mary. 1984. *Pure Lust: Elemental Feminist Philosophy.* Boston: Beacon Press.

Daremberg, C., and E. Saglio. 1896. *Dictionnaire des antiquités grecques et romaines d'après les textes et les monuments II(2).* Paris: Librairie Hachette et Cie.

Davies, Jacqueline MacGregor. 1988. "Pornographic Harms." In L. Code et al., eds., *Feminist Perspectives: Philosophical Essays on Method and Morals*. Toronto: University of Toronto Press.

Davies, John K. 1981. *Wealth and the Power of Wealth in Classical Athens*. New York: Arno Press.

———. 1971. *Athenian Propertied Families*. Oxford: Clarendon.

Delacoste, Frédérique, and Priscilla Alexander, eds. 1987. *Sex Work: Writings by Women in the Sex Industry*. Pittsburgh: Cleis Press.

De Lauretis, Teresa. 1987. *Technologies of Gender*. Bloomington: Indiana University Press.

———. 1986. "Feminist Studies/Critical Studies: Issues, Terms, and Contexts." In *Feminist Studies/Critical Studies*, 1–19. Bloomington: Indiana University Press.

———. 1984. *Alice Doesn't*. Bloomington: Indiana University Press.

Delbrück, R. 1929. *Die Consulardiptychen und verwandte Denkmäler* I–II. Studien zur spätantiken Kunstgeschichte im Auftrage des Deutschen Archäologischen Instituts. Berlin: Walter de Gruyter.

Delivorrias, A., with G. Berger-Doer and A. Kossatz-Deissman. 1984. "Aphrodite." *Lexicon Iconographicum Mythologiae Graecae* 2: 2–151.

Della Corte, F. 1982. "Le leges Iuliae e l'elegia romana." *Aufstieg und Niedergang der Römischer Welt* 2.30.1: 539–58.

Delphy, Christine. 1981. "For a Materialist Feminism." *Feminist Issues* 1.2: 69–76.

Desrousseaux, A. M., ed. and trans. 1956. *Athenaeus, Deipnosophistae*. Paris: Société d'Édition "Les Belles Lettres."

Detienne, Marcel, and Jean-Pierre Vernant. 1978. *Cunning Intelligence in Greek Culture and Society*. Trans. by J. Lloyd. Atlantic Highlands, N.J.: Humanities Press.

Deubner, Ludwig. 1956. *Attische Feste*. Berlin: Akademie-Verlag.

Diamond, Irene. 1980. "Pornography and Repression: A Reconsideration of 'Who' and 'What.'" In Lederer 1980, 187–203.

Dijkstra, Bram. 1986. *Idols of Perversity: Fantasies of Feminine Evil in Fin-de-siècle Culture*. New York: Oxford University Press.

Dixon, Suzanne. 1988. *The Roman Mother*. Norman: Oklahoma University Press.

———. 1982. "Women and Rape in Roman Law." *Kønsroller, parforhold og Samlivsformer: Arbejdsnotat nr. 3*. Women's Research Center in Social Science, Copenhagen.

Doane, Mary Ann. 1987. *The Desire to Desire*. Bloomington: Indiana University Press.

Doane, Mary Ann, Patricia Mellencamp, and Linda Williams, eds. 1984. *Re-Vision: Essays in Feminist Film Criticism*. Frederick, Md.: University Publications of America.

Dodds, E. R. 1959. *Plato: Gorgias*. Oxford: Oxford University Press.

Donaldson, Ian. 1982. *The Rapes of Lucretia: A Myth and Its Transformations*. Oxford: Oxford University Press.

Donnerstein, E. 1984. "Aggression against Women: Cultural and Individual Cases." In Malamuth and Donnerstein 1984, 19–52.

Douglas, Mary. 1984. *Purity and Danger*. London: ARK Paperbacks.

Dover, K. J. 1984. "Classical Greek Attitudes to Sexual Behavior." In J. Peradotto and J. P. Sullivan, eds., *Women and the Ancient World: The Arethusa Papers*, 143–57. Buffalo: SUNY Press.

———. 1978. *Greek Homosexuality*. Cambridge, Mass.: Harvard University Press.

———. 1974. *Greek Popular Morality in the Time of Plato and Aristotle*. Berkeley: University of California Press.

———. 1972. *Aristophanic Comedy*. Berkeley and Los Angeles: University of California Press.

DuBois, Page. 1988. *Sowing the Body: Psychoanalysis and Ancient Representations of Women*. Chicago: University of Chicago Press.

———. 1982. *Centaurs and Amazons: Women and the Pre-history of the Great Chain of Being*. Ann Arbor: University of Michigan Press.

Dunbabin, K. M. D. 1978. *The Mosaics of Roman North Africa: Studies in Iconography and Patronage*. Oxford: Clarendon Press.

Duncan, C. 1982. "Virility and Domination in Early Twentieth-Century Vanguard Painting." In Broude and Garrard 1982, 292–313.

Dunkle, J. R. 1971. "The Rhetorical Tyrant in Roman Historiography: Sallust, Livy and Tacitus." *Classical World* 65: 12–20.

Dunning, E. 1986. "Social Bonding and Violence in Sport." In Elias and Dunning 1986, 224–44.

DuPlessis, Rachel Blau. 1985. *Writing beyond the Ending*. Bloomington: Indiana University Press.

Düring, Ingemar. 1936. *De Athenaei Dipnosophistarum Indole atque Dispositione. Apophoreta* Lundström. Goteburg.

Duster, T. 1971. "Conditions for Guilt-Free Massacre." In Henry and Sanford 1971, 25–36.

Dworkin, A. 1987. *Intercourse*. New York: Free Press.

———. 1981. *Pornography: Men Possessing Women*. New York: Putnam, Perigee.

Earl, Donald. 1967. *The Moral and Political Tradition of Rome*. Ithaca: Cornell University Press.

———. 1961. *The Political Thought of Sallust*. Cambridge: Cambridge University Press.

Easterling, P. E., and B. M. W. Knox, eds. 1985. *The Cambridge History of Classical Literature I: Greek Literature*. Cambridge: Cambridge University Press.

Echols, Alice. 1983. "The New Feminism of Yin and Yang." In Snitow et al. 1983, 439–59.

Effe, Bernd. 1977. *Dichtung und Lehre. Untersuchungen zur Typologie des antiken Lehrgedichts*. Zetemata 69. Munich: C. H. Beck.

Ehrenberg, V. 1951. *The People of Aristophanes*, 2d ed. Oxford: Blackwell.

Elias, N., and E. Dunning, eds. 1986. *Quest for Excitement: Sport and Leisure in the Civilizing Process*. Oxford: Basil Blackwell.

Ellmann, Mary. 1968. *Thinking about Women*. San Diego, New York, London: Harcourt Brace Jovanovitch.

Enk, P. J. 1962. *Sextus Propertii Elegiarum Liber Secundus*. Leiden: A. W. Sijthoff.

Eysenck, H. J. E. 1982. "Sex, Violence, and the Media: Where Do We Stand Now?" In Malamuth and Donnerstein 1982, 305–18.

Faccenna, D. 1956–1958. "Rilievi gladiatorii." *Bullettino della commissione archeologica comunale di Roma* 76 (*Bullettino del museo della civiltà romana* 19): 37–75. Rome: "L'Erma" di Bretschneider.

FACT Book Committee. 1986. *Caught Looking*. New York: Caught Looking Inc.

Fantham, Elaine. 1986. "Women in Antiquity: A Selective (and Subjective) Survey 1979–84." *Échos du Monde Classique/Classical Views* 30 (n.s. 5): 1–24.

———. 1983. "Sexual Comedy in Ovid's *Fasti:* Sources and Motivation." *Harvard Studies in Classical Philology* 87: 185–216.

———. 1975. "Sex, Status and Survival in Hellenistic Athens: A Study of Women in New Comedy." *Phoenix* 29: 44–74.

Ferguson, Frances. 1987. "Rape and the Rise of the Novel." *Representations* 20: 88–112.

Ferguson, M. W., M. Quilligan, and N. J. Vickers, eds. 1986. *Rewriting the Renaissance:*

The Discourses of Sexual Difference in Early Modern Europe. Chicago: University of Chicago Press.

Fetterley, Judith. 1986. "Reading about Reading: 'A Jury of Her Peers,' 'The Murders in the Rue Morgue,' and 'The Yellow Wallpaper.' " In Elizabeth A. Flynn and Patrocinio P. Schweikart, eds., *Gender and Reading: Essays on Readers, Texts, and Contexts,* 147–64. Baltimore: Johns Hopkins University Press.

———. 1978. *The Resisting Reader.* Bloomington: Indiana University Press.

Ffolliott, S. 1986. "Catherine de'Medici as Artemisia: Figuring the Powerful Widow." In Ferguson et al. 1986, 227–41.

Film Comment. 1984. "Pornography: Love or Death." Vol. 20, November–December: 29–49.

Finley, M. I. 1980. *Ancient Slavery and Modern Ideology.* New York: Viking.

Flacelière, Robert. 1962. *Love in Ancient Greece.* Trans. by J. Cleugh. New York: Crown.

Fletcher, John. 1986. "Poetry, Gender, and Primal Fantasy." In V. Burgin, J. Donald, and C. Kaplan, eds., *Formations of Fantasy,* 109–41. London and New York: Methuen.

Foley, Helene P. 1988. "Women in Greece." In M. Grant and R. Kitzinger, eds., *Civilization of the Ancient Mediterranean: Greece and Rome,* 1301–18. New York: Scribner's.

———. 1982. "The 'Female Intruder' Reconsidered: Women in Aristophanes' *Lysistrata* and *Ecclesiazusae.*" *Classical Philology* 77: 1–21.

———. 1981. "The Conception of Women in Athenian Drama." In *Reflections of Women in Antiquity,* 127–68. New York, London, Paris: Gordon and Breach.

———. 1978. "'Reverse Similes' and Sex Roles in the *Odyssey.*" *Arethusa* 11: 7–26.

Forcione, A. K. 1972. *Cervantes' Christian Romance.* Princeton: Princeton University Press.

Fortenbaugh, W. W. 1977. "Aristotle on Slaves and Women." In J. Barnes, M. Schofield, and R. Sorabji, eds., *Articles on Aristotle. 2. Ethics and Politics,* 135–39. London: Duckworth.

Foucault, Michel. 1986. *The Care of the Self: Volume 3 of The History of Sexuality.* Trans. by Robert Hurley. New York: Random House.

———. 1985. *The Use of Pleasure: Volume 2 of the History of Sexuality.* Trans. by Robert Hurley. New York: Random House.

———. 1982. "The Subject and Power." *Critical Inquiry* 8 (Summer): 777–95.

———. 1979. *Discipline and Punish: The Birth of the Prison.* Trans. by A. Sheridan. New York: Vintage Books.

———. 1978a. *The History of Sexuality: Volume 1: Introduction.* Trans. by Robert Hurley. New York: Random House.

———. 1978b. "The West and the Truth of Sex." *Sub-Stance* 20.5: 5–8.

Foucher, L. 1964a. "Sur les mosaïques de Zliten." *Libya Antiqua. Annual of the Department of Antiquities of Libya* 1: 9–20.

———. 1964b. "Venationes à Hadrumète." *Oudheidkundige Mededelingen uit het Rijksmuseum van Oudheden te Leiden* 45: 87–115. Leiden: Rijksmuseum.

———. 1963. "Découvertes archéologiques à Thysdrus en 1961." Tunis: Secrétariat d'État aux Affaires Culturelles et à l'Information.

———. 1960. *Inventaire des mosaïques. Atlas archéologique, Sousse, feuille* LVII. Tunis: Institut National d'Archéologie et Arts.

Francis, E. D., and M. Vickers. 1983. "*Signa Priscae Artis:* Eretria and Siphnos." *Journal of Hellenic Studies* 103: 49–67.

Frank, R. I. 1982. "Augustan Elegy and Catonism." *Aufstieg und Niedergang der Römischer Welt* 2.30.1: 559–79.

Frankfort, H. 1970. *The Art and Architecture of the Ancient Orient.* Baltimore: Penguin Books.

Freijeiro, A. B. 1950. "Mosaicos romanos con escenas de circo y anfiteatro en el Museo Arqueológico Nacional." *Archivo Español de Arqueología* 23: 127–42. Madrid: Instituto Diego Velázquez.

Frel, J. 1983. "Euphronios and His Fellows." In W. G. Moon, ed., *Ancient Greek Art and Iconography*, 147–58. Madison: University of Wisconsin Press.

Friedl, E. 1967. "The Position of Women: Appearance and Reality." *Anthropological Quarterly* 40: 97–108.

———. 1962. *Vasilika: A Village in Modern Greece*. New York: Holt, Rinehart and Winston.

Friggeri, R., and C. Pelli. 1980. "Vivo e morto." *Tituli* 2: 97–172. Rome: Edizioni di Storia e Letteratura.

Fröhner, Wilhelm. 1872. *Les Musées de France (Recueil de monuments antiques)*. Paris: J. Rothschild.

Furtwängler, Adolf. 1874. *Eros in der Vasenmalerei*. Munich: T. Ackermann.

Galinsky, G. Karl. 1975. *Ovid's Metamorphoses: An Introduction to the Basic Aspects*. Berkeley and Los Angeles: University of California Press.

Gamel, Mary Kay. n.d. "The Aesthetics of Dismemberment I: Philomela's Tongue." Unpublished manuscript.

Gardner, Jane F. 1986. *Women in Roman Law and Society*. Bloomington: Indiana University Press.

Garland, Robert. 1987. *The Peiraeus: From the Fifth to the First Century* B.C. London: Duckworth.

Garrard, M. D. 1989. *Artemisia Gentileschi: The Image of the Female Hero in Italian Baroque Art*. Princeton: Princeton University Press.

———. 1982. "Artemisia and Susanna." In Broude and Garrard 1982, 147–71.

Gaselee, S. 1917. *Achilles Tatius with an English Translation*. London and New York: William Heinemann and G. P. Putnam's Sons.

Gauckler, P. 1910. *Inventaire des mosaïques de la Gaule et de l'Afrique II. Afrique proconsulaire (Tunisie)*. Paris: Académie des Inscriptions et Belles-Lettres, Ernest Leroux.

Geertz, C. 1974. "From the Native's Point of View: On the Nature of Anthropological Understanding." *Bulletin of the American Academy of Arts and Sciences* 28: 26–45.

———. 1973. *The Interpretation of Cultures*. New York: Basic Books.

Gentili, G. V. 1956. *La Villa Erculia di Piazza Armerina. I Mosaici figurati*. Rome: Edizioni Mediterranee (Collana d'arte sidera).

Gerschmann, K. H. 1975. *Chariton-Interpretationen*. Diss., Münster.

Ghali-Kahil, L. B. 1955. *Les enlèvements et la retour d'Hélène*. École Française d'Athènes, *Travaux et Memoires* 10. Paris: Boccard.

Ghislanzoni, E. 1908. "Il rilievo gladiatorio di Chieti." *Monumenti antichi della reale accademia dei lincei* 19: 542–614. Milan: Ulrico Hoepli.

Gilbert, Sandra M., and Susan Gubar. 1979. *The Madwoman in the Attic*. New Haven: Yale University Press.

Gilligan, Carol. 1982. *In a Different Voice: Psychological Theory and Women's Development*. Cambridge, Mass.: Harvard University Press.

Ginouvès, R. 1962. *Balaneutikè: Recherche sur le bain dans l'antiquité grecque. Bibliothèque des Écoles Françaises d'Athènes et de Rome* 200.

Gjerstad, E. 1973. *Early Rome*, Vols. 5 and 6. Lund: Skrifter Utgivna av Svenska Institutet i Rome.

Glass, Philip. 1988. "Usher and Einstein, Pharaohs and UFOs: An Interview with Philip Glass." *Fanfare* 11.6: 65–77.

Goldberg, J. 1986. "Fatherly Authority: The Politics of Stuart Family Images." In Ferguson et al. 1986, 3–32.

Golden, Mark. 1988. "Male Chauvinists and Pigs." *Échos du Monde Classique/Classical Views* 32 n.s. 7: 1–12.

Gombrich, E. H. 1969. *Art and Illusion: A Study in the Psychology of Pictorial Representation.* Bollingen Series 35.5. Princeton: Princeton University Press.

Goold, G. P. 1983. "The Cause of Ovid's Exile." *Illinois Classical Studies* 8: 94–107.

Gordon, A. E. 1983. *Illustrated Introduction to Latin Epigraphy.* Berkeley: University of California Press.

Gould, J. 1980. "Law, Custom and Myth: Aspects of the Social Position of Women in Classical Athens." *Journal of Hellenic Studies* 100: 38–59.

Gordon, Bette. 1984. "Variety: The Pleasure in Looking." In Vance 1984, 189–203.

Götte, E. 1957. *Frauengemachbilder in der Vasenmalerei des 5. Jahrhunderts.* Diss., Munich, published Aachen.

Grant, Michael. 1975. *Eros in Pompeii: The Secret Rooms of the National Museum of Naples.* New York: William Morrow. (Published in Great Britain as *Erotic Art in Pompeii.*)

———. *1967. Gladiators.* London: Weidenfeld and Nicolson.

Green, Peter. 1982. *Ovid: The Erotic Poems.* Harmondsworth: Penguin.

Greifenhagen, Adolf. 1976. "Fragmente eines Rotfigurigen Pinax." In L. Bonfante, H. Heintze, and C. Lord, eds., *In Memoriam Otto J. Brendel: Essays in Archaeology and the Humanities,* 43–48. Mainz: Von Zabern.

———. 1957. *Griechische Eroten.* Berlin: De Gruyter.

Griffin, Jasper. 1976. "Augustan Poetry and the Life of Luxury." *Journal of Roman Studies* 66: 87–105. Reprinted with modifications in J. Griffin, *Latin Poets and Roman Life* (Chapel Hill: University of North Carolina Press, 1985), 1–31.

Griffin, Susan. 1981. *Pornography and Silence: Culture's Revenge against Nature.* New York: Harper & Row.

———. 1978. *Woman and Nature: The Roaring Inside Her.* New York: Harper & Row.

Gubar, Susan. 1987. "Representing Pornography: Feminism, Criticism, and Depictions of Female Violation." *Critical Inquiry* 13.4: 712–41; reprinted in Gubar and Hoff 1989, 47–67.

Gubar, Susan, and Joan Hoff. 1989. *For Adult Users Only: The Dilemma of Violent Pornography.* Bloomington: Indiana University Press.

Gulick, C. B. 1927–41. *Athenaeus: The Deipnosophistae.* Cambridge, MA: Loeb Classical Library.

Guthmann, V. O. 1965. *Kreuznach und Umgebung in Römischer Zeit.* Kreuznach: Verlag des Vereins für Heimatkunde.

Guthrie, W. K. C. 1981. *A History of Greek Philosophy, Volume VI. Aristotle: An Encounter.* Cambridge: Cambridge University Press.

Hadas, Moses. 1953. *Three Greek Romances: Longus, Xenophon, Dio Chrysostom.* Indianapolis: Bobbs-Merrill.

Hägg, Thomas. 1983. *The Novel in Antiquity.* Berkeley: University of California Press. (= *Den Antika Romanen,* Uppsala, 1980.)

———. 1971. *Narrative Technique in Ancient Greek Romances.* Stockholm: Svenska Institutet i Athen.

Hallett, Judith P. 1985. "Buzzing of a Confirmed Gadfly." *Helios* 12.2: 23–37.

———. 1979. "Sappho and Her Social Context: Sense and Sensuality." *Signs* 4: 447–64.

———. 1978. "*Morigerari:* Suetonius, *Tiberius,* 44." *L'Antiquité Classique* 47: 196–200.

Halperin, David M. 1990. *One Hundred Years of Homosexuality*. New York: Routledge.
————. 1989. "Sex before Sexuality: Pederasty, Politics, and Power in Classical Athens." In M. B. Duberman et al., eds., *Hidden from History: Reclaiming the Gay and Lesbian Past,* 37–53. New York: New American Library.
————. 1986. "Plato and Erotic Reciprocity." *Classical Antiquity* 5: 60–80.
Halperin, David, John J. Winkler, and Froma Zeitlin, eds. 1990. *Before Sexuality: The Construction of Erotic Experience in Ancient Greece*. Princeton: Princeton University Press.
Hammond, M. 1958. "Plato and Ovid's Exile." *Harvard Studies in Classical Philology* 63: 347–61.
Haraway, Donna. 1985. "A Manifesto for Cyborgs: Science, Technology, and Socialist Feminism in the 1980's." *Socialist Review* 80: 65–107.
Harmon, A. M. 1925. *Lucian, with an English translation*. Vol. 4. New York: Putnam.
Harrison, Evelyn B. 1979. "Apollo's Cloak." In M. B. Moore and G. Kopcke, eds., *Studies in Classical Art and Archaeology,* 91–97. Festschrift P. von Blanckenhagen. Locust Valley, N.Y.: J. J. Augustin.
Haslam, Michael W. 1981. "Narrative about Tinouphis in Prosimetrum." *P. Turner* 8: 35–45.
Hatch, E. 1983. *Culture and Morality: The Relativity of Values in Anthropology*. New York: Columbia University Press.
Haugsted, I. 1977. "Kvinder i Athen." In H. S. Roberts, ed., *En Kvindes Chancer i Oldtiden. Opuscula Graecolatina* 13, 49–166. Copenhagen: Museum Tusculanum.
Heath, John R. 1986. "The Supine Hero in Catullus 32." *Classical Journal* 82.1: 28–36.
Hegel, G. W. F. 1910. *Phenomenology*. Trans. by J. B. Baillie. London: S. Sonnenschein.
————. 1920. *Aesthetik*. Trans. by F. B. Osmaston as *The Philosophy of Fine Art*. London: G. Bell and Sons.
Heidegger, Martin. 1959. *An Introduction of Metaphysics*. Trans. by Ralph Manheim. New Haven: Yale University Press.
Heilbrun, Carolyn. 1979. *Reinventing Womanhood*. New York: Norton.
Heiserman, A. 1977. *The Novel before the Novel*. Chicago: University of Chicago Press.
Helbig, W. 1868. *Wandgemälde der vom Vesuv verschütteten Städte Campaniens*. Leipzig: Breitkopf und Hartel.
Hemker, Julie. 1985. "Rape and the Founding of Rome." *Helios* 12: 41–47.
Henderson, Jeffrey. 1988. "Greek Attitudes towards Sex." In M. Grant and R. Kitzinger, eds., *Civilization of the Ancient Mediterranean: Greece and Rome,* 1249–63. New York: Scribner's.
————. 1987a. *Aristophanes: Lysistrata*. Oxford: Oxford University Press.
————. 1987b. "Older Women in Attic Old Comedy." *Transactions of the American Philological Association* 117: 105–29.
————. 1980. "*Lysistrate:* The Play and Its Themes." *Yale Classical Studies* 26: 153–218.
————. 1975. *The Maculate Muse: Obscene Language in Attic Comedy*. New Haven and London: Yale University Press.
Henig, M. 1983. *A Handbook of Roman Art: A Comprehensive Survey of All the Arts of the Roman World*. Ithaca: Cornell University Press.
Henry, Madeleine. 1985. *Menander's Courtesans and the Greek Comic Tradition*. Frankfurt: Peter Lang.
Henry, W. E., and N. Sanford, eds. 1971. *Sanctions for Evil*. San Francisco: Jossey-Bass.
Hermary, Antoine. 1986. "Trois notes d'iconographie." *Bulletin de Correspondance Hellénique* 110: 219–30.

Hermary, Antoine, H. Cassimatis, and R. Vollkommer. 1986. "Eros." *Lexicon Iconographicum Mythologiae Graecae* 3: 850–942.

Herter, Hans. 1960. "Die Soziologie der antiken Prostitution im Lichte des heidnischen und christlichen Schrifttums." *Jahrbuch für Antike und Christtum* 3: 70–111.

Hess, T. B., and L. Nochlin. 1972. *Woman as Sex Object: Studies in Erotic Art, 1730–1970* (*Art News Annual* 38). New York: Macmillan.

Heurgon, Jacques. 1973. *The Rise of Rome*. Trans. by J. Willis. Berkeley: University of California Press.

Higonnet, Margaret. 1986. "Speaking Silences: Women's Suicide." In S. R. Suleiman, ed., *The Female Body in Western Culture*, 68–83. Cambridge, Mass.: Harvard University Press.

Hilton, Margery. 1969. *Interlude in Arcady*. Toronto: Harlequin Books.

Himmelmann-Wildschütz, Nikolaos. 1959. *Zur Eigenart des Klassischen Götterbildes*. Munich: Prestel.

Hoff, Joan. 1989. "Why Is There No History of Pornography?" In Gubar and Hoff 1989, 17–46.

Hollein, H.-G. 1988. *Bürgerbild und Bildwelt der attischen Demokratie auf den rotfigurigen Vasen des 6.-4 Jahrhunderts v. Chr.* Diss., Hamburg. Frankfurt a. M.: Peter Lang.

Hollis, A. S. 1977. *Ovid: Ars Amatoria Book I*. Oxford: Oxford University Press.

———. 1973. "*Ars Armatoria* and *Remedia Amoris*." In J. W. Binns, ed., *Ovid*, 84–115. London and Boston: Routledge and Kegan Paul.

Holzinger, K. 1928. "Erklärungen umstrittener Stellen des Aristophanes." *Studien Wien* 208.5: 37–49.

Hopkins, Keith. 1983. *Death and Renewal: Sociological Studies in Roman History* II. Cambridge: Cambridge University Press.

Horney, Karen. 1932. "The Dread of Woman." *International Journal of Psychoanalysis* 13: 348–60.

Humphrey, J. 1986. *Roman Circuses: Arenas for Chariot Racing*. London: B. T. Batsford.

Hunter, R. L. 1983. *A Study of Daphnis and Chloe*. Cambridge: Cambridge University Press.

Ilberg, J. 1911. "Die Überlieferung der Gynäkologie des Soranos von Ephesos." *Abhandlungen der phil.-hist. Klasse der königlichen sächsischen Akademie der Wissenschaften* 28: 1–121.

Irigaray, Luce. 1985. *Speculum of the Other Woman*. Trans. by G. Gill. Ithaca: Cornell University Press.

———. 1985. *This Sex Which Is Not One*. Trans. by C. Porter and C. Burke. Ithaca: Cornell University Press.

———. 1981. *Le corps-à-corps avec la mère*. Montreal: Les Éditions de la Pleine Lune.

Jaeger, Werner. 1948. *Aristotle: Fundamentals of His Development*, 2nd ed. Oxford: Oxford University Press.

Jebb, R. 1971. *Sophocles Antigone*. Amsterdam: Hakkert.

Jed, Stephanie H. 1989. *Chaste Thinking: The Rape of Lucretia and the Birth of Humanism*. Bloomington: Indiana University Press.

Jehlen, Myra. 1981. "Archimedes and the Paradox of Feminist Criticism." *Signs* 6: 575–601.

Jennison, G. 1937. *Animals for Show and Pleasure in Ancient Rome* (*Publications of the University of Manchester* 258). Manchester: University Press.

Jex-Blake, K. 1896 (1982). *The Elder Pliny's Chapters on the History of Art*. Revised reprint of 1976 edition by R. V. Schoder, S. J. Chicago: Ares.

Johns, Catherine. 1982. *Sex or Symbol? Erotic Images of Greece and Rome*. Austin: University of Texas Press.

Johnson, P. 1984. "The Mosaics of Bignor Villa, England: A Gallo-Roman Connection." *III Colloquio Internazionale sul Mosaico Antico* (R. F. Campanati, ed.): 405–10.

Jones, W. H. S. 1963. *Pliny: Natural History*. 10 vols. Cambridge: Harvard University Press.

Joplin, Patricia Klindienst. 1985. "Epilogue: Philomela's Loom." In D. Wood Middlebrook and M. Yalom, eds., *Coming to Light: American Women Poets in the Twentieth Century*, 254–67. Ann Arbor: University of Michigan Press. Longer version: "The Voice of the Shuttle Is Ours," *Stanford Literature Review* 1 (1984): 25–53.

———. 1990. "Ritual Work on Human Flesh: Livy's Lucretia and the Rape of the Body Politic." *Helios* 17: 51–70.

Joyce, James. 1946. *Ulysses*. New York: Random House.

Kaempf-Dimitriadou, Sophia. 1979. *Die Liebe der Götter in der attischen Kunst des 5 Jahrhunderts v. Chr., Antike Kunst*. Beiheft 11.

Kähler, H. 1973. *Die Villa des Maxentius bei Piazza Armerina*. Berlin: Gebrüder Mann Verlag.

Kaibel, G., ed. 1887–1890. *Athenaeus, Dipnosophistae*. 3 vols. Leipzig: Teubner.

Kampen, Natalie. 1986. "Reliefs of the Basilica Aemilia: A Redating." Paper delivered at Brown University conference "Roman Women: Critical Approaches."

Kaplan, Cora. 1986. "*The Thorn Birds:* Fiction, Fantasy, Femininity." In V. Burgin, J. Donald, and C. Kaplan, eds., *Formations of Fantasy*, 142–66. London and New York: Methuen.

Kaplan, E. Ann. 1983. "Is the Gaze Male?" In Snitow et al. 1983, 309–27.

Kappeler, Susanne. 1986. *The Pornography of Representation*. Minneapolis: University of Minnesota Press.

Kehrberg, I. 1982. "The Potter-Painter's Wife. Some Additional Thoughts on the Caputi Hydria." *Hephaistos* 4: 25–35.

Kelman, H. 1973. "Violence without Moral Restraint: Reflections on the Dehumanization of Victims and Victimizers." *Journal of Social Issues* 29: 25–61.

Kendrick, Walter. 1987. *The Secret Museum: Pornography in Modern Culture*. New York: Viking Penguin.

Kennedy, George. 1963. *The Art of Persuasion in Greece*. Princeton: Princeton University Press.

Kenney, E. J. 1982. "Ovid." In *The Cambridge History of Classical Literature*, Vol. II, Part 3: The Age of Augustus, 124–61. Cambridge: Cambridge University Press.

Kent, S., and J. Morreau, eds. 1985. *Women's Images of Men*. New York: Writers and Readers Publishing.

Keuls, Eva C. 1985. *The Reign of the Phallus*. New York: Harper & Row.

Kitzinger, E. 1965. "Stylistic Developments in Pavement Mosaics in the Greek East from the Age of Constantine to the Age of Justinian." In *La Mosaïque Gréco-Romaine* I (G. Picard and H. Stern, eds.): 341–52.

Klinger, D. M. 1983. *Erotische Kunst der Antike. Band 7*. Nürnberg: DMK–Verlags–Gmbh.

Knigge, U. 1964. "Ein rotfiguriges Alabastron aus dem Kerameikos." *Mitteilungen des Deutschen Archäologischen Instituts, Athenische Abteilung* 79: 105–13.

Koch-Harnack, Gundel. 1983. *Knabenliebe und Tiergeschenke. Ihre Bedeutung im päderastischen Erziehungssystem Athens*. Berlin: Gebr. Mann.

Kock, Theodor. 1880–88. *Comicorum Graecorum Fragmenta*. 3 vols. Leipzig: Teubner.

Kolodny, Annette. 1985. "A Map for Rereading: Gender and the Interpretation of Literary Texts." In Showalter 1985, 46–62.

Kondoleon, C. 1986. "Art and Spectacle in Roman Cyprus." Paper presented at the 12th Annual Byzantine Studies Conference, Bryn Mawr College. *Abstracts of Papers* 2.

Kraemer, Ross. 1979. "Ecstasy and Possession: The Attraction of Women to the Cult of Dionysus." *Harvard Theological Review* 72: 55–80.

Krauskopf, I. 1977. "Eine attische schwarzfigurige Hydria in Heidelberg." *Archaeologischer Anzeiger:* 13–37.

Kristeva, Julia. 1982. *Powers of Horror*. New York: Columbia University Press.

Kuhn, Annette. 1985. *The Power of the Image: Essays on Representation and Sexuality*. London and Boston: Routledge and Kegan Paul.

———. 1982. *Women's Pictures: Feminism and Cinema*. London: Routledge and Kegan Paul.

Kurtz, D. 1985. "Beazley and the Connoisseurship of Greek Vases." *Greek Vases in the J. Paul Getty Museum* 2: 237–50.

Lacan, Jacques. 1977. "One: The Mirror Stage as Formative of the Function of the I as Revealed in Psychoanalytic Experience (1949)." In *Écrits: A Selection*, 1–7. Trans. by A. Sheridan. New York: W. W. Norton.

Lacey, W. K. 1968. *The Family in Classical Greece*. Ithaca: Cornell University Press.

Lancha, J. 1984. "L'Iconographie d'Hylas dans les mosaïques romaines." *III Colloquio internazionale sul mosaico antico* (R. F. Campanati, ed.): 381–92.

Lange, Lynda. 1983. "Woman Is Not a Rational Animal: On Aristotle's Biology of Reproduction." In S. Harding and M. Hintikka, eds., *Discovering Reality*, 1–15. Dordrecht: Reidel.

Larson, Shirley. 1986. *See Only Me*. Toronto: Harlequin Books.

Lassus, J. 1971. "La salle à sept absides de Djemila-Cuicul." *Antiquités Africaines* 5: 193–207.

———. 1950. "Le thème de la chasse dans les mosaïques d'Antioch." In E. Arslan, ed., *Arte del primo millenio. Atti del II° congresso per lo studio dell'arte medioevo*, 141–46.

Lavin, I. 1963. *Antioch Hunting Mosaics and Their Sources (Dumbarton Oaks Papers XVII)*. Washington, D.C.: Dumbarton Oaks Center for Byzantine Studies.

Leach, E. W. 1988. *The Rhetoric of Space: Literary and Artistic Representations of Landscape in Republican and Augustan Rome*. Princeton: Princeton University Press.

Lederer, Laura, ed. 1980. *Take Back the Night: Women on Pornography*. New York: Bantam.

Lefkowitz, Mary R. 1981a. "Critical Stereotypes and the Poetry of Sappho." In *Heroines and Hysterics*, 59–68. London: Duckworth. Orig. in *Greek, Roman, and Byzantine Studies* 14: 113–23.

———. 1981b. *The Lives of the Greek Poets*. London: Duckworth.

Lefkowitz, Mary R., and Maureen B. Fant. 1982. *Women's Life in Greece and Rome*. Baltimore: Johns Hopkins University Press.

Lerner, Gerda. 1986. *The Creation of Patriarchy*. New York: Oxford University Press.

Leschi, L. 1953. *Djemila, Antique Cuicul*. Algiers: Direction de l'Intérieur et des Beaux-arts.

Lesky, Alban. 1971. *Geschichte der griechischen Literatur*, 3rd ed. Bern.

———. 1966. *A History of Greek Literature*, 2nd ed. Trans. by J. Willis and C. de Heer. New York: Crowell.

Lever, Katherine. 1956. *The Art of Greek Comedy*. London: Methuen.

Levi, D. 1947. *Antioch Mosaic Pavements* I–II. Princeton: Princeton University Press.

Levin, D. N. 1977. "To Whom Did the Ancient Novelists Address Themselves?" *Rivisti di Studi Classici* 25: 18–29.

Lévi-Strauss, Claude. 1969. *The Elementary Structures of Kinship*. Boston: Beacon Press.

———. 1966. *The Savage Mind*. Chicago: University of Chicago Press.

Levy, Edmond. 1976. "Les Femmes chez Aristophane." *Ktema* 1: 99–112.

Lewis, D. M. 1955. "Notes on Attic Inscriptions (II), XXIII: Who Was Lysistrata?" *Annals of the British School in Athens* 1: 1–13.

Lewis, Thomas S. W. 1982–83. "The Brothers of Ganymede." *Salmagundi* 58–59: 147–65.

Licht, Hans. 1932. *Sexual Life in Ancient Greece*. Trans. by J. H. Freese. London: Abbey Library.

Lintott, A. W. 1968. *Violence in Republican Rome*. Oxford: Clarendon Press.

Linz, D., E. Donnerstein, and S. Penrod. 1987. *The Question of Pornography*. New York: Free Press.

Lloyd, G. E. R. 1983. *Science, Folklore, and Ideology: Studies in the Life Sciences in Ancient Greece*. Cambridge: Cambridge University Press.

———. 1968. *Aristotle: The Growth and Structure of His Thought*. Cambridge: Cambridge University Press.

Lobel, E. 1972. *Oxyrhynchus Papyrus* 39: 51–54, no. 2891, with Plates I and III.

Lodge, David. 1984. *Small World*. New York: Warner Books (reprint 1986).

L'Orange, H. P. 1973. *Likeness and Icon: Selected Studies in Classical and Early Medieval Art*. Odense: Odense University Press.

Loraux, Nicole. 1990. "Herakles: The Super-male and the Feminine." In Halperin et al. 1990, 21–52.

———. 1987. *Tragic Ways of Killing a Woman*. Trans. by A. Forster. Cambridge, Mass.: Harvard University Press.

———. 1981a. "L'acropole comique." *Les enfants d'Athena: Idées atheniennes sur la citoyenneté et la division des sexes* (Paris): 157–96.

———. 1981b. "Le lit, la guerre." *L'Homme* 21: 37–87.

———. 1978. "Sur la race des femmes et quelques-unes de ses tribus." *Arethusa* 11: 43–87.

Lorde, Audre. 1984. "The Master's Tools Will Never Dismantle the Master's House." In *Sister Outsider*, 110–13. Trumansburg, N.Y.: Crossing Press.

Lovejoy, A. O., and G. Boas. 1935. *Primitivism and Related Ideas in Antiquity*. Vol. 1 of *A Documentary History of Primitivism and Related Ideas*. Baltimore: Johns Hopkins University Press.

Luce, T. J. 1977. *Livy: The Composition of His History*. Princeton: Princeton University Press.

Luck, Georg. 1967–77. *P. Ovidius Naso Tristia*. Vol. 1, text and translation, 1967. Vol. 2, commentary, 1977. Heidelberg: Carl Winter.

Luppe, Wolfgang. 1974. "Nochmals zu Philaenis, *Pap. Oxy.* 2891." *Zeitschrift für Papyrologie und Epigraphik* 13: 281–82.

Lyne, R. O. A. M. 1980. *The Latin Love Poets*. Oxford: Oxford University Press.

MacCormack, Geoffrey. 1975. "Wine-Drinking and the Romulan Law of Divorce." *Irish Jurist* 10: 170–74.

MacKinnon, Catharine. 1989. "Sexuality, Pornography, and Method: Pleasure under Patriarchy." *Ethics* 99: 314–46.

———. 1987. *Feminism Unmodified: Discourses on Life and Law*. Cambridge, Mass.: Harvard University Press.

———. 1985. "Pornography, Civil Rights and Speech: Commentary." *Harvard Civil Rights–Civil Liberties Law Review* 20: 1–70.

———. 1983a. "Feminism, Marxism, and the State: An Agenda for Theory." In Elizabeth Abel and Emily Abel, eds., *Signs Reader: Women, Gender and Scholarship,* 227–56. Chicago: University of Chicago Press. Reprinted from *Signs* 7: 515–44.

———. 1983b. "Feminism, Marxism, and the State: Toward Feminist Jurisprudence." *Signs* 8: 635–58.

Maclean, Marie. 1987. "Oppositional Practices in Women's Traditional Narrative." *New Literary History* 19: 37–50.

McLeish, Kenneth. 1980. *The Theatre of Aristophanes.* London: Thames and Hudson.

McNally, Sheila. 1978. "The Maenad in Early Greek Art." *Arethusa* 11: 101–36.

Mahjoubi, M. A. 1968? [uncertain]. *Les cités romaines de Tunisie.* Tunis: Société Tunisienne de Diffusion.

———. 1967. "Découverte d'une nouvelle mosaïque de chasse à Carthage." *Comptes Rendus de l'Académie des Inscriptions et Belles-Lettres:* 264–78. Paris: Librairie C. Klincksieck.

Maiuri, A. 1953. *Roman Painting.* Geneva: Skira.

Malamuth, Neil M., and Victoria Billings. 1984. "Why Pornography? Models of Functions and Effects." *Journal of Communication* 34: 117–29.

Malamuth, N. M., and E. Donnerstein, eds. 1984. *Pornography and Sexual Aggression.* San Diego and New York: Harcourt Brace Jovanovich.

Manuli, Paola. 1983. "Donne mascoline, femmine sterili, vergini perpetue: la ginecologia greca tra Ippocrate e Sorano." In S. Camprese, P. Manuli, and G. Sissa, eds., *Madre Materia: Sociologia e biologia della donna greca,* 149–92. Turin: Boringheri.

Marcadé, Jean. 1965. *Roma Amor: Essays on Erotic Elements in Etruscan and Roman Art.* Geneva: Nagel.

———. 1962. *Eros Kalos.* Geneva: Nagel.

Marcovich, M. 1975. "How to Flatter Women: *P. Oxy.* 2891." *Classical Philology* 70: 123–24.

Marcus, Jane. 1984. "Still Practice, A/Wrested Alphabet: Toward a Feminist Aesthetic." *Tulsa Studies in Women's Literature* 3: 79–97.

———. 1983. "Liberty, Sorority, Misogyny." In C. G. Heilbrun and M. R. Higonnet, eds., *The Representation of Women in Fiction: Selected Papers from the English Institute, n.s. 7 (1981),* 60–97. Baltimore and London: John Hopkins University Press.

Marini, Giuseppe Luigi. 1971. *Il Gabinetto Segreto del Museo Nazionale di Napoli.* Turin: Ruggero Aprile Editore.

Marks, Margaret C. 1978. *Heterosexual Coital Position as a Reflection of Ancient and Modern Cultural Attitudes.* Ann Arbor: University Microfilms.

Marvin, G. 1986. "Honour, Integrity and the Problem of Violence in the Spanish Bullfight." In Riches 1986, 118–35.

Mathieu, N. C. 1973. "Homme-Culture, Femme-Nature?" *L'Homme* 13.3: 101–13.

Matz, D. S. 1977. *Epigraphical Evidence relating to the Roman Gladiatorial Establishment.* Diss., University of Minnesota.

Mau, August. 1902 (reprint 1973). *Pompeii: Its Life and Art.* Trans. by F. W. Kelsey. Washington, D.C.: McGrath.

Mayo, Penelope C. 1967. *Amor Spiritualis et Carnalis: Aspects of the Myth of Ganymede in Art.* Diss., New York University.

Meese Commission. 1987. *Final Report of the Attorney General's Commission on Pornography.* Tennessee: Rutledge Hill Press.

Merkelbach, R. 1972. "φαυσώ?" *Zeitschrift für Papyrologie und Epigraphik* 9: 284.

Merlin, A., and L. Poinssot. 1934. "Deux mosaïques de Tunisie à sujets prophylactiques (Musée de Bardo)." In *Monuments et mémoirs* 34 (Fondation Eugéne Piot): 17–176. Paris: Ernest Leroux.

Meyer, M. 1988. "Männer mit Geld. Zu einer rotfigurigen Vase mit 'Alltagsszene.' " *Jahrbuch des Deutschen Archäologischen Instituts* 103: 87–125.

Michelini, Ann. 1987. *Euripides and the Tragic Tradition.* Madison: University of Wisconsin Press.

Miller, M. C. 1989. "The *Ependytes* in Classical Athens." *Hesperia* 58: 313–29.

Miller, Nancy K. 1986. "Changing the Subject: Authorship, Writing, and the Reader." In T. de Lauretis, ed., *Feminist Studies/Critical Studies,* 102–20. Bloomington: Indiana University Press.

———. 1981. "Emphasis Added." *PMLA* 96.1: 36–48.

Mitchell, Juliet. 1975. *Psychoanalysis and Feminism.* New York: Vintage Books.

Modleski, Tania. 1988. *The Women Who Knew Too Much.* New York: Methuen.

———. 1982. *Loving with a Vengeance: Mass Produced Fantasies for Women.* London and New York: Methuen.

Molinié, G. 1979. *Chariton: Le Roman de Chairéas et Callirhoé.* Paris: Les Belles Lettres.

Moore, M. B. 1985. "Giants at the Getty." *Greek Vases in the J. P. Getty Museum* 2: 21–40.

Moore, M. B., and M. Z. Philippides. 1986. *Attic Black-figured Pottery. Agora* 23.

Morey, C. R. 1938. *The Mosaics of Antioch.* London: Longmans, Green.

Morez, Mary. 1977. "The Woman Is the Dominant Figure." In J. B. Katz, ed., *I Am the Fire of Time: The Voices of Native American Women,* 126–27. New York: E. P. Dutton.

Morgan, Robin. 1980. "Theory and Practice." In Lederer 1980, 134–40.

Mozley, J. H. 1979. *Ovid. The Art of Love, and Other Poems,* 2nd ed. revised by G. P. Goold. Cambridge, Mass.: Harvard University Press.

Mulvey, Laura. 1975. "Visual Pleasure and Narrative Cinema." *Screen* 16.3: 6–18.

Musurillo, H. 1972. *The Acts of the Christian Martyrs.* Oxford: Clarendon Press.

Myerowitz, Molly. 1985. *Ovid's Games of Love.* Detroit: Wayne State University Press.

North, Helen. 1966. *Sôphrosunê: Self-Knowledge and Self-Restraint in Greek Literature.* Ithaca: Cornell University Press.

Norwood, Gilbert. 1931. *Greek Comedy.* London: Methuen.

Ogilvie, R. M. 1965. *A Commentary on Livy, Books 1–5.* Oxford: Oxford University Press.

Okin, Susan. 1979. *Women in Western Political Thought.* Princeton: Princeton University Press.

Ortner, Sherry B. 1978. "The Virgin and the State." *Feminist Studies* 4.3: 19–35.

———. 1974. "Is Female to Male as Nature Is to Culture?" In M. Zimbalist Rosaldo and L. Lamphere, eds., *Woman, Culture, and Society.* Stanford: Stanford University Press.

Ostriker, Alicia. 1985. "The Thieves of Language: Woman Poets and Revisionist Mythmaking." In Showalter 1985, 314–38.

Ovadiah, R., and A. Ovadiah. 1987. *Hellenistic, Roman and Early Byzantine Mosaic Pavements in Israel.* Rome: "L'Erma" di Bretschneider.

Owen, S. G. 1924. *P. Ovidi Nasonis Tristium Liber Secundus.* Oxford: Clarendon Press.

Pace, B. 1955. *I Mosaici di Piazza Armerina.* Rome: Casini Editore.

Padgug, R. A. 1979. "Sexual Matters: On Conceptualizing Sexuality in History." *Radical History Review* 20: 3–23.

Page, Denys. 1955. *Sappho and Alcaeus.* Oxford: Oxford University Press.

Pally, Marcia. 1985. "Object of the Game." *Film Comment* 21.3: 68–73.

———. 1984. "'Double' Trouble." *Film Comment* 20: 12–17.

Parke, H. W. 1977. *Festivals of the Athenians*. Ithaca: Cornell University Press.

Parker, Holt N. 1989. "Another Go at the Text of Philaenis (P. Oxy. 2891)." *Zeitschrift für Papyrologie und Epigraphik* 79: 49–50.

Parkin, D., ed. 1985. *The Anthropology of Evil*. Oxford: Basil Blackwell.

Parlasca, K. 1959. *Die römischen Mosaiken in Deutschland (Römische-Germanische Forschungen 23)*. Berlin: Walter de Gruyter.

Parrish, D. 1985. "The Date of the Mosaics from Zliten." *Antiquités Africaines* 21: 137–58.

Parsons, P. J. 1971. "A Greek Satyricon?" *Bulletin of the Institute of Classical Studies of the University of London* 8: 53–68.

Patterson, Cynthia. 1986. "*Hai Attikai*. The Other Athenians." In M. Skinner, ed., *Rescuing Creusa: New Methodological Approaches to Women in Antiquity*, special issue of *Helios* n.s. 13: 49–67.

———. 1981. *Pericles' Citizenship Law of 451–50 B.C.* New York: Arno.

Pauly, A., and G. Wissowa. 1894–. *Real-encyclopädie der klassischen Altertumswissenschaft*. Stuttgart: Metzler.

Pearson, J. 1973. *Arena: The Story of the Colosseum*. New York: McGraw-Hill.

Peckham, Morse. 1969. *Art and Pornography*. New York: Basic Books.

Perry, Ben Edwin. 1967. *The Ancient Romance*. Berkeley and Los Angeles: University of California Press.

Pfohl, Stephen. 1990. "The Terror of the Simulacra: Struggles for Justice and the Postmodern." In *New Directions in the Study of Justice, Law, and Social Control*, 207–63. New York: Plenum Press.

Phillipides, S. N. 1983. "Narrative Strategies and Ideology in Livy's 'Rape of Lucretia.'" *Helios* 10.2: 113–19.

Phillips, E. D. 1973. *Greek Medicine*. London: Thames and Hudson.

Phillips, Jane E. 1982. "Current Research in Livy's First Decade: 1959–1979." *Aufstieg und Niedergang der Römischer Welt* 30.2: 998–1057.

Picard, Gilbert. 1968. *Roman Painting*. Pallas Library of Art. Volume IV. Greenwich, Conn.: New York Graphic Society.

Picard, G., and H. Stern, eds. 1965. *La mosaïque gréco-romaine* I. *Colloques Internationaux du Centre National de la Recherche Scientifique, Paris, 29 août–3 septembre 1963*. Paris: Centre National de la Recherche Scientifique.

Pickard-Cambridge, Arthur W. 1968. *The Dramatic Festivals of Athens*, 2nd ed., rev. by John Gould and D. M. Lewis. Oxford: Clarendon Press.

———. 1962. *Dithyramb, Tragedy and Comedy*, 2nd ed. Oxford: Clarendon Press.

Pinzer, Maimie. 1977. *The Maimie Papers*, ed. by R. Rosen and S. Davidson. Bloomington: Indiana University Press.

Plepelits, K. 1977. *Chariton von Aphrodisias: Kallirhoe*. Stuttgart: Anton Hiersemann.

Pöhlmann, E. 1973. "Charakteristik des römischen Lehrgedichts." *Aufstieg und Niedergang der Römischer Welt* 1.3: 813–901.

Poinssot, L., and P. Quoniam. 1952. "Bêtes d'amphithéâtre sur trois mosaïques du Bardo." *Karthago. Révue d'Archéologie Africaine* 3: 129–65.

Pollitt, J. J. 1986. *Art in the Hellenistic Age*. Cambridge: Cambridge University Press.

———. 1972. *Art and Experience in Classical Greece*. Cambridge: Cambridge University Press.

Pomeroy, Sarah B. 1988. "Greek Marriage." In M. Grant and R. Kitzinger, eds., *Civilization of the Ancient Mediterranean: Greece and Rome*, 1333–42. New York: Scribner's.

————. 1977. "Tekhnikai kai Mousikai: The Education of Women in the Fourth Century and in the Hellenistic Period." *American Journal of Ancient History* 2: 51–68.

————. 1975. *Goddesses, Whores, Wives and Slaves: Women in Classical Antiquity.* New York: Schocken Books.

Raaflaub, Kurt A. 1986. "The Conflict of the Orders in Archaic Rome: A Comprehensive and Comparative Approach." In *Social Struggles in Archaic Rome,* 1–51. Berkeley: University of California Press.

Rabinowitz, Nancy Sorkin. 1989. "Theseus and Hippolytos: Renegotiating the Oedipus." In P. Yaeger and B. Kowaleski-Wallace, eds., *Refiguring the Father: New Feminist Readings of Patriarchy.* Carbondale: Southern Illinois University Press.

————. 1987. "Female Speech and Female Sexuality: Euripides' *Hippolytos* as Model." *Helios* 13.2: 127–40.

————. 1976. *From Force to Persuasion: Dragon-Battle Imagery in Aeschylus' Oresteia.* Diss., University of Chicago.

Rabinowitz, Peter. 1987. *Before Reading: The Politics of Interpretation.* Ithaca: Cornell University Press.

Radway, Janice. 1984. *Reading the Romance: Women, Patriarchy and Popular Literature.* Chapel Hill: University of North Carolina Press.

Ray, William. 1984. *Literary Meaning: From Phenomenology to Deconstruction.* Oxford and New York: Basil Blackwell.

Reardon, Brian P., ed. 1989. *Collected Ancient Greek Novels.* Berkeley: University of California Press.

————. 1982. "Theme, Structure and Narrative in Chariton." *Yale Classical Studies* 27: 1–28.

Reckford, Kenneth J. 1987. *Aristophanes' Old-and-New Comedy.* Chapel Hill and London: University of North Carolina Press.

Reeve, Michael, ed. 1986. *Longus: Daphnis and Chloe.* Leipzig: Teubner.

Reilly, J. 1989. "'Mistress and Maid' on Athenian Lekythoi." *Hesperia* 58: 411–44.

Reinach, A. 1921. *Recueil Milliet: Textes grecs et latins relatifs à l'histoire de la peinture ancienne.* I. Paris: Klincksieck.

Renard, M., ed. 1962. *Hommages à Albert Grenier* (*Collection Latomus* LVIII). Brussels-Berchem: Latomus.

Renard, M., and R. Schilling, eds. 1964. *Hommages à Jean Bayet* (*Collection Latomus* LXX). Brussels-Berchem: Latomus.

Rich, Adrienne. 1986. "Blood, Bread, and Poetry: The Location of the Poet." In *Blood, Bread, and Poetry: Selected Prose, 1979–1985,* 167–87. New York and London: W. W. Norton.

Rich, B. Ruby. 1986. "Review Essay: Feminism and Sexuality in the 1980's." *Feminist Studies* 12.3: 527–81.

Richardson, Lawrence Jr. 1988. *Pompeii: An Architectural History.* Baltimore: Johns Hopkins University Press.

————. 1976. *Propertius Elegies I–IV.* Norman: University of Oklahoma Press.

Richardson, N. J., ed. 1974. *The Homeric Hymn to Demeter.* Oxford: Clarendon Press.

Riches, D., ed. 1986. *The Anthropology of Violence.* London: Basil Blackwell.

Richlin, Amy. 1984. "Invective against Women in Roman Satire." *Arethusa* 17.1: 67–80.

————. 1983. *The Garden of Priapus: Sexuality and Aggression in Roman Humor.* New Haven: Yale University Press.

————. 1981. "Approaches to the Sources on Adultery at Rome." In H. P. Foley, ed., *Reflections of Women in Antiquity,* 379–404. London and New York: Gordon and Breach.

Richter, G. M. A. 1970. *The Sculpture and Sculptors of the Greeks*. New Haven: Yale University Press.

Ridgway, B. S. 1977. *The Archaic Style in Greek Sculpture*. Princeton: Princeton University Press.

Riese, A., and F. Bücheler. 1894. *Anthologia Latina* I. Leipzig: Teubner.

Robert, L. 1949. "Monuments de gladiateurs dans l'orient grec." *Hellenica, Recueil d'Épigraphie, de Numismatique, et d'Antiquités Grecques* 7: 126–51. Paris: Librairie d'Amérique et d'Orient, Adrien-Maisonneuve.

————. 1948. "Monuments de gladiateurs dans l'orient grec." *Hellenica, Recueil d'Épigraphie, de Numismatique, et d'Antiquités Grecques* 5: 77–99. Paris: Librairie d'Amérique et d'Orient, Adrien-Maisonneuve.

————. 1946. "Monuments de gladiateurs dans l'orient grec." *Hellenica, Recueil d'Épigraphie, de Numismatique et d'Antiquités Grecques* 3: 112–50. Paris: Librairie d'Amérique et d'Orient, Adrien-Maisonneuve.

————. 1940. *Les gladiateurs dans l'orient grec (Bibliothèque de l'école des hautes études, fascicule 278)*. Paris: Librairie Ancienne Honoré Champion.

Roberts, H. E. 1972. "Marriage, Redundancy or Sin: The Painter's View of Women in the First Twenty-Five Years of Victoria's Reign." In Vicinus 1972, 45–76.

Robertson, M. 1976. "Beazley and After." *Münchener Jahrbuch des bildenden Kunst* 27: 29–46.

Robinson, D. M., and E. J. Fluck. 1937. *A Study of Greek Love-Names*. Baltimore: Johns Hopkins University Press.

Rocchetti, L. 1961. "Il mosaico con scene d'arena al Museo Borghese." *Rivista dell'Istituto Nazionale d'Archeologia e Storia dell'Arte* 10: 79–115.

Rose, Valentin. 1863. *Aristoteles Pseudepigraphus*. Leipzig: Teubner; reprint Hildesheim: Olms.

Rose, W. D. 1953. *Aristotle*. London: Methuen.

Rosellini, Michele. 1979. "*Lysistrata:* Une mise-en-scène de la feminité." In *Aristophane: Les femmes et la cité*, 11–32. Paris: Les Cahiers de Fontenay.

Rosen, Ruth. 1982. *The Lost Sisterhood: Prostitution in America, 1900–1918*. Baltimore: Johns Hopkins University Press.

Rostagni, A. 1944. *Suetonio. De Poetis e Biografi Minori*. Turin: Chiantore.

Roth, C. L. 1893. *C. Suetoni Tranquilli Quae Supersunt Omnia*. Leipzig: Teubner.

Roth, M. 1982. "Pornography and Society: A Psychiatric View." In M. Yaffé and E. C. Nelson, eds., *The Influence of Pornography on Behaviour*, 1–25. London and New York: Academic.

Rubin, Gayle. 1984. "Thinking Sex: Notes for a Radical Theory of the Politics of Sexuality." In Vance 1984, 267–319.

————. 1975. "The Traffic in Women: Notes on the 'Political Economy' of Sex." In R. Reiter, ed., *Towards an Anthropology of Women*, 152–210. New York: Monthly Review Press.

Rukeyser, Muriel. 1978. "Myth." In *The Collected Poems*, 498. New York: McGraw-Hill.

Rumpf, A. 1951. "Parrhasios." *American Journal of Archaeology* 55: 1–12.

Rush, Florence. 1980. "Child Pornography." In Lederer 1980, 71–81.

Russ, Joanna. 1985. "Pornography by Women for Women, with Love." In *Magic Mommas, Trembling Sisters, Puritans and Perverts: Feminist Essays*, 79–100. Trumansburg, N.Y.: Crossing Press.

————. 1983. *How to Suppress Women's Writing*. Austin: University of Texas Press.

Russell, D. A., and M. Winterbottom. 1972. *Ancient Literary Criticism: The Principal Texts in New Translations*. Oxford: Oxford University Press.

Russell, Diana E. H. 1980. "Pornography and Violence: What Does the New Research Say?" In Lederer 1980, 218–38.

Ryberg, I. S. 1955. *Rites of the State Religion in Roman Art. Memoirs of the American Academy in Rome* 23.

Saïd, Suzanne. 1983. "Féminin, femme et femelle dans les grands traités biologiques d'Aristote." In Edmond Lévy, ed., *La femme dans les sociétés antiques*, 93–123. Strasbourg: Université de Strasbourg.

———. 1979. "L'Assemblée des Femmes: Les femmes, l'economie et la politique." In *Aristophane: Les femmes et la cité*, 33–69. Paris: Les Cahiers de Fontenay 17.

Salmon, J. B. 1984. *Wealthy Corinth: A History of the City to 338 B.C.* Oxford: Clarendon Press.

Salomonson, J. W. 1965. *La mosaïque aux chevaux de l'antiquarium de Carthage* (*Études d'Archéologie et d'Histoire Ancienne Publiées par l'Institut Historique Néelandais de Rome*, I). La Haye: Imprimerie Nationale.

Sammons, J. T. 1988. *Beyond the Ring: The Role of Boxing in American Society.* Chicago: University of Illinois Press.

Saslow, James. 1986. *Ganymede in the Renaissance.* New Haven: Yale University Press.

Saussure, Ferdinand de. 1976. *Course in General Linguistics.* New York: McGraw-Hill.

Saylor, C. 1987. "Funeral Games: The Significance of Games in the *Cena Trimalchionis.*" *Latomus, Revue d'Études latines* 46: 583–602.

Schaps, David M. 1979. *Economic Rights of Women in Ancient Greece.* Edinburgh: University of Edinburgh Press.

———. 1977. "The Woman Least Mentioned: Etiquette and Women's Names." *Classical Quarterly* 27: 323–30.

Schefold, Karl. 1981. *Die Göttersagen in der klassischen und hellenistischen Kunst.* Munich: Hirmer.

———. 1978. *Götter- und Heldensagen der Griechen in der spätarchaischen Kunst.* Munich: Hirmer.

———. 1972. *La peinture pompéienne: Essai sur l'évolution de sa signification.* Collection Latomus 108. Brussels (Originally *Die pompejanische Malerei.* Basel: Benno Schwabe, 1952.)

———. 1957. *Die Wande Pompejis: Topographisches Verzeichnis der Bildmotive.* Berlin: Walter de Gruyter.

Scheibler, I. 1983. *Griechische Töpferkunst.* Munich: Beck.

Schipper, H. 1980. "Filthy Lucre: A Tour of America's Most Profitable Frontier." *Mother Jones,* April: 31–33, 60–62.

Schor, Naomi. 1986. "Reading Double: Sand's Difference." In N. Miller, ed., *The Poetics of Gender,* 248–69. New York: Columbia University Press.

Scobie, A. 1979. "Storytellers, Storytelling and the Novel in Greco-Roman Antiquity." *Rheinisches Museum* 122: 229–59.

Sedgwick, Eve Kosofsky. 1985. *Between Men: Homosocial Desire and English Literature.* New York: Columbia University Press.

Seeberg, A. 1971. *Corinthian Komos Vases. Bulletin of the Institute of Classical Studies of the University of London* Suppl. 27.

Seltman, Charles T. 1923–25. "Eros in Early Attic Legend and Cult." *Annual of the British School at Athens* 26: 88–105.

Sergent, Bernard. 1984. *Homosexuality in Greek Myth.* Trans. by A. Goldhammer. Boston: Beacon Press.

Shapiro, H. A. 1987. "Kalos Inscriptions with Patronymic." *Zeitschrift für Papyrologie und Epigraphik* 68: 107–18.

————. 1986. Review of Keuls 1985. *American Journal of Archaeology* 90: 361–63.

————. 1985. "Greek 'Bobbins': A New Interpretation." *Ancient World* 11: 15–20.

————. 1981a. *Art, Myth, and Culture: Greek Vases from Southern Collections*. New Orleans: New Orleans Museum of Art.

————. 1981b. "Courtship Scenes in Attic Vase-Painting." *American Journal of Archaeology* 85: 133–43.

Shaw, Michael. 1975. "The Female Intruder: Women in Fifth-Century Drama." *Classical Philology* 70: 255–66.

Shawn, Wallace, and André Gregory. 1981. *My Dinner with André: A Screenplay*. New York: Grove Press.

Short, J. Jr., and M. Wolfgang, eds. 1972. *Collective Violence*. Chicago: Aldine Atherton.

Showalter, Elaine, ed. 1985. *The New Feminist Criticism*. New York: Pantheon.

————. 1982. "Feminist Criticism in the Wilderness." In E. Abel, ed., *Writing and Sexual Difference*, 9–35. Chicago: University of Chicago Press.

Sichtermann, Hellmut. n.d. *Ganymed*. Berlin: Gebr. Mann.

————. 1956. "Hyakinthos." *Jahrbuch des Deutschen Archäologischen Instituts* 71: 97–123.

Silverman, Kaja. 1988. *The Acoustic Mirror*. Bloomington: Indiana University Press.

————. 1984. "*Histoire d'O:* The Construction of a Female Subject." In Vance 1984, 320–49.

————. 1980. "Masochism and Subjectivity." *Frameworks* 12: 2–9.

Simon, Erika. 1985. "Early Classical Vase-Painting." In C. G. Boulter, ed., *Greek Art Archaic into Classical*, 66–79. Leiden: Brill.

————. 1983. *Festivals of Attica*. Madison: University of Wisconsin Press.

Sissa, Giulia. 1983. "Il corpo della donna: lineamenti di una ginecologia filosofica." In S. Camprese, P. Manuli, and G. Sissa, eds., *Madre Materia*, 83–145. Turin: Boringheri.

Skinner, Marilyn B. 1987a. "Classical Studies, Patriarchy and Feminism: The View from 1986." *Women's Studies International Forum* 10.2: 181–86.

————. 1987b. "Rescuing Creusa: New Methodological Approaches to Women in Antiquity." *Helios* 13.2: 1–8.

————. 1986. "Classical Studies vs. Women's Studies: *Duo moi ta noêmmata.*" *Helios* 12.2: 3–16.

Slater, Philip. 1968. *The Glory of Hera*. Boston: Beacon Press.

Smith, D. J. 1983. "Mosaics." In Henig 1983, 116–38.

Smith, M. S., ed. 1975. *Petronii Arbitri Cena Trimalchionis*. Oxford: Clarendon Press.

Smith, Rowland, trans. 1901. *The Greek Romances of Heliodorus, Longus and Achilles Tatius*. London: George Bell and Sons.

Snitow, Ann Barr. 1983. "Mass Market Romance: Pornography for Women Is Different." In Snitow et al. 1983, 245–63.

Snitow, Ann Barr, Christine Stansell, and Sharon Thompson, eds. 1983. *Powers of Desire*. New York: Monthly Review Press.

Snyder, Jane McIntosh. 1989. *The Woman and the Lyre: Women Writers in Classical Greece and Rome*. Carbondale: Southern Illinois University Press.

Soble, Alan. 1986. *Pornography: Marxism, Feminism, and the Future of Sexuality*. New Haven: Yale University Press.

Sommerstein, Alan. 1985. *Aristophanes, Peace*. Warminster: Aris and Phillips.

————. 1980. "The Naming of Women in Greek and Roman Comedy." *Quaderni di Storia* 11: 393–418.

Sourvinou-Inwood, Christiane. 1987. "A Series of Erotic Pursuits: Images and Meanings." *Journal of Hellenic Studies* 107: 131–53.

———. 1978. "Persephone and Aphrodite at Locri: A Model for Personality Definitions in Greek Religion." *Journal of Hellenic Studies* 98: 101–21.

———. 1973. "The Young Abductor of the Locrian Pinakes." *Bulletin of the Institute of Classical Studies of the University of London* 20: 12–21.

Spatz, Lois. 1978. *Aristophanes*. Boston: G. K. Hall.

Spelman, Elizabeth V. 1983. "Aristotle and the Politicization of the Soul." In S. Harding and M. Hintikka, eds., *Discovering Reality*, 17–30. Dordrecht: Reidel.

Spivak, Gayatri Chakravorty. 1981. "French Feminism in an International Frame." *Yale French Studies* 62: 154–84.

Steele, Jessica. 1984. *Tomorrow—Come Soon*. Toronto: Harlequin Books.

Steinem, Gloria. 1980. "Erotica and Pornography: A Clear and Present Difference." In Lederer 1980, 35–39.

Stern, Leslie. 1982. "The Body as Evidence: A Critical Review of the Pornography Problematic." *Screen* 23: 38–60.

Stibbe, C. M. 1972. *Lakonische Vasenmaler des sechsten Jahrhunderts v. Chr.* Amsterdam: North Holland.

Stigers, E. S. 1981. "Sappho's Private World." In H. P. Foley, ed., *Reflections of Women in Antiquity*, 45–61. London and New York: Gordon and Breach.

Stone, Laura M. 1981. *Costume in Aristophanic Comedy*. New York: Arno.

Stroh, W. 1979. "Ovids Liebeskunst und die Ehegesetze des Augustus." *Gymnasium* 86: 323–52.

Suleiman, Susan Rubin. 1986. "Pornography, Transgression and the Avant-garde: Bataille's *Story of the Eye*." In N. K. Miller, ed., *The Poetics of Gender*. New York: Columbia University Press.

Sullivan, John P. 1986. *The Satyricon and the Apocolocyntosis*, rev. ed. Harmondsworth: Penguin.

———. 1968. *The Satyricon of Petronius: A Literary Study*. Bloomington: Indiana University Press.

Sutton, R. F. 1989. "On the Classical Athenian Wedding. Two Red-figure loutrophoroi in Boston." In *Daidalikon: Studies in Memory of R. V. Schoder, S.J.*, 331–59. Wauconda, Ill.: Bolchazy-Carducci.

———. 1985. Review of Koch-Harnack 1983. *American Journal of Archaeology* 89: 183–84.

———. 1981. *The Interaction between Men and Women Portrayed on Attic Red-figure Pottery*. Ann Arbor: University Microfilms.

Syme, Ronald. 1959. "Livy and Augustus." *Harvard Studies in Classical Philology* 64: 27–87.

Talese, Gay. 1980. *Thy Neighbor's Wife*. Garden City, N.Y.: Doubleday.

Tatum, J. 1989. "The Arena in the Roman Novel." Paper presented at International Conference on the Ancient Novel: Classical Paradigms and Modern Perspectives, Dartmouth College.

Thébert, Yvon. 1987a. "Private Life and Domestic Architecture in Roman Africa." In P. Veyne, ed., *A History of Private Life from Pagan Rome to Byzantium*, 313–409. Cambridge, Mass., and London: Belknap Press of Harvard University Press.

———. 1987b. "The Roman Empire." In *A History of Private Life* (see ibid.), 5–234.

Theweleit, Klaus. 1987. *Male Fantasies*. Vol. 1. Trans. by S. Conway. Minneapolis: University of Minnesota Press.

Thompson, Sharon. 1984. "Search for Tomorrow: On Feminism and the Reconstruction of Teen Romance." In Vance 1984, 350–84.

Thornley, George. 1657. *Daphnis and Chloe by Longus*. Reprinted as revised by J. Edmonds, 1924. London and New York: William Heinemann and G. P. Putnam's Sons (Loeb Classical Library).

Thurston, Carol. 1987. *The Romance Revolution*. Urbana and Chicago: University of Illinois Press.

Toynbee, J. M. C. 1973. *Animals in Roman Life and Art*. Ithaca: Cornell University Press.

Travlos, J. 1971. *Pictorial Dictionary of Ancient Athens*. New York: Praeger.

Tsantsanoglou, K. 1973. "The Memoirs of a Lady from Samos." *Zeitschrift für Papyrologie und Epigraphik* 1: 183–95.

Tumolesi, P. S. 1980. *Gladiatorium paria. Annunci di spettacoli gladiatorii a Pompeii*. Rome: Edizioni di Storia e Letteratura.

Utter, Robert, and Gwendolyn Needham. 1936. *Pamela's Daughters*. New York: MacMillan.

Vaio. John. 1973. "Manipulation of Theme and Action in Aristophanes' *Lysistrata*." *Greek, Roman, and Byzantine Studies* 14: 369–80.

Vance, Carole S., ed. 1984. *Pleasure and Danger: Exploring Female Sexuality*. Boston and London: Routledge and Kegan Paul.

Verducci, Florence. 1985. *Ovid's Toyshop of the Heart*. Princeton: Princeton University Press.

Vermeule, Emily. 1969. "Some Erotica in Boston." *Antike Kunst* 12: 9–15.

Vernant, J.-P. 1990. "One . . . Two . . . Three: Eros." In Halperin et al. 1990, 465–78.

Versnell, H. S. 1987. "Wife and Helpmate. Women of Athens in Anthropological Perspective." In J. Blok and P. Mason, eds., *Sexual Asymmetry: Studies in Ancient Society*, 59–86. Amsterdam: Gieben.

Veyne, Paul. 1987. "The Roman Empire." In *A History of Private Life from Pagan Rome To Byzantium*, trans. by A. Goldhammer, 5–234. Cambridge, Mass., and London: Belknap Press of Harvard University Press.

Vicinus, M., ed. 1972. *Suffer and Be Still: Women in the Victorian Age*. Bloomington: Indiana University Press.

Vickers, Brian. 1973. *Towards Greek Tragedy*. London: Longmans.

Vickers, Nancy. 1982. "Diana Described: Scattered Woman and Scattered Rhyme." In E. Abel, ed., *Writing and Sexual Difference*, 95–110.

Vilborg, Ebbe, ed. 1955. *Achilles Tatius Leucippe and Clitophon*. Stockholm: Almquist and Wiksell.

Ville, G. 1981. *La gladiature en occident des origines à la mort de domitien. Bibliothèque des Écoles Françaises d'Athènes et de Rome* 275. Rome: École Française de Rome.

———. 1965. "Essai de datation de la mosaïque des gladiateurs de Zliten." In Picard and Stern 1965, 147–55.

———. 1964. "Les coupes de Trimalcion figurant des gladiateurs et une série de verres 'sigillés' gaulois." In Renard and Schilling 1964, 721–33.

———. 1960. *Les jeux de gladiateurs dans l'empire chrétien (Mélanges d'Archéologie et d'Histoire* 72). Paris: École Française de Rome, E. de Boccard.

Volbach, W. F. 1976. *Elfenbein Arbeiten der Spätantike und des frühen Mittelalters*. Mainz am Rhein: Verlag Philipp von Zabern.

Vorberg, Gaston. 1932 (reprint 1965). *Glossarium Eroticum*. Originally published Stuttgart: Püttmann. Reprints Hanau: Müller and Kiepenheuer; Rome: Bretschneider.

Walkowitz, Judith. 1980. *Prostitution in Victorian Society: Women, Class and the State*. New York: Cambridge University Press.

Walsh, P. G. 1961. *Livy: His Historical Aims and Methods.* Cambridge: Cambridge University Press.

Walters, H. B. 1926. *Catalogue of the Engraved Gems and Cameos, Greek, Etruscan and Roman, in the British Museum.* London: British Museum.

Walton, Michael. 1987. *Living Greek Theater: A Handbook of Classical Performance and Modern Production.* New York: Greenwood Press.

Ward-Perkins, J. B. 1981. *Roman Imperial Architecture.* New York: Penguin Books.

Warren, L. B. 1973a. "Etruscan Women: A Question of Interpretation." *Archaeology* 26: 242–49.

———. 1973b. "The Women of Etruria." *Arethusa* 6: 91–101.

Watson, Alan. 1975. *Rome of the XII Tables.* Princeton: Princeton University Press.

Watson, G. R. 1952. "Theta Nigrum." *Journal of Roman Studies* 42: 56–62.

Weart, S. W. 1989. "Learning How to Study Images as Potent Forces in Our History." *Chronicle of Higher Education* 35.26: A44.

———. 1988. *Nuclear Fear: A History of Images.* Cambridge, Mass.: Harvard University Press.

Webster, T. B. L. 1972. *Potter and Patron in Classical Athens.* London: Methuen.

Wehgartner, I. 1983. *Attisch Weissgrundige Keramik.* Mainz: Philipp von Zabern.

Weitzmann, Kurt. 1977. *Late Antique and Early Christian Book Illumination.* New York: Braziller.

Wells, C. 1984. *The Roman Empire.* Stanford: Stanford University Press.

Wendel, Carolus, ed. 1914. *Scholia in Theocritum Vetera.* Leipzig: Teubner.

Wender, Dorothea. 1973. "Plato: Misogynist, Paedophile and Feminist." *Arethusa* 6: 75–90.

Wheeler, A. L. 1924. *Ovid: Tristia. Ex Ponto.* Cambridge: Loeb Classical Library.

Whitman, Cedric H. 1964. *Aristophanes and the Comic Hero.* Cambridge, Mass.: Harvard University Press.

Wibberly, Mary. 1979. *Love's Sweet Revenge.* Toronto: Harlequin Books.

Wilamowitz-Moellendorff, Ulrich von, ed. 1958 (1927). *Aristophanes Lysistrate.* Berlin: Weidmann.

Williams, D. 1983. "Women on Athenian Vases: Problems of Interpretation." In A. Cameron and A. Kuhrt, eds., *Images of Women in Antiquity,* 92–106. New York: Croom Helm.

Williams, Gordon. 1978. *Change and Decline.* Berkeley: University of California Press.

Williams, Linda. 1984. "When the Woman Looks." In M. A. Doane et al., eds., *Re-Vision: Essays in Feminist Film Criticism,* 83–99. Frederick, Md.: University Publications of America.

Williams, R. 1971. "Literature and Sociology: In Memory of Lucien Goldmann." *New Left Review* 57: 3–18.

Willis, Ellen. 1982. "Feminism, Moralism, and Pornography." In Snitow et al. 1983, 460–67.

Wills, G. 1988. "Blood Sport." *New York Review of Books,* February 18: 5–7.

Wilmowsky, D. von. 1864. *Die Villa zu Nennig und ihr Mosaik.* Bonn: A. Marcus.

Wilson, R. J. A. 1983. *Piazza Armerina.* Austin: University of Texas Press.

Winkler, John J. 1990. *The Constraints of Desire: The Anthropology of Sex and Gender in Ancient Greece.* New York and London: Routledge.

———. 1988. "The Novel." In M. Grant and R. Kitzinger, eds., *Civilization of the Ancient Mediterranean: Greece and Rome,* Vol. III, 1563–71. New York: Scribner's.

———. 1985a. *Auctor & Actor: A Narratological Reading of Apuleius's The Golden Ass.* Berkeley: University of California Press.

———. 1985b. "The Ephebes' Song: *Tragôidia* and *Polis.*" *Representations* 11: 26–62.

———. 1982. "The Mendacity of Kalasiris and the Narrative Strategy of Heliodorus' *Aithiopika.*" *Yale Classical Studies* 27: 93–157.

———. 1981. "Gardens of Nymphs: Public and Private in Sappho's Lyrics." In H. Foley, ed., *Reflections of Women in Antiquity*, 63–89. London and New York: Gordon and Breach.

Winterbottom, M. 1974. *The Elder Seneca II. Controversiae VII–X. Suasoriae.* Cambridge, Mass., and London: Harvard University Press.

Wiseman, T. P. 1985. *Catullus and His World: A Reappraisal.* Cambridge: Cambridge University Press.

Wollmann, H. 1917. "Retiarier-Darstellungen auf römischen Tonlampen." *Römische Mitteilungen des Deutschen Archaeologischen Instituts, Römische Abteilung* 32: 147–67. Berlin: W. Regenberg.

Wuilleumier, P., and A. Audin. 1952. "Les médaillons d'appliqué gallo-romains de la vallée du Rhône." *Annales de l'Université de Lyon* (IIIᵉ série) 22. Paris: Société d'Édition "Les Belles Lettres."

Wycherley, R. E. 1978. *The Stones of Athens.* Princeton: Princeton University Press.

Zeitlin, Froma I. 1990. "The Poetics of Eros: Nature, Art and Imitation in Longus' *Daphnis and Chloe.*" In Halperin et al. 1990, 417–64.

———. 1986. "Configurations of Rape in Greek Myth." In S. Tomaselli and R. Porter, eds., *Rape*, 122–51. Oxford: Basil Blackwell.

———. 1985a. "Playing the Other: Theater, Theatricality, and the Feminine in Greek Drama." *Representations* 11: 63–94.

———. 1985b. "The Power of Aphrodite: Eros and the Boundaries of Self." In P. Burian, ed., *Directions in Euripidean Criticism*, 52–111. Durham: Duke University Press.

———. 1982. "Cultic Models of the Female: Rites of Dionysus and Demeter." *Arethusa* 15: 129–57.

———. 1981. "Travesties of Gender and Genre in Aristophanes' *Thesmophoriazousae.*" *Critical Inquiry* 8.2: 301–27. In E. Abel 1982, 131–57.

———. 1978. "The Dynamics of Misogny: Myth and Mythmaking in the *Oresteia.*" *Arethusa* 11: 149–84.

Zevi, E. 1937. "Scene di gineceo e scene di idillio nei vasi greci della seconda metà del secolo quinto." *Memorie. Atti della Accademia Nazionale dei Lincei, Classe di scienze morali, storichi e filologiche* 6: 291–369.

Zillman, D., and J. Bryant. 1984. "Effects of Massive Exposure to Pornography." In Malamuth and Donnerstein 1984, 115–38.

CONTRIBUTORS

Shelby Brown has recently held a Getty Fellowship to research ancient art depicting events of the Roman arena. Her excavation experience includes work in Italy, Greece, and North Africa, and she has published on human sacrifice in ancient Carthage.

Helen E. Elsom has been Visiting Assistant Professor of Classics at Cornell University. She works in England as a free-lance writer and political activist.

Madeleine M. Henry is Assistant Professor of Classical Studies at Iowa State University. Her publications include work on prostitutes in Greek comedy, and she is now working on a review essay on recent applications of feminist theory to classical antiquity.

Sandra R. Joshel teaches at the New England Conservatory, on ancient history and on film, women's studies, and mythology. She is the author of *Work, Identity, and Legal Status at Rome.*

Terri Marsh has often been Visiting Assistant Professor of Classics, most recently at Wake Forest University, and is now at work on *The Dialogues of Xanthippe,* a feminist revision of fifth-century Athens.

Holly Montague is Assistant Professor of Classics at Amherst College. She is at work on a study of Cicero's rhetoric.

Molly Myerowitz teaches Classics at Howard University. She is the author of *Ovid's Games of Love* and of articles on ancient cultural history and classical literature. She translates Ovid's poetry and is herself a poet.

Holt N. Parker is Assistant Professor of Classics at the University of Arizona. His previous work has been in linguistics, and he is currently at work on an edition of the Greek medical writer Metrodora.

Nancy Sorkin Rabinowitz is Professor of Comparative Literature at Hamilton College. She has published widely on Greek tragedy and is at work on a book, *Euripides' Traffic in Women.*

313

Amy Richlin is Associate Professor of Classics and Women's Studies at the University of Southern California. She has published on Roman satire and sexuality, including *The Garden of Priapus,* and on Roman women, and she is now working on a book on Roman witches.

H. A. Shapiro is Associate Professor of Humanities at Stevens Institute of Technology. He is the author of *Art and Cult under the Tyrants in Athens* and articles on Greek vase painting.

Robert F. Sutton, Jr., is Associate Professor of Classical Studies at Indiana University— Purdue University at Indianapolis. A specialist in ancient pottery, he has excavated in Italy and Greece, is publishing ceramic discoveries from three surface surveys in Greece, and is preparing a study of the imagery of heterosexuality on Attic vases.

Bella Zweig is Lecturer in Humanities at the University of Arizona. Her interests include comparative work on Classics and Native American cultures, especially on women, and she is now working on studies in Greek tragedy and ritual.

Index